Bournemouth
St. Peter's

A

Bournemouth St. Peter's

IAN McQUEEN

Dorset Publishing Company
MILBORNE PORT
SHERBORNE DORSET

TO SHEILA
AND THE CHILDREN

First published 1971 by
Dorset Publishing Company
Milborne Port
Sherborne Dorset

SBN 902129 09 0

Printed in Great Britain by
F & M Naish & Co
at Benfleet, Essex

Contents

Preface

A KEEN interest in Church and local history, coupled with my family's continuous association with St. Peter's for over a century (having provided in that time four churchwardens who served the parish for a total of forty years), made it natural that I should want to write this book. It has taken a long time to complete, and would never have got far beyond a beginning without the help and encouragement that I was given by so many people. They are especially:

The Rev. W. H. Fox Robinson and the Rev. Dr. Gordon Roe, for stimulating my endeavours at the outset;

Dean Hedley Burrows and Bishop A. L. E. Williams, for the immense trouble to which they put themselves when I sought their assistance;

The Borough Librarian of Bournemouth and his Reference Library staff not only for their patience and courtesy, which I regret to say I have grown used to taking for granted, but also for their personal interest and many practical suggestions, not least in selecting and lending most of the photographs;

Ronald Hines, my predecessor as vicar's warden, and Martin Maycock, my wife's brother-in-law, for their constructive criticisms and wise counsel;

Nicholas Taylor, for discovering so much unknown material about St. Peter's and leading me to many helpful sources;

The churchfolk of St. Peter's and St. Swithun's, particularly my late grandmother, Mrs. Ethel Palmer, my great aunt Miss Evelyn Keep, Mrs. E. M. Whitten, Miss J. Deane, Miss Linda Stanley, Mrs. Marion Taylor, Cyril Maynard, George Head, Jim and Ted Keep, Leonard South and Michael Peterson;

John Ruston and Rodney Legg, for their scholarly guidance and kind tolerance of an author's foibles.

I. MCQ.

Bournemouth.
May, 1971.

CHAPTER I

Bournemouth Before St. Peter's

THE EARLIEST known mention of Bournemouth appears in the Christchurch Cartulary of 1407. Thereafter the name is found in various maps and documents in spelling which differs from time to time. There is an interesting reference to the place in a survey conducted in 1574 which reports, "we find at Bournemouth within the west bay at Christchurch a place very easy for the enemy to land, there containing by estimation one quarter of a mile in length, being void of all inhabiting." And uninhabited Bournemouth remained until the nineteenth century, useful only to the smugglers who found its beach and deserted chine entirely suitable for their clandestine activities.

During the Napoleonic wars soldiers were stationed at Christchurch for the purpose of guarding the vacant coast between that place and Poole. They also assisted the Preventive Officers of Excise in their operations against the smugglers. For part of this time the soldiers of the Dorset Rangers patrolling the district were under the command of Captain Lewis Dymoke Grosvenor Tregonwell, who was later to build Bournemouth's first house. Before this, the only building in the locality for several miles around the chine was a decoy house, called Bourne House, situated to the north of the lonely road between Christchurch and Poole, a little to the west of where The Square now is. The decoy house, built during the eighteenth century for sporting purposes, was also used unofficially by the smugglers. It is known that some game shooting did take place at Bournemouth because the third Earl of Malmesbury recalled that in 1826 he shot an old blackcock on the ground where St. Peter's Church was later built. In his *Memoirs of an Ex-Minister* the Earl wrote:

> The principal stronghold round which the smugglers operated was the sea-shore and hollow cliffs that run from Christchurch Head to Poole, then a district of gorse and heath for ten miles, with fir-woods above them. In this wild country black game were abundant, and in 1826 I shot an old black cock on the very spot where St. Peter's Church at Bournemouth now stands. This waste was a favourite resort and breeding-ground of the Hen-harrier, a very destructive species of hawk. They built their nests under the furze bushes and from these impenetrable places used to issue forth and plunder the cultivated country outside for many miles . . . In 1830

> there were not more than half a dozen houses and cottages where now one of our largest and most fashionable sea-side places stands, with its usual accompaniments of clergymen, doctors, lawyers . . . It was in this at that time very wild country that as boys we disported ourselves, and imbibed an eternal affection for it and its traditions.

In the early part of the nineteenth century Bournemouth was part of the vast parish of Christchurch, and lying mainly within the Chapelry and Tything of Holdenhurst in the Liberty of Westover, whose Lord of the Manor was Sir George Ivison Tapps. Most of the wild, barren heathland around Bourne Chine was included in the Christchurch Enclosure Award of 1805, as a result of which Sir George Tapps obtained by allotment or purchase great tracts of land on which much of the centre of Bournemouth now stands. He did not acquire this land with the object of carrying out any development on a large scale, though even at this early stage he must have realised the potential value of owning an extensive estate in such a pleasant locality. Tapps had the barren heath thickly planted with pine trees; these trees substantially changed the whole character of the place and greatly influenced its eventual development. In 1809 an inn was built, called originally the Tapps Arms, but later the Tregonwell Arms.

The first dwelling house at Bournemouth was The Mansion, later known as Exeter House after the Marchioness of Exeter who stayed there, erected in 1811 by Lewis Tregonwell. This house stood on the site of the present Royal Exeter Hotel which still incorporates part of the fabric of the original building. Tregonwell, a Dorset squire, had been attracted by the beauties of the lonely chine and empty shore while serving in the Dorset Rangers. In 1810 he brought his wife on a visit to Bournemouth and she liked the place so much that she suggested that he might buy some land there and build a house for their summer residence. Tregonwell thereupon purchased a site of 8½ acres between the decoy house and the sea, along the east side of what is now Exeter Road, and their house was built during the following year. The Tregonwells occupied it for the first time in April 1812.

Tregonwell particularly enjoyed the quiet sea-bathing facilities of Bournemouth and next built a group of cottages for summer letting to people who wanted to take advantage of the sea and pleasant surroundings which the place provided. He then envisaged building an estate of houses as private residences, buying further land for this purpose and engaging a surveyor to plan the development. After his death in 1832 his widow Henrietta and his surviving sons, St. Barbe and John, continued with the work he had started.

Sir George Tapps died in 1835. His son, Sir George William Tapps-Gervis, decided to follow Tregonwell's example and lay out a building estate on part of his own land. Gervis was forty years old when he succeeded to his father's baronetcy. Already the local Member of Parliament (he sat for Christchurch from 1832 to 1837 and had previously represented New Romney) he took a keen interest in the betterment of his property and played a very important part in the development of Bournemouth as a seaside town. He employed as his architect a young man from Christchurch called Benjamin Ferrey who had just started a practice in London. Ferrey drew up plans for what was called The Marine Village of Bourne which included provision for a Church.

Gervis was more ambitious than Tregonwell and envisaged the building of a complete seaside town. Bournemouth's position was considered very favourable for a watering-place, particularly as a resort for invalids and as a winter residence for persons in delicate health who required a warm climate and sheltered atmosphere during the colder months of the year. The transformation of the open heath into thickly wooded pine forests had greatly contributed to the health-giving properties of the area and Bournemouth was soon to become known as a suitable spot where the old and infirm could live.

One of Ferrey's designs, executed about 1836 and exhibited at the Royal Academy, is now displayed in the lobby of the Russell-Cotes Art Gallery in Bournemouth. It shows a suggested lay-out of villas covering the hill on the eastern side of the Bourne stream, and an octagonal Church in Early English Gothic style. This design shows the eight-sided Church occupying a position close to that of the present St. Peter's, but much higher up the hill. It depicts a building with lancet windows in groups of three, an ornamented porch on the south-west face, and a turret and spire over all. It is a pity that, when this scheme was discarded, Ferrey was not allowed to build the Church, because his design possesses an artistic merit which was almost totally lacking in the building which was actually erected only a few years later.

The site which Ferrey proposed for the Church was criticized in some detail by Dr. A. B. Granville in *The Spas of England* (1841), a book in which the doctor warmly welcomed the development of Bournemouth as "the very first invalid sea-watering place in England." It must be remembered, however, that at this time Bournemouth was coming to be recognised as a winter health resort and not as a place for summer holidays. On the subject of the Church Granville forecast that if it was built in the exposed position suggested by Ferrey the invalids would "be blown away in endeavouring to reach the House of God." He went on:

> In a colony of invalids, the Temple of God should be in a quiet, secluded and rural spot. It should be easily accessible to all — to the villagers in health who are occupied to the last minute with household affairs — to the valetudinarian who cannot walk far — to the feeble and the cripple who can only creep or must be carried; and all of whom ought, above all things, to eschew exposure of every description. Such a spot I pointed out for that purpose, on the estate of Mistress Tregonwell on the eastern bank. There a plain, unassuming but spacious and well-built rural church, without any pretensions to Gothic naiseries (for who can bear a church in a Gothic dress that is not as big as Lincoln, Wells or York Minster?) should be erected near the entrance to the Park Villas, whereby the invalid inhabitants of the Park Villas would have it near to them; close to a spot where the villagers' community would be principally settled, on the margin of the brook at the foot of Gordon Villas, that attendance may be made easy to the dwellers therein as well as to the villagers; and lastly, not far removed from the present and any other detached villas along the lower and upper roads; thus leaving no excuse to any class of inhabitants and visitors (as they will have, if the church is built on the top of the hill) for not attending service.

While waiting for a Church of their own to be built the early residents of Bourne Tregonwell, on the west side of the Bourne stream, and the Marine Village of the Gervis estate, on the east side, had to travel several miles to Poole, Holdenhurst or Christchurch when they wanted to attend a service. Occasionally services would be held in Bournemouth if a clergyman happened to be staying in the district, but such visits were infrequent. It was only with the development of the Gervis estate that any proper provision was made for the religious needs of the community.

As early as 1837 it was provided in one of the Gervis building leases that as soon as the ground landlord should erect a Church or chapel for divine worship according to the rites of the Church of England the lessee should pay an additional rent of £1 per annum for the use of a pew or three sittings. In 1838 a pair of semi-detached cottages at what is now The Square (about where Bobbys' shop now stands) were knocked into one and fitted up for use as a temporary Church on Sundays and as a schoolroom on weekdays.

This temporary Church was small in size, too small in fact to accommodate two-thirds of the residents and visitors, and must have looked rather odd. A pointed turret, containing the single bell, was fixed to the apex of the roof and whilst some of the windows had been enlarged and given rounded arches in an attempt to create a romanesque appearance the other windows were left as they were, flat, small and square. The upper floor of one of the cottages was left intact as a minstrels gallery, but unfortunately no details survive of what instruments were played there. It may be but fanciful to suppose that Bournemouth once boasted characters such as those who cannot fail to delight the reader of Hardy's *Under the Greenwood Tree*. The Rev. Hugh Wyndham, ordained deacon in 1836 and priest in 1839, was the usual clergyman, and the Sunday services were held at 11 a.m. and 3 p.m. At about this time a Sunday School was started and the churchpeople of Holdenhurst used to walk over to Bournemouth on Sunday afternoons to teach in it. The day school was kept by the Misses Hoare.

When the temporary Church was no longer needed for services it was retained as the schoolroom for the National day school and the Sunday School. It was also used for public meetings and the first Vestry meetings of the "District Chapelry of Bournemouth" were held there. When the growing numbers of children led to the erection of the new St. Peter's Schools, the old building was sold to Miss Georgina Talbot, the owner of the Talbot Village Estate, who had it pulled down and used some of the stone in the construction of the Talbot Village schools.

Once started, the building of seaside villas at Bournemouth progressed quickly, with the result that within a few years the need for a permanent Church was a pressing one. This need soon found its expression in the first St. Peter's.

CHAPTER II

Building The First St. Peter's

IN 1841 Sir George Gervis began to erect a permanent Church, the first St. Peter's, on the site of the present building. He employed as his architect John Tulloch, of Poole and Wimborne, who had been responsible for a number of other Churches in the locality, including the original St. Peter's at Parkstone (1833). He had also designed those of Lytchett Minster, Dorset (1834), Holt, Dorset (1836) and East Boldre, Hants (1839) and had inserted the nave galleries at Blandford in 1836-37. His next commission after St. Peter's was the new Church at Pennington, Hants, which he built in 1843.

The foundation stone of the first St. Peter's was laid on Tuesday, 28th September, 1841, after a service led by the Rev. Hugh Wyndham in the temporary Church. In spite of very bad weather, a procession set out at noon from the Bath Hotel, composed of workmen, persons bearing vessels containing corn, wine and oil, the bricklayer, the architect, clergymen, gentlemen and tenantry. At the site a service was read by the Rev. William Francis Burrows, Vicar of Christchurch, and two hymns were sung. The inscription on the cornerstone read:

> This Church was built at the sole expense of Sir George William Tapps Gervis, Bart., of Hinton Admiral, in the County of Hants, and proprietor of this estate. This chief corner stone was laid on the 28th September, 1841, by Mrs. Tregonwell of Cranbourne Lodge, Dorset and Bournemouth. Dedicated to St. Peter. The Rev. W. F. Burrows, Vicar. The Rev. Hugh Wyndham, Officiating Minister.

Mrs. Tregonwell was not even present when the stone bearing her name was laid. She was prevented from attending because of the unfavourable weather and Mr. Wyndham deputised for her. The proceedings ended with a formal dinner at the Bath Hotel at which Wyndham presided and Samuel Bayly, who was to become the first people's warden at St. Peter's, an office he held from 1845 until 1848, was vice-chairman. Bayly was Bournemouth's first property speculator and played a large, if unprofitable, part in Bournemouth's early building development. Born in Blandford in 1798, he received only a very meagre education. However, he possessed a restless and inquiring nature which more than compensated for the lack of formal schooling. He ran such a successful drapery business in Christchurch that he was able to retire with a competence by the time he was forty. Having built Hengistbury House as his residence, Bayly was encouraged by a commercial friend from London to engage in the building speculations at Bournemouth which led to his downfall. He fared well for a few years and was responsible for the erection of the Belle Vue Hotel where he went to live, the Bathing Establishment nearby, and many other early buildings. Unfortunately his financial resources became overstrained and eventually he was forced into bankruptcy. He died in 1864 and was buried in St. Peter's churchyard. It is also interesting to note that Peter Tuck, churchwarden of St. Peter's in 1854-55, who, with his father, was a prominent builder and contractor to the Gervis estate, preserved the working tools used for the laying of the foundation stone of the Church and they were used again in 1877 when the first stone was laid of the Masonic Hall in St. Michael's Rise.

The second edition of *The Visitor's Guide to Bournemouth,* published in 1842, says of the new Church that "It will be a small, neat structure, consisting of a nave and chancel, free from any superfluous ornament. It will afford accommodation for 350 persons; and the plan is so arranged, that transepts may be added when the inhabitants shall be so increased as to require an enlarged building. A window of painted glass will adorn the east end. The church is erecting at the sole expense of the wealthy baronet, who is the owner of the soil, from a design by Mr. J. Tulloch, architect, Poole."

Sir George Gervis originally intended that the new Church should be completed and consecrated in May 1842, but the building was still unfinished when he died on 26th August of that year, at the early age of forty-seven. There was no building contract and the work had been done simply upon verbal instructions given from time to time. Gervis left an infant heir (Sir George Elliott Meyrick Tapps Gervis, later known as Sir G. E. M. Tapps Gervis Meyrick, Third Baronet, born 1827) and no provision in his will, which had remained unaltered since before his succession to the baronetcy, for the completion and endowment of the still unfinished Church. Furthermore, the Bishop of Winchester refused to consecrate the building until it was adequately endowed and had a substantial income from pew rents. The Gervis trustees were therefore placed in considerable difficulty and the situation had to be resolved by the Court of Chancery.

In 1843 the Court referred the case to Master Duckworth with instructions to report upon the deceased benefactor's intentions in regard to provision for the Church. This report was eventually produced on 29th May, 1844, and was confirmed by an Order of the Chancery Court a month later. The Court found that Gervis had intended to complete the Church at his own expense, to endow it with a rent-charge of £50 per annum, to set aside a piece of land not exceeding 1½ acres as a churchyard and to provide up to two acres of further land for a parsonage house and garden. It was also reported that the pew rents then exceeded £120 and that completion of the Church would tend to increase the value of the Gervis estate at Bournemouth. The trustees were then given permission by the Court to spend £350 in completing the Church and were empowered to promote a private Bill in Parliament which would enable them to endow it. Without delay an Act was passed (receiving the Royal Assent on 6th August, 1844) "to enable the Trustees of the Will of Sir George William Tapps Gervis Baronet deceased to convey a Church at Bournemouth in the County of Southampton to Her Majesty's Commissioners for building new Churches and to endow the same."

This special statute for St. Peter's (7 & 8 Vict., cap. 27) firstly gave the Gervis trustees power to convey the site of the Church and churchyard to the Church Building Commissioners. Secondly the trustees were authorised to convey further land for a parsonage, subject to satisfactory arrangements being made for building the house and laying out the garden at a cost of not less than £1,500. Thirdly, provision was made for endowing the Church with a rent-charge of £50, with a further rentcharge of £6 for repairs. Fourthly, the Act laid down that the Right of Nomination to the Church should be vested in the trustees of Sir George Gervis and his or their heirs and assigns.

With the legal difficulties now removed, the Gervis trustees completed and endowed the new Church, and it was consecrated by Bishop Sumner of Winchester on 7th August, 1845. The District assigned to the "Chapelry of Bournemouth" covered a large tract of land which was very thinly populated. It extended along the coast from Branksome Park to Boscombe Chine, a distance of 3½ miles, and it stretched a long way inland, including within its boundary part of the land on which Winton was later built. The land for the Church and Churchyard was conveyed by the Gervis trustees to the Church Building Commissioners by a deed dated 14th June, 1845. The site was described as part of Allotment No. 33 in the Christchurch Inclosure Award. The plan of the plot from this deed shows a frontage of 225 feet and a width at the rear of 240 feet. The side boundaries measured 335 feet on the north and 320 feet on the south.

In spite of the delays in getting the Church completed and consecrated the building was licensed for services and opened in the summer of 1844. Mr. William Edward Rebbeck, who was agent for the Tregonwell estates in Bournemouth, acted as Parish Clerk and made arrangements for the services in conjunction with Mr. George Abraham Crawley, solicitor to the trustees of the Gervis estate. Crawley was also one of the trustees, the others being Messrs. O. J. A. F. Meyrick and E. L. Pemberton. There was some difficulty about the Parish Clerk's remuneration, which had been fixed by Sir George Gervis at £5 per annum, and Rebbeck recorded that "when the new Church was opened in June, 1844 Mr. Tulloch stated that the trustees would not allow me any salary" (presumably because of the uncertain legal position), but the Gervis estate did in fact pay him up to July, 1845. Some of the correspondence which passed between Crawley and Rebbeck at this time has fortunately been preserved and it throws a great deal of light on the way the affairs of the Church were run. At the beginning of 1845 Rebbeck compiled his account for the previous year:

Bourne.
The Trustees of the Late Sir G. Taps Gervis Bart.
Dr. to W. Rebbeck

June 28th	Expences (sic) of going into Poole by request of Mr. Tulloch about coverings &c. for the church		2	6
Pd.	for 2 large Hassocks for Pulpit and Reading desk		7	0
	Carriage of Do. from Wimborn		1	0
	White Chamber for Vestry		1	3
Pd.	Mr. Bloomfield for assisting at the singing when the Church was opened		4	9
	Do. Second Sunday		3	0
25th	Removing the Stove from the Church to School Room, 5 men, Horse & Waggon		5	0
Nov. 23rd	Removing Do. to the Church		5	0
	4 days assisting about the flue of Stove at the Church by order of Mr. Tulloch		8	0
	Bier (sic) for Men at Do.		1	6
	1 Cwt. of Coal for Church		1	9
Pd.	Mr. Sydenham for 100 Advent Hymns for Church		1	9
Pd.	Do. for 4 Violoncello strings for Do.		3	4
		£2	8	7
	1 Years salary as Clerk Due May 1844	5	0	0
		£7	8	7
	2 Cwts. coal		3	0
		£7	11	7

No comment was made about the beer bought for the men who helped with the stove when Crawley paid the bill on behalf of the Gervis trustees:

Whitehall Place
27 March 1845

Sir,

Inclosed I send you a draft on Coutts & Co. for £7 11s. 7d. the amount of your account for which I will thank you to send me a stamped receipt as paid "by the Trustees of Sir Geo. Gervis's Estate in discharge of the annexed account" & I shall then be able to annex it to the account. I am by no means sure that these expenses ought not to be paid by the Pew Renters amongst themselves, but I will pay them on the present occasion, & will make enquiries respecting it of Mr. Tulloch when I write to him.

Messrs. Tice & Co. of Christchurch will no doubt give you cash for the enclosed draft.

I am Sir
Yours &c.
Geo. A. Crawley.

The Christchurch bankers mentioned in the last sentence of Crawley's letter were Messrs. Tice & Welch, a firm founded in 1839 which amalgamated with the Wilts and Dorset Banking Company in 1849. The Wilts and Dorset Company was later taken over by Lloyds Bank.

Rebbeck continued to arrange the services at the new Church, engaging such local or visiting clergymen as happened to be available. The Gervis trustees assumed responsibility for the fees which Rebbeck requested from time to time. The exchange of letters between Crawley and Rebbeck printed below is of particular interest because not only are several of the clergymen named but also it is made clear how the arrangements operated.

20 Whitehall Place
19th April 1845

Sir,

I have this morning received your letter, and enclose three Post Office orders amounting together to £11 5s. being the Stipend for the duty performed at Bournemouth for the days mentioned in your letter.

The Stipend allowed to Mr. Tidemore and to the preceding Curates was 50s. a week or 25s. for each Service — and as in the present case there was an additional Service on Good Friday the sum I have sent will I conceive be divided as follows

Mr. Hammond	2 Services	2	10
Mr. Wilson	3 Do.	3	15
Mr. Timson	2 Do.	2	10
Mr. Blandford	1 Do.	1	5
Mr. Buller	1 Do.	1	5
		£11	5

I will thank you to pay these sums to the above mentioned Clergymen and obtain their Receipts which you will be good enough to transmit to me.

I am, Sir,
Your obedient Servant,
Geo. A. Crawley.

Bourn, April 22nd.

Sir,
I received your letter on Sunday last containing the post office Order for £11 5s. I yesterday went into Poole, Parley and Holdenhurst and have enclosed your Mr. Wilsons, Mr. Bullers and Mr. Hammonds receipts. I have also enclosed a letter Mr. Timson desired me to forward you. I shall feel greatfull if you allow him to fulfill the kind intention he mention in his letter to you. I have not forwarded Mr. Blandfords money as I think you will find in reference to my note of the 18th that Mr. Blandford did two services on the 11th March and you remitted me £1 5s. only so that £1 5s. is now due to him.

I am very respectfully,
Your obedient Servant,
W. E. Rebbeck.

No other record has been found concerning the curacy held by Mr. Tidemore. The only priest of that name mentioned in the *Clergy List* for 1845 was the Rev. James Tidemore, perpetual curate of Netherthong, Yorks., so he may have been a visitor to Bournemouth who undertook the duties during his stay. Mr. Hammond was probably the Rev. W. Hamond (sic) who was assistant curate of Christchurch with Holdenhurst in 1845. Mr. Wilson was the Rev. Robert Otway Wilson, B.D., Vicar of St. Paul's Church, Poole, from 1833 to 1853. It is not quite certain who Mr. Timson was. The name does not appear in the *Clergy Lists* for 1845 and 1848 and the form of receipt which Rebbeck prepared for Timson to sign calls him "the Revd. E. Timson." A Rev. W. Timson is mentioned in Mate & Riddle's *Bournemouth 1810-1910,* pp. 92 and 240, as having officiated occasionally at services in the temporary Church at The Square and as having had a house built on the East Cliff in 1848 on land leased from the Gervis estate. Unfortunately we do not know what Mr. Timson said in the letter which Rebbeck forwarded to Crawley.

Mr. Blandford was the Rev. William West Blandford, M.A., Oxon., assistant curate of Witchampton, Dorset. He was eventually paid the additional £1 5s. 0d. due to him, but not until November, 1845, and then only after further correspondence. Mr. Buller was the Rev. Henry John Buller, M.A., Rector of West Parley, Dorset, from 1839 to 1874. He wrote to Rebbeck on 6th April, 1845:

Mr. Henry Buller will have much pleasure in offering his services at a quarter before three o'clock tomorrow & will be in Bournemouth at that hour, unless he hears from Mr. Rebbeck to the contrary this evening.

There is no record of the Rev. Hugh Wyndham having officiated at the first St. Peter's after it was licensed for services in 1844. In the absence of positive evidence, the probability must be that he had left Bournemouth by this time, because by 1845, according to the *Clergy List* for that year, he was acting as assistant curate of St. Basil's Church at Toller Fratrum, Dorset.

In the alphabetical list of clergymen in the *Clergy List* for 1845 appears the name of R. W. K. Wood, M.A., against which is the designation "Incumbent of Bournemouth". The section of the same publication headed *List of Benefices* then gives "Christchurch-Bournemouth. R. W. K. Wood, 1844." Presumably, therefore, Wood succeeded Wyndham at some time during 1844, but where he came from and where he went are unknown. In any case there seems little doubt that he was not strictly entitled to be called Incumbent at that stage.

Although the first St. Peter's was an enterprise initiated solely by Sir George Gervis and carried on after his death by his trustees, Mrs. Henrietta Tregonwell was also very interested in the establishment of the permanent Church. It was she who had the honour of being invited to lay the foundation stone and was most disappointed when bad weather on the day of the ceremony in 1841 prevented her from going out and she had to depute the Rev. Hugh Wyndham to do it for her. She had one particular personal reason for being impatient at the delays caused by the death of Sir George Gervis since she wanted to bring the bodies of her late husband and infant son, Grosvenor Portman Tregonwell, to the new churchyard for reinterment. She herself was getting old, and with increasing infirmity she feared she might die without accomplishing her wish.

There is an interesting letter in St. Peter's Archives which she wrote to Rebbeck at Midsummer, 1845. Rebbeck, it will be remembered, was both Parish Clerk at St. Peter's and Mrs. Tregonwell's agent for Bournemouth, so the letter gives him instructions in both capacities.

Cranborne,
June 24th, 1845.

Rebbeck,
I think you may receive the Ground Rent from Peter Tuck, as Mr. Pearce has not received the Ground Rents of Bourne that I can recollect. I am *quite ill* with Influenza. I attribute it to my taking off my Gown and sitting in a Draft of air up Stairs the day before

> I left Bourne. Yesterday I remained in Bed, the Phlegm lodges on my Chest, & I am rather short-breathed. I am weakened with Perspiration - Blister, &c.
> John and Mrs. J. T-ll went to Salisbury to'day. They return on friday or thursday according as I am; when I move it will be to Bourne. Have you heard *what day* the new Church will be consecrated? I am *now more* anxious than ever about this, as Mr. Churchill wrote about having the Vault pulled down, that is against the Chancel of Anderson Church and I have begged that it may not be done before next month, as we have *promised* that our Church shall be consecrated, and then *you know what* my intention immediately is to do, and this I wrote to Mr. Churchill. You may name it to Mr. Bennett. I am not well enough to write to him at present.
>
> I am, &c.,
>
> H. Tregonwell.
>
> Have the down Stairs Bedroom thoroughly well aired before we return, get the Salisbury Bedstead painted directly, & if the smell of the Paint goes off it may be put up in that Room with the white furniture from Salisbury — my Son will send some Bedding from Sy. by the Carrier to Bourne soon. Mr. & Mrs. Northcote & Baby are at Ensham. Grass cut in our Park to'day. The letter you named did not arrive to'day. - H.T-ll.

Immediately after the consecration of St. Peter's Mrs. Tregonwell started making the arrangements for the removal of the bodies of Lewis and Grosvenor Tregonwell from the family vault at Anderson. A new vault was prepared and made ready in St. Peter's churchyard for the reception of the remains which were reinterred on 26th February, 1846. These re-burials are not mentioned in the extant registers of St. Peter's, but those of Winterbourne Anderson tell the full story. In the burial register for the years 1772-1812, now deposited in the County Record Office at Dorchester, is the following entry:

> Grosvenor Portman Tregonwell son of Lewis Dymock Tregonwell, Esq. of Cranborne and Harriet his wife was buried in the family vault on the first of June 1807. 10 weeks old.

On the following page of the register is this note:

> I hereby certify that the body of Grosvenor Portman Tregonwell was removed from the family vault in this parish on the 26th day of February, 1846 and was carried to Bournemouth. Edward Dansey, Curate of Winterbourne Anderstone.

We are reminded by these records that Anderson was formerly known as Anderstone (a corruption of *St. Andrew's tun*), and that Mrs. Henrietta Tregonwell was also known as Harriet. Her daughter was also named Henrietta and one of the daughters of her son

John was called Harriet. The entry relating to the "Founder of Bournemouth" appears in the register book of burials which is still in use at Anderson:

> Lewis Dymock Grosvenor Tregonwell, Cranborn Lodge. Buried 26 Jan. 1832. Age 73. W. H. R. Churchill, Rector. N.B. This body was removed from the family vault in this parish to Bournemouth on the 26th day of February 1846. Edward Dansey, Curate of Anderstone.

Mrs. Tregonwell selected a pleasant spot in the churchyard, in the middle of the path near the top of the Thirty-nine Steps, as the site for the new grave, surmounting it with a large altar tomb of simple but pleasing design. Brass plates affixed to the monument record the names and particulars of the seven members of the Tregonwell family who are buried there. The principal inscription reads:

> Sacred to the Memory of Lewis Dymoke Grosvenor Tregonwell, Esquire, of Anderson, and Cranborne Lodge, in the County of Dorset, who departed this life at the latter of these residences on the 18th day of January, 1832, aged 73 years. Also of Grosvenor Portman Tregonwell, his son, who died an infant, on the 29th May, 1807. Their remains were removed from Anderson to this spot on the 26th day of February, 1846, Bournemouth, which Mr. Tregonwell was the first to bring into notice as a watering place by erecting a mansion for his own occupation, having been his favourite retreat for many years before his death.

Within two months Henrietta Tregonwell herself died and was buried with her husband and baby. Hers is the first burial entry in the registers of St. Peter's. On the other side of the tomb another inscription plate was fixed:

> Sacred to the Memory of Henrietta, relict of L. D. G. Tregonwell, Esquire, of Anderson and Cranborne Lodge, in the County of Dorset, and daughter of Henry William Portman, Esquire and Ann, his wife, of Bryanstone House, Dorset, who departed this life at her residence at Bournemouth, on the 15th of April, MDCCCXLVI. Aged 76 years. Sincerely regretted by a large circle of friends.

John Tregonwell succeeded to his father's Bournemouth estate where Rebbeck continued to act as agent. The account book between these two, covering the period from June 1846 to Rebbeck's death (and thereafter with Rebbeck's son), recently came to light and is now available for consultation at Bournemouth Central Library. Several entries in it relate to St. Peter's. We see that Rebbeck made a number of payments for pew rents and other Church subscriptions. Among the earlier items appear the following:

1847				
Jany. 11	Balance for Pew Rents as per Receipts	2	13	4
May 15	Paid Rev. A. M. Bennett Easter Offering		10	0
May 15	One weeks Pew Rent as per Receipt		3	0
Sep. 17	Pd. Rev. A. M. Bennet subscription to school	1	0	0
	Do. Do. Do. for organist		10	0
1848				
May 18	Paid Rev. A. Bennett Easter Offering		10	0
July 14 & 15	Pd. Churchwardens for Quantity of Grass from Church Yard		15	6
Oct.	Subscription to organist		10	0
	Do. to school	1	0	0
Dec. 18	Pew Rent as per Receipt		4	0
1849				
June 3	To Easter Offerings to Clergyman		10	0

By the time it was completed, or very soon afterwards, the first St. Peter's was already too small for the needs of the rapidly growing community. Its total length from east to west was about 75 feet and its width about 26 feet. The seating accommodation for worshippers is given by Mate & Riddle in *Bournemouth 1810-1910* as 270 places, 150 of which were on the floor and 90 in a gallery at the western end. *Bright's Illustrated Guide to Bournemouth* (1888) states there was accommodation for "about 250" people. Mate & Riddle go on to say that, "Being erected rather as a temporary structure, the Church was small and ill-suited to the requirements of residents and visitors." It contained two pulpits, both exactly alike, on either side of the Church; one was used for taking the service and the other for preaching. There were neither ornaments nor decorations to relieve the drabness of the interior, for such things were held in those times to be the frivolous and unjustified practices of the Church of Rome. The seats consisted partly of box pews and partly of plain benches. A coal stove inside the building provided the only heating. Presumably a small band made music in part of the gallery, as witness the reference to the four violoncello strings which Rebbeck bought in 1844 from Mr. Sydenham's Library and Reading Room near the beach. (Sydenham stocked soda water, tea, coffee and pianos in addition to books and newspapers!) Harry Crumpler, sacristan of St. Peter's from 1873 to 1936, recalled that the singing was led by a flute, clarionet and bass viol. There was also an organ installed in the gallery, built by a Mr. J. Duncan of Poole, who came over to Bournemouth every Sunday to play it. Duncan's workshops were in the lower part of the present Poole High Street near the Quay. His organ was later removed from the gallery to a new position at the east end of the nave.

The architectural style in which the new Church was built, mock Gothic, has been almost universally condemned, particularly by the clergy of the period. The first incumbent, the Rev. Alexander Morden Bennett, called it "a very poor structure" and Carter refers to it as a "poor, modern chapel of ease." Dr. J. H. Overton, writing of the mock Gothic Churches of the period in his *English Church in the Nineteenth Century,* said of Tulloch and his fellow architects: "They built their churches first, and began to study the principles of church architecture afterwards. There are probably no churches which are more of a puzzle and a despair to architects and clergymen than the churches built in the early part of the nineteenth century. Unmitigated ugliness and hopeless inconvenience are their chief characteristics."

The first St. Peter's had its main entrance at the west end. There were lancet windows on each side of the west door and along the south and north walls of the Church. Above the west door was another window, divided by the simplest of tracery into two main lights. Over this window was a clock, the first, and at the time the only, public clock which Bournemouth possessed. Perched on the western end of the roof was a small, square bell-tower with circular turrets at the corners, capped by a short, thin steeple. The apex of the roof at the east end of the building was surmounted by a stone cross.

The design and appearance of the new Church proved to be so unpleasing and the appointments so inconvenient that it came as no surprise to local residents when they heard that steps were soon to be taken to alter and enlarge it, with the eventual object of building an entirely new edifice which would be both worthier as a House of God and more in keeping with the character of the town and the religious needs of the population. And the pioneer in this work was the first Vicar, Alexander Morden Bennett.

CHAPTER III

The Arrival Of Morden Bennett

AS WE have seen, the situation at St. Peter's in the summer of 1845 was that the new Church had been completed and licensed for divine worship but not yet consecrated. The Bishop of Winchester, the Right Rev. Charles Richard Sumner, in whose diocese the Church had been built, refused to perform the consecration ceremony until he was satisfied that an incumbent had been appointed who was willing to take charge. The endowment was a mere £50 per annum and the income from pew rents less than £200. There was no parsonage and, although the Gervis trustees had generously provided a fine plot of land for the purpose, the house still had to be built at the expense of the clergyman presented to the Church. The minimum sum stipulated as the cost of the parsonage and laying out the grounds was £1,500. It is no wonder, therefore, that these responsibilities, coupled with the lack of any assurance that the growth of Bournemouth would be maintained, led several clergymen to refuse to take the living.

Apparently news got about of the difficulties of filling the vacancy at St. Peter's and at least one clergyman was under the impression that a paid summer holiday at the seaside would be rather pleasant. On 3rd June 1845, writing to Rebbeck from an address near Andover, he said:

> Sir,
> Having heard that a Clergyman is wanted for the duties at Bournemouth I write to you, at the suggestion of Mr. Ledgard of Poole, to beg that you will be good enough to let me know whether this will be the case in the months of August & September, & if so whether my services for 3 or 4 weeks at that time would be accepted and if so on what terms—and whether there is a house for the clergyman, or if one can be obtained & at what rent. My family consists of a party that would require 5 or 6 bed rooms & 2 sitting rooms. Begging you to excuse the trouble of this letter, & that which it seeks to put you to, for your taking which for me I shall be truly obliged.
>
> I am, Sir,
> Your obedient Servant,
> C. R. Dallas.

The search for a full-time incumbent continued. A man was

needed of the highest principles, and with an earnest pioneering spirit, who was prepared to launch himself into the unknown with an ugly little Church in his care, and yet be willing to spend his own private means in carrying out his pastoral duties. In other words, it needed a paragon of virtue and ability, and a rich one at that.

When one considers the many drawbacks, which must have combined to make St. Peter's one of the least attractive livings in the whole of England, it is quite astonishing, and something for which successive generations have good reason to be thankful, that the incumbent was no less a man than the Rev. Alexander Morden Bennett. Over a quarter of a century later, in October 1871, Morden Bennett wrote of Bournemouth as it was when he arrived. "This town was scarcely known as a watering-place; there were but a few lodging-houses, scarcely any dwellings for the poor, and only one small Church in which we met together for common acts of worship."

The incumbent's then very young son, Alex. Bennett, came to Bournemouth with his family in 1845 and some of his reminiscences sixty years later were reported in *The Bournemouth Graphic*. The only school he could remember was the Sunday school, held in the building which had been the old temporary Church. Nor were the scholars very numerous. Indeed, on the first Sunday on which Morden Bennett drove over from Mudeford to enter the duty, so few were they that, as he walked from the Belle Vue Hotel where he had put up his horse, he overtook the teacher with the key in one hand and holding the solitary pupil by the other! It is true there was a Church, and well did Alex. Bennett remember it, "with four castellated excrescences, one at each corner of the roof, and a tiny spire. And then inside the western gallery there was the village orchestra—sackbut, psaltery, and all kinds of music." The consecration was on a bright summer's day, when the Church was packed, and Bishop Sumner came to Bournemouth for the first time. When the plate was handed round, Alex. Bennett put in a bright half-sovereign which his grandfather had given him for the purpose.

In the summer of 1845 Morden Bennett was thirty-six years old, having been born at Morden College, Blackheath, where his father was college treasurer, on 11th October, 1808. He had studied at Worcester College, Oxford, taking his B.A. degree in 1830 and his M.A. in 1832. He had been ordained deacon in 1831 and priest in the following year.

Morden Bennett's first assistant curacy was at Withington, near Cheltenham, in the diocese of Gloucester. At the age of twenty-seven, while assistant curate at Hampton Lucy, Warwick, he married a London parson's daughter, moving soon afterwards first to South Cadbury, Somerset, where he held another assistant curacy, and then to Shepton Mallet, in the same county, where he was temporary priest-in-charge. His wife died while they were at Shepton and Morden Bennett then moved to London as assistant curate at All Souls, Langham Place. After only a short stay at Langham Place he moved to the Portman Chapel in Baker Street, London, as assistant priest, an appointment he relinquished on coming to Bournemouth.

The Portman Chapel at this period was one of the outposts of the Oxford Movement, then only just feeling its way within the Establishment and making few friends among the leaders of the Church. The ideas which Morden Bennett must have acquired at the Portman Chapel found their expression at St. Peter's in a gradual development over the years, for although Morden Bennett was a courageous, thinking priest of the modern school he never attempted to force his personal views upon an unready or unprepared congregation. Many of the practices and customs which he started at St. Peter's became traditions which are still upheld to this day, and when he died in 1880, far from there being any reaction against his churchmanship, a storm broke around the person of his successor who was not trusted to carry on Morden Bennett's work without interruption.

The Oxford Movement had started as a protest against the neglect and self-satisfied conservatism which were paralysing the Church. It was dedicated to securing the proper performance of clerical duties and ritual observances. It held that the Church of England was not an institution subject to the state but a part of the visible Holy Catholic Church having an unbroken connection with the primitive church. The sacraments, which had been sadly neglected in many parishes, were once again given their due prominence. The adherents of the Oxford Movement came to be called Tractarians, after the Tracts which their leaders published setting out their views.

It was in 1845, the year Morden Bennett came to St. Peter's, that the Oxford Movement split when Newman and his supporters seceded to Rome. However, John Keble and other Tractarians who remained within the Anglican Church, supported by increasing numbers of young priests like Morden Bennett, continued with their proposals for reform which were principally designed to assert the authority and dignity of the Church. In these men the spirit of the Oxford Movement was able to survive, the clergy setting the example in being particularly zealous in performing their duties, carrying out rubrical directions and striving to win the hearts of their people.

In time changes were made in the performance of public worship with the object of bringing about a higher level of reverence at divine service and a revival of life in the Church as a whole. In Bournemouth Morden Bennett was to pursue these policies at a steady but fairly leisured pace. Outwardly, at least, he was not in the vanguard of reform; his beliefs and ideals were only put into practice at St. Peter's after due deliberation and careful preparation. He would lead his congregation with a firm hand but would refrain from taking any step until he was sure that his people would follow him. This sensible caution resulted in several changes in the worship of St. Peter's having to wait until they could be introduced confidently by his successors.

One circumstance which may have prompted Morden Bennett's decision to accept the living of St. Peter's was that early in 1845 he married again, and his second wife had close local associations. She was Miss Mariamne Elizabeth Hopkins, daughter of Captain Henry Hopkins of Christchurch and sister of the Rev. Frederick Hopkins, who was curate of Holdenhurst from 1847 to 1858 and vicar of the same place from 1877 to 1903. At all events Morden Bennett agreed to come to St. Peter's, and so began a highly successful incumbency which lasted for thirty-five years.

What kind of a man was this Morden Bennett, who has left his imprint on the life of Bournemouth as surely as have Gervis and Tregonwell? First and foremost, he was a man of deep, compelling religious faith, a man with an urgent and real sense of the mission of the Church and of its intimate and telling impact on the lives of Christian people. He was, it is believed, the first incumbent in the Winchester diocese to introduce the daily celebration of the Eucharist. Secondly, he was a man of vision and purpose, accurately forecasting the steady development of Bournemouth into a thriving centre of population and ensuring through his personal efforts that the Church would be ready to welcome the new people as they arrived, rather than the other way round. It is said that on several occasions when a new family came to reside in his parish he was in the house even before the furniture had been arranged. Thirdly, he was a man who clearly appreciated the role which the Church should play in local affairs, particularly in education and the relief of those unable to manage for themselves, and he quickly became one of the most respected citizens of the new town which he helped in no small measure to create. His name has been linked with those of Tregonwell and Gervis as one of the three founders of Bournemouth, though the official histories of the town have given him less recognition than he deserves. Fourthly, he was a man devoted exclusively to the difficult and exacting task he had undertaken; in the words of Sir Henry Taylor, "The Vicar thinks of nothing but his duties—laborious and devoted, with a singular austerity of manner and aspect. He looks like the Commination Service incarnate." Fifthly, he was a man quite unworried and unconcerned by the fact that he was not, and could never be, a popular figure. Some people thought him pompous. It was said that, although he had "no ease or charm of manner to help him," he nevertheless succeeded in inspiring whole-hearted support for his many schemes and enterprises by sheer moral courage and strength of character. He was not a great preacher. "Such utterances of his as have been preserved are dull and heavy with quotation from hymn and Bible, and yet those who remembered him have said that his preaching was fired with the love of Christ and suffused with simple sanctity." Lastly, he was a man of the family, both his own personal family, which he guided through several periods of sadness which afflicted his domestic life, and his family of parishioners, who looked up to him as the father-figure that he certainly was. When Morden Bennett died, the *Bournemouth Directory* said of him, "there is no man now living in Bournemouth or who has ever been connected with it, that is, or was, more universally respected than he. His stern and uncompromising character may in some instances have prevented him from being regarded with that affection with which some men are—still everybody admired his unswerving determination to carry out in its entirety every scheme which he took in hand." His own sacristan, Harry Crumpler, wrote of him, "If ever there was a true hard-working Priest in God's Church, Alexander Morden Bennett was one of the most indefatigable, earnest, Christian-minded clergymen it has ever been the lot of a congregation to possess."

On hearing that Morden Bennett had accepted the Gervis trustees' invitation to St. Peter's, Bishop Sumner came to Bournemouth on 7th August 1845 to perform the ceremony of consecrating the new Church. The new incumbent, whose official title was that of perpetual curate, quickly made arrangements to move to the district and lived temporarily at Mudeford while his new home was being built. After a winter of riding to and from his parish across the desolate wastes between Christchurch and Bourne Chine, he must have been very glad to take up his new residence in the growing village when the parsonage was ready for occupation in 1846.

The piece of land provided for the parsonage by the Gervis trustees was a fine one. Situated on high ground above the churchyard and commanding beautiful views of the sea and the Purbeck Hills beyond, it was an excellent spot for a family house and this is what Morden Bennett made it. The architect was Edmund Pearce of Canford, who was later responsible for the St. Peter's schools and for the south aisle which Morden Bennett added to the Church. For the construction of the cellar of the parsonage Pearce obtained some heavy stonework from the ruins of Southampton Castle which was being disposed of at that time. The new parsonage later became known as the vicarage, but the original title is perpetuated to this day in the name of Parsonage Road.

One of the first changes which Morden Bennett made at St. Peter's after his arrival to start his ministry was to remove one of the Church's two pulpits and in its place to erect a "reading pew" and vicarage pew combined. The family sat at the back of the pew and the incumbent, taking the service, in front.

Details of the services held at St. Peter's during Morden Bennett's first few years are given in the *Bournemouth Guide* of 1850: "Divine service commences on Sundays at 11 o'clock in the forenoon, and at 4 in the afternoon, except during a portion of the winter when the afternoon service commences at three o'clock. There is also a service commencing at eight o'clock daily throughout the year."

It is clear from this extract that one of Morden Bennett's first actions after his arrival in Bournemouth was to introduce a daily celebration. The incumbent's Tractarian leanings were accordingly made apparent from the very beginning of his ministry at Bournemouth, and at a time when many parsons held Holy Communion services as seldom as once a month. As previously stated, St. Peter's was probably the first Church in the Diocese of Winchester to have its daily celebration of the Eucharist, a tradition which has continued to the present day.

Another innovation was the provision of the clock mentioned in the last chapter. Its face was high up on the west wall of the Church near the apex of the roof immediately below the bell-tower. Installed in 1848 by Messrs. Thwaites & Read of Clerkenwell, London, this was the first public clock which Bournemouth ever possessed. It is now fixed in the ringing chamber half way up the tower of the present St. Peter's, facing inwards, so that only the bell-ringers can tell what time it says. However, it still strikes the hours and remains in good working order.

Morden Bennett quickly made his mark on the religious life of

Bournemouth. A visitor in about 1850 described the growing town as "a High Church Colony, squatted amongst the sunny chines between Poole and Christchurch; Puseyism flourished like the rhododendrons in the thicket hard by: everyone turned round to the east at the creed: funerals were conducted on approved High Church principles with wooden biers and violet palls."

The first Vestry Meeting of *The District Chapelry of Bournemouth* was held on 20th November 1845 when Morden Bennett nominated Edward Castleman, a member of an old Dorset family who had acquired property in Bournemouth, as one churchwarden; the other, selected by the Vestry, was Samuel Bayly, the property speculator who had been concerned with the laying of the foundation stone in 1841.

Morden Bennett then turned to the task of making his Church and his ministry more worthy of their respective functions, by enlarging the building, founding schools, and taking the Word of God and the practice of religion outside the boundary of his own parish into the neglected rural areas beyond.

CHAPTER IV

Bennett's Early Years

MORDEN BENNETT quickly settled down to the pioneering work which was needed at Bournemouth and soon began to take a prominent part in the affairs of the local community. His first scheme for the extension of the Church's influence in the parish was the establishment of a Church school. Although the population of the district in 1846 was only about six hundred, Morden Bennett insisted on the great importance of setting up proper educational facilities and started appealing for donations. He was helped in raising the money by one of his parishioners, Miss Harriet Daniell, who published four drawings of local views at £1 12s. 0d. a set "in aid of the Fund for Schools and School-houses at Bournemouth." Unfortunately, Miss Daniell died on 21st February, 1849, before the building work on the new school had commenced, and was buried in St. Peter's churchyard six days later. A separate drawing by Miss Daniell of Morden Bennett's new parsonage was also published at about the same time and is reproduced in this book.

Generous support for the school building fund was soon forthcoming and Morden Bennett instructed Edmund Pearce to prepare the plans. A piece of land for the school was obtained from the Gervis estate adjoining the north-east side of the site of the Church. The foundation stone of St. Peter's school was laid on 30th June 1850 by Lady Louisa Ponsonby, the wife of the Rev. the Hon. Walter Ponsonby, Vicar of Canford Magna, who later became Earl of Bessborough. By 1851 the resident population of Bournemouth had increased to 695 and, with the progress of the new town's development, many more people were coming to swell these numbers, so it was just as well that a school awaited them.

Morden Bennett held very decided views about the need for denominational Christian education and throughout his life he not only strove to establish more and more Church schools but also did his best to prevent or hinder the setting up of Board Schools within the district upon the ground that they might attract children away from the schools maintained by the Church. It is largely due to Morden Bennett's personal influence in these early days that not until the twentieth century were there any schools in Bournemouth other than those managed by the Church or privately. St. Peter's school was enlarged in 1859-60.

In 1871 Morden Bennett amplified his opinions about the necessity for Church schools. He wrote:

> In a school where there is no religious teaching, the instruction which is given is serviceable as far as the child's welfare in this world is concerned; but in a school where importance is attached to religion, the child is taught to keep up a sense of God's presence at all times: to perform all his social duties on the principle of love, and is thus prepared for an entrance into that glorious kingdom which has been purchased for us by our Lord and Saviour Jesus Christ, so that he may be happy for ever. Therefore, I say, that the Church school is to be preferred to the Board school, because in the Church school much attention is paid to religious teaching; in the Board school religion is not altogether excluded (thank God), but it is treated as a matter of secondary importance.

St. Peter's school flourished for eighty-five years until in 1936 it was decided that there was no longer any real need for an elementary school in the centre of Bournemouth. By that time most of the old houses had become converted into shops and offices or replaced by modern commercial premises, and the residential population had mostly moved to the outskirts of the town. The design and amenities of the school were in any case exceedingly old-fashioned and the expense of carrying out the necessary alterations and renovations could hardly be justified. Accordingly the property reverted to the Meyrick estate as ground landlords and the buildings were demolished to make way for a modern commercial block.

The new St. Peter's school had only just been completed and opened when Morden Bennett noticed the educational and spiritual needs of a growing but sadly neglected community of artisans, workmen and smallholders who lived in a settlement of cottages to the north of Bournemouth at a place called Moordown. Nobody had previously troubled to consider that these people lacked the most fundamental ministry of the Church; Morden Bennett not only saw the problem but he resolved to fill the need and in so doing accurately perceived that this poor neighbourhood would one day become a vital part of Bournemouth's urban growth.

The mission, which was designed to serve the residents of the hamlets of Moordown, Redhill and Muscliffe, was started in a farm cottage at Moordown. Then, in 1853, Sir George Tapps Gervis, the Lord of the Manor, gave Morden Bennett a piece of land alongside the road from Bournemouth to Wimborne for the erection of a permanent school-chapel. This was the year of Morden Bennett's introduction to the rising young ecclesiastical architect, George Edmund Street, and the Moordown Church was the first of his many commissions in the Bournemouth area.

With his customary energy Morden Bennett quickly collected most of the money he required and issued the following notice:

MOORDOWN SCHOOL-CHAPEL

Moordown, in the Parish of Holdenhurst, Hants, comprises a tract of heath-land on which many poor families are settled, who are two miles distant from their parish church. It is proposed, under the sanction of the Vicar, on this spot to erect a schoolroom, which the Bishop has consented to license for an occasional service. It is hoped that the privileges of the Church being thus brought near to these poor people, may serve, by God's blessing, to improve their spiritual and moral condition, or may at least afford consolation to the aged and infirm.

The surrounding population amount to 300.

The Contract for the Building (exclusive of Architect's commission, law expences etc.) amount to:	£359	8	0
The contributions amount to:	£261	5	8½
Deficiency in the building account:	£98	2	3½

A. MORDEN BENNETT,

May 12th, 1853. Perpetual Curate of Bournemouth.

The school-chapel at Moordown was completed early in 1854. One of its tiny windows was glazed with coloured panes depicting St. John the Baptist, and the building became known as St. John-in-the-Wilderness. It was a small, modest structure, with a chancel which was curtained off during the week so that the main part of the building could be used as a school. Within ten years fifty scholars were in daily attendance at the school under the care of a certified mistress from the training college at Salisbury.

In the summer of 1865 £150 was spent on enlarging the school-chapel twenty feet eastwards so as to provide a greater number of sittings, because the attendance at services had increased to such large numbers that many people were unable to obtain admission. Even the enlarged building later became too small for the increased residents who populated the growing district and it was replaced in 1874 by the present Church of St. John the Baptist. The old chapel was retained as the school until modern schools adjoining the new Church were opened. The original building was then sold for commercial purposes and is now used as showrooms and offices by Willis (Bournemouth) Limited, builders merchants, who continue to call their premises Old St. John's Buildings.

Before returning to Morden Bennett's work at St. Peter's Church it may be interesting to give one example of the way in which he entered into the secular life of the community. In 1847 he was, with his two churchwardens, Samuel Bayly and Richard Elgie, one of ten local gentlemen who met at the Bath Hotel for the purpose of having a discussion with Decimus Burton, the new architect to the Gervis Estate, about plans for the further development of Bournemouth and particularly about the provision of a pier or jetty. At this meeting general agreement seems to have been reached that a landing place would be a desirable addition to the local amenities, but shortage of money put an end to the scheme for the time being. Eventually, in 1855, a jetty was erected, and this was replaced by the first pier in 1861. The pier was built by the Bournemouth Improvement Commissioners, a body constituted in 1856 to administer the local government, and it is noteworthy that the resolution to proceed with the work was proposed by Henry Dickinson and seconded by Robert Kerley who were respectively churchwardens of St. Peter's in 1855-56 and 1856-57.

The other churchwarden for 1856-57 was Thomas Kingdon, one of the earliest legal lights of Bournemouth and first clerk to the Improvement Commissioners. His annual salary as clerk was a mere £25 and he resigned after two years over a dispute about additional fees which he contended he was entitled to receive. He lived in a house built on the site of Bournemouth's present Town Hall.

In 1853-54 Dr. E. V. Mainwaring, one of the first medical men to be attracted to Bournemouth, was the people's churchwarden. He lived at 5 Richmond Terrace, a property which is now part of the Norfolk Hotel. Mainwaring died in 1855 and lies buried in St. Peter's churchyard. His widow herself died on the very day of the doctor's funeral. Robert Kerley, churchwarden in 1856-57, was later the donor of the site of Holy Trinity Church, where stained glass windows to his memory were placed in the chancel in 1872. Kerley was chairman of the Bournemouth Improvement Commissioners from 1865 to 1867.

One of the earliest baptisms to take place at St. Peter's was of a motherless baby boy who was destined to become famous in the world of music, Hubert Parry. His mother, whose health was poor, came to Bournemouth early in 1848 for the birth of her second child. The baby was born on 27th February 1848 but Mrs. Parry only survived her confinement by a fortnight. She was buried at St. Peter's on 18th March and two days later young Hubert was christened, being taken back to his family home at Highnam Court, Gloucestershire. It is interesting to note that the boy's father, Thomas Gambier Parry, was known as "a keen supporter of the 'high-church' movement." Perhaps he encouraged Morden Bennett, whose own leanings in that direction had not as yet greatly influenced the worship at St. Peter's. Mrs. Parry's grave is just to the east of the Church, near the churchyard steps. On one side are those of Harriet Daniell and Walter Scott Evans; on the other that of a later vicar, George Stopford Ram and members of his family.

Hubert Parry distinguished himself as one of the foremost English musicians. He gained fame and admiration as composer of operas, oratorios and orchestral music. Knighted in 1898, he was created baronet four years later, but as he left no male heir the title died with him. On his death in 1918, at the age of seventy, he was buried in the crypt of St. Paul's Cathedral. In 1923 a memorial tablet was unveiled in the old Winter Gardens, *in memory of Charles Hubert Hastings Parry, Bt., C.V.O., D.C.L., Mus.Doc. Born in this town February 27, 1848. A great musician whose influence on British music will always be remembered.*

This tablet was stored at the Bournemouth Public Library when the old Winter Gardens was pulled down in 1935. In 1964 it was re-erected at the present Winter Gardens. St. Peter's is proud to have the name of such a famous composer on the first page of its Register of Baptisms.

Having launched the school building project at St. Peter's, Morden Bennett turned to the task of enlarging and improving the Church. By 1850 the population of Bournemouth was nearly seven hundred and the Church was not only far too small but lacking in any architectural or artistic attraction. The incumbent demanded further money to enable him to erect an aisle and a small vestry on the south side of Tulloch's building and was soon in a position to instruct Edmund Pearce to draw the plans and proceed with the work. (It was fortunate that throughout his ministry at St. Peter's Morden Bennett could count on having many rich people among his congregation who were prepared to participate generously in all his building projects. Had the situation been otherwise there is little doubt that St, Peter's as we know it today would never have been brought into existence.) Lady Gervis laid the foundation stone of the south aisle on 21st May, 1851. In addressing the large concourse of people who witnessed the ceremony Morden Bennett stated that the new aisle "would serve as an adjunct to the present building until additional accommodation should be required, when another aisle would be erected; and, if it should afterwards be necessary to provide further accommodation, the body of the Church would be elongated."

The new south aisle was a simple enough structure, consisting merely of a new outside wall, in which were inserted four windows, with a lean-to roof. A tiny vestry was added at the east end. The cost of the extension was £1,250. Its great interest is that it is the oldest part of the present St. Peter's and the only part of the main body of the Church not designed by George Edmund Street, the famous ecclesiastical architect to whom Morden Bennett later entrusted the work of building the new Church.

The south aisle is now quite different in character from the remainder of Street's Church, though it harmonises well enough with what was built afterwards. The design and shape of Pearce's windows, for instance, are very similar to those later designed by Street for the clerestory.

When it was built in 1851 as an addition to Tulloch's Church the south aisle must have seemed a great improvement upon the rest of the building and quite an adornment to it. Pearce designed his windows of two lights each, trefoilated in the head, with a quatrefoil filling up the space between the top of the lights and the circumscribing arch. These windows, glazed by William Wailes, portray events in the life of St. Peter. The two middle ones were paid for by the congregation as a memorial to Morden Bennett's wife and daughter. The brass inscription on the wall reads:

> In memory of Mariamne Elizabeth Bennett, the beloved wife, and Elizabeth Ann Bennett, the only daughter of Alexander Morden Bennett, Incumbent of this Church. These windows were presented to the Church by the congregation as a testimonial of esteem and token of sympathy towards their pastor in a season of severe affliction, 1852.

The other windows were erected in memory of members of the McCobb and Monro families. There was also a similar window at the west end of the south aisle which was removed in 1874 when the western transepts or vestibules were added.

The south aisle windows, designed in the style of the thirteenth century, are not very satisfactory examples of glass painting and there is no record that Wailes was ever again employed on any work for St. Peter's. At a later period, when Street was actively engaged in building the new St. Peter's, he proposed several times that he should be allowed to replace the south aisle with one of his own design. Street's final design for St. Peter's illustrated in *The Builder*, 1870, and reproduced on the cover of Nicholas Taylor's *Guide*, 1962, shows a series of twelve lancets, matching the windows in the north aisle. Morden Bennett always refused to agree to any alteration and this may well have been due to the sentimental attachment he had to the middle windows in memory of his wife and daughter.

Mrs. Mariamne Elizabeth Bennett died in December 1852, at the early age of thirty-seven, and their young daughter died the following month. Widowed for a second time and left with two young sons, Morden Bennett was almost overcome by these successive bereavements and devoted himself still more to his pastoral work. It was in 1851 that he decided this work was sufficient to justify the employment of an assistant curate. Morden Bennett's first curate was the Rev. George Irving Davies, who left Bournemouth in 1852 when he was succeeded by the Rev. H. L. Dodds who remained at St. Peter's until 1855. A second curate, Edward Kelson Yeatman, was appointed in 1853, but he emigrated to Australia during the following year and later became Rector of Auburn in the Diocese of Adelaide.

This period also accounts for the burial in St. Peter's churchyard of the two most famous women who lie there. The first of these was Mary Wollstonecraft Godwin, authoress of *A Vindication of the Rights of Women* and other works, who was married to William Godwin, atheist political revolutionary and writer. She was the first Englishwoman to fight for the rights of her sex and was also noted for her philosophy of free love which she openly practised before her eventual marriage. Mary Godwin died in childbed in April 1797, but the child, a daughter, survived and was named after her mother. She appears to have inherited many of her mother's feminist ideas, went off to Italy with Percy Bysshe Shelley the poet in 1814 and married him two years after his first wife had committed suicide by drowning herself in the Serpentine. Mary Woolstonecraft Shelley's best-known works are *Frankenstein* (1818) and the collected edition of her late husband's poems (1847). After the poet's death in 1822 she returned to England and died in London early in 1851.

By this time their son, Sir Percy Florence Shelley, had succeeded to his grandfather's baronetcy and was living at Boscombe Manor. He was responsible for bringing his mother's body to Bournemouth and having it buried in a vault built for the purpose in St. Peter's churchyard. Soon afterwards, the remains of her parents, William and Mary Godwin, were brought from St. Pancras churchyard in London and reinterred in the same tomb. Although the St. Peter's burial register does not mention the Godwins, Mary Shelley's burial is recorded as having taken place on 8th February 1851. The St. Pancras registers contain no reference to the exhumations of the Godwins, but a search at the Bishop of London's Registry has revealed that the removal of their remains "to the Churchyard of

Bournemouth Parish Church" was authorised by a Faculty issued on 5th February 1851 to the Proctors of Sir Percy Shelley.

In 1854, Sir Percy Shelley commissioned Henry Weekes, the famous portrait-sculptor, to carve a monument to his parents. This memorial in white marble, one of the sculptor's finest works, depicts the drowned body of the poet, supported by his widow. Weekes' sculpture was originally intended for St. Peter's Church, but Morden Bennett took the view that it might attract unwelcome publicity and make the Church too much of a show-place. Sir Percy Shelley then offered it to Christchurch Priory, where it may be seen to this day, affixed to the north wall of the tower. The inscription underneath, which ends with a stanza from Shelley's poem *Adonais,* reads:

> To the Memory of Percy Bysshe Shelley, Poet. Born at Field-Place in the County of Sussex, August 4, 1792. Drowned by the upsetting of a boat in the Gulf of Speggia, July 1822. His ashes are interred in the Protestant burial ground at Rome. Also to the Memory of Mary Wollstonecraft Shelley his wife. Born August 30, 1797. Died February 1, 1851. Her remains are interred together with those of her father William Godwin, and her mother Mary Wollstonecraft Godwin, in the Churchyard at Bournemouth.
>
> 'He hath outsoared the shadow of our night:
> Envy and calumny and hate and pain,
> And that unrest which men miscall delight,
> Can touch him not and torture not again;
> From the contagion of the world's slow stain
> He is secure, and now can never mourn
> A heart grown cold, a head grown grey in vain,
> Nor, when the spirit's self has ceased to burn
> With sparkless ashes load an unlamented urn.'

CHAPTER V

Bennett Engages An Architect

BY THE year 1853 the growth of Bournemouth was progressing with such strength that it seemed obvious to Morden Bennett that here were the beginnings of what would one day become a great and important town. He was determined that the Church of this town should be a worthy building and sufficient in size to accommodate the increasing population. The addition of the south aisle had eased the initial problem, but it was clear that the stage would soon be reached when further extensions would be impossible. Tulloch's building, quite apart from its ugly appearance, was not sound enough structurally to serve as the basis for extensive improvements, and the incumbent realised that the most sensible course to adopt was to erect a completely new Church. The first essential was to engage a leading ecclesiastical architect to prepare the plans.

Morden Bennett turned for advice to his friend John Leybourne Popham, Vicar of Chilton Foliat in Wiltshire, who suggested a consultation with a brilliant young architect, George Edmund Street, who had recently been appointed Diocesan Architect for Oxford. Morden Bennett immediately acted upon this advice and an introduction was arranged. Popham, having rendered better service to St. Peter's than he possibly ever knew, disappears from our story.

Street was only twenty-nine years old and practising in Oxford when Morden Bennett first asked him to design the new St. Peter's. He was already on record (in *The Ecclesiologist* for 1850, in an article "On the Proper Characteristics of a Town Church") as attacking the imitative architects like Gilbert Scott for reproducing the architecture of mediaeval village churches, whose plans were inconvenient for the large congregations of the new industrial towns. In 1853 Street was working on Cuddesdon Theological College, the plans of which had been finished and the building recently started. Two years later, in 1855, he moved his offices to London. Within a very short time he had made his name as one of the leading architects of the day and he remains justly famous as the principal exponent of the Gothic revival in English architecture of the nineteenth century.

Added to his purely professional skills Street was a sincere and convinced Christian. As he said himself: "Christian Art is never properly developed except by an essentially Christian intention on the part of the artist, as well as on the part of those who employ his talents. The church architect must thoroughly believe the doctrines of the Church for which he builds, and must lead a life of — to say the least — fair conformity to her rules and discipline. He must also be fairly acquainted with her ritual and usages."

Morden Bennett and Street found complete sympathy with one another in their religious views and this harmony soon ripened into a lifelong friendship. St. Peter's was the first commission for a town Church ever entrusted to Street. Urged on by his client's great enthusiasm he made it a perfect example of the feelings and aspirations of the Oxford Movement which he supported and with which Morden Bennett was so closely associated. The whole design was envisaged so as to draw the eye of the worshipper towards the altar and to provide a rich setting for beautiful ornaments and fittings.

The new St. Peter's could not be built as a whole because of the great expense involved, so Street's plans provided for the building work to be carried out in stages. Architect and parson worked together on their Church for over twenty-five years; within a year of its completion both were dead.

Street prepared his first plans for St. Peter's in 1853, incorporating Pearce's south aisle into his own design. Provision was made for a tower and spire at the western end of the building, not where they were later actually erected but further eastward. At this stage the western transepts or vestibules were not included in the design.

The first work which Street actually carried out for Morden Bennett was to build the school-church of St. John-in-the-Wilderness at Moordown which has already been mentioned. In 1855 his first work at St. Peter's, the addition of a north aisle to Tulloch's Church, was started. The local Guide for 1856 reported: "The new aisle is fast approaching completion, and it reflects great credit on the present respected and zealous incumbent, that he should have determined on so judicious a plan for securing the erection of the Church; each portion is to be proceeded with only after the money sufficient to defray the cost of building has been collected."

Street's north aisle presents a very different aspect to Pearce's south aisle. Instead of four broadly-spaced two-light windows, Street provided twelve lancet windows, the eight easterly ones having their sills placed higher from the ground and therefore being smaller than the others. The effect of this arrangement is to direct the eye eastward and was doubtless very carefully contrived by the architect. The next few years saw these windows glazed with representations of the twelve apostles in coloured glass, each figure holding a scroll on which is written a sentence of the Creed. Brass plates beneath the windows record the names of the persons in whose memory they were inserted.

Street was never really satisfied with the fact that Pearce's south aisle differed so fundamentally in style from his own north aisle, and his completed design for St. Peter's incorporated a new south aisle with twelve more lancet windows to match those on the north side. Morden Bennett always refused to allow his architect to proceed with this part of the plan, but it is not clear whether this reluctance was on the ground of economy or because it would have meant disturbing Mrs. Bennett's memorial windows. After Morden Bennett died, when a memorial to him was under consideration, Street prepared preliminary sketches for a magnificent side chapel to be built onto the south aisle which would have involved removing all of Pearce's windows except the Monro window depicting Peter's denial of Our Lord which is the one next to the south porch. In this design (certainly not one of his best efforts) Street abandoned all thoughts of lancets and suggested four large three-light windows facing south and one fine four-light window facing west.

Following the completion of the north aisle in 1856 Mr. Duncan's organ was moved down from the gallery and placed in a new position at the east end of the nave.

Soon afterwards Street designed the font which was given to the Church, "In Memory of James Meyrick. Presented by his Mother. 15th October 1854." Lest it should be thought from the ambiguity of the inscription that the font was made in 1854 it must be added that the date given is that of James Meyrick's death. He was thirty-seven years old when he died and was buried in St. Peter's churchyard four days later. He was probably a relation of the patron, who added Meyrick to his surname of Gervis, at about this time.

The font is octagonal in shape and supported by eight pillars, four of stone and four of polished Purbeck marble. The base and upper part are made of Caen stone. The sculptor, who later collaborated with Street in executing many other carvings for St. Peter's, was T. W. Earp of Lambeth. At least one contemporary critic thought highly of it. Writing of the Mediaeval Court section of the Great International Exhibition of Art and Industry held at South Kensington in 1862 a reviewer in *Building News* said, "It is difficult to understand upon what principle the selection has been made; why Mr. Street's Bournemouth font should be excluded, whilst his St. James the Less font cover is admitted . . ." This quotation may provide a clue as to the date of the font; it appears rather unlikely that such remarks would have been made about it if it had been a fixture at St. Peter's for upwards of five years.

After completing the north aisle of St. Peter's the next task which Morden Bennett entrusted to Street was the building of a new mission Church and school at Pokesdown. The original Pokesdown mission had been founded in 1857 as yet another outpost of religion and education in a neglected rural area. Pokesdown at this time consisted of a little collection of thatched houses and cottages with a population of only seventy. Between that place and Bournemouth over the vast, bare heath stretched the Christcurch Road, deserted except for three lonely houses and an inn at Boscombe known by the sign of the Ragged Cat. The permanent Church at Pokesdown, dedicated to St. James the Greater, was begun in 1858, followed by the inevitable church school, both designed by Street. Here again, Morden Bennett rightly forecast the ultimate development of this district, which would make his mission of the focal point of the religious life of a busy suburb.

The site of St. James' was presented by the Lord of the Manor and patron of St. Peter's, Sir George Meyrick, and the cost of the original building was £1,750, a sum which Morden Bennett was able to raise quite quickly from his rich parishioners. Although it was extended later to accommodate the larger congregations of the growing district, the Pokesdown Church was never intended to be a "town" Church, and even as late as 1888 (by which time the north aisle had been added) it was referred to as "one of the most beautiful little village churches in the county."

Pokesdown was in 1860 constituted a parish in its own right and one of its early vicars, the Rev. Thomas Anderson, who held the living from 1868 until his retirement in 1886, was previously one of Morden Bennett's curates at St. Peter's. There is a more modern link in the person of a more recent vicar of St. Peter's, the Rev. W. H. Fox Robinson, who was the incumbent of St. James' from 1947 to 1953.

Very little is known about the non-clerical staff of St. Peter's during its early history. There is no record of how long Rebbeck continued to function as parish clerk after Morden Bennett was appointed perpetual curate, but he was still in correspondence with the Gervis estate solicitors about his salary as late as 1847, though this concerned the income he should have received for his services several years previously. Nevertheless, Rebbeck maintained a close connection with the Church and continued to act as agent for

Tregonwell's Bournemouth estate. Rebbeck is one of the persons commemorated in the south window of the south-western transept. He died in 1879 and his body lies in the churchyard. Rebbeck's was the last funeral service taken by Morden Bennett before he himself died early in the following year.

There was succession of organists, possibly serving in an honorary capacity. Morden Bennett is reported to have changed organists frequently, but the only names which have come down to us are those of Miss Pattison and Mr. Baine.

Francis Graham was the first sexton whose name has been preserved in the extant records of the parish, and he might have been forgotten altogether had it not been for the fact that he disgraced himself. On 27th November, 1858, the churchwardens, William Rogers and Richard Stephens, met Morden Bennett at the parsonage and it was resolved that "in consequence of gross neglect of duty after repeated warnings" Graham should be "dismissed from his office as Sexton on December 31st next ensuing." One wonders why Graham should have been given a clear month's notice instead of suffering immediate dismissal if his conduct had been as bad as the circumstances suggest; perhaps the churchwardens feared they might be unable to fill the vacancy in time for Christmas.

We are now faced with the difficulty of deciding who was the first sexton of St. Peter's. This title has always been said to belong to William Ames, whose monument in the churchyard bears this inscription: *"William White Ames. Born 5th November, 1820. Entered into Rest, 30th March, 1884. He faithfully discharged the duties of Sexton to this Church for twenty years. 'Lord I have loved the habitation of Thy House'."* The conflict becomes apparent when it is noted that Ames did not hold the office of sexton up to the date of his death, for he was succeeded by Harry Crumpler in 1873. If we deduct twenty years from 1873 we arrive at a date prior to the dismissal of Graham. Perhaps the answer is that Ames' years of service were not continuous, or it may be that some of the twenty years mentioned on his tombstone were spent as assistant to Crumpler. Crumpler clearly held office from 1873, as is indicated on "his" window at the east end of the north transept which was erected during his lifetime and must be presumed to be accurate.

The matter is further complicated by the wording of an anecdote published in 1914 by T. A. Compton, M.D., B.A., in a little booklet entitled *Southbourne's Infancy*. Dr. Compton, who had been Morden Bennett's medical attendant, wrote this:

> When Mr. Bennett first became Vicar of St. Peter's, Bournemouth, the majority of the congregation had been accustomed to leave

> before the Church Militant Prayer, at Morning Service on Sunday. This the Vicar wanted to stop, but found difficulty in doing so. At this time, and for many years afterwards, the Verger was an old man of very prepossessing appearance, with beautiful long, snow-white hair, which gave him a truly patriarchal appearance. He was a thoroughly good Churchman, much liked by everyone. He was devoted to the Vicar, for whom he would have done anything. One Sunday, after Service, Mr. Bennett called him into the vestry and said, "Ames" (the man's name), "why did you not stop the people going out at the wrong time?" The response was very naturally, "How could I help it, sir?" "I'll show you," said the Vicar. "Bring your Prayer Book and come down with me to the porch door." The two having arrived there, and the door closed by the Vicar, the latter said, "Now kneel down, Ames, with your feet against the door," facing a supposed congregation coming out. "Read over to yourself several Collects. Now supposing I am one of the many wanting to go out; how can I or any other person of decent feeling upset such a venerable old man as you are saying his prayers?" This plan was actually carried out the next Sunday, and its absolute success assured, so that after a few Sundays no one ever got up to try to go out!

This amusing story seems to indicate that Ames was sexton when Morden Bennett came to Bournemouth, but, if so, he would have been under thirty years of age and could hardly have been described with any accuracy as "a venerable old man". It may also be noted that Morden Bennett was over twelve years older than Ames. If the incident has any truth in it, it is possible that it may refer to some previous sexton or verger and that Dr. Compton made a mistake about the name. However, if the mention of the porch is correct, this must presumably refer to the south porch which was not built until 1859, soon after Francis Graham was sacked and at a time when Ames was still under forty.

Leonard South, sacristan of St. Peter's from 1937 to 1963, who worked for many years as assistant to Crumpler and knew him well, suggests that the apparent conflict is due to a lack of precision in the terms employed. He says that in the middle of the nineteenth century there were two officials, one, called the sacristan or verger, who was responsible for the interior and the goods, vestments and ornaments of the Church and for attending the clergy, and the other, called the sexton, who was employed to toll the bell, blow the organ and dig the graves. On this reckoning Ames and Crumpler were vergers and Graham a sexton. This explanation of the difficulty may well be the right one, especially when one considers the great amount of grave-digging that had to be done, particularly later on during the -sixties and -seventies when the number of funerals averaged nearly two a week. Nevertheless, it still does not cope with the arguments that "sacristan" and "sexton" are the same word, and that Graham and Ames were both called sextons by their contemporaries.

The reader now has all the evidence which has so far been found and must judge for himself whether or not Ames was the first sexton (or verger) of St. Peter's.

Very soon after the addition of the north aisle and the building of the new Church of St. James at Pokesdown Morden Bennett had collected enough money from his latest appeal for subscriptions to carry out the next stage of his building programme. In 1859 the clerestory was added with a high hammerbeam roof, both designed by Street. The clerestory windows "consist of pairs of lights under a continuous arcade, and show the influence on Street of Early French Gothic; their sills are splayed downwards most effectively to give a greater impression of height. Bands of red sandstone and colonettes of Purbeck marble add richness to the Bath stone tracery." The clerestory windows also bear a strong superficial resemblance to Pearce's four windows in the south aisle below.

When the work had been finished the old roof of Tulloch's original Church was removed, with the result that the nave was almost entirely new. Practically nothing was left of Tulloch's mock-Gothic structure of 1841-44.

In 1859 Street also built the beautiful and exquisite south porch which has served ever since as the principal entrance to the Church. The architecture is similar in style to the remainder of the Church, and the doorway and the capitals of the columns are richly carved. The doorway, indeed, bears some resemblance to that in the porch at Christchurch Priory. The windows, of which there are four on either side, are set off to great advantage by small arcades formed of shafts of Purbeck marble.

On Christmas Day, 1859, Dr. Walter Kerr Hamilton, Bishop of Salisbury, came to St. Peter's and officiated at the re-opening of the enlarged Church. The first stage of Street's re-planning for St. Peter's had been completed.

To recall what the Church looked like at this time it must be remembered that there was no tower or spire, and the west end of the building terminated practically level with the new south porch. Henry Morden Bennett, the Vicar's son, described it in his reminiscences as being "all height and no length." The font was placed just to the left of the south entrance and there were no wall paintings to be seen in the nave. The altar was sited at the extreme eastern end of the Church, where Street was to build the chancel steps a few years later. There were box pews on the north side of the nave and benches on the south side. The lectern, portable and made of wood, was placed in the middle of the Church at the east end of the centre aisle. There were two candles on the altar, but no cross. The east window was a simple pointed arch divided into three lights. The pulpit (the one which Morden Bennett retained on his arrival in 1845) stood in the south aisle. The small vestry built by Pearce in 1851 still stood at the east end of the south aisle.

The scene was now set for the second stage of Morden Bennett's building programme, erecting a new chancel to house a fine new altar as the focal point for every worshipper.

CHAPTER VI

Morden Bennett's Middle Years

DURING MOST of the eighteen-fifties Morden Bennett ran the growing parish with the help of only one assistant curate. John Maguire held this position from 1855 to 1856 and Alfred Brook from 1857 to 1859. With the establishment of new Churches at Moordown and Pokesdown and the opening of a mission beyond the river Stour at East Parley the incumbent's resources were taxed to the utmost and in 1860 he appointed two assistants who remained on the permanent staff for many years, Samuel Robinson Waddelow and Edward Wanklyn. In 1863 they were joined upon his ordination as priest by the vicar's son, Alexander Sykes Bennett. Around these three men Morden Bennett built up a large clerical staff of excellent quality.

Waddelow, who served as senior priest at St. Peter's until his death in 1875, probably exerted a greater influence in the town than any curate before or since. His work for Bournemouth's sick people, especially in connection with the National Sanatorium and later with the establishment of The Firs Home, made him greatly beloved and respected throughout the locality. He was honoured with appointment as a colonial bishop in 1866 but, having accepted the office and whilst awaiting the day of his consecration, he was forced to withdraw on medical advice. His early death in 1875 brought profound sorrow to his large circle of friends.

Wanklyn spent over fifteen years at St. Peter's before becoming first vicar of St. Michael's when the parish became independent of St. Peter's in 1876. He died in 1881. Wanklyn's brother James opened Bournemouth's first private school for gentlemen's sons, at Exeter House, now part of the Royal Exeter Hotel. James Wanklyn, a clergyman as well as a schoolmaster, also used to assist at St. Peter's.

Alexander Sykes Bennett, having taken his degree at Exeter College, Oxford, and served two years as deacon at Wilton, returned to Bournemouth in 1863 and assisted his father at St. Peter's until the latter's death. He had a great deal to do with the mission Churches and often rode over to East Parley on horseback to celebrate Holy Communion, crossing the Stour by the ferry at Red Hill. He was later very closely associated with the daughter-

Church of St. Swithun where he was the first priest-in-charge. He was so popular in the parish that when Morden Bennett died the congregation petitioned the patron that he should be presented to succeed him but (as we shall see) the patron had other ideas and instead Alex. Bennett became the first vicar of St. Stephen's.

Morden Bennett and his assistant clergy never allowed themselves to take for granted the privileges and blessings of their growing Church and expanding congregation. These things were treated uncompromisingly as a challenge to their pastoral zeal and as a message from God which had to be answered. The immediate response was the further enlargement of St. Peter's and the foundation of more Churches.

There were still many small communities on the rural outskirts of Bournemouth which had no regular religious services and no opportunity for educating their children and young people. In 1857, at about the same time as the inauguration of the Pokesdown mission, Morden Bennett started a new venture at East Parley Green, a quiet spot south of the Christchurch Road near the western end of what is now Hurn Airport. The new mission, which was designed to serve the hamlets of Blackwater, Hurn and West Hurn as well as East Parley itself, was started in a small mud cottage. This cottage was uninhabited and about to be pulled down when Mordern Bennett heard of it. There were large fissures in the walls, and the only means of keeping the building up was a wooden prop at the back. The school which was founded as part of this mission was carried on under these difficult conditions for six years and services were performed in the cottage by St. Peter's clergy every Sunday during the period except in fine weather in the summer when they were held on the Green in the open air.

East Parley at this time was a scattered agricultural neighbourhood and, although a permanent school-chapel was built a few years later, this was the only one of Morden Bennett's missions to escape transformation into the religious centre of a closely-packed urban community. Nevertheless, its part in the life of that remote corner of the huge parish of Christchurch was no empty one, and has proved to be a source of much comfort to the inhabitants of this rural spot.

By 1862 the mud cottage had fulfilled its usefulness and Morden Bennett felt that more permanent arrangements for conducting the work of the mission were justified. He commissioned Street to design a school-chapel with a schoolhouse adjoining and fortunately a copy of the architect's original drawing has been preserved. This shows the chapel as later built and a schoolhouse of two storeys connected to the north side of the nave and facing west. The school-house proved to be beyond the means of the founder, so Street and Morden Bennett had to content themselves with erecting the chapel only. This building, seating up to two hundred persons and costing £900, was opened for worship on 21st July 1863 and dedicated to St. Barnabas, the Cypriot who, as related in the *Acts of the Apostles,* sold an estate and "brought the money and laid it at the Apostles' feet." Morning and evening services were held on Sundays, with Holy Communion once a month. The St. Peter's clergy also travelled over to East Parley during the week to visit the poor.

The chapel of St. Barnabas is still in use and stands north of the Christchurch Road very close to the western entrance of Hurn Airport. The design is simple, but Street has created an unusual feature by sharply raising the level of the tiny chancel which is approached from the nave by a flight of steps. Portable partitions separated the chancel from the nave so that on weekdays the nave was transformed from a Church into a school.

As early as the end of 1865 Morden Bennett was able to look back on the start of his missionary endeavours: "We have seen in this parish what may be done among a neglected and uncared for population by sending for the ministers to carry to the houses of our poor the glad tidings of the gospel, and the comforts of our Holy Religion as well as to minister the word and sacraments on a Sunday. Beginning often without a building even wherein to hold a service on the Lord's day, we have seen congregations gathered together on the village green; then a school established, and lastly a school chapel, or, as in one instance, a handsome church built, in which all, from the least to the greatest, may worship God in the beauty of holiness, and after the manner of their forefathers." The "handsome church" must be a reference to St. James' Church at Pokesdown, built by Street in 1858. East Parley, and the first Church of St. John the Baptist at Moordown, would correctly be called school-chapels or school-churches.

A fascinating description of the harvest festivities of a century ago has been preserved. On Thursday, 7th September 1865 a harvest thanksgiving service was held in the school-chapel of East Parley;

"Then all adjourned, some walking and some in carriages, to a large field, lent for the purpose by Mr. Elliot. A brass band, hired from Kinson for the occasion, marched in front of the company assembling in the fields, and then it took up its place in a waggon. A part of the field had been separated off by hurdles so as to form a banquetting hall, where the tables were arranged, and covered with the whitest of cloths, which contrasted well with the bright green carpeting of grass. The tables were shaded from the sun by the trees, which was a most agreeable arrangement. When all had taken their seats, silence was obtained, and the Rev. A. M. Bennett said the grace, and then every one in earnest regaled themselves with tea, cake, and bread and butter, which was most abundantly supplied, and the best of its kind. During the repast the band played some gay lively tunes — suggestive of dancing — and gradually the tea tables were deserted for that part of the field where the games and amusements were prepared. All the clergy present mixed with and promoted the merry-making. For a time the band played its polkas and country dances, and no dancers came, all the young men being engaged with the boys in running races, and leaping hurdles, and in trials of strength and other athletic games, as well as scrambling for apples and balls, which fell as a shower from one part of the field to the other, to the imminent peril of hats and heads. But, after a time, dancing began in good earnest, and it was very pleasant to see the old English country dance footed away merrily on the green grass. Every one looked and seemed happy, and even the smallest children had some amusement prepared for them. Soon after eight o'clock the sports ceased, and it is hoped all returned home, not only with a most pleasant remembrance of a day's enjoyment, but with a thankful heart to God the Lord of the Harvest who had given them all things richly to enjoy."

The harvest festivities of 1865 were largely experimental but proved so successful that the activity was repeated in subsequent years. A substantial meal was normally provided for the families of the labourers followed by rural sports and games. A writer in 1867 commented that this seemed to be "a rational mode in which Christians may express their gratitude to the Lord of the Harvest for the annual supply of their temporal wants." The merrymaking usually continued until after sunset.

Another activity in which Morden Bennett took a great interest was the founding of the Bournemouth Volunteer Rifle Corps in 1860. He was chaplain to the Volunteers and the commanding officer was Charles Allen King of Branksome Dene, churchwarden from 1860 to 1864. The other churchwarden, William Rogers, was the quartermaster, and he is also noted for having in later years served as Lieutenant of the first Bournemouth Fire Brigade, eventually succeeding to the Captaincy. Morden Bennett himself was one of the most energetic promoters of the Volunteers, presiding at several of the early meetings and being credited with having done a considerable amount of personal recruiting. He and his churchwardens certainly set a fine example.

In 1861 there arrived in Bournemouth Sir Henry Taylor, the famous colonial administrator and man of letters. He said some very nice things about the town (for example, "The place is beautiful beyond any seaside place I have ever seen except the Riviera"), built a house known as The Roost (now called Rawden) in Hinton Road and settled down with his family. He became associated with Morden Bennett in many public works, particularly the National Sanatorium of which he was a generous benefactor. Taylor, who is noted for having been recommended for a life peerage in the bill which Lord Russell unsuccessfully presented to Parliament in 1869 and for his "clear, just and tolerant" mind, was not always kind when speaking of his adopted home. He wrote that on his arrival in Bournemouth the residents comprised "two clergymen, two doctors, three widows and six old maids. Of these, the doctors and two of the widows have families. The clergymen and the old maids have none." The clergymen are presumably meant to be the widower Morden Bennett and the bachelor Waddelow. Taylor does not record what view the vicar's sons took of the aspersions cast upon their origin, but he goes on to describe the curate as "handsome, dutiful and soft." Was this Waddelow or Wanklyn?

In the 1962 *Guide* Sir Henry is referred to as that "distinguished civil servant and poet, who lived his last twenty-five years in Bournemouth. Taylor's father, a radical who admired William and Mary Godwin, was bankrupt, and his sons were self-educated. Henry rose rapidly in the Colonial Office, and, under Lord Bathurst, became one of the chief authors of the policy of 'amelioration' of slavery as against simple abolition. He frequently debated against John Stuart Mill and other Benthamite supporters of William Wilberforce. He was knighted in 1859. Twelve years earlier he had refused the permanent under-secretaryship in succession to Sir James Stephen, because he wished to continue the literary career, which, like Matthew Arnold, he combined with that of an administrator. Taylor's single important book was a blank-verse drama called 'Philip van Artevelde' (1834). This was famous in its day because in it Taylor created for the drama the same historical atmosphere with which Walter Scott had saturated the novel. As Leslie Stephen wrote, 'Taylor was a warm admirer of Wordsworth and Southey and belonged to their school, with such differences as distinguish the dweller in Downing Street from the recluse of the Lakes.' His friends included Tennyson and Carlyle, and in particular the poet Aubrey de Vere. To his house in Hinton

Road came Benjamin Jowett and Dean Church, and also Robert Louis Stevenson, who came to live at Alum Chine in 1884."

This forthright, vigorous old man lived on at The Roost for a quarter of a century until he died in March 1886 at the age of 85. He was buried in St. Peter's churchyard, his monument remaining in full view of the Church until the Chapel of the Resurrection was built alongside in 1925. Taylor's eldest daughter, Eleanor, married the Rev. Charles Seymour Towle, a friend and protege of Morden Bennett who became vicar of St. John's Moordown (1873-1886) and St. Clement's Boscombe (1892-1908).

In 1859 a new organist was appointed for St. Peter's. He was Mr. J. H. Caseley, who relinquished the post of assistant organist of Worcester Cathedral in order to come to Bournemouth. With a thorough training in great Church music behind him Caseley took the lead in forming the Vale of Avon Church Choral Society whose first festival, which was also the first choral festival ever held in the Diocese of Winchester, was held in St. Peter's on 1st May 1862. Several choirs from the surrounding district took part and although in later years some of those who had participated in it looked back at this beginning as a humble attempt, it set the pattern for the grander festivals that followed.

After holding two festivals in each of the first two years, it became usual to hold one festival annually, in the spring or early summer. A few years later, in conjunction with the North Hants Choral Association (founded in 1863) and the South Hants Association (founded in 1865) The Vale of Avon Society started the Winchester Diocesan Choral Association which held festivals in the Cathedral every two or three years. Fifty-five choirs, comprising in all over 900 choristers, sang at the first diocesan festival in 1866. Apart from St. Peter's, the most usual festival place in the Vale of Avon were Christchurch, Ringwood, Lyndhurst and Fordingbridge. Sixteen choirs were taking part by 1865 and over twenty by 1868. At the June festival at Lyndhurst in 1868 St. Peter's sent a choir of 22 voices, only Ringwood and Christchurch sending more.

These choral associations were formed with the laudable object of promoting the use of Church Music in the celebration of Divine Worship, but nevertheless they were looked upon by many with feelings almost of suspicion. It must be remembered that this was a time of much dispute within the Established Church about matters of ritual and ceremony.

A particularly trivial point of tension arose after the introduction at St. Peter's of Thomas Helmore's *Manual of Plainsong*. On 3rd August 1867 the *Wiltshire County Mirror* carried a report describing an "Anti-Ritual Meeting" at Salisbury at which the principal speaker declared that:

> It had been objected that when they spoke of Ritualism they did not define what they meant; he could tell them. In the parish church of Bournemouth, in which he desired to worship with many others, the Service, he was told, was monotoned, but he called it droned. (Hear, hear.) The best he could say of it was, that, like the rest of the system, it was a poor and paltry imitation of the manner in which the Services of the Church of Rome were performed. (Hear, hear.)

However trivial the Anti-Ritualists' complaints about plainsong may have been, there were many people in Bournemouth, both residents and visitors, who found genuine difficulty in worshipping at St. Peter's. The practices introduced by Morden Bennett under Tractarian influence alienated many of the Evangelical persuasion who felt that another Church should be founded in the town which would more nearly cater for their tastes. As *The Bournemouth Visitors Directory* pointed out:

> It is an undeniable fact that many families are deterred from coming to Bournemouth at all, while many others will not remain here, notwithstanding the evident genial influences of its climate, solely because they do not find a Church of England in which they can worship God in accordance with the belief and usage to which they have long been accustomed and are ardently attached.

Popular demand for the establishment of a separate parish true to the spirit of Evangelicalism grew stronger, with bitterness and tension not entirely absent on either side. Morden Bennett's reaction was to oppose those who wanted to break away, presumably in the hope that one day all would be united in support of the type of worship he was introducing at St. Peter's.

One example of the trouble arose in 1865, when Morden Bennett decided that the altar candles should be lighted at celebrations of the Holy Communion. With the object of pacifying those parishioners who were scrupulous about this practice and preferred a simpler mode of worship, Morden Bennett arranged that the candles should only be lighted at the early celebrations and that two later celebrations would be held each week with the candles unlighted. This compromise failed entirely to satisfy the critics and the incumbent reiterated his view that the candles ought to be lighted "as our Church directs, to signify the presence of our Lord in the Sacrament, in His twofold nature as God and man."

The tensions between Tractarianism and Evangelicalism concerning the ceremonies of the Church led to many disagreements becoming prevalent at this time in various parts of the country.

As the Reverend Benjamin John Armstrong, the Norfolk diarist, recorded in 1866, "Nine Counsel, of whom five are Q.C.s, have pronounced the Eucharistic vestments and the two Altar lights at the celebration to be strictly legal, and incense not legal."

When Bournemouth's 'Ritualist' St. Clement's Church was opened, the Bishop, who supported the Evangelical movement, refused to proceed with the Consecration Service until the candles on the reredos were extinguished and the Communion wafers replaced by bread.

Harry Crumpler, Morden Bennett's faithful sacristan from 1873, saw the dispute as a demand on the part of the Evangelicals to "have the service nearly all read, and above all, the sermon preached in a black gown." The prevailing practice at St. Peter's during this period was for the minister to preach in a surplice on weekdays, but to wear academicals on Sundays.

Fortunately, good sense on both sides prevented any irremediable rift within the Anglican community of Bournemouth, and plans were laid for building Holy Trinity Church on a site at Madeira Vale given for the purpose by Robert Kerley, the former churchwarden of St. Peter's. John Tregonwell, son of "the Founder of Bournemouth," was one of the first trustees.

A District for the new Church was carved out of that originally granted to St. Peter's and was gazetted on 5th November 1867, following an Order in Council of the previous day. By December of that year a temporary Church was made ready for use and an incumbent appointed. The erection of the permanent Church, to plans in the Lombardo-Gothic style by C. J. Ferguson of Carlisle, was started soon afterwards and the consecration ceremony was performed on 28th September 1869 by none other than the Right Rev. Bishop Vincent William Ryan, the Evangelical leader and former Bishop of Mauritius, whose subsequent appointment as Vicar of St. Peter's was to provoke such a storm of protest.

Many Bournemouth churchpeople of Evangelical leanings, who had never found themselves in harmony with the influence of Keble and Pusey which prevailed at St. Peter's, transferred their allegiance to Holy Trinity and its first Vicar, the Rev. Philip Frank Eliot, later to become Dean of Windsor, whose eloquent preaching attracted large numbers to his Church. However when the Evangelical supporters died they usually had to return to St. Peter's which boasted the only churchyard in the Bournemouth of those days. Even the most cursory glance at St. Peter's burial register for the years up to the opening of the Wimborne Road Cemetery at Rush Corner (now called the Cemetery Junction) in 1878 reveals the repeated signature of Mr. Eliot who came very often to St. Peter's to bury the deceased members of his flock. John Tregonwell was buried in the family vault at St. Peter's in 1885.

Although Morden Bennett did all he could to uphold the standards of churchmanship in which he believed, he was not above showing toleration. Crumpler gives an instance of his charitable disposition towards those who differed from him in religious views. "When the Congregational Church was being built there came a severe wind which blew down some of the walls and Mr. Bennett, hearing of this, sent them a cheque for £5 towards their loss; he was in every sense of the word a true Catholic Churchman."

The foundation of Holy Trinity came just in time to relieve two elements of pressure upon St. Peter's. In the first place, it reconciled all feelings of bitterness between those who supported the churchmanship of Morden Bennett and those who preferred Evangelicalism. Secondly, the new Church provided a thousand extra sittings for the accommodation of Bournemouth's ever-increasing population. One important effect upon the life of St. Peter's was that it no longer had to try to provide a spiritual home for those who steadfastly refused to accept Morden Bennett's views and who opposed him at every opportunity. Consequently, a much more pleasant atmosphere among the laypeople was able to prevail.

When an appeal for public subscriptions was made in 1870 to provide six new bells in Morden Bennett's honour Lord Wolverton (George Grenfell Glyn, second Baron Wolverton, 1824-1887, Liberal statesman and personal friend of W. E. Gladstone) wrote:

> I have a great respect for Mr. Bennett and differences of opinion on some points have never induced me to omit the opportunity of showing it when it could be done with propriety. I thought Mr. Bennett was hard upon us when he so strenuously endeavoured to stop the progress of the promoters of the Church of Holy Trinity; however, that is gone by and I shall willingly add my name to the alphabetical list of supporters of the proposed peal of bells.

Though founded amid some acrimony, Holy Trinity soon established itself as a worthy rival to St. Peter's. The hard feelings of the early years were soon forgotten, but it was noticed that "The parishioners of Holy Trinity could be distinguished on Sundays because they carried a Bible while those of St. Peter's carried a Prayer Book and Hymns Ancient and Modern (then the correct badge for High Churchmen)."

CHAPTER VII

Building The Chancel

THE GREAT achievement of Morden Bennett's middle years at St. Peter's was the further extension of the Church by the addition of the chancel and eastern transepts with vestries adjoining. The Tractarian leanings of both architect and incumbent ensured that the choir and sanctuary would become the dominant features of the interior, the eyes of every worshipper in all parts of the building being directed towards the altar.

Street's first design for the east end of St. Peter's made no provision for the transepts, the north chancel aisle being intended to house the vestry and organ chamber. A second design was prepared in 1860 which formed the basis for the work which was soon to start, but several modifications were later introduced involving a third set of plans.

The 1860 design was reproduced in *Building News* and this picture is reprinted as Plate IV in Nicholas Taylor's *Guide to St. Peter's* (1962). Taylor points out that in both earlier designs, compared with that actually finished in 1864,

> The details were made cruder and simpler by being 'back-dated' some forty years. The mouldings were less multiple, and the capitals were 'stiff-leaf' of *c*.1260 instead of the 'naturalistic foliage' of *c*.1300 which was actually carried out. The choir stalls were to be chunky and primitive, with no dividing wall or gates from the nave except three steps. The reredos would have depicted the Last Supper, and above the chancel arch there would have been a magnificently archaic and 'early Christian' Last Judgement, instead of the present Rood Painting. The sanctuary vaulting would have been striped in red and white stone. The east window's tracery, containing curious panels of sculpture at the base of its lights, would have been much more forceful, though less sophisticated, than that actually executed in 1864.

The principle feature of the design is undoubtedly the huge chancel arch, of lofty proportions and extending across almost the whole width of the nave. The chancel is thus seen as a part of the Church rather than as an appendage to it. And the altar, though far distant from the congregation, thereby achieves a prominence it would otherwise lack.

It was in 1860, just after the re-opening of the Church following the addition of the south porch, clerestory and new roof, that

Morden Bennett opened the fund for building the chancel. Transepts on both sides, made necessary on account of the increased population since the original design was prepared, were to be erected at the same time, together with a new vestry to replace the one at the east end of the south aisle built by Pearce in 1851. The new vestry was built on two floors at the east side of the north transept, the lower part being for the clergy and the upper part (reached by a spiral staircase) for the choir.

Writing in the *Bournemouth Parish Magazine* for July 1865, after completion of the additional work, the incumbent pointed out that the transepts:

> were not in the original design, but it was found absolutely necessary to add them in consequence of the increasing demand for sittings at the Church. The situations of the transepts with regard to the chancel is, it is true, somewhat novel, yet not altogether without precedent, or without its advantages, for not only does it enable the altar to be widely and distinctly seen, but also the pulpit to be placed in a situation where it is within view of the greater portion of the congregation.
>
> The cost of the transepts has added very greatly to the estimated cost of the building; but if it has added to the expense, it has also enhanced its beauty. This is especially noticeable in the interior, where the effect of the two pointed arches on either side of the chancel is most pleasing. And this is just as it should be, for it is most agreeable to all our ideas of reverence for the honour and glory of God that the beauty of the interior of a church should never be sacrificed to a fair exterior, for, as has well been said, 'that is no fit shrine for God's service, where the only thought has been to make a fair shew to the outer world, and no care has been taken to make the interior symbolic, and an *act of sacrifice to Him*.

At this time Morden Bennett pointed out that the cost of the building, including architect's commission, clerk of the works, fittings, consecration fees, earthworks, printing, and other incidentals, had amounted to £6,000, of which £472 was still required. He entertained no doubt that the remaining money would be quickly found, and was already embarking on plans for the tower and steeple.

The extensions eastward were erected in 1863 and 1864. The contractors were Messrs. Rogers & Booth of Gosport and the clerk of the works was Mr. Davison. On the Vigil of St. Thomas' Day, 20th December 1864, the enlarged Church was consecrated by Bishop Sumner of Winchester (his first visit to the parish since the consecration of Tulloch's original Church in 1845) and early in the morning of St. Thomas' Day Holy Communion was celebrated in the new sanctuary for the first time.

The richly-coloured reredos, of Our Lord in Majesty, worshipped by Holy Angels, was the work of T. W. Earp of Kennington Road, London, a sculptor favoured by Street for work of this kind. Morden Bennett wrote of the design:

> By the position in which He is placed, we are reminded that He is present in that Sacrament of His body and blood. As His right hand is lifted up (Luke xxiv., 50), we are taught to seek His blessing through that Sacrament. As He bears in His left hand the orb, surmounted by the Cross, we are reminded that all who hope for Salvation through Him, must confess the faith of Christ crucified.

Earp was also responsible for the pulpit, which he carved to Street's design in 1861-62. It was exhibited and much admired during the summer of 1862 when it was on display at the Great International Exhibition of Art and Industry at South Kensington. It was brought to Bournemouth and placed in the Church when the Exhibition closed. A critical description of the new pulpit appeared in the *Building News* of the time, commencing, "No finer work ever came from Mr. Street's hands, no better carving ever left Mr. Earp's." The figure of the Angel which supports the desk bears a scroll with the text, "How shall they preach, except they be sent."

Street's earlier drawing of the pulpit shows a much shorter Angel and a smaller desk. The revised design is infinitely more impressive and the architect deserves full praise for having had second thoughts.

For some peculiar reason there is no mention of the pulpit in the *Catalogue of the Great International Exhibition*. Street and Earp exhibited in both the Ecclesiological Society section and in the Architectural section, but neither is recorded as showing a pulpit. However, in the text of J. B. Waring's *Masterpieces* shown at the 1862 Exhibition, there is a reference to the pulpit (probably a late addition) and also to the design for St. Peter's Church which was exhibited by Street.

The High Altar for the new sanctuary was carved in 1860 by G. H. W. Butler, whose name appears in a flowing script on the underside of the table-top. The only way to see the inscription is to crawl beneath the Altar with a torch.

Street's design for the east window was radically altered between 1860 and 1864. The earlier drawing, as reproduced in *Building News* and Taylor's *Guide*, shows the five principal lights as much shorter than those actually inserted. The tracery above is less boldly drawn in the original and is almost fussy in its detail. The tracery in the later design actually used takes a stiff, geometrical form and is a very fine and imposing piece of work. The huge circle above the middle lights, containing a cinquefoil in the centre between five trefoils, is a most pleasing improvement upon the rather delicate vagueness of the architect's original idea.

The glass in this window has been fully described by Octavius Curtis:

> The glazing of the east window is perhaps the finest in the Church. It was executed by the well-known firm of Clayton & Bell, after designs by G. E. Street, R.A., and cost £319. The Passion of our Blessed Lord is the subject represented. In the upper part of the first compartment we have introduced our Lord's triumphal entry into Jerusalem. In the lower part David, with the head of Goliath — the enemy of God's people. In the second, the betrayal of our Lord: Cain rising up against his brother, Abel being depicted underneath. The Crucifixion, and Moses lifting up the Serpent in the Wilderness, are represented in the third compartment. In the fourth the descent from the Cross, and underneath Naomi, Ruth, and Orpah mourning for the dead. The fifth compartment contains the entombment of Christ; underneath which is Joseph, illtreated by his brethren and let down into the pit. In the circle above is introduced 'The Lamb that was slain and is alive again,' worshipped by angels, after the description by St. John in the Book of Revelation. The highest compartments are filled by the emblems of the first and third persons of the Holy Trinity, the Dove being surmounted by rays of heavenly light. It will have been noticed that the types from the Old Testament are situated in the lower part of the window, while the antitypes from the New are represented above. We cannot but admire the colouring of this window, though some will regret the archaic character of the drawing. The first compartment was presented to the Incumbent by the congregation in January, 1866, another being raised by past and the then present Curates of the Church. The other compartments were filled during Whitsun week, 1866, at the cost, principally, of the congregation.

A detailed description of the new chancel and transepts, enlivened with artistic criticism and architectural comment of the most valuable kind, appears in Taylor's *Guide*. No attempt has been made here to do more than mention some of the more interesting features and their historical associations. The leading papers of the time, such as *The Builder, The Ecclesiologist,* and *Building News,* took great interest in the gradual building of St. Peter's, as witness the number of reports and pictures which appeared in their pages. The most perceptive comments at this particular time are contained in *The Ecclesiologist's* long description of 1866, the final paragraph of which is quoted by Taylor and repeated here:

> Decidely the least satisfactory thing in the design considered as a whole, is the position of the transepts. We are more and more

> strongly of opinion that transepts should spring not from the chancel of a church, but from the nave. In this case the comparative meagreness of the transepts, with their large surfaces of blank plastered wall, is an eyesore from the nave, when contrasted with the beauty of the chancel. Again they decidedly swallow up the voice. We know few modern churches which are so unsuccessful acoustically. The lessons are nearly inaudible in the nave; and even the choir . . . is not heard through the whole building. Again the people seated in the transepts and choir-aisles must miss the sermon altogether. On the other hand, the effect of the choir-aisles is not only admirable in an artistic point of view, but they afford great facilities for the recession of communicants from the altar. The fact that the sanctuary is vaulted deserves all praise. But we could wish that the chancel proper had been vaulted too. The wooden roof of this part, with its quasi-lantern effect, is not satisfactory; and the vaulted sanctuary, from the fact that its outer roof is lower than that of the nave, is decidedly too low for internal effect. But, in spite of these criticisms, this church must be regarded as one of the very best of our time.

Another duty performed by Bishop Sumner when he came to consecrate the new eastern parts of St. Peter's Church in December 1864 was the consecration of an addition to the churchyard of 1½ acres. St. Peter's churchyard was the only consecrated burial ground in Bournemouth at this time, and the demand for grave spaces was increasing year by year.

On Whit Tuesday 1864 the churchwardens, Edmund Christy and William Rogers, attended in the Vestry at 2 p.m. for the purpose of allotting seats in the Church in its enlarged state. They decided that nobody should be allowed to rent more seats than they could occupy and that no seats could be reserved after a service had started. Priority for obtaining sittings would be given to people living within the District and seats were not to be allotted to individual houses but should be occupied by the persons to whom they were rented. Notices were to be placed on the pews to include the injunction that "Strangers are requested not to take possession of any seats except such as are offered to them by the Churchwardens."

The whole of the benches and chairs in the south transept and south chancel could be rented by the year at 25/- per seat or £6 per bench holding five persons. The seventeen rows of benches on each side of the nave and in the south aisle, together with the chairs parallel with them in both north and south aisles, should be let at the same rate. Four rows of benches in the nave and south aisle, together with the chairs parellel with them, should be let to tradespeople at the rate of 35/- per annum for five sittings. Three rows of benches in the nave and two in the south aisle were to be available for domestic servants at £1 for five seats.

There were also 300 free seats "for the use of the poor." These comprised all the benches in the north aisle and north transept and the chairs at the west end of the Church. At the west end the sexes were divided, men sitting on the south side and women on the north, thus following the continental Catholic practice.

Frequent references to the pew rents appear in the Parish Magazine and Vestry minutes. Efforts were continually being made to increase the endowment of the benefice so that when sufficient provision had been made all seats could be free.

It seems that the right to sittings once allotted was jealously guarded and that a private traffic in seats went on, though without any official approval. In 1865 Morden Bennett points out:

> I am doing all in my power to turn the present building to account, by opening it for divine service five times every Sunday; and I ask you, for the love of Christ, to accommodate one another by placing your seats at the disposal of the Churchwardens whenever they are not occupied by your respective families or households.

And in July 1867 a special Vestry meeting was called by the churchwardens to pass a resolution that seats should not be transferred from one person to another without the sanction of the churchwardens. At the same time it was arranged that there should be one scale of pew rents for annual lettings and another for shorter periods.

Two letters from Morden Bennett on this subject are preserved in St. Peter's Archives; one is to Richard Stephens dated 7th October 1870 and the other to the Vicar's Warden, Matthew Webb, dated 6th November 1876. They read as follows:

> My dear Stephens,
> Since I saw you at Holdenhurst last week I have been thinking about the letting of seats at St. Peter's Church.
> You are probably aware that at the first consecration of the Church in 1845 a scheme was prepared by the Ecclesiastical Commissioners, with the approval of Bishop Sumner, fixing the rates at which the seats should be let, and by this scheme we have been guided from that time to this.
> Some few years ago, I think it was in 1865, when you expressed a desire that the Church should be made free, I consulted Bp. Sumner on the subject. The opinion which he gave was that it ought not to be done until an Endowment was provided.
> My desire has been, from first to last, that the system of pew rents should be abolished, & I should be very thankful if it could be done now. The chief difficulty is in meeting the annual expenses,

which amount to £600 or £700 per an., as you will see by the Account Book now in the hands of Mr. Webb.
I do not think there is any probability of raising this amount by the offertory in addition to the sum already collected.
I should be very thankful if you would kindly consult the members of the congregation on the subject, so as to take action upon it.
There is no doubt that the amount produced by the letting of seats at the present time is small in proportion to the numbers of the congregation, and it is reasonable to say that, if the Agency was in the hands of a person who was free from other occupation, a larger sum would be realised.
I am therefore inclined to think that the most practical plan to pursue would be to pass a resolution to the effect that, considering the labour & attention required in managing the agency connected with the letting of the seats in St. Peter's Church, it is desirable that it should be put into the hands of a person who could give his whole time to the matter.
I am doubtful whether it would be wise to offer this agency to the school master as I think his time is too fully occupied. I was told last week that the rents were likely to produce a larger sum during the present season in consequence of the increased demand.

Believe me
Yrs. sincerely
A. Morden Bennett.

Dear Webb,
During the last four months the rents for seats at St. Peter's Church have amounted to much less than last year:

1875	208	8	9
1876	187	10	5
	20	18	4

Believe me
Yrs. very truly
A. Morden Bennett.

As we shall see in a later chapter, the pew rents at St. Peter's were not abolished until the twentieth century.

A famous Victorian churchman, who became associated with St. Peter's at this time and whose link with the Church has been perpetuated ever since, was John Keble, Vicar of Hursley. He had been one of the pioneers of the Oxford Movement and Professor of Poetry at Oxford University. His best-known book, *The Christian Year,* was one of the most successful publications of the age.

Because of his wife's failing health Keble accompanied her to Bournemouth for the winter of 1865-66. They lived at a house called Brookside in Exeter Lane, near Bournemouth Pier. Every morning Keble walked to St. Peter's for the daily celebration and usually occupied a seat in the recently built south transept.

Early in the morning of 29th March 1866 Keble died at Brookside, and his funeral at Hursley was attended by a vast congregation who gathered together to honour the memory of one of the most devout Englishmen of all time.

The notice of Keble's death in the *Bournemouth Parish Magazine* for April 1866 asked prophetically:

> Is it too much to expect that some memorial will be found hereafter, connected with St. Peter's Church, Bournemouth, more closely than a churchyard tomb—some memorial which shall make known ever to future generations of visitors and inhabitants therein assembling, that here died among us JOHN KEBLE, looking for the resurrection of the dead, and the life of the world to come.

The following month's *Magazine* contained a definite proposal for the suggested memorial, a stained glass window in the south wall of the transept where Keble had usually sat. It was already decided that the subjects should illustrate the Te Deum. The sum of £95 had already been collected towards the estimated cost of £200.

So many subscriptions were received that there was enough money over to glaze the windows at the east end of the transept with pictures illustrative of the Resurrection. The two windows, executed by Clayton & Bell, were set in place early in 1867. The Te Deum window has a portrait of Keble in the lower right corner, depicting him robed in cassock, surplice, hood and stole.

These windows were by no means the only monuments erected to this great man. Keble College at Oxford was founded only a few years after his death and, at St. Peter's, the south transept was later refurnished as a side chapel and named after him.

The Keble windows are just two examples of the many fittings, furnishings and adornments which were added to St. Peter's immediately after the completion of the eastern end of the Church. The iron gates leading from the nave into the chancel were made by Mr. Leaver to Street's design in 1866 and the iron and brass screens separating the chancel from the transepts soon afterwards.

A great work of art, alas no longer to be seen, was the sanctuary panelling, made by Morris, Marshall & Co. of Queen Square, Bloomsbury, and affixed in 1867. The panels were made up of enamelled tiles, representing Angels, designed by Sir Edward Burne-Jones. The colours were burnt into the tiles, so as to ensure permanence and prevent fading, but by 1899 the painting had become so powdery that it was impossible even to trace the design. Nicholas Taylor refers to the loss of the Burne-Jones Angels as "an artistic tragedy" and it is to be regretted that no clear photograph or drawing of these mosaics has been preserved. A similar fate befell Burne-Jones' panels in the north and south sides of the sanctuary which were brought to St. Peter's in the same year.

Nevertheless, Burne-Jones is still represented at St. Peter's by the Monro window in the south transept in which Christ is depicted at the Sea of Tiberias. Apparently Burne-Jones drew the figures and William Morris designed the background patterns and lettering. Morris, who had been articled to Street in 1856, later achieved renown as a pioneer of British socialism.

In 1869 the sanctuary arcades were added. They were not an afterthought on Street's part, as they had been included in the earlier plans. Why they were delayed and not built with the rest of the chancel is a mystery. These double arcades of interlaced arches form the sedilia, and the design seems to have been copied from Lincoln Cathedral, which Street knew well. It is very fortunate that the arcades were not forgotten, for by this time Street and Morden Bennett were both heavily engaged on the next stage of their building.

CHAPTER VIII

Circa 1870

THE YEARS around 1870 mark a further period of increased parochial activity at St. Peter's and another addition to the Church.

Soon after the completion of the new eastern parts of the Church the organ was moved from the nave into the north transept and surrounded by curtains. But it was nearly worn out and had insufficient power to be clearly heard throughout the enlarged Church. As a temporary measure a large second-hand organ was purchased until enough money could be raised to buy a new one. The second-hand instrument, by Bates of London, came from the Vauxhall Gardens and remained in use until 1870, when it was sold to a non-conformist chapel in Brighton. It was so huge that it occupied the whole of the north transept. The Bates organ was an ugly looking instrument which offended the eye of the vicar, and an appeal was launched for funds to provide a case for it and to decorate its front pipes. These embellishments were never done, possibly because there was a succession of organists at short intervals just about this time, possibly because of the decision to buy an entirely new instrument as soon as sufficient money was available. Though some of the stops on the Bates organ were good ones the instrument taken as a whole does not seem to have been worthy of the Church. One of the organists described it as a dear old rattle-trap. In 1869 Morden Bennett ordered a fine new organ by Henry Willis of the Rotunda Organ Works, costing £700, which was installed during the following year.

The Church organists were changed even more frequently than the organs provided for their use. Caseley, who had been appointed in 1859, was succeeded by William Henry Beare, who died in 1867 at the early age of thirty and lies buried in the churchyard. In the next two years Beare's brother and a Mr. Taylor successively came and went. Finally, in 1869, Morden Bennett engaged a highly competent musician, Thomas Alfred Burton, who brought about a welcome improvement in the music of St. Peter's during the next decade. Burton's musical activities were not confined to the Church; but he and Alex. Bennett were noted for the active parts they took in the entertainments of the Bournemouth Amateur Musical Society.

Leachman's book on St. Peter's contains a long section about the music, mainly contributed by Burton, including one exquisite anecdote concerning the new Willis organ. Burton wrote:

> On my appointment, Mr. Bennett told me he was getting funds for a new instrument, and he showed me Willis' specification. One of the stops on the Choir Organ was *Viol d'Amour,* but this was sternly rejected by the Vicar as being unsuitable for a church organ. However, Willis and I plotted in secret to keep the stop, though calling it *Viol da Gamba.* I really believe if Mr. Bennett had known that the despised *Viol d'Amour* was doing duty as an innocent *Gamba,* he would have sent for a carpenter and had it nailed up, as he once threatened to do with the *Open Diapason* on the Great in the original organ; and this he certainly would have done had he been certain of the offender. I used to think he had an idea that the *Viol of Love* was lurking about somewhere in disguise.

The Willis organ, which had three manuals and 1,292 pipes, was given a gala opening on St. Luke's Day, 1870. Burton gave a recital, including in the concert an anthem specially composed for the occasion. It was a fine instrument, both in its musical quality and in the beauty of its pipes, which were decorated with coloured diaper work in 1873. These pipes filled the arches leading from the organ chamber to the remainder of the north transept and to the sanctuary.

The new organ was so good that the deficiencies of the choir were quickly noticed. Alex. Bennett's appeal speaks for itself:

> Additional voices are needed in the choir. There is not sufficient power to fill the Church. The defect is more apparent since the erection of the New Organ. Are there no young men of willing mind ready to offer themselves in singing God's praise? Of course, regularity at practice is indispensable. Are there no boys of the higher or middle classes who would value a training in music? Names should be sent without delay . . .

An innovation of 1869, the year of Burton's arrival at St. Peter's, was the congregational music rehearsal which had been tried a few years previously without great success. So far as we know, the idea was Morden Bennett's, though he may well have received some hint or encouragement from the newly-appointed organist. In a sermon preached in October 1869, the incumbent pointed out that in spite of having a choir to lead the singing "everyone present should feel that he has a duty to perform in this matter." The first congregational practices were held in the School-room at 4 p.m. on Saturdays, starting on November, and proved very successful. So much so that, by the following month, there had been "a very sensible improvement in the way the hymns are rendered in the time of Service," and the music practices are being held in Church. It is not known how long these arrangements were continued; one must assume from the lack of any further record that the initial enthusiasm soon wore off.

Another innovation of this period was the Choir Home, which opened in 1865 and lasted for very much longer than the music practices for the congregation! Half the choirboys lived at the Home, ruled by a resident Matron, and attended St. Peter's School. The other boys lived at their homes in the town.

A novelty of 1865 which has continued down to the present day was the Parish Magazine. The first issue of the *Bournemouth Parish Magazine,* dated June 1865, starts with a few prophetic words which have been fully justified by the events of later years:

> Why should not Bournemouth, a place which is continually increasing, and rising in importance, have its Magazine as well as its Directory? At some future day we may have a Mayor and Corporation, we may have our central terminus for converging railways, or send one or two representatives to Parliament. Let it not therefore be thought presumptuous to commence a Parish Magazine.

The principal objects of this was to "form a record of events connected with the District Church." The early issues of the Magazine consisted merely of eight pages of local news and pastoral instruction bound up around the particular month's copy of *Parish Magazine,* a syndicated publication of religious Victoriana under the editorship of the Rev. J. Erskine Clarke, Vicar of St. Michael's, Derby. At the beginning of 1867 the local matter was published under the title of *The Vale of Avon and Bournemouth Magazine* and contained news of other parishes in the district, as well as Bournemouth. The Rev. W. H. Lucas, Vicar of Sopley, was responsible as editor for collecting material from the various parishes concerned, but items from St. Peter's filled almost half the pages. At the end of 1867 another change was made; starting with the issue for January 1868, *The Bournemouth Parish Magazine* was published for Bournemouth, Pokesdown, Moordown and Parley; and Ringwood, Sopley, Hinton and neighbouring parishes printed their local news in *The Vale of Avon Parish Magazine,* of which Lucas remained the editor.

The rearrangement of 1868 proved not entirely satisfactory and in January 1871 *The Bournemouth and Vale of Avon Parish Magazine* was born. Although the "Vale of Avon" parishes made regular contributions to the new publication, most of the news items concerned St. Peter's. Copies of the Magazine might be obtained at Sydenham's and Gavin's Libraries, and of Edward Offer, Printer, Commercial Road.

1866 was the year of the first contested election for churchwarden at St. Peter's. At the Annual Vestry Meeting on 3rd April, William Rogers and Matthew Webb were both nominated as people's warden. Rogers had previously served as churchwarden from 1857 to 1865 and Webb was later to be Vicar's warden from 1868 to 1877. Morden Bennett, as chairman of the meeting, declared a majority in favour of Webb, but the supporters of Rogers demanded a poll, which was arranged for Thursday, 12th April, at the National School Room between 9 a.m. and 4 p.m. At an adjourned meeting of the Vestry "at nine o'clock" on 12th April (unfortunately we do not know whether this was before the poll or afterwards) Webb expressed a wish to retire and Rogers was declared duly elected.

St. Peter's was treated to the unusual spectacle of a contested election for people's warden only three times more during the rest of the nineteenth century, and these contests were in consecutive years, 1874, 1875 and 1876. In 1874 Gustavus Lane, who had been warden since 1870, was proposed for re-election and David Sydenham, who had been Lane's predecessor for the year 1869-70, was nominated to oppose him. The Vestry minute does not specifically state the result of the election, but as Sydenham was later proposed and elected as a sidesman and Lane is known to have been churchwarden immediately before the 1875 Vestry meeting, it seems certain that Lane was the successful candidate in 1874. The list of churchwardens prepared by James Druitt which appears in Leachman's *St. Peter's* appears to be inaccurate in naming Sydenham as people's warden for 1874-75.

The same gentlemen were again nominated in the two following years. In 1875 Lane was the winner by five votes to two, though in the next year Sydenham mustered twenty-four supporters to Lane's twenty. In 1877 Walter Scott Evans, an outfitter with a business in Commercial Road, was the only candidate to fill Sydenham's place and was unanimously elected. He continued to hold the office until his death over thirty years later, with the exception of two years when he served as Vicar's warden. Scott Evans is remembered as one of the great churchwardens of St. Peter's and evidently carried out his duties most conscientiously. For instance, it was reported in the *Parish Magazine* for November 1882 that when the new cross was fixed to the top of the spire, "Our excellent Churchwarden, Mr. W. Scott Evans, in his capacity as custodian of the fabric, made the perilous ascent to the top of the spire, which neither the Vicar nor his brother Churchwarden ventured to do."

The St. Peter's School buildings, erected to Edmund Pearce's designs in 1850, soon became too small to accommodate all the children who wished to attend. A house in Orchard Lane was taken for an Infant School, but by 1866 the premises were required for demolition. A large room for the infants' classes was then built on a site adjoining St. Peter's National School, opportunity then being taken to complete the unfinished block of buildings by the addition of a classroom, cloakroom, porch and offices, involving an outlay of £900. Even though the urgency of the undertaking necessitated some haste in starting the work, Morden Bennett was able to report that he had been given nearly half the money before the building had even begun.

In 1867, just before the closure of the Orchard Lane school, forty infants were enrolled, under the charge of Miss Newman, formerly a pupil-teacher at Christchurch. In the same year there were 90 children attending St. Peter's National School, taught by Mr. G. Price, a certificated master, assisted by his wife and Miss Stein, a certificated mistress.

There was also an evening school for "Labouring Lads of 12 years and upwards" who were charged threepence a week for three evenings' instruction every week during the winter season. Thirty-nine lads attended during the winter of 1864-65. By 1869 the evening classes were being held four times each week, the subjects offered being Reading, Writing, Arithmetic, English Grammar and Composition, Geography, History, Euclid and Algebra. The tuition fees was raised to sixpence per week and "early application for admission to Mr. T. Thompson" was advised.

Another social service administered from St. Peter's during the period around 1870 was the Children's Clothing Club and Shoe Club "for the benefit of the deserving poor in Holdenhurst, Moordown, East Parley and Pokesdown, as well as Bournemouth."

The schoolchildren of this time were always given a summer treat, this popular event often being held on St. Peter's Day. The magazine reports of these functions make very interesting reading. On 29th June 1867,

> Soon after half-past two all our young friends from Moordown, Pokesdown, and Bournemouth, scholars past and present, assembled in the field adjoining the Westover Pleasure Grounds, for the purpose of rendering full and ample justice to the cheer provided for them. This year they all sat down under the shade of a large tent to the number of 425. This number would have been still larger had the Parley contingent made its appearance, but this was not to be. Illness which had broken out in the parish rendered it more prudent to defer their treat till a later day. When tea was finished, and the bread and butter and cake had all disappeared, a procession was formed and with banners flying the whole body marched to the Cranborne gardens, placed at their disposal through the kindness of the proprietor. There they gave themselves up to two or three hours thorough enjoyment. The boys ran races, scrambled for

balls, and nuts. While the girls in another part of the gardens devoted themselves to amusements more peculiarly their own. There was however a feature in this year's gathering which we welcomed with pleasure, and that was the introduction of music into the entertainment. While the rest of the children were enjoying their games some of the scholars of St. Peter's School, and some of the choir of the School-church at Moordown, gathered themselves together, each choir in a separate part of the gardens, and sang some glees, rounds and madrigals, with much taste and skill. Before returning home, the children repaired in a body to St. Peter's Church where a short service was held, and after a few words of counsel and advice given by the Incumbent with reference to the events of the day, they were dismissed with the Blessing.

In the summer of 1869 the school treat was held at Hinton Admiral, on the estate of the patron and Lady Gervis. All the children aged seven and over from the schools at Bournemouth, Moordown and Pokesdown rode to Hinton in waggons lent for the occasion by Messrs. R. Seare of Muscliffe, D. Burt of Moordown, Cox of Malmesbury Farm and Hayter of Bournemouth. The magazine account relates that, "on arriving at the gates of the Park a procession was formed, and headed by the band we marched up in great style to the house, music playing and banners flying. We were not left long waiting before the bugle sounded, summoning us to dinner, to which we sat down in number about 340, including about thirty children from Christchurch, and an equal number from the village school." During the afternoon there were races, cricket matches, sack-jumping and other games, and after tea the party adjourned to the park, "where several fire balloons were sent up with great success." The entertainment ended with three cheers for Sir George and Lady Gervis.

Our ancestors were seldom slow about embarking (literally) on novel pursuits. In May 1871, Bournemouth's first regular steamship, the *Heather Bell,* began her six seasons of pleasure trips from the pier. Within two months of this innovation, on the Feast of the Dedication, the treat for the children of the local Church schools consisted of a trip on the *Heather Bell* to Studland and Old Harry Rocks. The schoolchildren from St. Peter's, St. Clement's, St. Michael's and St. John's, Moordown, who went on this outing, numbered over four hundred, despite the ship being credited with a carrying capacity of only 246. The men who accompanied the party had dinner together afterwards.

St. Peter's Day was not observed solely as a day of pleasure for the children. To the congregation it was a day of religious observance and social gatherings. In the eighteen-sixties it was the custom of the people year after year to invite the incumbent to meet them over tea in the evening. It was hoped the practice would never be discontinued, as it served "as a bond of union between the Pastor and his flock and promotes good feeling between them." These parties used to be held in the schoolroom, with a musical entertainment and the usual refreshments. Unfortunately, the population of the town increased so rapidly that there was insufficient room at the school for everybody to sit down at once, so the concerts had to be stopped. It appears they were revived soon afterwards, because in 1873, when 29th June fell on a Sunday, the "entertainment" was put off until the following day.

There is never a reference to strong drink being served at parochial functions. Probably it never was. Morden Bennett acted as chairman of the local branch of the Church Temperance Association, and his assistant clergy were prominent members. Total abstinence was not a part of the Association's creed, except as a remedy for "inveterate habits of intemperance" or as an example to others. Nevertheless, it is doubtful whether Morden Bennett would ever have touched alcoholic liquor, save possibly within the privacy of the Parsonage.

The year 1869 saw two changes in religious observance connected with the services. One was the introduction of the Sung Eucharist, which had to be explained very meticulously to the congregation before all members would accept it. In a three-page article in *The Bournemouth Parish Magazine* for June 1869, Morden Bennet set out his reasons for wanting to start this type of service.

> The Holy Communion may be regarded as the highest form of Christian worship, and therefore it seems to be most fitting that we should bestow all suitable dignity upon It, and make use of all such external aids as are best calculated to excite our feelings of devotion. . . . Surely when we thus draw near to our Heavenly Father with grateful hearts, we must be convinced that music will be a powerful aid in giving expression to our feelings. . . . But if a doubt should still remain on the mind of any one, whether a choral service is suitable for the celebration of the Holy Communion, it may be remembered that our Blessed Lord sang a hymn with His Apostles at the time of the institution of this Sacrament. . . . It must appear to any one who reflects calmly upon the subject, that the Choral Celebration gives greater dignity to the service. And it may be safely asserted that as we become accustomed to it, we shall find it a great help to our devotions, so that we may reasonably hope that it will fit our minds for the presence of Christ, and prepare us for the service of Heaven.

St. Peter's Day that year was observed with a Choral Celebration at 8 a.m. If Morden Bennett succeeded in establishing the Sung Eucharist, he had to bow to superior authority when trouble started again over the candles. As we saw in Chapter Six, two candles had been lighted on the altar at early celebrations of Holy Communion since 1865; though, (in the Incumbent's words) "to accommodate my services to all, as far as I could, without introducing any excess of ceremonial, but keeping strictly within the bounds of moderation," the candles were left unlighted at the later celebrations. The critics remained unconvinced and unsatisfied, and difficulties arose at many Churches throughout the land. A case was brought before the Court of Arches in 1868 to test the legality of placing lighted candles upon the altar and judgement was given in favour of allowing the practice. Morden Bennett made no change in the arrangements at St. Peter's, preferring to do what he could to placate those residents and visitors who felt aggrieved at seeing the candles lighted.

The opponents of "high ritual" appealed to the House of Lords just before Christmas, 1868, and succeeded in obtaining a reversal of the previous decision. Morden Bennett still made no change in the observances at St. Peter's, but the Archdeacon was soon on his track and asking for information. The vicar delivered a reasoned reply, complaining of the system which allowed a temporal Court to decide spiritual causes, and adding:

> It is my wish to pay Canonical obedience to my Diocesan, as I am bound. I am therefore fully prepared to pay attention to any directions which you as Commissary and Archdeacon may have to give me in his name. If any change is to be made in the mode of conducting the service, I should prefer that the responsibility of making it should rest with those who are set in authority over me. I should also feel better satisfied, if the order came from the Chief Pastor of the Diocese, than if it proceeded from a temporal Court; and others, perhaps, might sympathise with me.

The ailing Bishop Sumner considered this appeal, but felt he was bound to require Morden Bennett to discontinue the practice of lighting the candles except when they were needed for providing light. This episcopal direction was, of course, obeyed.

Morden Bennett was not alone in complaining about the anomalous legal position affecting matters of ritual and observance which had been steadily introduced into the worship of the Church of England by Tractarian priests. The law itself was far from certain and had frequently to be tested by applications to the Courts which themselves were led on several occasions to reverse their previous decisions. The greatest point of objection was that the Courts to which such cases were referred, notably the Judicial Committee of the Privy Council, were secular tribunals and not spiritual ones.

The trouble over the candles at St. Peter's only represented one small aspect of a much wider problem. Clergy who were more advanced than Morden Bennett in their ritualistic ways were being challenged over such matters as the use of incense and vestments and over the ceremonial practices observed when celebrating Holy Communion. In no sense was Morden Bennett an extreme Anglo-Catholic ritualist, though undoubtedly he was in general sympathy with their more moderate aspirations and would himself have introduced a higher ritual at St. Peter's if he had thought his congregation ready to accept it.

Between 1867 and 1871 several Court judgements were given against the ritualists, but the effect of these decisions, coming as they did from a tribunal of the state, was to excite greater dislike of the Judicial Committee among the clergy and this indirectly led to an increase of ritual usages rather than the reverse. Changes in the legal procedure made during 1874 did not affect the main complaint that temporal Courts were deciding spiritual issues. Low churchmen banded themselves together to resist any change and litigation increased, checked only by the bishops more frequently using their power to veto proceedings.

As late as 1877 the Judicial Committee gave the clear and most specific decision that the cope and the surplice were the only lawful vestments for the Church of England. But the turbulent climate of the time is perhaps best illustrated by recalling that in 1878-81 four priests were sent to prison for failing to obey orders made by Courts against whose authority and jurisdiction they had protested. It was not until ten years later, after favourable judgements had been given by the Archbishop of Canterbury and the Judicial Committee in the case of Bishop King of Lincoln, that ritualist clergy could hope with any confidence that their sincerely held beliefs were likely to be tolerated. Even when Eucharistic vestments were eventually introduced at St. Peter's in the early years of the twentieth century they were technically unlawful though by then generally accepted by the bishops.

In case the modern reader should be surprised that matters like these should have been the cause of so much argument and dissension such a relatively short time ago, let it be recalled that the principal issues in Bishop King's case were whether it was proper to have lighted candles on the altar, whether it was lawful for the celebrant to mix water with the wine in the chalice during the service, whether he was allowed to take the eastward position (facing the altar) for the celebration, whether he could permit the *Agnus Dei* to be sung after the consecration, and whether it was legal for him to make the sign of the cross in the air. Modern priests and congregations may accept these things as matters of course, but in Morden Bennett's time they were looked upon by a great many people as particularly wicked.

CHAPTER IX

The Tower And Vestibules

"ALL THAT is needed to render the Church one of the grandest structures in the South of England, is the Tower, which is to be erected at the West End, and surmounted with a spire." So wrote Morden Bennett in the Spring of 1869. Three years previously, not long after the completion of the chancel and transepts at the eastern end of St. Peter's, the incumbent had obtained Street's design for a tower and steeple and was starting to raise the money, then estimated at £3,500. He referred to the tower as "a most important appendage to the Church, and a conspicuous ornament to the place." He suggested that every resident member of the congregation should make himself responsible for a certain sum towards the building fund, payable by instalments over four years.

By the end of 1868, £2,600 had been subscribed, and it was decided to proceed at once with building the tower. Plans for the steeple or spire were deferred. The tower was not to be erected immediately adjoining the west door of the Church, but a distance of twenty feet away, so as to leave room for the vestibule, or western transept. This would serve as a sort of foyer to facilitate the entrance and exit of the congregation, at the same time providing accommodation for an additional 140 worshippers when the Church had to be filled to capacity.

Both tower and spire were in Street's original design for St. Peter's of 1853. This is made clear from a description in *The Ecclesiologist* for February, 1855. The decision to move the tower westward, so as to leave space for a transept or vestibule, must have been made at a very late stage, probably not earlier than 1866. Philip Brannon's engraving of St. Peter's in the Fifth Edition of his *Guide* (1860) shows the Church not as it then was but apparently as it was intended to be. The chancel, tower and spire, none of which had been begun, are all shown, but the tower is connected to the nave, leaving no room for the vestibule, nor is a vestibule or western transept mentioned in the accompanying text. Furthermore, Morden Bennett's notice about the tower and steeple, dated March 1866, certainly makes no reference to the proposed addition.

There was an urgent need for new accommodation at this period, because, although Holy Trinity had just been built, neither St. Swithun's nor St. Stephen's had been begun and St. Michael's existed only as a temporary wooden building, seating 400. At the same time, it must have been clear to Street and Morden Bennett that when further central Churches had been built St. Peter's congregation would be slightly reduced in size. Street therefore devised the ingenious solution of a western transept which could be used at first as an extension of the nave but eventually as a vestibule or foyer between the nave and west door — the sort of space that is badly lacking in most town Churches, where congregations have difficulty making their way out after the main service on Sundays.

As the fund for building the tower had already been opened, Morden Bennett preferred to proceed with that part of the Church first, and leave the vestibule to be filled in afterwards.

The contract for the tower was awarded to Messrs. Dove Brothers of Islington at a price of £2,995, but the total cost of the enterprise, including contingent expenses, was estimated at £3,300. The work of putting in the underground foundations was begun on 25th January 1869, but the builders soon ran into unexpected trouble. The sandy soil extended far lower than had been thought, with the result that an extra fifteen feet of earth had to be excavated before it was safe to pour in the concrete bed on which the tower was to rest. This additional preparatory work increased the estimates by £120 and delayed the laying of the foundation stone from February until April.

13th April was fixed for the foundation stone ceremony and Lord Henry Scott, Member of Parliament for the Southern Division of Hampshire, was invited to officiate. Owing to illness, Lord Henry was unable to attend, so the ceremony was performed by Lady Gervis and the address given by Richard Stephens, a former churchwarden. As we shall see later, Lord Henry was not forgotten, but was invited in 1874 to lay the first stone of the vestibule.

At the conclusion of the service which followed the laying of the foundation stone, Morden Bennett entertained seventy ladies and gentlemen to luncheon in the schoolroom, at which the incumbent made a speech in which he referred to the total cost of the tower as £5,000. The vestibule and steeple would involve spending £5,000 more, and this did not include the bells.

Perhaps we have here a clue to Morden Bennett's financial wizardry, for such it undoubtedly was. Over and over again we see that the first mention of a project is coupled with an estimate which is soon greatly increased. It defies belief that the true figures, or at least realistic ones, were not available from the outset, and one is driven to the conclusion that the original underestimates were published deliberately. Presumably, Morden Bennett found from experience that a high figure was likely to provoke opposition and might discourage members of the congregation from making donations.

Morden Bennett never embarked on any scheme (and the tower was no exception) without first raising most of the money beforehand. He had a great fear of getting into debt and adhered to the principle that any advance must be carried out in stages, as the funds required could be made available. His usual method was to raise a fairly substantial part of any fund privately before the public was told anything about it. Undoubtedly, this encouraged others to subscribe liberally and served as a bulwark against any voice which might be raised in opposition.

Morden Bennett's practice in money matters was simple and straightforward; his appeals for funds were unashamedly directed to the rich, who were told to dig deeply into their pockets. They had money to spare and God needed it. Fortunately, rich parishioners were quite numerous at this time and the incumbent always seemed able to obtain what he required without much difficulty. He clearly preferred to collect large gifts from the affluent, rather than smaller contributions from the poorer elements of the community. He was exceedingly generous himself and sometimes would offer £50 or £100 of his own money if a certain number of others would do the same. Furthermore, he played with great subtlety upon the pride of those wealthy Victorians who could not bear to see a subscription list circulated in which they appeared less generous or less rich than their neighbours.

Crumpler pointed out that many men of Morden Bennett's means "would have retired to live in ease and luxury. He was a man of wonderful tact in all business transactions, and for many years he kept all the accounts of the different churches in a most straightforward manner and was always able to answer any question that might be put to him. On one occasion he was asked by a gentleman how much he had after he had paid all the expenses. In reply he said, 'If you really wish to know, last year I had 9½d. left for myself.' "

The tower was completed in 1870 and, as it stood some distance away from the remainder of the Church, a wooden covered way was made to connect them. Contemporary pictures of St. Peter's at this period show that the Church presented rather an odd appearance. The top of the tower looked unfinished, as it was in fact, and the space between Church and tower gave the impression of untidiness or of an unhappy afterthought.

By the time the tower was finished, Morden Bennett was laid up with a serious illness, largely caused through overwork. The strain of his busy and exacting life during the previous quarter-century was having its effect. The finances of his many enterprises were not entirely satisfactory and he can hardly be blamed for worrying about them. A letter to his warden, Matthew Webb, which is preserved in St. Peter's Archives, gives an indication of some of these difficulties. It is dated 18th February 1870 and reads:

Dear Webb,
On referring to the accounts of the different institutions under my charge I find that at Midsummer last there was a considerable balance against me in each of these accounts; and I am very desirous that this should not occur again, at least to the same extent. You are aware that in the accounts of St. Peter's Church there was a deficiency of £130. The following statement will show what the deficiency was on the other accounts, though with regard to St. Michael's Church, the Sanatorium and Pokesdown School this will not occur again as I am to a great extent relieved from responsibility in their case.

St. Michael's Church	£29
St. Clement's Mission	35
East Parley Services	26
Sanatorium Chapel	31
Moordown Services (here the expenses are partly met by an endowment)	4
	125
St. Peter's School	28
Moordown School	36
Parley School	33
St. Michael's School	13
Pokesdown School	5
St. Clement's School	2
	£242

If you can suggest any arrangement by which the finances of these Institutions can be managed by a committee of gentlemen as has been done with St. Peter's Church I should be very thankful to be relieved of so heavy a burden which you will observe is in *addition* to my own subscription.

Believe me,
Yours very truly,
A. Morden Bennett.

The heavy burden was not easily lifted from Morden Bennett's shoulders and his illness in 1870 and 1871 prevented him from doing any work at all for many months. But a rest cure at Great Malvern, followed by periods of recuperation abroad and at the home of relations enabled him to return to his parish by Whitsun, 1871. He was then given the new bells, which had just been hung in the tower, as a testimonial to his "zeal and unwearied efforts for the welfare of Bournemouth and its inhabitants."

It had always been intended that a peal of bells should be placed in the tower, which was built with a circular stairway in the north wall leading to the ringing chamber above. The incumbent's serious illness was seized upon as an ideal opportunity of honouring him and providing the bells at the same time. An appeal throughout the town was organised by Richard Stephens, donations being sent in by many notable people to swell the large fund collected from the townsfolk of Bournemouth. Sir George Gervis, referring to Morden Bennett's "exertions and liberality," subscribed £25, and Samuel Wilberforce, the new Bishop of Winchester, recorded that he found it very gratifying to hear of dissenters joining with churchmen in such good work.

The bells were manufactured by John Taylor & Co., the well-known Loughborough bell-founders, and they delivered them to Stephens at the end of February, 1871, invoiced thus:

We respectfully hand you the weight of the six largest bells we forwarded on Saturday last for St. Peter's Church, Bournemouth.

cwt.	qtr.	lbs.
6	3	18
8	0	8
9	2	14
11	1	8
14	1	6
19	2	10
69	3	8

We trust they will safely arrive and when completed prove to your perfect satisfaction.

Morden Bennett returned from spending the winter abroad in time for the dedication of the new bells on the Tuesday in Whit week, 1871. A brass plate under the tower commemorates the occasion:

To the Glory of God and as a Mark of Respect and Esteem for the Rev. Alexander Morden Bennett, M.A., Vicar of St. Peter's District,

Six Bells were hung in this Tower by the Inhabitants of Bournemouth. — Whitsuntide 1871.

The brass commemorative plate was supplied by Hart, Son, Peard & Co., to the order of the architect. The original account for £18 16s. 6d., certified by Street as correct, is preserved in St. Peter's Archives. The exchange of letters passing between Stephens and Morden Bennett concerning the testimonial are printed in Leachman's *St. Peter's,* pp. 29-31.

When the Vicar returned to his full duties in September, 1871, he discovered there was still a debt of £400 on the building fund of the tower. Offering personal contributions totalling £40 if others would do the same, he challenged his congregation to meet the deficiency without further delay. He got the money, of course.

Morden Bennett's doctor, in *Southbourne's Infancy,* tells a revealing story about the vicar's struggle to regain his faculties during his illness:

After his first paralytic seizure, when over sixty, he gradually improved in a satisfactory manner and was generally quite a cheerful patient. After some weeks, however, I noticed one morning the uselessness of his right hand was evidently much upon his mind. Now Mr. Bennett used to write a wonderfully clear, almost copperplate hand, and the thought that he might never do so again was naturally a great trial. On this special morning he told me in a rather sad voice, "I shall never write again." Recognising the importance of removing by any means if possible this feeling of depression, I said to him, "Mr. Bennett, you *will* write again, with your left hand, at any rate, and I dare say just as well as formerly with your right."

The words were hardly out of my mouth, when the patient said, "Nurse, bring me pencil and paper." When these were put before him, he asked me what he should do. I told him, "Oh, begin first with downward strokes, then pothooks, as they do in the Infant School."

After he had filled a small page with strokes of sorts, I stopped him, and said: "Now no more to-day. Try again to-morrow."

Mr. Bennett then remarked so cheerfully, when I looked at his first trial with his left hand, "You will see the end lines are much better than the first ones"; and so they were. From that moment I felt sure he would be able to write again, but never indeed expected what eventually happened, *viz.,* that after some months he produced the same old copper-plate writing with his left hand! Later on, moreover, regaining power on his right side altogether, he could write equally well with either hand.

I think when the result is considered my tarradiddle was quite pardonable!

The need for the vestibule was now becoming more urgent and, with the warning of his recent illness prominently in his mind,

Morden Bennett was determined to do whatever he could to ensure that the Church would be completed during his lifetime. The Building Fund Report, printed in *The Bournemouth and Vale of Avon Parish Magazine* for December 1872, confirms that all the expenses for the tower had been paid and it was then proposed to join the tower to the main building, at a further outlay of £2,200. Contributions exceeding £500 were already in hand and the work would commence as soon as two-thirds of the expenditure had been promised. The Vicar and churchwardens explained that:

> This addition to the Church, which may be described as a Vestibule or Narthex, would externally assume the appearance of a Double Transept with a North and South Gable, and would internally afford additional accommodation to the congregation, which is much needed. It would be a cause of reproach if the Church should remain long in its present unfinished state, after so much has been expended upon it.

The western transepts, as they now become to be called (the idea of a vestibule fading regrettably into oblivion), were built in 1874, being opened and dedicated that same year. Nicholas Taylor has referred to them as being "among the few really satisfying works of Street's last ten years, after he had exhausted himself in designing the Law Courts in London." Lord Henry Scott promised to lay the foundation stone in April, but again he was prevented from coming and the stone was laid by Morden Bennett himself.

Upon the completion of the western transepts, the font was moved from its old position just inside the south door and replaced in the south-west transept, which has since served as a baptistery.

In the Summer of 1871 a new lectern was offered to the Church as a memorial gift by Colonel Williams. A handsome design was prepared by Mr. Potter, of London, in the form of an eagle with outstretched wings, which was executed in brass and placed in the Church at Easter, 1872. The old wooden lectern had stood for many years in the centre of the nave gangway where it blocked the view of the altar and reredos for many of the congregation. The new lectern was therefore placed at the extreme south-east corner of the nave.

Two other offerings made to the Church at about the same time were the lych-gate and the churchyard cross. The latter was designed by Street after the style of the 12th century and put up during the Summer of 1871. Four of the eight panels around the octagonal base contain sculptured foliage of a rather ordinary kind, but there are fine sculptures on the other panels depicting respectively the Nativity, the Crucifixion, the Ascension and the

Martyrdom of St. Peter. Earp was again responsible for the carving.

The picturesque lych-gate, meaning the gate of the dead, where the bier was generally rested, was also erected in 1871 to Street's design. It was built entirely of oak and serves as a charming entrance to the churchyard. By 1878 the churchyard was so full that it had to be closed for ordinary burials and reserved for residents of 20 years standing. The years 1873-77 had seen nearly two burials a week at St. Peter's. The town's new cemetery at Rush Corner, which had its first funeral on 29th April, 1878, was opened just in time.

During the time between the building of the tower and western transepts a start was made on the frescoes inside the Church. The first of these was the decoration of the blank wall over the chancel arch. Street's original idea for this painting was *Our Lord in Majesty,* but this subject was used for the reredos, so *The Crucifixion* was chosen for the chancel arch. The design was displayed in the Church during Lent, 1873, and the work was begun by Clayton & Bell in May the same year, and finished in July. Cartoons of the figures were drawn in London and sent down to Bournemouth as soon as they were ready, so they could be copied on the wall. A new method of wall-painting was adopted so as to ensure the permanence of the fresco so far as possible and minimise the deleterious effects of the atmosphere. The colours were mixed with an adhesive preparation of gelatine and no lime was used. The cost of the fresco amounted to £150.

The new fresco was so successful that Morden Bennett and several members of his congregation thought it would be fitting to have similar pictures painted above the arches in the nave. It was decided to introduce two or more allegorical subjects from the New Testament, the first of which, depicting *The Good Shepherd,* was to be a memorial to Samuel Wilberforce, the famous and beloved Bishop of Winchester, who had just died.

Samuel Wilberforce, 1805-73, was the third son of William Wilberforce, the philanthropist and suppressor of the slave trade. He is best remembered as Bishop of Oxford from 1845 until 1869, when he succeeded Sumner at Winchester. Though opposed to ritualistic extremes, Wilberforce was himself a High Churchman, holding views far more sympathetic towards the level of worship being evolved at St. Peter's than those of the Evangelical Sumner. At Oxford Wilberforce had acquired a national reputation for his ability to reconcile diverse opinions and had exercised a considerable influence on the Tractarian movement by his efforts at composing the differences between the traditionalists and the Puseyite leaders. His well-known nickname "Soapy Sam" represented the public's recognition of his capacity for evasion in contentious matters, Lord Westbury having described one of Wilberforce's synodical judgements at Oxford as "a well-lubricated set of words, a sentence so oily and saponaceous that no one could grasp it." The Bishop, never at a loss when presented with an opportunity of exercising his ready wit, commented that he owed his nickname to the fact that though he was often in hot water he always came out with clean hands.

It will be recalled that it was Wilberforce, while at Oxford, who appointed Street as his diocesan architect and thus became his first patron. He was known as an exceedingly active bishop; *The Monitor* for January, 1878, said of him:

> He set himself the task of becoming acquainted with and known to every priest and every church, and almost every congregation in his diocese. He was said with truth to be an ubiquitous bishop, for the celerity and rapidity of his movements were surprising.

He was killed by being thrown from his horse in July, 1873, and the Church mourned a good man, noted far and wide for his devotion to duty. Because of the more essential need to raise funds for the western transepts, it was not until 1877 that the nave frescoes at St. Peter's were executed, at a cost of over £300, or more than twice the figure spent on the chancel arch. And by that time everybody seems to have forgotten the original object of Bishop Wilberforce's memorial. *The Good Shepherd* does, however, appear in the easternmost spandril of the arches on the north side of the nave. The other seven pictures also illustrate subjects from the New Testament.

CHAPTER X

The Mission Extended

WE NOW go back a little in time in order to complete the account of the mission work and church building in Bournemouth which derived its impetus, and a great deal of its finance, from the efforts of Morden Bennett and the St. Peter's congregation.

From about 1865 the population of the Moordown area began to increase rapidly and the school-chapel was no longer big enough for the needs of the locality. Many acres of land at Winton were laid out for housing and the new residents had to choose between the school-chapel in one direction and St. Peter's Church, quite a long distance away, in the other. In 1867 the Moordown school had seventy children, under the charge of Mr. C. Bower, a certified master, formerly of St. Mark's College, Chelsea, assisted by his sister. Morden Bennett noted in his magazine that with each of the schools in his control, "there is a Sunday School connected. The girls are instructed in plain needlework, in order to fit them for domestic service. The schools are chiefly supported by the Congregation of St. Peter's Church."

Numbers continued to grow and, having undertaken the spiritual charge of the villages of Winton and Moordown (those "two workmen's suburbs to the north of Bournemouth" as the local guide book stated), the Rev. W. W. Herringham in 1872 purchased the land on which the present St. John's Church and Vicarage now stand, which he afterwards conveyed to Morden Bennett who had in the meanwhile bought further land at the rear, which in due course became the site of the new school.

The new St. John's was designed by Street, and on 6th August 1873 the foundation stone was laid by the Earl of Malmesbury who had himself been largely responsible for the growth of the population on account of his having disposed of so much of his land for house-building. Morden Bennett made an earnest appeal to his people for funds and was met, as usual, with a liberal response. The Church was finished and consecrated in 1874. The new parish of Moordown was created, partly from St. Peter's and partly from Holdenhurst, by Order in Council dated 20th March 1874. A huge area was allocated, bounded on the west by the County boundary all the way from Talbot Road to the River Stour, on the north by the river, Muscliffe Lane and Castle Lane, on the east by the whole length of Charminster Road, and on the south by Wimborne Road and Talbot Road. Parts of the original St. John's parish were later taken over towards creating districts for St. Augustine's, St. Alban's, St. Luke's, St. Francis' and Holy Epiphany. The first Vicar to be appointed was the Rev. Charles Seymour Towle, a former assistant curate of St. Peter's. Later on he became Vicar of St. Clement's.

The establishment of the National Sanatorium for the treatment of consumption and diseases of the chest was another important venture in which Morden Bennett played a prominent part, but the building of the chapel there is most closely associated with the name of Waddelow, his senior curate, who made it his particular concern. Street was engaged as architect and the chapel, dedicated to St. Luke the physician, was opened on St. Luke's day, 18th October,1866. Because money for the project was short (there was still an outstanding debt of £400 in the summer of 1867) certain appendages, including the heating, had to be left out. It is reported that, while waiting for this deficiency to be remedied, the new chapel was so cold in winter that patients could not bear the temperature, and services were held, as formerly, in the corridor.

Another artisans' suburb growing quickly at this time was Springbourne. In the *Parish Magazine* for May, 1867 appeared a paragraph headed "Rapid Growth of Bournemouth":

> The town is extending in every possible direction — North, East and West. The increase in the number of new dwellings on Boscombe Heath is very noticeable. Here a piece of ground has been secured for Church purposes, 2 acres for a Church and Churchyard, and 2 acres for a school and playground, or any other buildings that may be required, the plot of ground is advantageously situated in a central position. On the North is the new Colony of Springbourne, where the land is judiciously laid out for the dwellings of the labouring classes, and the population is rapidly increasing; on the South East are the houses on the allotments of the Freehold Building Society; on the cliff, directly South, is the new residence of Sir H. Drummond Wolff. And on the adjoining land other villas are likely to be built shortly.

By the end of the summer of 1867 a subscription list for raising a building fund had already been opened, but Morden Bennett was not content to lose any pastoral opportunity while waiting for the fund to reach a sufficient figure to enable the main project to proceed. "In order to lose no time in meeting the Spiritual wants of the increasing population in the part of this district which is now called Springbourne," he wrote, "a building has been secured." This was a room consisting of the shell of three unfinished cottages (now 290, 292 and 294 Holdenhurst Road) hired for use as a Mission Room until the new Church on Boscombe Heath could be built. Opened for service on Sunday 10th November 1867, with a Celebration at 8 a.m. and Evening Prayer with sermon at 6.30 p.m., the new mission served to collect together a nucleus of Anglicans in the neighbourhood and to minister to their needs until more permanent arrangements could be made. There was accommodation for 180 worshippers and at the first evening service every seat inside was taken so that latecomers had to join in from the porch.

Among the St. Peter's congregation Morden Bennett appealed enthusiastically for the St. Clement's Mission Room. "This may be regarded as purely Missionary work," he reported, "there being no fund whatever, either for the buildings or for the services, but such as may be raised by the freewill offerings of the people."

In *A Little Book about S. Clement's, Bournemouth,* published in 1923, it is stated that by the end of 1867 a schoolroom had been erected at the expense of Miss E. Mordaunt and Morden Bennett, who were desirous that a charity should be legally and properly constituted as Church of England Schools in connection with St. Clement's Church. By 1871 they had founded St. Clement's Home, a small orphanage for girls. By its side was the schoolroom, or "the little Dames' School" as it was then called.

A local gentleman, Edmund Christy, who had been churchwarden of St. Peter's from 1864 to 1866, offered to pay for the permanent Church of St. Clement and to endow it, provided Morden Bennett consented to a separate district being formed. This being agreed, Morden Bennett laid the foundation stone in 1871, and the building, designed to seat no less than 700, was ready for consecration in the spring of 1873. St. Clement's soon achieved what was little less than notoriety because of the "high-church" ritual of its services. There was even a spot of difficulty at the consecration, for which candles were lit on the reredos and wafers provided for the Communion. The Bishop of Winchester, "Soapy Sam" Wilberforce, refused to carry on until the candles were extinguished and the wafers replaced by bread. Wilberforce wrote in his diary (15th April 1873) that it was "all most disturbing." He was so greatly put off his stride by the doings of St. Clement's that during the Communion he spilled some of the consecrated wine which "for 45 years I have *never* done," and which "quite overset me."

The Rev. George Douglas Tinling, who died in 1880 at the early age of 36, was the first incumbent. St. Clement's adopted the continental Catholic practice of separating the sexes, men on the south side, women on the north. A Convent of the Sisters of Bethany was attached to the Church in 1875.

In 1866 the need was felt for a school and place of worship on the western side of central Bournemouth. Morden Bennett secured a plot of ground on the site of the present Devon Towers Hotel and Street was commissioned to build the first St. Michael's Church. This was a Purbeck stone and timber structure, 70 feet long and 47 feet wide, modelled in the style of a mediaeval French barn, with a huge roof reaching almost to the ground. The dedication, on the second Sunday in Advent 1866, was conducted by the Rt. Rev. Horatio Powys, Bishop of Sodor and Man, who later died in Bournemouth and had a window to his memory installed in the present St. Michael's Church. Morden Bennett pushed forward with a scheme for the erection and endowment of a permanent Church. George Durrant, Esq., of Norwich, gave £500 and an acre of land on the north side of Poole Road. As soon as £3,000, the amount required by the Ecclesiastical Commissioners, was raised, part of St. Peter's parish was set aside as a separate district for St. Michael's. Norman Shaw, who had been a pupil of Street, was engaged as the architect for the permanent Church, Morden Bennett laying the foundation stone on 4th August 1874.

After the first portion of the new building had been completed and consecrated Street's 'barn' was pulled down, but not before it had given its name to the present St. Michael's Road. It is regrettable that, while so many undistinguished buildings of the period have been allowed to survive, this curious edifice (the only one of its kind which Street ever attempted) had to be demolished. Edward Wanklyn of St. Peter's became the first vicar of St. Michael's. In 1877 the schools were built on land given by Mr. W. Clapcott Dean, £2,000 having been contributed by Mr. Durrant. The chancel of the Church was consecrated in 1883 and the tower dedicated in 1901.

By 1878 Morden Bennett had started five more missions, four within St. Peter's parish and the other at Branksome, a school-chapel which was the predecessor of the present St. Aldhelm's Church. This last connection was a most curious one, because Branksome is over the county boundary and in the neighbouring diocese of Salisbury. One wonders how it was that a vicar of St. Peter's should have had any connection with it, but Morden Bennett was not the kind of man who could see a need and then sit back and do nothing about it. It is a known fact that in the

1870's, and possibly earlier, Morden Bennett used to go along after Evensong at St. Peter's to the waste ground opposite Bourne Valley potteries, and there he conducted services for the growing community of people who forgathered each Sunday among the stacks of pottery pipes. Not content with this open-air ministry, Morden Bennett then proceeded to build a school-chapel in Langley Road, Lower Parkstone. This was erected in 1875 to Street's design, and although used as a school during the week, it was kept as a place of worship on Sundays.

There is a possible explanation for this link with Branksome, for at that time Branksome Park was owned by Henry Bury, who went to live at Branksome Tower in about 1869. This district was then in the parish of Kinson, but the Bury family worshipped at St. Peter's, travelling there by coach across the long stretch of heath where is now the built-up area between Westbourne and St. Michael's Church. Bury must have been very conscious of the need for a place of worship in the 750 acres which comprised the Branksome Park estate, and it seems more than probable that he and Morden Bennett would have discussed the matter together, especially in the early years of the decade when Bury was selling much of his land for building. It was in 1875, the year in which the school-chapel was built, that Bury laid the foundation stone of All Saints' Church, Branksome Park, and Morden Bennett took part in the service. In his address he referred to the lack of accommodation for the poorer people except on the outskirts of the town, and in doing so indicated the responsibility of local landowners for providing them with places of worship. The district around the potteries was evidently in his mind, and so it came about that, resulting from his early efforts, the foundation stone of St. Aldhelm's Church was laid in 1892.

Within St. Peter's parish St. Martin's Mission in Orchard Street and St. Margaret's Mission in Holdenhurst Road were opened "among the dwellings of the poor," as Morden Bennett expressed it in a *Parish Magazine* article. Apparently the vicar and his assistant clergy found it difficult to persuade the poorer and less well educated parishioners to come to the services at St. Peter's, which presented the image of a rich men's or gentlemen's Church, so religion and education were sent out to the populace. Another Mission Room was opened in 1877 at Seamoor Road, Westbourne, and an infant school was started there in 1878. The room was placed at Morden Bennett's disposal by Mr. Joy, which the incumbent "took as a great favour as Mr. Joy was not a churchman."

This mission eventually became transformed into St. Ambrose, a daughter-Church of St. Peter's until it became a separate parish in 1922. The foundation stone of a permanent building for St. Ambrose, as a chapel-of-ease to St. Peter's, was laid on 27th November 1879. This building was in Alumhurst Road and the cost, including the site, was £800. The chancel, nave and vestry were soon completed and an appeal launched for a further £1,000 to build an extension of the nave to accommodate three hundred persons. As we shall see in a later chapter this was by no means the final development of St. Ambrose, for only a few years afterwards a much finer site was acquired and the erection of the present Church commenced.

The only other new Church founded by Morden Bennett which has not yet been mentioned was St. Swithun's which was built to serve the East Cliff side of the parish. Sir George Gervis gave a triangular piece of land for this purpose, stipulating to the incumbent that it should never be formed into a separate parish but should always remain attached to the mother-Church of St. Peter's. Norman Shaw, the architect of St. Michael's, was instructed to prepare plans for building the Church in stages as needs and finance might dictate. The foundation stone was laid in 1876 by Lady Eden and the first portion, comprising only the chancel of the present building, opened and consecrated just before Christmas the same year. The material used was Purbeck stone, with dressing of Corsham free stone. A temporary nave supplied accommodation for the growing congregation until funds would allow of the permanent structure being erected. Lady Eden presented the reredos, representing the Crucifixion in *basso relievo* in the centre, with two panels on either side containing other New Testament subjects and the whole surmounted by a handsome canopy.

The vicar's son, Alex. Bennett, became St. Swithun's first Priest-in-charge. In *The Story of Bournemouth* David Young relates that in 1876 the famous novelist John Galsworthy, then nine years old, was sent to a preparatory school in Bournemouth where he remained until at fourteen he went on to Harrow. The school was *Saugeen,* situated not far from St. Swithun's Church, which the boys attended, and where some, including Galsworthy, sang in the choir.

CHAPTER XI

The End Of An Era

STREET'S DESIGNS for St. Peter's had always included a spire. Though of necessity this part of the building had to be left until last, Morden Bennett was particularly keen on securing the "crowning glory" for his Church. Apart from adding lofty grandeur to the finished structure it would serve to remind residents and worshippers of things above, lifting their eyes and their minds towards the heavens. Street's final plans for the spire were adopted in 1878, not without some misgiving on the part of several local residents who claimed that it would be blown down in the first severe south-west gale. The Building Committee was just on the point of seeking tenders for the work when Street made an astonishing suggestion, namely that the proposed spire should not be built, but that a shorter steeple, combined with a lantern, should be erected instead.

It seems odd if Street should have thought upon reconsideration that the spire might be an artistic mistake. One can only assume (and this seems to be borne out by the available evidence) he felt that a lantern would be better suited to the exposed position. Even so, it is hard to imagine an architect of such skill and eminence as Street, who had already built a spire for a Church at Eastbourne which was showing no signs of collapse, doubting his ability to design one for Bournemouth which would be capable of withstanding the elements.

Whatever the correct explanation of Street's suggested change of plan may have been, the St. Peter's Building Committee refused to entertain the proposal of a lantern, saying there was a general feeling among the subscribers in favour of the original design. The *Bournemouth Visitors Directory* reported on 4th January 1879 that Street's only fear for the spire was "with regard to the gales which prevailed at every seaside place," but as he had successfully erected a spire at St. Saviour's, Eastbourne, he did not see why they should not have one at St. Peter's. The Building Committee accordingly instructed the architect to obtain estimates from three competent builders.

Six tenders were submitted for building the spire:

James Peerless of Eastbourne	£3,050
Stevens & Barlow of Bristol	£2,999
Dove Brothers of Islington	£2,967
Adamson & Sons of Putney	£2,965
S. Clark of Bournemouth	£2,946
Wall & Hook of Brimscombe	£2,560

The Gloucestershire firm whose price was so much lower than the others was duly engaged. The first stone was laid by the Hon. Miss C. Meyrick on Tuesday 25th March 1879, in the middle of a snowstorm. The spire, surmounted by a copper cock (an allusion to the patron Saint) with a large cross above it, was completed by the end of the year. The total cost eventually reached a figure of £3,100.

Octagonal in shape, the spire has walls two feet two inches thick at the lowest level, tapering to less than twelve inches in thickness near the top. The interior diameter of the bottom of the spire is fourteen feet. Its height from the top of the tower to the capstone is 86 feet.

As Leachman was not slow to observe when writing in 1915, the spire "still happily bids defiance to any raging gales that come its way." However, the prognostications of those who expected the spire to collapse were not completely groundless, for in 1880, during a severe gale, the cross and weathercock did get blown down. In 1882 a new and much lighter cross was designed by Street's son and placed in position where it has stood safely ever since. But it was thought prudent not to replace the cock.

While the spire was being built Street arranged to fill the four niches at the top of St. Peter's tower with statues by Earp depicting the Four Fathers of the Western Church, St. Gregory, St. Augustine of Hippo, St. Jerome and St. Ambrose. These statues, in pale grey stone, were brought from Earp's workshops and placed in position on the tower in November 1879. A good view of two of them can be obtained from the restaurant of Messrs. Beales.

The portrayal of the four Latin Doctors seems to have been a favourite subject of Street at this time. A few years earlier he had been working on Bristol Cathedral and selected a similar set of statues for the exterior of the new north porch he built there. The Bristol statues, which were not by Earp but by Frank Redfern, were set up in February 1876, having been executed at a cost of £450. Leachman and Taylor both assert that Redfern's statues were removed from Bristol following protests by vigilant Protestants and Low Church Clergymen and brought to St. Peter's. But this is not so. At the same time Street was also working on the rebuilding of East Heslerton Church in Yorkshire and the rejected

Bristol statues were taken there, where they still adorn the tower.

The completion of the spire, with its cross standing 202 feet above the ground, was the occasion for great rejoicing, and a Service of thanksgiving was held at St. Peter's on 18th December 1879 to mark the successful termination of the building of the Church. It was a proud moment. The choir was augmented by members of the Amateur and Philharmonic Societies, the *Te Deum* was sung, Morden Bennett gave an address, and the proceedings ended with the singing of the *Hallelujah Chorus*.

The rejoicing was short-lived. Early in January Morden Bennett was taken ill with serious pulmonary and cardiac conditions which his doctor, and a specialist brought from London, diagnosed as hopeless. Just a few days later, on Monday, 19th January, 1880, he died. Not only his friends and congregation but the whole of Bournemouth was saddened by the news and plunged into gloom. It was estimated that at his funeral no less than three thousand people crowded into St. Peter's Church and churchyard to pay their last respects. One of his intimate friends, in a tribute published in the *Parish Magazine,* wrote "Those who are capable of estimating the magnitude of his work are deploring the loss of an experienced priest — of one who was eminently fitted to organise and to extend the Church's work; but the poor are simply saying, 'We have lost a friend'."

Morden Bennett's body was laid to rest close to the Church he had built, served and loved, on the southern side of the churchyard steps. The grave is marked by a simple stone with a cross on it and the brief inscription:

> Alexander Morden Bennett, Priest.
> First Vicar of Bournemouth.
> Born OCT. XI A.D. MDCCCVIII.
> Entered into Rest JAN. XIX MDCCCLXXX.
> Looking for the Mercy of Our Lord Jesus Christ, Amen.

Morden Bennett's name has long been legendary in the annals of Bournemouth, for in nearly thirty-five years as vicar he unmistakably impressed his personality and integrity on the life of the whole town. It is no exaggeration to say that much of Bournemouth's flourishing growth and development was directly due to his efforts. What at first sight seems somewhat surprising is not the honour and respect in which he was held by all his contemporaries, but that a man so determined, uncompromising and austere should at the same time have earned the friendship of almost all who knew him. His love of God, coupled with his deep concern for all humanity, which showed itself clearly in his daily life and actions, undoubtedly explains why. But, as Crumpler pointed out, a man who was all that Morden Bennett was had problems to contend with when dealing with the materialism of the world. "So exact and true was he," wrote Crumpler, "that he expected to find others the same but so often got disappointed."

Two large windows were installed at St. Peter's in Morden Bennett's memory, one on the north side of the vestibule given by the congregation and the other on the south side of the tower by his two sons. The "Bennett Memorial Window" in the western transept was executed by Clayton & Bell and depicts eight scenes from the Book of the Revelation. With the money which was left over after paying for the window the congregation purchased a set of Sacramental plate, to be used by the clergy when visiting the sick. The "Founder's Window" under the tower was designed by Street and also manufactured by Clayton & Bell. This interesting window shows six great Church-builders, Aaron with the tabernacle, Solomon with the temple, Lanfranc with Canterbury Cathedral, Walkelin with Winchester Cathedral, Flambard with Christchurch Priory and Morden Bennett with St. Peter's Church.

While on the subject of stained-glass windows it is worth noting Morden Bennett's far-sightedness in approving the design for the "Minstrel Window" which was placed in the north transept, near the organ, in 1874. In one of the lights of this window is pictured a choral Celebration, with the priest fully robed. Although coloured Eucharistic vestments did not come into use at St. Peter's for another forty years there is no doubt that Morden Bennett approved of them and might, had he lived longer, have succeeded in persuading his congregation to accept them. It is not easy, in an age which accepts vestments as a matter of course, to imagine the controversy which would probably have been stirred up in Morden Bennett's time if he had worn them. He felt, perhaps, that this window was a fitting and tactful way of quietly expressing his own opinion.

Morden Bennett's friends considered that a stained-glass window was hardly a sufficient memorial and began to think of what they could provide which would be more substantial and permanent. The first suggestion was to erect a magnificent side-chapel at St. Peter's and Street was asked to prepare the preliminary sketches. Street's design, reproduced in Leachman's book, was for a chapel adjoining the south aisle and south-eastern transept. It represented Street's last attempt before he died to do away with Edmund Pearce's windows in the south aisle which Morden Bennett, in his lifetime, had never allowed him to touch. Surprising as it may seem, however, Street's proposal would have left the south aisle window nearest the porch intact, though the Wailes lights in memory of Mrs. Bennett further to the east would have been removed. At this period Street was suffering from overwork and nervous strain; hardly surprisingly, his memorial side-chapel was a poor design, probably the work of an assistant.

The side-chapel scheme was eventually abandoned in favour of building a completely new Church and of offering its first incumbency to Alex. Bennett, with future patronage vested in the Keble College Advowson Trustees. It was said in the committee's circular that "the Church accommodation in Bournemouth is still inadequate to the growing needs of the town," which is a statement difficult to accept at its face value when related to the site ultimately chosen, which was only a very short distance from St. Peter's, Holy Trinity and St. Michael's. Thus was founded the Bennett Memorial Church of St. Stephen, designed by Pearson and said by many to rival and even surpass St. Peter's in architectural and artistic merit. St. Stephen's, in the time-honoured tradition of "Bennett" Churches, had its beginning in a temporary building which was consecrated by Dr. Harold Brown, Bishop of Winchester, on 14th August 1881. In his sermon at the consecration service the Bishop went to some length in comparing Morden Bennett with Noah, the builder of the ark, pointing out that the deceased vicar would go down in local history as a great builder and organiser. The memorial stone of the permanent St. Stephen's was laid the same day. The builders were Messrs. Abley, of Salisbury, and the first portion to be completed was consecrated in 1885. Alex. Bennett served as vicar of the new parish until 1911, his Church becoming noted for its services in a high ritual, of a kind which his father had never dared to introduce at St. Peter's.

We must now examine the turbulent events which surrounded the appointment of Morden Bennett's successor at St. Peter's. He would not be an easy man to follow. As the Rev. E. J. G. Forse wrote of Morden Bennett in 1935, "He set an indelible impression upon the presentation of religion, and an almost impossible standard of life and work for succeeding incumbents."

CHAPTER XII

Vicar Trouble

IT IS sad to recall that Morden Bennett's death heralded a period of unhappiness and strife in the parish life of St. Peter's. And the feuding and bitterness reached serious proportions before the beloved Vicar was even buried.

It will be remembered that the right of patronage was vested in Sir George Meyrick, and it was a most unseemly lack of tact and decency on his part which precipitated a struggle which lasted nearly two years. Lady Meyrick had a brother, the Reverend Edward Harland, an elderly clergyman of low-church learnings, who had for thirty years held the living of Colwich in Staffordshire. He was also a Prebendary of Lichfield Cathedral and Chaplain to the Earl of Harrowby. No sooner had Morden Bennett breathed his last than news reached Bournemouth that the patron intended appointing his brother-in-law to fill the vacancy.

Bournemouth was shocked, not only by the churchmanship of the proposed Vicar, which amounted to a substantial threat to the traditions of St. Peter's which Morden Bennett had built up so lovingly, but more by the haste with which Sir George Meyrick acted. His intentions were noised abroad in the parish within hours of the late incumbent's death and it was obvious he had made his plans while Morden Bennett was still suffering from his last illness. To the people of St. Peter's, who had confidently expected Alex. Bennett to succeed his father, it seemed as if the patron was preparing at one stroke to force the parish into Evangelicalism and provide a comfortable preferment for his brother-in-law. The congregation could scarcely have been worse insulted in its hour of sorrow. The news seemed unbelievable.

A group of the leading parishioners immediately decided to present a petition to the patron. No less than 730 signatures were collected in the space of two days "representing all classes from Lord Faversham to the mule drivers in this place, and all shades of opinion." After the usual respectful preamble the petition went on: "We of course do not presume (unless by your favour allowed) to suggest a particular clergyman to fill this important post, but we venture to make our earnest request to you, that in the choice of a new Vicar, such provision may be made as shall not prove unsatisfactory to the large congregation which have hitherto worshipped so happily and harmoniously, in St. Peter's Church; and that the vast work which has been set on foot and organised by Mr. Bennett, both in this town and in the eight districts formed under his care, may still be continued as he would have wished." News of the petition reached the ears of the Bishop who on 25th January wrote to Sir George Meyrick representing to him the feelings of the town and the wishes of the congregation.

A Parish Meeting was hastily called for the purpose of deciding what to do about the petition. The views of the petitioners were endorsed and Lady Meyrick was asked to give Dr. Salt, one of the Churchwardens, and the Reverend Rowland Hill, the Senior Curate, an appointment to call on her to present the petition. Lady Meyrick replied on 22nd January (be it noted this was only three days after Morden Bennett's death) saying she thought it would not be advisable to receive the deputation, and that it would save trouble to everyone if she mentioned that Sir George had already offered the living to a clergyman, of whose acceptance she had little doubt.

Nevertheless, Salt and Hill drove out to Lady Meyrick with the petition on the 23rd when Harland was confirmed as the patron's nominee. The Churchwardens and sidesmen then met to draft a letter to the prospective Vicar which was sent to him on the following day. They pointed out that "there do exist shades of difference of religious opinion which, in the delicate relations of a pastor to his parishioners, may seriously mar the harmony of his intercourse with them," and went on to suggest that the living ought to have been offered to Alex. Bennett.

Harland replied on the 26th: "When you know me better, you will, I believe, find that I am not likely to disturb the comfort of the congregation of St. Peter's. . . . At my age I cannot expect very long to stand in the way of future arrangements; but so long as it pleases God to permit me to serve Him as Vicar of St. Peter's, it will be my great desire to carry on Mr. Bennett's plans, and to continue his work."

On the same day (26th January) Sir George Meyrick wrote formally to the Churchwardens confirming his offer of the living to Mr. Harland and asking for details and particulars of the value of the benefice. Judging from the terms of the patron's letter, Harland's acceptance does not appear to have been definite at that stage. "I have offered the living of St. Peter's to Mr. Harland, and I think he will accept it, and, as a matter of business, it is my duty to ask you for the information as to the value of the living, etc., which I must send to him before I can ask for his final answer."

Walter Scott Evans, the people's warden, couched his reply in not very warm terms. ". . . So far as I am aware, it does not come within the range of the legal or usual duties of churchwardens, to supply detailed information as to the financial matters of the church of which they are churchwardens. Our late respected Vicar of St. Peter's, with the assistance of an honorary treasurer, kept all the church accounts under his own personal control, but as I happen to be the treasurer, I have extracted from my books the details you require, which I offer out of courtesy as a private individual, and not in my official capacity, and therefore I am not to be considered responsible for their accuracy; for our late dear Vicar, I know, paid from his own private purse, accounts which should have been charged to the church."

The *Bournemouth Visitors' Directory,* in its issue for 31st January (the day Sir George Meyrick wrote to the Churchwardens saying that Harland had accepted the living), reports a Parish Meeting held on the 28th at which Scott Evans made it clear that the object the Churchwardens had in mind was that Alex. Bennett should succeed his father. The Churchwardens "have endeavoured by all fair and legitimate means to bring that about. No one could approve of the way in which the new Vicar had been appointed (*Hear, hear.*), but the appointment having been made and accepted he, speaking for himself, would meet him cordially, and try, so far as in him lay, if the Vicar acted as he said he would act, to do his best that harmony might not be stayed."

The congregation was still very far from satisfied and feelings of rancour persisted between the patron and the parishioners of St. Peter's. Quite apart from their own views about the indecent haste in which the new appointment had been made and the underlying reasons which appeared to be behind it, the parishioners were understandably anxious for Alex. Bennett's future. It seemed grossly unfair and morally indefensible that this fine priest, who had assisted his father with such loyalty and ability for so many years, should be driven away by one man's caprice from the town and people he loved and had served with great distinction. It was to his credit that Alex. Bennett had never taken the least part in the acrimonious meetings and correspondence, but was quite prepared to accept with fortitude whatever the future might hold in store for him. As he could not take over the incumbency of St. Peter's why not create a separate parish of St. Swithun's (where he was already priest-in-charge) and appoint him its first Vicar?

The patron flatly refused to have anything to do with this suggestion. He wrote that, "When I gave the land for St. Swithun's, — and before the building was commenced — it was on the express understanding with Mr. Bennett that it should never be made a separate district, so as to cut off the East Cliff from the mother Church, and before your meeting was held I wrote this as my unaltered opinion to a gentleman who, I observed, was present at the meeting. Under these circumstances I ought not to allow the feelings of the moment — glad as I should be to join in any expression of esteem for Mr. A. S. Bennett, to weigh with me against what I deliberately believe to be for the permanent good of the Church at Bournemouth. Upon this principle I take my stand, but I must add that I consider my rights and duties as a patron — which I am bound to maintain and exercise honestly and fearlessly — have been completely ignored, and I regret extremely that by the action of others, I should have been placed in a position of apparent antagonism towards Mr. Alex. Bennett, for whom I have a very great regard."

The *Bournemouth Visitors' Directory* commented, "Sir George is quite correct in his opinion that 'the rights and duties of a patron' should receive due consideration, and we are sure the officials and congregation of St. Peter's are desirous of fully respecting them. But the feelings and wishes of the congregation and parishioners are also entitled to respect, and surely had Sir George Meyrick been a little less precipitate in filling up the vacancy occasioned by the late Mr. Bennett's death much of the difficulty which has since arisen would have been avoided."

Prebendary Harland took up his duties during March and preached at the Easter services. At the Annual Vestry Meeting Scott Evans appealed for an end of the recent bitterness. "A new vicar is now amongst us, and as he has showed us that he wishes to continue the grand and good work of St. Peter's Church as before, we shall all give him our most hearty co-operation and genuine support." However by June it was apparent that the trouble had not completely died down. Rumours were circulating about prospective changes in the celebration of the Holy Communion and a petition was prepared asking the Vicar to adopt no change whatever.

Harland soon decided that he would be unable to work harmoniously at St. Peter's. In July he finally resolved not to accept the living and returned to Staffordshire to resume his work at Colwich. Unfortunately the feelings of the congregation were not to be placated, because the patron offered the incumbency to Vincent William Ryan, a churchman noted for his pronounced Evangelical views, who had been the first Anglican Bishop of Mauritius.

Ryan, who was born in 1816, held the degrees of B.A., M.A. and D.D. of Oxford University and had started his parochial career as curate and then incumbent of St. Anne's Parish in Alderney. After a further period as curate of Edgehill, near Liverpool, he was appointed Principal of the Church of England Metropolitan Training Institution at Highbury in 1850, going from there in 1854 as Bishop of Mauritius, a place in which his familiarity with the French language was specially useful. When he went to Mauritius there were only two clergymen at Port Louis and one missionary in the country districts. Ryan was successful in building up quite a flourishing church organisation there, being responsible for the erection of a number of churches and schools before he finally left that diocese in 1867.

On his return to England Ryan became Archdeacon of Suffolk and the Rector of St. Nicholas' Church, Guildford. On his appointment to St. Peter's he had been Vicar of Bradford in Yorkshire since 1870.

He was no stranger to Bournemouth, though his previous visits to the town only served to accentuate his position as a prominent member of the Evangelical party. On 28th September 1869, soon after returning from Mauritius, he had acted as Commissary for the Bishop of Winchester and consecrated the new chancel and nave of Holy Trinity Church. More recently, on 4th September 1878, he had been to Holy Trinity again, this occasion being the service of dedication and thanksgiving on the completion of the tower, at which he preached the sermon. As one of the leaders of the Evangelical party within the Church of England Bishop Ryan found no favour with the prevailing views at St. Peter's and the Parish Magazine for August 1880 contains an editorial which must have made him feel most unwelcome.

"The patron still seems determined to thwart our wishes" by appointing Bishop Ryan whose "views and opinions are diametrically opposed to those that have been associated with our Church and Parish for one third of a century. Now an effort is being made to lower the standard of our services, to bring all Church teaching in this district to the same level, and to deprive us of the worship and services, which we have learnt to love. The Bishop of the Diocese has expressed his regret that this should be so; and we on our part cannot pretend to welcome in any way one whose very coming will be the signal for the removal of the landmarks laid by our late dear Vicar, in strict conformity with the Prayer Book and the Bible."

Nevertheless Ryan was inducted to the living on 7th August. In the result nobody was satisfied. The parishioners of St. Peter's still smarted under what they considered an unjust betrayal of the principles laid down by Morden Bennett, and the Evangelical party, who thought they had won a great victory, were highly disappointed at the moderation displayed by Ryan in his new cure.

The comings and goings of vicars were reflected in an unprecedented number of changes among the assistant clergy. Alex. Bennett awaited the building of St. Stephen's Church as a memorial to his late father where he was to be instituted and inducted as the first Vicar. Rowland Hill and Henry Fraser (one of Morden Bennett's later appointments) left the parish in 1880. The same year saw the advent of no less than eight assistant curates, seven of whom left during either that year or 1881. Hill, who as we have seen championed the cause of Alex. Bennett when the living of St. Peter's was offered to Harland, spent a short period at St. Michael's Church in Bournemouth before going as assistant to Alex. Bennett at St. Stephen's from 1881 to 1885 when he was appointed Rector of Frome St. Quentin.

Bishop Ryan came to St. Peter's determined to weather the storm of protests that had surrounded his appointment. He decided only gradually to introduce any changes from the traditional worship which he thought to be necessary. In this he kept faith with his new congregation to such an extent that he won a considerable measure of loyalty and indeed respect. Nevertheless there were many who found themselves unable to accept him whole-heartedly and his position in the parish was never a happy one.

The most stirring opposition to Ryan's activities at St. Peter's came from his so-called friends, the supporters of the Evangelical party. They spoke of him in most uncomplimentary terms, accusing him of giving concessions and compromises amounting to "a very serious dereliction of duty, which is likely to have a disastrous effect on Bishop Ryan's ministry in this place." His retention of the practice of turning to the east at the Creed was considered objectionable, and he also received the blame for anything his curates chose to do which failed to meet with approval from "the proper custodians of Protestant interests."

As an example of the type of pressure with which the new Vicar had to deal here are a few paragraphs from a letter written by the Reverend W. W. Phelps in December 1880 to Colonel Rowlandson, the Chairman of the Bournemouth branch of the Church Association.

> The Vicar of St. Peter's, Bournemouth, Bishop Ryan, has been led by one of his curates (the Rev. Mr. Lambert) into the serious mistake of offering St. Swithun's pulpit for an Advent sermon to be preached on Friday week by a clergyman who is a member of the Holy Cross Society, and also of the Confraternity of the Blessed Sacrament, and also of the English Church Union, a society which at the present moment is in active rebellion against the supremacy of the Crown, and is advising the clergy to adopt forbidden vestments all over the land. The gentleman to whom I allude is the Rev. E. E. Dugmore, vicar of Parkstone, near Poole.
>
> The greatest possible detriment to the cause of Evangelical truth and to the honour of Christ will arise should the contemplated arrangement take effect, and the hopes of those who regarded the coming of Bishop Ryan to this town as an era of blessing will be frustrated.
>
> I only heard of the fact yesterday and felt it to be so urgent a matter that I called last night at the Vicarage and respectfully remonstrated with Bishop Ryan.
>
> The names of two other decided friends of Ritualism, one of whom, namely the Rev. W. H. Lucas, Rural Dean of this district, preached last week at the notorious St. Clement's Church in this town, appear in the list of Advent preachers at St. Swithun's; this, of course, I regret, but I feel that the selection of Mr. Dugmore, being as he is a member of the Holy Cross and English Church Union, is a graver scandal still.
>
> Personally, I feel I have done my duty in this matter. A Protestant sentry is bound to challenge an intruder into the camp, and I am solemnly pledged by my ordination vow with all diligence to banish and drive away all false doctrine contrary to God's word. "Faithful are the wounds of a friend, but the kisses of an enemy are deceitful." It may be, the opposition Bishop Ryan has encountered in making his false move will help to release him from the chain of some dangerous influences which at present surround him, and will quicken him to enter upon a course in harmony with the convictions of his conscience and the traditions of the party with which he has always hitherto been identified. He must lead and not follow his congregation.

It is perhaps not surprising that Bishop Ryan, finding himself out of favour with substantial numbers of churchmen in both factions, came to the conclusion that Bournemouth was not the place for the continuation of his ministry. With some relief he accepted the Rectory of Middleham in the Diocese of Ripon, upon the basis that he would make himself available to help with the episcopal duties in that place. In 1883 he became Rector of Stanhope, in County Durham, where he died on 11th January 1888.

It was during Ryan's short tenure of the living at St. Peter's, in February 1881, that the Founder's Window was erected as a memorial to Morden Bennett. And St. Peter's was honoured at

Evensong on the sixth of that month by the presence of Her Majesty the Queen of Sweden.

Ryan left St. Peter's in June 1881. His farewell was kinder than his welcome had been. "During the year of his residence amongst us he won the respect and esteem of persons of every shade of religious opinion." Tactfully forgotten was the fact that he had also failed to gain the confidence of such persons. Once again the future was in the hands of Sir George Meyrick. Who would he appoint this time?

CHAPTER XIII

The Peacemaker

WHEN SIR George Meyrick nominated Bishop Ryan as vicar in the summer of 1880 it was not generally known that another clergyman had been offered the living but had turned it down. This other was the Rev. George Stopford Ram who had been vicar of St. Anne's, Highgate, for the previous twelve years. Ram was a graduate of Wadham College, Oxford, and had held a number of appointments in the London area. There can be no doubt that if Ram had accepted St. Peter's in 1880 he would have found a ready welcome from his congregation and the parish would have been spared the undignified disputes which marred the incumbency of the Evangelical Bishop. Ram, however, preferred to stay where he was at Highgate.

Upon Ryan's resignation the patron again approached Ram, who he believed was "a thoroughly acceptable man," and this time Ram agreed to come. In making the appointment Sir George Meyrick pointed out that his great desire was, and always had been, to place a man in charge of St. Peter's who would be loyal to the Church of England, neither falling short of, nor going beyond her teaching, and at the same time one who would as far as possible consult the comfort and promote the peace of the congregation, by continuing the ritual to which that congregation had long been accustomed, within the limits of the law.

Ram's first message to his new parishioners made it clear that he had no intention of disturbing any of the usages which had become established under Morden Bennett. "It may be well for me to state at once," he wrote, "that in my opinion a clergyman ought not to accept a cure of souls unless he is prepared to respect the usages of the church and the feelings of the congregation over which he is placed." Needless to say, the people of St. Peter's were delighted and looked forward to Ram's early arrival in Bournemouth to take up his duties.

Though Ram was unable to give up his old parish until December he took an early opportunity of coming to Bournemouth and making himself known. His first visit, during which he stayed as the guest of Alex. Bennett and took part in the opening service of the Bennett Memorial Church of St. Stephen, was in October 1881.

He was inducted to St. Peter's just before Christmas, on 23rd December. It seemed as if a peacemaker had arrived at last.

George Stopford Ram was a well-connected clergyman of very good family. Born on 18th June 1838, he was the eldest son of the Rev. Abel John Ram, M.A., Oxon., of Clonattin and Ballytegan, County Wexford, Rector of Rolleston, Burton-on-Trent and an Honorary Canon of Rochester Cathedral. His mother was Lady Jane Ram, formerly Stopford, daughter of the third Earl of Courtown; through her, Ram was a great-grandson of the third Duke of Buccleuch. The Irish estates of the Ram family were acquired early in the seventeenth century by the Right Rev. Thomas Ram, D.D., who went to Ireland in 1599 as chaplain to the Earl of Essex and later became Bishop of Ferns and Leighlin, a see which he held from 1605 until 1633. These estates were sold in 1916 by the Rev. E. D. S. Ram, eldest son of the St. Peter's vicar.

At the age of twenty-seven Ram married the Honourable Charlotte Anne O'Brien, daughter of Lord Inchiquin, and together they produced no less than ten children, three sons and seven daughters. Not surprisingly, one of the first complaints made by the Ram family upon their arrival at St. Peter's was that the vicarage was not large enough. Tragedy struck the Ram family just after their arrival in the parish when on 5th February 1882 their nine months old twin son Abel Bernard died.

In 1883 Ram insisted on having the parsonage enlarged, saying it was too small and too inconvenient in its arrangements for a family residence. Since the Rams had so many children to accommodate, in addition to themselves and their domestic servants, it is hardly surprising that they found it too small. Furthermore, very few improvements and repairs had been carried out by Morden Bennett during his long residence there. According to the vicar it was an absolute necessity to alter and enlarge it, in fact almost to rebuild it. The alterations carried out at this time cost the parish £1,562 16s. 8d. The Church offerings on Palm Sunday 1883 were devoted to the enlargement fund, and Sir George Meyrick kindly contributed £500 towards the expense. After the initial building work had been finished a further £131 19s. 8d. was spent on modernising the "sanitary appointments" and £439 14s. 0d. on three additional rooms. It was during Ram's tenure that the parsonage became known as the vicarage, though the original title is perpetuated in the name of Parsonage Road.

While the work on the vicarage was being carried out the Ram family lived at Hilfield, a large house in Bath Road near the Lansdowne which was pulled down only a few years ago to allow for the erection of the block of flats known as Buckingham Mansions.

By the time Ram was inducted St. Peter's had a new organist. Just before Morden Bennett died, late in 1879, Burton decided to retire in order that he could devote more time to his numerous professional engagements. He accepted instead the appointment of organist at Holy Trinity where his services would only be required on Sundays. To fill Burton's place at St. Peter's came Duncan Hume, who had been a pupil under the organist of Chichester Cathedral and who was the son of the Rector of Meon Stoke.

Another familiar figure missing from St. Peter's by the time Ram arrived was the original parish clerk of pre-consecration days, William Edward Rebbeck. He died in December 1879 and his funeral was the last Morden Bennett conducted before he himself died.

There were many changes in the clerical staff. The assistant clergy appointed by Harland and Ryan all took posts elsewhere and, as we have seen, Alex. Bennett took over the new living created for him at St. Stephen's. Ram needed to employ a third assistant priest at St. Peter's, the additional expense of £150 per annum being provided by the churchwardens from the offertory, helped by a yearly subscription from one of Morden Bennett's later vicar's wardens, Charles J. Nixon.

Among the new clergymen appointed were William Paxton Thorp and George Herbert West, who looked after St. Swithun's, and H. S. K. Bellairs, who was priest in charge of St. Ambrose. From 1883 J. R. Husband took over responsibility for St. Swithun's and from 1885 Duncan Travers for St. Ambrose. When Travers left Bournemouth to resume missionary work in Central Africa and Zanzibar in 1888 St. Ambrose was placed in the charge of J. I. Patterson, a former curate at Chatham, who, as will later appear, may justly claim to be the founder of the present St. Ambrose parish. Husband subsequently became vicar of John Keble's parish at Hursley. He died in 1948 and is buried at Wimborne Road cemetery at Bournemouth.

Ram had in succession three senior assistant curates at St. Peter's. The first was Percy Brent who revived the St. Margaret's Mission in Orchard Street and was appointed vicar of Enfield in 1883. Next was Gavin Saxby, formerly Fellow of St. Augustine's College at Canterbury and Principal of St. Boniface's Missionary House at Warminster, who was inducted to the living of Monks' Kirby in 1885. Finally, Frank Buxton replaced Saxby and remained at St. Peter's until after Ram's death.

It has already been noted that Walter Scott Evans was people's warden throughout the whole of Ram's time at St. Peter's. Dr. Salt, Morden Bennett's last nominee, continued as vicar's warden until 1887 when James Druitt, a well-known local solicitor, was appointed.

There were two very important burials at St. Peter's during the 'eighties, one providing an interesting link with the New World, the other a macabre, secretive affair with strong literary associations.

The connection with North America concerns Major-General Richard Clement Moody, R.E. (1813-1887) who died in Bournemouth and was buried in the churchyard on 2nd April 1887. His address in the Burial Register is given as the Bath Hotel. Moody's grave is to the right of the steps leading up the churchyard and behind the Shelley tomb. Nicholas Taylor in his *Guide* writes of Moody:

> At the age of twenty-eight he became the first Governor of the Falkland Islands, where he stayed for eight years. He introduced tussock-grass into England. While Commandant of Royal Engineers in North Britain (1854-58), he produced a detailed scheme for the restoration of Edinburgh Castle. This interest in architecture was brought to fulfilment in his next and most important job (1858-63), as the first Lieutenant-Governor of the Canadian colony of New Caledonia, which in 1866 amalgamated with Vancouver Island to form British Columbia. Moody planned the colony's first capital, New Westminster, when its site was still virgin forest, and he pioneered much of the colony's road system. In executive authority he was overshadowed by the autocratic Governor Sir James Douglas (whose name is immortalised in the fir tree), but his five years' planning was rewarded when the Canadian Pacific Railway's first terminus was called Port Moody in his honour. In 1866, he retired from the Army to Lyme Regis, and died suddenly twenty-one years later, when visiting Bournemouth. Moody was one of an unknown generation of Victorian planners, many of them, like him, officers of the Royal Engineers, who created 'New Towns' in the newly conquered British colonies. In 1958, a centenary service was held at his grave, attended by the Bishop of New Westminster, who was at the Lambeth Conference, and its civic dignitaries, who flew over specially for the occasion. A plaque at the foot of the grave commemorates this.

The other burial of particular note during this period was of the heart of Percy Bysshe Shelley, the atheist poet. The story goes that, after Shelley's drowning in the Gulf of Spezia in 1822 and the barbaric burning of his body on the beach, his heart, which had been snatched from the flames, was brought back to England where it came into the possession of his daughter-in-law, Lady Shelley. She kept the heart, shrivelled like an apricot, in an urn or casket at Boscombe Manor, according to one account behind silk curtains in an alcove of her drawing-room with a red lamp always burning in front of it. Another description says that Lady Shelley had it sewn in a cushion which she kept by her bed at night and in the sanctum during the daytime. When Sir Percy Shelley died in 1889 the poet's heart was secretly placed in the son's coffin and buried in the family vault in St. Peter's churchyard. Another story has it that the heart was not buried in the vault until Lady Shelley herself died in 1899, but the burial in Sir Percy's coffin is the more generally accepted. Yet another version of this curious story is that the heart was placed in the tomb after the baronet's death by Canon M. W. F. St. John, Lady Shelley's nephew, when he had eventually managed to persuade his aunt to have it taken from its shrine at Boscombe Manor and decently buried. Thus it has transpired that St. Peter's churchyard has become the last resting place of all that remains in England of one of her greatest poets.

The main entrance to the churchyard was completed in 1882 by the provision of a pair of stone piers and walls opposite the western end of the Church. A pair of heavy oak gates was then hung on the piers. All these were designed by A. E. Street and erected by Wall & Hook, the contractors who had built the spire.

The principal additions to the interior of St. Peter's during Ram's incumbency were the frescoes in the spandrils above the arches in the sanctuary. Towards the end of 1885 instructions were given to Messrs. Clayton & Bell to prepare coloured sketches of saints and angels for the decoration of those walls, the work to be carried out under the supervision of Mr. (later Sir) Arthur Blomfield. The first portion, consisting of the frescoes on the south side, was started in June 1886. Members of the congregation were asked to subscribe for the cost as memorials to deceased relations. The series was not finished until 1889 when the corresponding frescoes in the spandrils on the north side of the sanctuary were completed.

At this same time Blomfield was advising on the provision of a baptistery. A fund for the project was opened in 1885, when nearly £390 was collected, but the idea seemed to lack the whole-hearted support of the congregation and was eventually abandoned. Blomfield's proposal, submitted in 1887, was to build the bapistery in the form of an apse at the western end of the south aisle. The expense of this would be more than had originally been estimated and Blomfield wisely suggested that no definite plan should be settled until the available funds had been substantially increased.

It may be worthwhile at this stage of the narrative to mention the regular services held at St. Peter's under Ram, as they appear set out in the local guidebook of the time:

> *Services on Sunday.*—Holy Communion, 8 a.m.; Matins with Litany and Sermon, 11 a.m.; Celebration of the Holy Communion, 12.30 p.m.; Evensong with Sermon, 3 p.m.; Children's Services with Catechising, 4.15 p.m.; Second Evensong with Sermon, 7 p.m. There is a choral celebration once a month after Matins, and on the first and third Sundays an early celebration at 6 a.m. Holy Baptism on the first and third Sundays in the month at 4.15 p.m.
> *Holy Days.*—Holy Communion, 8 a.m.; Matins and Sermon, 11 a.m.; Second Celebration of Holy Communion, 12 noon; Evensong, 5 p.m.
> *Week Days.*—Holy Communion, 8 a.m. and 12 noon on Thursdays; Matins, 10 a.m.; Litany on Wednesdays and Fridays at 12 noon; Evensong, 5 p.m.; Churchings on Wednesdays and Fridays at 12 noon, and on Mondays and Thursdays at 5 p.m., notice of which must be given before the service.
> Number of sittings, 1250. Free seats, 470. The character of the service is moderately high.

It will be noted that Morden Bennett's practice since 1871 of starting the morning service at 10.30, which was done with the object of ensuring that the Holy Communion was celebrated not later than 12 noon, was not followed by his successors. Furthermore, it will be observed that Ram held only one choral celebration each month.

On 18th June 1889 St. Peter's was chosen as the venue for the first Annual Festival of the Bournemouth Church Choral Union which had just been formed by local parishes as the successor to the old Vale of Avon association. Over four hundred choristers and choirmen took part.

When one remembers the tensions and difficulties which existed at St. Peter's when Ram arrived it says a great deal for his character and personality that within a very short time he managed to gather about him a contented congregation with whom he strove in a most harmonious partnership to consolidate and even to extend the excellent foundation on which Morden Bennett had built the parish. Always kind and courteous to all with whom he came in contact, and with an easier and more natural charm of manner than Morden Bennett had possessed, Ram quickly endeared himself to the people of Bournemouth and throughout his ministry maintained the happiest association with his flock. Mrs. Ram, too, was much beloved and respected; the gay parties which they gave at the vicarage are still recalled with great pleasure by some of the oldest parishioners. One of Ram's particular loves, and a facet of his work for which he had a special talent, was visiting the sick, who were greatly helped by his practical sympathy and cheering presence. He founded a Communicants' Guild for women and also the St. Mary's Guild, a Wednesday afternoon Bible class for young domestic servants. The sincere spiritual guidance which he gave to the women attending the meetings of those institutions was helpful and stimulating. Ram's own tact and wisdom, aided of course by the rapidly increasing population of the town, ensured ever greater attendances at services and other parish activities. In 1886 St. Peter's had, for the first time, more than one thousand Easter Communicants. Pew rents, always a fair guide in those days to the health of the parish, increased from £439 to over £600 during the year following Ram's induction.

Soon after Ram's induction the very close links which had hitherto bound the East Parley Mission of St. Barnabas to St. Peter's were severed, and although the St. Peter's clergy and churchwardens kept in touch with the Mission and helped it financially for many more years, its direction passed into other hands.

With Morden Bennett's death in 1880 the driving force behind the East Parley project had seemed to diminish, with the result that later in the same year Mr. Towle, Vicar of Moordown, took temporary charge of the district. The Rev. R. A. Chudleigh, Rector of the adjoining parish of West Parley in the next County of Dorset, offered to take permanent charge of the Mission, but only upon condition that he was released from responsibility for West Moors. In October 1880 the new Vicar of St. Peter's, Bishop Ryan, called a meeting of all interested parties at Bournemouth. The first problem was purely financial and an appeal was launched for an endowment of not less than £1,000. Morden Bennett himself had already raised a fund of £102 19s. 6d. Consols as a basis for the East Parley endowment and to this figure were added five gifts of £100 each, one from Alex. Bennett, one from Morden Bennett's estate, one from the Rev. Frederick Hopkins (Vicar of Holdenhurst and brother-in-law of Morden Bennett), one from the Rev. Zachary Nash (Vicar of Christchurch) and the other raised from collections at St. Peter's. Other donations were also received, among them the sum of £27 which was collected at St. Peter's following a sermon by Prebendary Harland in support of the endowment appeal.

Chudleigh's conditions for taking over the duties at East Parley were satisfied by a scheme which Ryan and his colleagues proposed whereby West Moors, together with Verwood and Three Legged Cross, which formed part of the large parish of Cranborne, should be united as a separate ecclesiastical district. After a number of further meetings and negotiations about details, delayed somewhat by Ryan's resignation and Ram's appointment to St. Peter's, the scheme took effect at the end of 1881. Ram approved the arrangements and became one of the trustees of the endowment fund, £500 of which was lent temporarily at 4 per cent interest to the Vicar of Cranborne so that money would be available to meet the expenses of constituting the new District around Verwood and West Moors. Donations for East Parley's endowment fund never quite reached the target figure of £1,000, though by the turn of the century quoted investments to this value were held by the trustees, capitalisation of interest and prudent re-investment having accounted for the difference.

The other two Churches of St. Peter's parish, St. Swithun's and St. Ambrose, were both extended during the time Ram was vicar. St. Swithun's was temporarily enlarged in 1883 so as to provide two hundred extra seats. This work, for which a local architect, H. E. Hawker, was engaged, cost £350. Mr. George was the builder. For the portion of the permanent St. Swithun's which had already been completed was made a new east window, designed by Messrs. Burliston & Gryllis of Newman Street, London, depicting the Wise Men and Shepherds at Bethlehem.

The first part of the permanent Church of St. Ambrose, started under Morden Bennett shortly before his death, was completed and an appeal launched in 1883 to raise the sum of £1,000 for the purpose of building a sufficient portion of the nave to accommodate three hundred persons. At the same time the idea of creating a separate District for St. Ambrose was canvassed, but not carried out. The new nave was built in 1883-84 to the plans of a Mr. Horner at a cost of £1,800. Mr. Pike of Springbourne was the builder.

Within ten years it became clear that further building would be needed and that a site nearer the centre of the district would be preferable. Mr. James Edward Cooper Dean, who owned a corner site in a most favourable position, generously donated the land and in 1894 the decision was taken to build an entirely new Church. Hodgson Fowler, an architect from Durham, drew the plans for the new St. Ambrose Church, and on 20th October 1899 Mrs. Abel Smith laid the foundation stone.

So successful was Ram in bringing peace, order and goodwill to St. Peter's that one is tempted to speculate how the parish might have continued its development under his leadership had it not been interrupted by his untimely death and the reign of a less talented successor. In the autumn of 1889 Ram and his wife went to Ireland to stay with their noble relatives, the vicar having been advised by his doctor to take a restful holiday as an antidote to the strain of overwork which he was experiencing. At Lord Inchiquin's seat, Dromoland Castle in County Clare, Ram became seriously ill with typhoid fever. Just as it seemed he was getting over the worst of the illness and recovering his health he suffered a sudden and fatal heart failure. He was only fifty-one.

Ram's body was brought back to St. Peter's and buried in the churchyard in the same grave as his baby son Abel, and next to Hubert Parry's mother. As had been the case with Morden Bennett the Church was not big enough to hold all the mourners who came from far and wide to attend the funeral. It was reported that the Church could have been filled more than twice over had there been room inside. The throngs of people who were unable to secure seats massed outside in the churchyard where they were organised by the officers and men of the Artillery and Rifles Volunteers.

So for the second time in ten years the people of St. Peter's mourned a beloved vicar. The epitaph on Ram's gravestone could scarcely have been more appropriately chosen. "The fruit of righteousness is sown in peace of them that make peace."

CHAPTER XIV

The Scholar Who Failed

IN JANUARY 1890, within two months of Ram's sudden death, a new vicar was appointed. This was Prebendary Cecil Edward Fisher, rector of Hagworthingham, Lincolnshire, a man of almost exactly the same age as Ram, both having been born in 1838. Fisher was inducted on 28th March 1890; and so began his fourteen years at St. Peter's, years of promise and success at the outset but years of disappointment and tragedy towards the end. When Leachman was writing his book about St. Peter's in 1915 Fisher was still alive and certain things were left unsaid. But, even in Leachman's pages, the sad memories of Fisher's failure can be perceived. It was not a happy time.

Fisher was noted as a scholar and had been elected a Student of Christ Church, Oxford. After serving as assistant curate in two Wiltshire parishes he was for fourteen years rector of North and South Stoke with Easton, Lincs., then from 1879 vicar of Grantham and from 1884 rector of Hagworthingham. Since 1877 he had held a prebendal stall at Lincoln Cathedral; after coming to Bournemouth he became an honorary canon of Winchester.

The new vicar's first year at St. Peter's was a happy and successful one. Fisher's churchmanship fitted him well as a worthy successor to Ram and Morden Bennett, and his scholarly explanations of the rituals and ceremonies of the Church gave his congregation a most thorough understanding of the religious significance surrounding the worship of St. Peter's. At the annual parochial tea-party of 1891 Scott Evans expressed the people's thankfulness to God for sending them such a good priest as their vicar. A reference to Fisher's successful first year in the parish was greeted with applause. For several years afterwards similar compliments were paid. In 1895, when the incumbent returned to Bournemouth from vacation in Italy the bells of St. Peter's rang out a happy welcome. "The Vicar's return is a source of universal joy to all," was one comment.

The decoration of the sanctuary at St. Peter's, begun under Ram, was continued. When the frescoes on the north wall of the sanctuary had been finished in 1889, Ram had decided that the sanctuary roof should also be decorated. The designs had been approved just before Ram died. As the provision of these frescoes had been so close to the deceased vicar's heart, Fisher and the congregation resolved to complete them as a memorial. Work on the sanctuary roof was started in September 1891 by Messrs. Powell & Sons of Whitefriars, under the supervision of G. F. Bodley, "the leading church architect of the generation after Street, and also a pupil of Scott." Nicholas Taylor has pointed out that if the sanctuary were not so dark it would be clear to the visitor that these frescoes are of considerable merit.

Soon afterwards, other frescoes were painted on the east wall, the chancel roof, and the west wall of the chancel arch. All these, which have become known as the Ram Memorial Frescoes, cost nearly £400. They were dedicated on 12th December 1891. In 1892 a brass inscription plate was placed near the pulpit reading, "To the glory of God and in loving memory of George Stopford Ram, M.A., Priest, Vicar of St. Peter's, Bournemouth, 1881-1889, the Frescoes on the roof of the Sanctuary are offered by some friends who have worshipped in the church. Dedicated Dec. 12th, 1891."

In January and February 1891 Fisher organised a Ten Days Mission to the Terrace Road District, conducted by one of his friends, the Rev. J. F. Flowers, rector of Bonby, Lincs. In February 1892 there was a similar mission, this time to the whole of St. Peter's District. Fisher soon arranged for the completion of the permanent St. Swithun's Church and this work, together with the erection of St. Swithun's Hall, was soon finished. Fisher also wanted a hall or parish room for St. Peter's and frequently spoke of the great and growing need for such a building, but he never managed to get it done and that task was left to his successor.

A notable event on 25th August 1892 was the first wedding from St. Peter's vicarge, when Fisher's daughter Violet married Mr. R. A. Cholmeley. As the bride walked down the aisle on her husband's arm her Sunday School children strewed flowers in their path. The Church bells were kept ringing at intervals until late in the evening.

In 1895 a new schoolmaster was appointed to take charge of St. Peter's School and Mr. C. T. Barker moved into the schoolhouse with his young family. His son Charles was assistant organist under Duncan Hume and later became organist of St. Ambrose Church. The St. Peter's organ at that time was hand-blown, the blower occupying a small room just outside the vestry door. Ernest Coombes, the son of the churchyard gardener and school caretaker, was paid 4d. per hour to manipulate the long blower blade and watch the small lead weight which travelled up and down indicating the amount of air in the bellows.

The schoolhouse also ran an informal organisation nicknamed "The Ecclesiastical Restaurant" whose job it was to serve breakfasts for the St. Peter's staff after the early morning celebrations. First to arrive was always Harry Crumpler, the sacristan. Fisher's preference was for soup and toast and one of his daughters would leave a tablet of soup at the schoolhouse on her way to the service. One of the assistant curates liked cider which he habitually drank facing the east!

Fisher was a short man with a somewhat wispy beard. One morning, a group of his daughters was waiting in the porch at the end of a service when two visitors came out. "Not a bad sermon," said one of the strangers, "but he did remind me of a goat, with his little beard." The daughters were most upset, but when the vicar was told he was quite unperturbed. "You should have replied that you were his *kids,*" he said with a smile.

For the services at St. Peter's Fisher advised holding fast to the doctrines of the Prayer Book, "swerving neither to the errors of Rome on the one side, nor to Puritanical fanaticism on the other, but waiting in patience and charity for that blessed gift of Unity to come in God's good time." He started holding a choral celebration every Sunday morning, normally at 9.45 a.m. "It will thus be in the power of many of our parishioners to join in offering every Sunday the great Christian sacrifice with the musical praise and thanksgiving which our highest act of worship demands."

It was then the custom at St. Peter's for the communicants to kneel in the chancel while waiting for their turn at the Altar-rail to receive the Blessed Sacrament, and not to stand as they do now. In 1897 one of the congregation presented two strips of rich red carpet to be placed in the chancel for the communicants to kneel on.

The famous authoress Phyllis Bottome, in her "fragment of autobiography" *Search for a Soul,* has given us a fascinating glimpse into the life of Bournemouth and St. Peter's at this time. Her father, the Rev. W. M. Bottome, an American parson from New York who had married an English wife and settled in England as a country vicar, spent a year at St. Peter's under Fisher deputising temporarily for the senior assistant curate who had had a breakdown. For part of the time the Bottome family lived opposite the Church in rooms over a confectioner's shop in The Quadrant. About her father's work at St. Peter's Phyllis Bottome wrote:—

> I don't know quite how well my father fitted into the ways of St. Peter's Church. He had to swallow his pride to become a curate

> again after nearly twenty years of being his own master; but the Senior Curate of St. Peter's was a very important person. On him fell the chief sermons and the major share of parochial responsibility. The Vicar was a clever but very sick man. There were three lesser curates beneath my father's sway, with whom we soon became awe-inspiringly intimate. None of them liked, nor I think *were* liked by, the Vicar; but my father, with his usual unconscious skill, got on with them all very easily. They were jealous of him, no doubt, but they soon found him almost startlingly harmless. He cared for none of the things they wanted and forgot to assume any authority over them. He preferred the less rich parishioners; he even took on with enthusiasm the Home for Incurables, where the poorer invalids, who could not afford hotels, villas, or even lodgings, were sent in a lump to die of T.B. and where they usually did die of it. It was true that my father preached the curates and even the Vicar off their legs, but he made no fuss about it, and was always willing to be fobbed off with "daughter" churches, leaving the pulpit of St. Peter's to the less oratorically gifted.
>
> The Vicar, however, soon insisted on my father's preaching at St. Peter's in the evening, when he found that he was so great a "draw". He often said sarcastic things to my father as he did to all his curates, but they were said with a smile; and my father always took them as jokes and repeated them with enthusiasm. Wit was always a pleasant thing to my father—his own or anybody else's; and he used to try his own jokes off on the curates, not always successfully.

The curates reminded Phyllis Bottome of

> . . . the flowers and fruit of California: so large, so luscious, so bright and vivid were those prosperous and pleasant young men! Everybody wanted the Bournemouth curates. They were an unfailing source of comfort, interest and entertainment to the invalids; and they acted as discreet safety valves for their anxious and often irritated relatives.

The senior priest at St. Peter's from 1894 to 1899 was the Rev. P. M. C. Johnstone, who came to Bournemouth after experience in Cornwall and South Africa. On leaving St. Peter's he was instituted as vicar of St. Michael's, Woolwich, but returned to Bournemouth in 1902 as vicar of St. Katherine's, Southbourne. He later became vicar of All Saints, Cheltenham, and an honorary canon of Gloucester Cathedral.

In November 1897 there were placed in St. Peter's the seven sanctuary lamps which hang before the Altar. They were given to the Church by Miss Sellon. Fisher was particularly grateful for these lamps and was at pains to explain to his congregation their proper meaning and significance:

> Those who enter into the symbolism of Christian worship will readily see how beautifully figurative as well as scriptural is the use of these lamps. The description which S.John gives in Rev.iv.5

> of the vision which he saw of the heavenly worship will at once occur to people's minds. "There are seven lamps of fire," he says, "burning before the throne, which are the *Seven Spirits of GOD*." And in Rev.v.6 he writes of the Lamb in the midst of the throne, from whom proceed "seven eyes, which are the *Seven Spirits of GOD*, sent forth into all the earth." Again in Rev.i.4 S.John sends a salutation of peace to the seven churches, not only from himself, but "from Him which is, and which was, and which is to come, and from the *Seven Spirits* which are before His throne." We know, of course, that there is but one Holy Ghost, but there are seven Spiritual Illuminations which come forth from Him. These are mentioned in Holy Scripture, these are "sent forth into all the earth," and these we receive at our Confirmation. It is probable that the seven lamps of which we read in the books of Exodus, which Bezaleel made by the commandment which God gave to Moses, for the Sanctuary of the Tabernacle, were typical of those S.John saw when the "door was opened in Heaven." The prophet Zechariah also tells us how an angel came to him and awoke him, and he saw amongst other things a golden candlestick and seven lamps. Thus we have for 1500 B.C. as well as in the description of the unceasing worship in Heaven, a Scriptural record of this beautiful symbolism. The Altar is Christ's earthly throne, where His presence is real but not visible, and when we kneel before it we should try to think of the "Lamb which is in the midst of the Throne in Heaven," of the glorious worship which surrounds it, and of the "seven lamps burning before it, which are the seven Spirits of God."

Leachman, writing in 1915, remarked that perhaps more questions were asked about these lamps than about anything else at St. Peter's, the prevailing Protestant idea being, apparently, that they were used in some mysterous way for the burning of incense. In the *Magazine* for June 1899, Fisher explained that the seven lamps typify the sevenfold gifts of the Holy Ghost:

> People sometimes come into S.Peter's Church and ask what is the meaning of the seven lamps. They ignorantly imagine that they indicate that the Blessed Sacrament is reserved in a tabernacle above the altar. Of course this is not our custom; if it were so there would be *one lamp, not seven*. The seven lamps are a symbol of the lamps of fire before the throne in heaven.
>
> Let us try to think more of that tribute, and of Him Whom S.John saw sitting upon it, and as we think of this remember that this same Lord Jesus Christ is spiritually but really present at our altars. What faith, what joy, what power would this give to our worship of the Lamb of God in the Holy Eucharist, before Whom the Cherubim and Seraphim and all the company of heaven prostrate themselves in adoration.

The schoolmaster's daughter has recalled that Miss Sellon asked to be allowed to go to St. Peter's at night to see the lamps alight as the sole lights in the Church. "I stood in the little group," Mrs. Whitten remembered, "a small child rather frightened of the dark."

Also in the Diamond Jubilee year was founded the Servants Needlework Guild which specialised in making articles of clothing to be sent to poor London parishes where the work done by the St. Peter's women was greatly welcomed. There were three simple rules of the Guild, 1. Each member to make one garment; 2. A subscription of 1/- a year to go towards materials, to be paid in advance; and 3. All garments to be sent in to Mrs. Patterson, Clavadel, by the last week in October.

The following year, 1898, is remembered particularly for the last Communion of the great Liberal statesman, William Ewart Gladstone, which he took one Thursday morning at St. Peter's only a few weeks before his death. Owing to his great age and extreme weakness Gladstone occupied the end choir stall, so as to be near the Altar rail. A brass plate now affixed there recalls the occasion. Phyllis Bottome was herself in Church that morning and at Mrs. Gladstone's request knelt beside the ailing old man and helped him to rise after he had made his Communion. She was formally introduced to Gladstone in the churchyard afterwards.

During 1898 it was realised that the Burne-Jones mosaic panels on the sanctuary walls had perished beyond repair and become almost entirely defaced. A parishioner's bequest was earmarked for the replacement of the two larger panels representing angels on each side of the Altar. Sir Arthur Blomfield was employed to direct the work and drawings of the proposed new panels were prepared by Messrs. Powell & Son of Whitefriars. The new designs for the side walls were the Marriage at Cana and the Last Supper on the north and the Feeding of the Five Thousand and the Supper at Emmaus on the south. These subjects were the same as the Burne-Jones originals of twenty years earlier but of different design, no attempt being made to copy the old panels. The new mosaics for the side walls of the sanctuary were to cost £45 each and, within a month of Fisher making an appeal for the money, it was all subscribed.

In order to ensure that the new work would not quickly perish as the previous panels had done, Powell's advised that they should be manufactured by the *opus sectile* process which they believed would be imperishable. Their confidence in this new method seems to have been fully justified, for, even if the new designs lacked the Burne-Jones artistry, they have lasted so far in excellent condition. The panels on the east wall were completed early in 1899 and dedicated on Saturday, 22nd April at the eight o'clock celebration. Three of the side panels were installed by the end of June, but the fourth was so damaged in transit to Bournemouth that it had to be sent back to the makers for restoration and was not placed in position until the end of July. At the same time the reredos was restored and re-gilded for the sum of £45 and the altar shelf added.

In 1899 Fisher sprang to the defence of burning incense in Church when this practice was assailed in Court as being contrary to the law of the Church of England:

> All church-people must be interested in knowing that the question of the ceremonial use of incense in our Church has been lately brought before the Archbishops' Court. Whatever may be the outcome of this particular investigation, it may surely be a matter of prayer that the minds of the Archbishops and Bishops may be directed to a right judgment in this, as well as other matters; and that so integral a part of the worship of heaven, so accurately described by S.John (Rev. iii, 3) under the guidance of the Holy Spirit, a practice so distinctly scriptural, and used by so large a portion of the Catholic and Apostolic Church, may be given to us as our due heritage; not by the law of a secular court (with which we have nothing to do), but by spiritual authority duly constituted.

The turn of the century is an appropriate moment in time to consider the position of St. Peter's as it then was. The living was worth only £150 and a house. The vicar was in poor health, taking the chaplaincy at Baveno in Italy whenever he could, in order to spend some time in a warmer climate. He was getting into debt and becoming more and more unpopular with his colleagues and congregation. There were even rumours of immorality, but probably these were unfounded; at least, one can discover no evidence to support them. Responsibility for keeping the parish going fell increasingly upon the shoulders of the senior assistant curate (from 1901 the Rev. Charles Seagrim, a very able and popular man) and the churchwardens. When the writer's grandparents, he a sidesman and she a churchwarden's daughter, married in 1903, the bride declared she would refuse to have the ceremony in St. Peter's if "that dreadful man," meaning the vicar, was going to touch her Collections and pew rents, always giving at least some indication of the health and happiness of the parish, fell seriously, with the result that debts were created and essential repairs to buildings could not be carried out. This regrettable situation persisted throughout the opening years of the twentieth century, eventually leaving Fisher's successor with the legacy, as Leachman put it, of many and serious tasks facing St. Peter's, debts to be paid off, schools enlarged and put in order, "and hope and enthusiasm rekindled throughout the parish." How much of this difficulty was due to Fisher's own manner and approach, and how much to his physical disabilities, is hard to say. But, unfortunately for all concerned, his ministry which had started so auspiciously was doomed to end in utter failure.

The year 1901 had only just begun when Queen Victoria died and a huge memorial service was held in St. Peter's, attended by the Mayor and Corporation (then only newly instituted as a County Borough), Magistrates, Police, Fire Brigade, Coastguards, Artillery Volunteers and Rifles Volunteers. The Bournemouth Municipal Orchestra massed in the north transept to swell the music for the sad occasion.

At the Easter Vestry, faced with the problems of higher expenses and decreasing income, Fisher made an appeal which sounds prophetic of the Envelope Schemes and Christian Stewardship Campaigns of a later age. "If only," said the vicar, "Church-people would lay by, Sunday by Sunday, some definite sum for Church purposes, and if prevented from attending the Service, send their accustomed offering to the Vicar or Churchwardens, a constant income would be assured." It is a little pathetic to note that apparently the vicar never considered that the reason people were staying away from Church might have something to do with his own behaviour. Only when it was too late did he pause to examine his own failings and admit the disaster of his ministry. In 1901 the parishioners were not inspired by his plea; the vicar had lost their confidence and the crisis drew nearer.

In the summer of 1901 the vicar and congregation felt outraged by the suggestion that part of the churchyard should be given up to make room for the new-fangled trams. It would be an "act of desecration" against the churchyard, said the people of St. Peter's, if the Bournemouth Corporation should succeed in obtaining an Act of Parliament to enable them to lay tramway lines through St. Peter's churchyard. A petition against this proposal was drawn up and presented to the authorities, but the march of progress could not be arrested.

This was not the only petition against proposed legislation presented during this period by the people of St. Peter's. In 1895 the Vestry Meeting had signed a petition addressed to the House of Commons protesting against the Welsh Church Disestablishment Bill which, so it was said, was "fraught with injustice to the Church and injury to the Nation." Then, in 1902, the Deceased Wife's Sister's Bill was before Parliament, proposing to allow a man to marry the sister of his deceased wife, which was then unlawful. Fisher invited his congregation to object to the suggested reform. "No words are strong enough," he wrote in the Magazine, "with which to protest against this iniquitous measure, which is not only contrary to the teaching of Holy Scripture, and of the Catholic Church, but also threatens to undermine the purity of the social condition of our community. Surely it is plain that if a woman may not marry the brother of her deceased husband, a man may not marry the sister of his deceased wife."

At the beginning of the new century St. Peter's was lit by gas lamps which gave insufficient light and were smelly as well. People complained that at evening services it was so dark in Church that they could hardly see to read their books and that the atmosphere produced by the gas was most unpleasant. The gas lighting system needed overhauling in any case. One evening the gas failed completely and the Church was plunged into darkness just as the choir was singing the anthem from Psalm 43, *O Send Out Thy Light*. Organist and choir, unperturbed by the sudden emergency, carried on to the end of the music.

The first step towards fitting electric light in the Church, decided the congregation, was to provide it in the nave. Mr. Jackson was employed as architect to design the brackets and electroliers for the new installation which was ready early in 1903 at a cost, excluding the architect's fees, of £187 17s. 0d. At the same time the ventilation was increased by inserting grilles in the west door. These improvements were at once noticed with satisfaction. The air was purer, the atmosphere cleaner, and the lighting much brighter. The extension of the electric lights in to the chancel had to be delayed because the bill for the nave lighting remained unpaid and the Church finances were in such a poor state that no more modern luxuries could be afforded. The chancel and sanctuary lights were not converted to electricity until 1906, under Fisher's successor, when the parish was once again moving forward and in a position to pay its way.

Fisher's incumbency at St. Peter's came to a sudden end in March, 1904. But the storm clouds had been gathering for some years and causing no little concern among the principal parishioners. The Vicar was living beyond his means and had developed a weakness for drink. Possibly these troubles were not entirely of Fisher's own making, for he was never completely well after the turn of the century. Nevertheless, the impact of his ministry was reduced to almost nothing and his activities had become grave embarrassments to the churchfolk of Bournemouth.

Fisher's craving for whisky was the worst of the trouble. This was developing into a scandal which proved difficult to hush up. It was rumoured, and probably true, that he satisfied his craving for drink on the unconsecrated altar wine when no other liquor was readily available. Parts of the churchyard became depositories for empty bottles, and on at least one occasion the Vicar was so drunk in the Vestry that the sacristan, Harry Crumpler, had to summon Scott Evans from his office to deal with the situation.

Walter Scott Evans, who by 1903 had been people's churchwarden for twenty-six years since his first election in the days of Morden Bennett, was one of Fisher's friends. To him Fisher had turned when beset with financial difficulties and Scott Evans had lent him over £2,000. In 1902 James Druitt, vicar's warden since the time of Ram, was replaced by Dr. Kinsey Morgan, and in 1903 the Vicar appointed Scott Evans to fill the doctor's place. Another man of strong character was needed to act as people's warden, and he was found in Charles William Keep, unanimously elected on the proposition of Messrs. Sydenham and Druitt. On accepting office Keep promised to promote the interests of St. Peter's in every possible way. One of these interests would have to be the uncongenial task of arranging to have the Vicar replaced.

Despite their friendship with Fisher the churchwardens could no longer ignore the serious disrepute which the Vicar was bringing upon himself and upon St. Peter's. Scott Evans and Keep had no alternative but to go to Winchester and report to the Bishop. With the co-operation of the Bishop and the Patron Fisher's resignation was quickly obtained and the vacancy filled forthwith. It was a sad and tragic end to a career which had in the main been so scholarly and successful.

The Parish Magazine for April 1904 announced the fact of the Vicar's resignation merely as part of a paragraph dealing with the appointment of his successor. Nowhere is there any expression of regret at Fisher's departure nor any mention of where he was intending to go on leaving Bournemouth. The congregation must have been heartily relieved at the prospect of being rid of him.

He took no further part in the activities of St. Peter's and left the Easter Vestry Meeting to his senior assistant curate Charles Seagrim, who himself left the parish later in 1904 to become Vicar of Ashmansworth, near Newbury. At Whitsun Fisher wrote his valedictory letter to the people of St. Peter's. Writing from his new home at Shirley Warren, near Southampton, he regretted being unable to say *good-bye* from the pulpit and asked the congregation to give their full trust and confidence to his successor. In one of the paragraphs he sadly alludes to the failings which led to his enforced resignation: —

> I am deeply conscious of many negligences, omissions and failures in my Ministry among you. Perhaps if it had pleased God to give me greater bodily strength, I might have done better. I humbly trust my will was bent the right way; and I know that, in your charity, you will make allowance for my physical weakness, and the many imperfections of my work.

Fisher settled at Southampton where, during his retirement, he acted as assistant priest at St. Michael's Church. He died in 1925 when nearly ninety years of age.

CHAPTER XV

Daldy Arrives

THE NEW vicar nominated for St. Peter's was a 38-year-old bachelor, Alfred Edward Daldy. He was no stranger to the parish, for he had preached several times at St. Peter's and at both daughter-Churches. Although Fisher's resignation did not take legal effect until 31st May Daldy's appointment was notified in March and the vicar-designate "himself announced this to Canon Fisher on 23rd March, showing his greatest consideration in desiring that he should be the first person to hear the tidings authoritatively from his own lips." The people were thankful to be told that "Mr. Daldy is a sound Churchman, and will carry on the work of St. Peter's upon the Catholic lines which, with brief exceptions, have obtained in the parish."

Daldy was unable to take up his new duties immediately, as he had agreed to undertake a mission in South Africa. Once his work there had been completed he left Cape Town on the s.s. Saxon on 22nd June, arriving in Southampton on 9th July. The institution and induction service on 28th July, conducted by the Bishop of Southampton and the Archdeacon of Winchester, was a great occasion. Most of the neighbouring clergy were there and the Mayor and Corporation of Bournemouth attended in state. The singing was led by the combined choirs of the three Churches, St. Peter's, St. Swithun's and St. Ambrose. A photograph published in the local press showed part of the procession walking along the south side of the Church in the afternoon sunshine.

The young Daldy, carefully and most suitably chosen for the incumbency at this difficult time, was well fitted for the task of leading St. Peter's out of the complacency of the Victorian age into the bright, new era of the twentieth century. Born in 1865, he was educated at Cranbrook School and Cambridge University, where he took his B.A. when he was only just nineteen. Four years later he obtained his M.A. It is quite remarkable that of the first ten vicars of St. Peter's Daldy was the only Cambridge man. The other nine were all "M.A., Oxon." Upon his ordination in 1888 Daldy went as assistant curate to St. Michael's, Bromley, later moving to take up a similar position at All Hallows, Barking. In 1897 he left London to become Diocesan Missioner at Winchester where he served under Randall Davidson until in 1903 the latter began his long reign at Canterbury. When Daldy gave up his post as Diocesan Missioner to come to St. Peter's a presentation fund of £232 18s. 3d. was raised for him, of which £34 10s. 0d. was used in the purchase of a suite of dining room furniture.

Advantage had been taken of the change of incumbent to carry out extensive repairs to the vicarage. These had not been finished by the time Daldy arrived. Several structural alterations were carried out, a new drainage system installed, and the building redecorated both inside and out. The cost of all this work came to over £800, and a further £100 was spent on a new fence. As the parish was still in low water financially the people were asked to contribute to a Vicarage Repair Fund. A bazaar and a sale of work were held to raise some of the money. It was reported that this bazaar was the first such function ever held by St. Peter's for its own parochial needs, but it set a precedent for many future events of a similar kind, the correctness of which was not seriously questioned until over half a century later.

The pronunciation of the new vicar's surname caused some confusion in the town. *The Bournemouth Graphic* reminded its readers that the first syllable should be pronounced as in "dally." On Daldy's second Sunday at St. Peter's a larger congregation than usual filled the Church to hear him preach. Speaking on the text "Thy Kingdom come" the new vicar said his aim was "to fulfil the purpose of God in this town," rather than simply to draw increased congregations and keep them united in heart. He believed the Church should not lose sight of its true ideals or the object of its existence by spending its energies on elaborate organisation or business-like exactness. One reporter of this sermon described Daldy as "not a great preacher, though few of his listeners could fail to be impressed by his earnest manner." The same paper remarked after Daldy's Harvest Festival sermon later in the year that the vicar seemed a man "of rare understanding and zeal."

One of the first changes made at St. Peter's by the new incumbent was to introduce coloured Eucharistic vestments. Some of the parishioners found it difficult to accept them and Daldy was faced with the not inconsiderable task of persuading his congregation that this was a valid Anglican practice and not wicked popery. Despite "some grave opposition" Daldy contrived, by use of his great personal charm and convincing explanations, not only to silence the critics but in many cases to bring them round to his own way of thinking. He was obviously a man who would rule his parish firmly and vigorously as Morden Bennett had done, and it says much for his character that he was able to do it with a loving Christian concern for his Church and people, who soon became devoted to him. Thus, following St. Clement's, St. Peter's was the second Bournemouth Church to use Mass vestments, starting with the early celebrations in the autumn of 1904. Strictly speaking, the use of the Eucharistic vestments at this time was illegal, though increasing numbers of priests were acting in the matter according to their individual consciences. Spiritual authority was given in 1908 in the report of five bishops *On the Ornaments of the Church and its Ministers* which concluded that these vestments were permitted, if not enjoined. Daldy also introduced Confession, which again was a complete departure from the practice of other Churches in the district except St. Clement's.

Daldy did much to consolidate a definitely Catholic tradition at St. Peter's, forging ahead along lines which Morden Bennett would evidently have followed. On 20th May 1910 there was a memorial service for the late King Edward VII at which the *Missa de Angelis*, a plainsong Mass of Roman origins, was sung. This would have been a very "high-church" type of service for those days. Then, in 1915, Daldy held a Sung Eucharist for Corpus Christi, yet another sign of his determined movement towards Catholic practice. The banner of the Confraternity of the Blessed Sacrament which hangs at St. Peter's also dates from about this time and clearly indicates the direction of Daldy's theological leanings. Support for the Confraternity at this period would have been regarded by some Protestants as close to treason.

When Daldy took over at St. Peter's the Sung Eucharist was celebrated at 9.45 every Sunday, but the new vicar decided for the future to start the service at 9.30 so as to give time for a sermon as required by the rubric in the Prayer Book. However, the celebrations with sermon only continued for about a year until, towards the end of 1905, Daldy reverted to the original time of 9.45 and abandoned the sermon. At the same time Matins was advanced from 11 o'clock to 11.15. Soon afterwards the choral celebrations were timed to start at 10 o'clock, which has been the most usual time ever since.

Daldy tried to discourage his congregation from communicating at the Sung Eucharist, asking his people to receive the Holy Communion at one of the early services or, if they were not well enough to come early, at 12.15 p.m., after Matins. He explained that the choral celebrations "are specially meant for praise and thanksgiving. Great inconvenience is often caused by people receiving unnecessarily at choral celebrations. Of course, we do not want a celebration without communicants, but in every way a plain service without music is the most fitting service at which to partake. Nor do I wish in any way to interfere with the 'liberty of the subject,' but I ask you to consider the question and do what you can to make the services orderly." Daldy is also on record in 1906 as complaining about communicants leaving the Church before the end of the service. Quite rightly he insisted upon their remaining in their places until the celebrant had left the Altar. The congregation had obviously forgotten the lesson of old Ames kneeling at the door saying his prayers!

The new vicar took a lively interest in civic and public affairs, quickly making his presence felt in the life of the town. "The Church has a function to perform towards the town," wrote Daldy in 1905. "It should be a power for righteousness, influencing civic, communal, and social life." Within a few months of his coming to Bournemouth Daldy was chairman of a meeting at the Prince's Hall in support of the Melanesian Mission, was principal speaker at a meeting of the Foresters, and supported a public meeting of the R.S.P.C.A. However, in spite of these public activities, in which he clearly displayed keen interest, it was not until the middle of October, when he had been in Bournemouth nearly three months, that he found the time to address his parishioners at St. Ambrose, and this was at the special request of the priest-in-charge on the occasion of a social gathering in the Parish Room.

Shortly before Christmas 1904 Daldy gave his people a social evening, with music and refreshments provided. Five hundred guests were invited, of whom about 350 attended. The function was an immense social success, with speeches by both vicar and Mayor, and was remembered for its good fellowship, cordiality and enthusiasm.

It is perhaps not surprising that the advent of a handsome young clergyman as vicar caused some speculation in the parish as to who would become the lady at the vicarage. Some of the young ladies of Bournemouth were not slow in endeavouring to attract Daldy's attentions, but their efforts were successful only to the extent of other parishioners referring to them as "the Band of Hope!" Daldy did soon find a wife, Mrs. Constance Mary van der Noot, widow of the Rev. Edgar van der Noot and daughter of Sir Algernon West, G.C.B. After their marriage in 1908 Mrs. Daldy took her full share in all the parish activities and some of the older members of St. Peter's still remember her with great affection. To celebrate the patronal festival each year she regularly presided over a garden party at the vicarage, where big bowls of strawberries and cream were served as her guests strolled over the wide lawns from which they could enjoy the magnificent views across the bay to the Purbecks.

It may have been at about this time, or perhaps earlier, that a story got about concerning St. Peter's which Cyril Maynard, chorister and choirman since 1908, was told while serving in India during the First World War. When the chaplain at Dalhousie heard that he came from St. Peter's he remarked that that was where the ladies went to Church followed by their footmen carrying their books. Cyril Maynard could only reply that this must have been before his time!

Not everyone who came to St. Peter's during this time was happy and prosperous. There were incidents of sadness as well. One day Harry Crumpler called Mrs. Barker, the schoolmaster's wife, to go to the Church to witness a wedding. After the service Mrs. Barker went to wish the couple every happiness, but the bride and groom parted at the Church door, one going one way and one the other. One wonders what tragedy lay behind that pathetic marriage.

Duncan Hume, organist since 1880, was sacked, despite having "attained the reputation of being one of the finest accompanists of Gregorian chants in the country" and having "gained for St. Peter's a renown for the high standard of its devotional music." At the beginning of February 1905 Daldy announced that with very great reluctance, and after seven months most anxious consideration, he had decided to make a change. Whatever the reason for Hume's dismissal may have been, it is clear that the organist had no wish to leave and that Leachman was more tactful than accurate in saying that Hume resigned. Daldy appealed for sympathy: "Mr. Duncan Hume is an old inhabitant and has many friends in Bournemouth. I am sure they will continue to be friendly to him at a time when he will specially need their help." Hume considered that he had received less than justice, particularly as rumours began to circulate as to why the vicar had thought it necessary to relieve him of his duties. "He tells me," wrote Daldy, "it has come to his knowledge that people have said he is leaving because of a grave moral fault. I wish most emphatically to give such statements my entire repudiation. Mr. Hume is leaving for no such reasons." But the vicar was still not saying in public what the real reasons were. However, it was a matter of notoriety in the parish that Hume's trouble was an addiction to alcohol. This had not only impaired his musical abilities but it is said that on one occasion he was so much the worse for drink that he fell off the organ stool.

To succeed Hume Daldy appointed James D. Chandler, Mus.Bac., F.R.C.O., organist and choirmaster at All Saints, Wokingham, who had been a pupil of Sir George Martin, organist of St. Paul's Cathedral. Chandler successfully maintained the high standards of St. Peter's music under five vicars and covering a period of over forty years.

Cyril Maynard has recalled what it was like to be a choirboy at this period:—

> From 1865 to 1925 there was a choir Home where eight boys, mostly from the London area, lived, and the rest of the boys lived locally and were known as Town boys. The main reason that I became a Home boy was that my father had been a Home boy. In his days the Choir Home was in Crowther Terrace, Upper Terrace Road, but it was later moved to 93 Old Christchurch Road. After attending an audition at 60 Berners Street, London, at which I had to sing Attwood's "Come Holy Ghost," I was chosen by Mr. J. D. Chandler, the organist and Choir-master, to fill a vacancy at the Choir Home and joined the choir on 1st June, 1908. I had to have an Eton suit, square and black tie for Sundays.
>
> St. Peter's services were very different to those at St. Barnabas, Clapham Common, where I had been in the choir. What impressed me most was the Sung Eucharist, at which the Celebrant was usually the Rev. E. W. Leachman, the banners, all of which used to be carried in processions, and the chancel being shut off with gates. On Sundays we attended the following services:— Sung Eucharist, 10 a.m. Matins and Sermon, 11.15 a.m., First Evensong and Sermon, 3 p.m. (boys only), Sunday School Service, 4 p.m. and Evensong and Sermon, 6.30 p.m. The Sunday School occupied most of the centre of the Church and we had to sit in front of the pulpit for the address or lesson. On weekdays boys only sang Evensong at 5.30 p.m. followed by choir practice each evening except Saturday, and we also sang the Litany on Wednesday and Friday at 12.5 p.m. On Saint's Days we sang the Eucharist at 11 a.m. On Sundays the Te Deum, Magnificat and Nunc Dimittis were sung to settings, but during Lent settings were not used and at the Eucharist we sang Merbecke or Missa de Angelis.

In 1905 the churchwardens abandoned the previous practice of collecting subscriptions to augment the meagre endowment and instead arranged to give the vicar the Easter offerings. That year Daldy received £180. It may be taken as some indication of the measure of his increasing popularity among the congregation of St. Peter's that the next year the vicar's Easter offerings totalled £340.

Fortunately for the parish Daldy quickly established himself as the true friend and trusted leader of his flock. He was the man of the moment, exactly the type of priest needed at that difficult time. The failings of his predecessor had left the people discouraged and lacking in enthusiasm. The parish required a reawakening of its missionary spirit and an energetic leadership from its vicar, both of which Daldy supplied in full measure. He soon became noted as a very kind friend and adviser to folk of all ages and every social position. His personal and very practical generosity to many of his poorer parishioners helped many families through difficult times and his example undoubtedly prompted many of the richer people to follow his lead. He realised only too well the sorry state in which Fisher had left the parish and in a purposeful way set about its conversion.

The way was not easy and yet another dispute awaited a solution when Daldy arrived. The vacancy in the benefice had provided a new opportunity to consider the question of removing St. Swithun's from the parish and creating a separate district. It will be recalled that this matter had been quite thoroughly canvassed on Morden Bennett's death, when the Patron had refused to hear of it, and again in 1896 under Fisher, who himself had the idea of making both St. Swithun's and St. Ambrose into parishes of their own. When it was known that Canon Fisher was leaving, the supporters of separation were not slow to act. Immediately his resignation was announced a committee was formed and steps were taken, by petitions and publicity, to effect the separation of St. Swithun's before a new vicar could be inducted. However, since the vacancy was such a short one, lasting only from 1st June to 28th July, Bishop Ryle of Winchester thought it inadvisable to proceed during that period, especially since a large number of parishioners were opposed to the change.

The congregation of St. Swithun's at this time was mainly composed of rich people living in the fine houses on Bournemouth's East Cliff. The district around the Church was purely residential in character. Moneyed parishioners were abundant, all the sidesmen came to Church in frock coats and top hats and the ladies in their silks rustled up the aisles. Worshippers were driven to the Church doors in their carriages and pairs. The atmosphere was one of Edwardian opulence. On one occasion when Winnington Ingram, the Bishop of London, came to Sunday Matins at St. Swithun's and preached for the East London Charity Fund the collection came to over £100, practically all in golden sovereigns.

The dispute over the separation of St. Swithun's was laid before Daldy as soon as he arrived in Bournemouth to commence his ministry. The problem was further complicated by the offer of

£15,000 (£10,000 for St. Swithun's and £5,000 for St. Peter's) for the purpose of endowment and the offer of a house to serve as a vicarage for the new parish. But these offers were made upon certain conditions, one of which was that the money would not come into the possession of the Church until the deaths of five testators and the house would not be made available until the owner's death. Meanwhile, the donors sought to stipulate that the separation should be effected immediately and that they should be given the right of first presentation at St. Swithun's.

Daldy went thoroughly into the reasons for and against the proposed division of the parish and had a long meeting with the committee, whose members tried there and then to convince him that the time had come for St. Peter's and St. Swithun's to part. According to the vicar, "The two questions to be decided were these: First, is it in the true interest of the Church that St. Swithun's should be a separate parish? Secondly, do the proposals to endow St. Swithun's and St. Peter's, and to provide a house at some future date, over-rate all other considerations? We know that money does not make wrong right, or unwisdom wisdom; but, where a question of expediency is concerned, money often rightly turns the scales."

When in October 1904 Daldy decided to write an open letter to all his parishioners to explain the issues and the various problems confronting him a sub-committee of the supporters of separation was appointed to meet him in order to revise his draft. However, the gentlemen on the sub-committee (Mr. Hutchings, Mr. W. Fisher, General Galloway, Sir J. Hanbury and Mr. P. L. Evans) refused to co-operate, apparently because they thought that the vicar should have espoused their cause with greater enthusiasm. In this letter Daldy wrote of his parish:

> The Parish is sharply divided into two parts. The first comprises the East Cliff and part of the town; the second is the District of St. Ambrose, partitioned off from the Mother Church by the Parish of St. Michael.
>
> St. Ambrose and District will, I think, obviously become a separate parish in the course of time, and I suppose it would not be seriously contended that St. Swithun's District should be separated and St. Ambrose District remain permanently a part of the Parish of St. Peter.
>
> We have then to consider the effect of the separation of St. Swithun's District upon the District around St. Peter's Church.
>
> The population of the two Districts is about 7,500. Separation would mean that St. Peter's would have a population of, say, 4,500. This would make St. Peter's one of the smallest parishes of Bournemouth. It would be smaller than the present District of St.

Ambrose. And although it is contended that the population of St. Swithun's is not "especially wealthy," yet there can be no doubt that the St. Swithun's District is far more wealthy than St. Peter's, and that the tendency is in the direction of St. Peter's becoming increasingly poorer.

Supposing the separation to take place you would have St. Peter's Parish, containing about 4,500 people, with the following responsibilities, supposing, that is, that it maintains what is at present provided: —

(*a*) A Church seating 1,250.
(*b*) St. Peter's Schools, among the largest in the town.
(*c*) A large and beautiful Churchyard.
(*d*) A Choir Home, providing daily sung Services.
(*e*) A considerable amount of additional work at the Hospital, Firs Home and St. Mary's Home.

It is contended on the one hand that the question of St. Peter's being reduced to one of the smallest parishes of Bournemouth is of little importance, because people in Bournemouth frequently do not go to their Parish Churches, and because St. Peter's would always have a strong following.

It is also contended that St. Swithun's District has not contributed more than £75 a year towards general Parish Funds for the last ten years, and that, in return for part services of an Assistant Curate.

In reviewing the position of St. Swithun's Church at this time Daldy reminded his congregation that there were no poor people living nearby and that it lacked both churchyard and school. Nevertheless, it was agreed at once that the people of St. Swithun's should have more control over their Church's affairs, particularly as regards finance, and that separate wardens would be appointed, even though, as a matter of law, the St. Peter's churchwardens would have to continue to act officially for the whole parish. Daldy dismissed criticisms that he had been unable to maintain adequate contact with his daughter-Churches by promising to attach senior priests to St. Peters, St. Swithun's and St. Ambrose, so as to free himself of much routine work and thus enable him to have more time to keep in close touch with all parts of his parish. Patterson remained in control of St. Ambrose. At St. Swithun's the priest appointed to take charge was the Rev. Ernest Marling Roberts, a very able assistant and most highly respected by all who knew him. When Roberts left Bournemouth in 1909 he became vicar of St. Philip's, Kensington, moving to St. Mary Abbots, one of London's richest and most important livings, in 1917. He was Rural Dean of Kensington from 1919. To succeed Roberts in charge of St. Swithun's Daldy appointed Kenneth McMaster.

On the vexed question of separation Daldy refused to be hurried. He promised an early decision, but not until he had given long thought and earnest prayer about the conflicting arguments and obtained the best advice. He besought his people "to maintain at all costs that spirit of unity and peace which is so essential for the well-being of our work . . . we cannot afford to lose the services and prayers of a single worshipper at our Churches."

Daldy delayed giving his final answer until the summer of 1905. By that time some of the heat had died down and Daldy had, through his personality and integrity, re-established that friendly, co-operative relationship between priest and people which had been so sadly lacking during Fisher's later years as vicar. The financial and other reforms which Daldy introduced placed St. Swithun's in as independent a position as St. Peter's had, but the incumbent came to the conclusion that from every point of view it would be harmful to constitute St. Swithun's as a separate parish. Daldy realised by now that even the most vehement of the separatists would eventually be prepared to accept his ruling. "It is neither to be expected or desired," he wrote, "that we should all hold exactly the same opinions, but by considerateness and forebearance we may hope to live and work quietly for our common Lord and Master."

Daldy's decision to preserve the *status quo* still failed to find favour in every quarter. By the beginning of 1906 he had to make a further appeal to his parishioners for unity and toleration. Under the heading of *The Co-ordination of our Churches* he wrote:—

> Those of you, my friends, who have not noticed it before will now be able clearly to see the lines upon which it is best, in my judgment, for the Churches of this parish to run. S.Peter's, S.Swithun's and S.Ambrose' are upon an equality, free to promote the kingdom of God on earth. They are linked together by being under one Vicar, by Committees and Organisations which concern the parish as a whole, and by (no small thing, I venture to think) being integral parts of the largest and most central parish in the town. Many of you, I know, do not agree with this policy, and that, I think, is to be expected. But at all events you will do me the credit of saying that it is intelligible and that it gives every part of the parish perfect freedom to move forward. In two not very unimportant matters we must wait for the completion of this plan. The question of the legal position of Churchwardens is not yet decided, and S.Ambrose' Church will not be consecrated till October. But neither of these matters interfere with the ordinary working of the parish.

At last the opposition was silenced. Not for nothing was Daldy to acquire a reputation as a priest who ruled his parish. But even in cases where the disagreement was substantial he had the ability and good sense to explain his own point of view with thoroughness, to treat his critics with every courtesy, and always to act himself like the true Christian gentleman he was. Alex. Bennett, still vicar of St. Stephen's, must often have been reminded of his own father, for in Daldy St. Peter's had once again a parson who would give his parish firm and effective leadership in the best traditions of Morden Bennett.

CHAPTER XVI

New Buildings And Improvements

AS SOON as Daldy assumed the incumbency of St. Peter's he insisted at once on improving and extending the material things of the parish, particularly those which had been neglected or not adequately pursued under his predecessor. Money was short, but this was largely due to Fisher's unpopularity which had caused many members of the congregation to contribute less than their proper share and had turned others away from the parish altogether. With enterprise and farsightedness reminiscent of his great predecessor Morden Bennett, Daldy started to put things right. In no small measure did he possess the gift of leadership. Anything which really needed doing he would see was achieved. His people followed his lead and reacted enthusiastically to his encouragement. John Garrett Leigh called Daldy "the apostle of reality."

When he took over the parish Daldy found not only a discouraged congregation but also the burdens awaiting him of completing and reorganising many aspects of Church life which had not been properly attended to for years. The Terrace Road Mission had been closed, St. Peter's School was in serious disrepair and needed enlarging, St. Ambrose School required complete rebuilding, the electric lighting at St. Peter's Church had to be finished, a side-chapel for the daily services was wanted, the Church of St. Ambrose had been left incomplete and unconsecrated, and St. Peter's was the only Church in the whole of Bournemouth without a parish hall. To help him carry out the various tasks which had to be performed Daldy gathered about him a fine team of young clergymen led by three senior priests, Leachman at St. Peter's, Roberts at St. Swithun's and Patterson at St. Ambrose.

The laity were more and more encouraged to take an active part in furthering the life of the Church, both within the parish and in the missionfield beyond, and were dissuaded from misdirecting their energies in petty squabbles and "parish-pump" politics. The people of St. Swithun's and St. Ambrose particularly, given wide freedom to conduct their own affairs, would be able to contribute far more to their own Churches and grow steadily less reliant upon, and less antagonistic towards, the things which were done for them and expected of them by the people of St. Peter's.

When Daldy appointed John Gregory White as his churchwarden in 1905 Scott Evans was re-elected as people's warden and gave the vicar his most loyal support until his sudden death in 1908 at the age of sixty-six. He had been churchwarden of St. Peter's continuously for over thirty years since his first election during the time of Morden Bennett and his death was a very great loss to the Church and parish for which he had done so much. Daldy recalled that Scott Evans had "stuck to the Church through the ups and downs of parochial life, and one vicar after another, in sunshine and darkness. There could not be found in Bournemouth any man who was so devout and had so entirely given himself to his Master as the late people's warden." Scott Evans, who left a widow, seven sons and five daughters, lies buried in the churchyard alongside one of the vicars he served, George Stopford Ram. As a memorial of his life and work a panel of coloured mosaic tiles was affixed to the wall of the north aisle near the entrance to the north transept depicting St. Paul preaching at Athens. Elected to replace Scott Evans was William John Palmer, a local wine merchant and the second of the present writer's great-grandfathers to serve as churchwarden, C. W. Keep having been the first. Palmer thus embarked on a long tenure of the people's wardenship lasting twenty years, through most of which he served in a happy partnership with James Druitt, who was reappointed vicar's warden in 1912. By this time Druitt had retired as Town Clerk and was an Alderman on the Borough Council. He was elected Mayor of Bournemouth for the year 1914-15.

An immediate worry in 1904 was the condition of St. Peter's School. Regular running repairs had not been carried out as they should have been and it was apparent that this state of affairs could not be allowed to continue. Furthermore, the large increase in Bournemouth's population which had taken place during Fisher's time, during which the town had successively been accorded the status of Borough and County Borough, meant a corresponding increase in the demand for education, so much so that a new classroom was needed. The preliminary estimate of the amount required to put the school in order was £915, but when the final figures were prepared the estimate was for a sum of no less than £1,600. By the summer of 1905 only £423 had been promised so Daldy and the school managers decided to do the repairs only and to postpone building the new classroom. "This will save for a time £300," wrote the vicar, "but the Class Room, although not among the requirements, is *most* necessary, and I hope its erection will not be long delayed." The repairs were so urgently needed that no further delay could be allowed while the money was found, and most of these repairs were carried out during the summer of 1905. The congregation rallied round and soon produced enough money to enable the bills to be paid. In the Church, the new electric lighting installation was completed in 1907, thus finally replacing all the old gas lighting.

Daldy re-opened the St. Peter's Mission in Terrace Road which Fisher had had to close because of falling support and lack of funds. It was soon flourishing again under the guidance of the young assistant curates. As regards St. Ambrose School the Church reached agreement with the Education Authority that each should provide accommodation for 150 children. The extensive enlargements which this arrangement involved meant an expenditure to the Church of £2,000, part of which was required for the purchase of the site. Daldy's appeal for the money which he needed for this project was made in a way that was reminiscent of Morden Bennett's outlook and approach. Daldy wrote:

> I cannot repeat too often that our aim is (1) to give the children *Education, i.e.*, the education of the whole man—body, soul, spirit. (2) to maintain at all costs *religious* education, not merely as an addition to other teaching, but as the basis of it all. For this I am asking you to make great sacrifices. At present we have only approached the edge. Let us consider, one and all, what we can do. What can I give up for the children's sake? There is no greater joy or privilege than offering what costs us much for the progress and blessing of the next generation.

Once this kind of lead was given the people of St. Ambrose themselves were most generous in their support, and a similar response was forthcoming over the completion of their Church building. Most of the actual building, to plans of the Durham architect, Hodgson Fowler, had been finished but substantial debts remained. Daldy insisted that these liabilities should be discharged as quickly as possible and the Church consecrated. In 1906 Mrs. Johnson paid £3,500 so that the tower could be erected as a memorial to her late husband. With its tower built and all the debts settled St. Ambrose Church was ultimately consecrated on 14th May, 1907. It was a great day for Patterson, the popular priest-in-charge, an important milestone along the road over which he led his district for so many happy years. He now redoubled his efforts for St. Ambrose (which he was now able to infuse with even more life and activity than before) so that, in due time, it might take its rightful place as one of the parish Churches of Bournemouth.

The year 1906 saw the transformation of the south transept at St. Peter's Church into a beautiful side-chapel dedicated to the memory of John Keble. During the previous year a generous benefactor to the Church, William Gibson, offered to pay all the expenses of converting the transept and building a new sacristy at the south-east corner. Sir Thomas Jackson, a former pupil of Scott and famed as the designer of the Examination Schools and other Oxford buildings, was engaged as architect. His plans were soon completed and approved whereupon the building contract was prepared and signed. Just as work was about to begin Gibson suddenly died and it was found that he had made no provision in his will to cover the expenses which the Church had undertaken. Fortunately Gibson's family generously agreed to confirm the arrangements and meet the expenses. Building operations started on 23rd April 1906 and the new Keble Chapel was opened by the Bishop of Southampton on St. Peter's Day just over two months later.

The only alteration affecting the exterior of the Church was the addition of the little sacristy where the priests' robes and communion plate are now kept. The porch and door which formerly led out of the transept, where the credence table now stands in the sanctuary of the chapel, were removed and the door re-erected as the outside entrance of the new sacristy. The space where it had previously been was blocked up. Access to the sacristy from the interior of the Church was made by inserting a door in the east wall of the "nave" portion of the chapel. An accompanying photograph of St. Peter's from the south-east, taken in 1880 just after Morden Bennett's death, shows the original porch and the space which is now filled in by the Keble Chapel sacristy. This picture may be compared with Kenneth Hoskin's more recent photograph of the same view which serves as the frontispiece to Nicholas Taylor's *Guide*.

The Keble Chapel was decorated and furnished inside to Jackson's designs. A flamboyant iron screen, in a style termed by Taylor as "Arts and Crafts Gothic," was put up between the chapel and the east end of the south aisle. This screen was made by Hart, Son, Peard & Co., as were the altar cross and candlesticks, which were the gifts of Mrs. Kidston, a member of the congregation. When the chapel was opened there was just a curtain behind the altar, but in 1907 the carved oak and panelled reredos, with its five painted figures, was presented in memory of Julia, widow of the Hon. John Ashley, who had died on 10th April 1907.

In his *Guide* Nicholas Taylor has described the wall paintings and other decorations which were added to the Keble Chapel in 1907-08 as inferior. "Not only are their ornamental patterns ugly," he wrote, "but they impede the sunlight, which should flow into the choir from the south side." The chapel also contains an inscription in memory of its chief donor William Gibson, recording that although he had hoped to carry out the beautifying of the transept during his lifetime it was, in fulfilment of his wish, completed by his sister and his brother's children. Daldy now had a suitable side-chapel for the weekday celebrations and other services for which only small congregations were expected. This has proved most convenient to priests and people alike. The chapel has also been much used and appreciated as a quiet and dignified place for private prayer.

Daldy now turned to the desirability of having a parish hall near St. Peter's Church. To him it was amazing that St. Peter's should be without a hall. St. Swithun's and St. Ambrose had had their halls in use for some time to the great benefit of the activities of those Churches. Daldy felt handicapped in his ministry in having no such accommodation available at St. Peter's. Fisher had earlier voiced a plea for a "parish room" soon after his arrival in Bournemouth, but nothing more tangible was achieved than the collection of a small fund. In July 1906 Daldy and his churchwardens were fortunate to find that a vacant site immediately opposite St. Peter's Church in Hinton Road was for sale. This was so suitable in every way that the opportunity was too good to be missed. The churchwardens and sidesmen met at once and decided to buy it. The price was £1,700 with an annual ground rent of £30, which Sir George Meyrick kindly offered to reduce to £15.

A faculty was applied for to divert £500 which had been collected towards a choir home to the cost of acquiring the hall. The total expense would be very substantial, but the general feeling in the parish was that, without spending too much money on embellishment, it should be possible to build a hall which would be worthy of St. Peter's. "It is better to do the thing well, even if we have to wait, than to build unsatisfactorily," was one of the remarks made at the time. In the result St. Peter's was to be able to provide itself with one of the most spacious buildings of its kind in the country.

Plans were prepared by the Church's Bournemouth architect, H. E. Hawker, for a building comprising a large hall seating about five hundred people, with platform and gallery, cloakrooms, two committee rooms, two retiring rooms and a kitchen. It was estimated that some £7,000 would be needed, of which only around £1,700 was in hand. By the end of 1906 Hawker's drawings were published and a determined appeal made for raising the money.

After two years in the parish Daldy had succeeded, as Morden Bennett had done, in finding the way not only into the hearts and souls of his congregation but into their wallets as well. Sufficient financial support was immediately forthcoming to justify a start being made on the erection of the hall in the early summer of 1907. Messrs. Jones & Seward were the building contractors and the foundation stone was laid by Lady Meyrick on St. Peter's Day. By 1908 the hall was open and ready for use. Ever since then it has proved to be a most useful centre for a wide variety of parish activities. Vestry and similar meetings no longer had to be held in the school, which was not really suitable for such functions, and permanent accommodation for a parish office was secured. As we shall see later in this narrative the hall has played a full and significant part in such important ventures as the St. Peter's Players, the Christopher Library, the Samaritans, the Sunday School and staff residences. Letting rooms at the hall when these were not required for Church purposes has generally more than offset the expenses of upkeep. After some sixty years it is perhaps relevant now to consider whether the interior might be substantially modernised and remodelled so as to make the hall even more useful for present-day parish needs.

An immediate benefit arising out of the completion of the hall was that the Society for the Propagation of the Gospel decided to come to Bournemouth in September 1908 and use it as the venue for a Missionary Summer School. Chief local organiser was the Rev. Harold Gordon Peile, M.A., who had been on the staff of St. Peter's for two years. Leachman, was was also concerned with many of the arrangements, has commented in his history of St. Peter's how valuable this missionary conference proved to be, not only to the S.P.G. but also to the parish as a whole. One direct result that Daldy probably never bargained for when he kindly offered his new hall for the Summer School was that his guests would enlist the services of the efficient Peile for a full-time position in their own organisation. Peile then left Bournemouth to become Clerical Organising Secretary of the S.P.G. for Schools and King's Messengers, an appointment he held until 1912 when he went out to Singapore where he was attached to the Cathedral staff. In 1919 Peile was appointed vicar of All Saints Church, South Acton, the parish where he had served his title when first ordained. So it can truly be said that one of the first direct results of building St. Peter's Hall was to send a priest to become a missionary.

When the hall building was complete arrangements were made for its management to be under the control of administrative trustees and a succession of vicars and prominent parishioners served in the trusteeship until in 1960 the Parochial Church Council became the trustee. The total cost of the hall and its site was just over £9,700, but all outstanding debts were paid off by 1914, by which time St. Peter's had spent a further £8,000 on yet another building enterprise, the new vestries and organ for the Church.

Before coming to these, however, there are certain other matters to relate, including an additional Church which temporarily joined the parish, Christ Church, Westbourne. This history of this curious Church goes back to 1899 when Ram was vicar of St. Peter's. In that year the Rev. George Morris felt there was an opening in Bournemouth for an Evangelical Church. He purchased a building behind the Westbourne Arcade in Seamoor Road which had originally been erected as a public hall. Morris is said to have been a former assistant curate of St. Peter's, but no evidence has been found in the Church records to substantiate this statement. It seems improbable that such an active Evangelical would have served happily under Morden Bennett or Ram, though possibly Morris had some connection with St. Peter's during the time of Harland or Ryan. However, his name does not appear in the magazine for 1880-81 among the large number of assistant clergy who came and went during those troubled years.

Morris fitted up his hall in Westbourne as a Church in the hope that as soon as it was ready for services the Bishop of Winchester would agree to have it licensed. St. Nathaniel's, as the building was called, was situated within the parish of St. Peter's, so the vicar's consent was also needed. Morris applied vainly for such permission first to Ram and then to Fisher. When both refused to co-operate he opened his chapel on a completely informal basis as an Independent Protestant Evangelical Church of England. Morris and his successors carried on a useful ministry at St. Nathaniel's for many years despite the denial of any official backing. The position of St. Nathaniel's was somewhat anomalous, for it was neither part of the Anglican Church nor affiliated to any other religious body.

In 1907 the Trustees approached Daldy about the possibility of having St. Nathaniel's regularised by the Bishop so that a priest of the Church of England could be licensed to officiate in it. Daldy agreed in principle and in 1908, with the Bishop's approval, an arrangement was made whereby St. Nathaniel's should change its name to Christ Church and become affiliated to St. Peter's. The Rev. E. A. Causton was the first licensed minister. The work of Christ Church went forward so successfully that in 1914 a new and much larger building was dedicated in the Alumhurst Road. Christ Church became independent of St. Peter's in 1921 when it was constituted a vicarage in its own right. The Rev. T. H. Lingley, who had been on the staff of St. Peter's since 1919, was inducted as the first incumbent. Christ Church remains to this day in the curious position of being within the Anglican Communion but of having no territory as a parish.

Soon after establishing himself in Bournemouth Daldy was twice honoured by the Diocese. In 1909 he was appointed Rural Dean of Christchurch (this deanery then also comprised the Bournemouth parishes) and in 1911 he became an Honorary Canon of Winchester. Daldy held these offices throughout the rest of his time at St. Peter's, relinquishing them only when he left the parish to take up duties of Residentiary Canon and Archdeacon of Winchester.

As was usual on occasions of great national rejoicing St. Peter's held a civic service in 1911 to celebrate the Coronation of Their Majesties King George V and Queen Mary. Mayor and Corporation attended in state, but there was departure from the normal procedure which angered at least one local resident who wrote to the *Echo* about it — there was no band! An indignant Mr. Henry Ebben of Boscombe Grange strongly protested at having his pleasure ruined because of the Mayor not having "his orchestra or some band to accompany him when on an important errand with the Council," pointing out that: "Last Sunday I was bitterly disappointed when I found the Coronation procession turned into a funeral one. I never remember the Corporation attending St. Peter's Church without a band, and I hope it will never again."

Had the Mayor at this time realised what sort of condition the St. Peter's organ was in he might not have risked going to Church without his band. By 1912 it had become clear that the old Willis organ was nearly worn out and hardly worth repairing. Daldy decided to try to procure a new one, which at the same time might incorporate a greater variety of stops and more modern apparatus. Contemporaneously with replacing the organ it was also decided to rebuild the vestries, which were far too small. Street's vestries of 1864 were on two floors, with choir vestry on the upper floor reached by a spiral staircase and clergy vestry at ground floor level.

In April 1913 the vicar launched an appeal for both the organ and the vestries. He was met with a most enthusiastic and generous response, though the expense was found to be much greater than he had originally thought. For instance, it had been hoped to have the organ built for about £2,300, but the contract with Messrs. Harrison & Harrison of Durham was in the sum of £2,376 and this figure did not include the electric discus blowing plant for which a separate estimate had to be obtained from Messrs. Watkins & Watson. The contract with Harrisons was made upon the basis that any valuable parts of the old instrument would be included in the new. It was stipulated that the contractors should be paid £500 upon instructions being given, £1,000 when the organ was delivered to the Church and the balance on satisfactory completion. So unsure were the vicar and churchwardens of when all this money would be available that they had written into the contract a provision that the work was not to proceed until such time as they thought they had sufficient funds in hand to justify making a start. As it turned out they need not have been so cautious, for although the total cost of the organ came eventually to over £2,700, when Mrs. Kidston heard the figure she came forward immediately to say that she would be pleased to settle it in full.

The detailed specification of the new organ was drawn up by Harrison in conjunction with Chandler and provided for an instrument of three manuals, thirty-two notes on the pedals and sixty-two drawstops. David Salwey has recorded that the late Mr. Arthur Harrison "took infinite pains with it, and had special difficulties to contend with owing to the distance of the instrument from the main body of the Church. Its position explains the different effect it has in the Keble Chapel to that from the main body of the Church. . . . In artistic design and execution there is no organ in Bournemouth to touch it, and all who love organs should hear it if the opportunity comes their way." In 1959, when Fox Robinson was vicar, a visitor to the Church who had been a friend of the builder told him: "Don't ever let anyone dismantle this organ. Only allow it to be cleaned. There can never be another Harrison — organ or organ-builder."

The organ was left caseless except for the plain dark pine panelling provided by the builders, but Ninian Comper, who was now Daldy's choice as the St. Peter's ecclesiastical architect, designed a special case for it, estimated to cost about £750. Unfortunately nobody came forward with the money for the case, so the organ was left as it was and Comper's drawing left to hang in the vestry. It would certainly improve the general appearance of the north transept if Comper's dignified design could some day be carried out.

The new vestries and organ chamber were designed by Hawker. A small room for the sacristan was provided on the ground floor next to the clergy vestry and rooms for the organ blower and storage in the basement. Messrs. Jenkins & Sons were the builders and Messrs. Aish & Co. carried out the electrical work. At the same time the heating apparatus was thoroughly overhauled and altered so as to provide for an even distribution of heat in the Church, and a large fresh air inlet was added. These heating improvements were carried out by Messrs. G. Haden & Sons of Trowbridge who had supplied the original heating plant in 1864, seventy years previously. All this work cost a lot of money, £8,000 in all, but by the end of 1914 Daldy was able to report that all but £200 had been paid or secured.

A number of other smaller additions and improvements were made to the Church at about this time, mostly under Comper's direction. Miss Bertha Evetts bequeathed £100 which was spent on a new screen between the north transept and the north aisle. Wooden font rails in the Jacobean style and a new lectern stand with iron railings were also given. The floor of the sanctuary was repaved with Fosterley marble and Hoptonwood stone in memory of George John Fenwick who had died in 1914, having been a parishioner for fifty years. Fenwick's family also provided a set of oak altar desks to replace Street's brass altar rail. It seems so out of character for Daldy to have consented to the removal of the tasteful and original altar rail, surely one of the most beautiful and attractive of the many fittings which Street designed for St. Peter's. Its replacement was an act of sheer vandalism which, even some fifty years later, is hard to forgive. The paving was installed by Messrs. Farmer & Brindley and the woodwork of Comper's ugly dark altar desks done by Messrs. J. McCulloch & Co.

While he was still alive and residing at *Crag Head* Fenwick realised that in 1913 Harry Crumpler had completed forty years' service as sacristan of St. Peter's. Fenwick suggested to Daldy that some permanent record of this honourable achievement should be placed in the Church and he gave the vicar £100 for the purpose only a few days before he died. Fenwick's money was used to install a new stained glass window, appropriately inscribed, for the east end of the north transept which was now empty because the old Willis organ had been removed. The design of the window was Comper's, representing the Annunciation of the Blessed Virgin Mary.

On 14th January 1915 the organ, vestries, Crumpler window,

altar desks and sanctuary pavement were dedicated by the Bishop of London. Chandler gave a recital to show off the capabilities of his new organ and, at a New Year Party afterwards, the parish said farewell to Mr. and Mrs. Leachman and gave a welcome to a new assistant curate Edward Blyth and his wife who had just returned to England after eleven years of chaplaincies in Egypt.

Daldy's senior priest at St. Peter's during this period of rebuilding and refurnishing was a bespectacled clergyman called Edgecombe Walter Leachman, now chiefly remembered as the parish historian. Leachman began his clerical duties as assistant curate of St. Clement's, Boscombe, from 1899 to 1901. From then until he joined the staff of St. Peter's in 1906 he worked at Camberley. He was already a keen writer. Prior to writing the history of St. Peter's he had a book *The Church's Object Lessons* and two shorter papers about prayer published by Messrs. Mowbray & Co.

St. Peter's Bournemouth came out at the end of 1915. Leachman explained in the preface that an article about the Churches of Bournemouth in *The Quiver* of February 1913 had amounted "almost to a challenge that someone should tell the story of the church of St. Peter, which has played such a prominent part in the deeper life of the town and district." He also disclosed that he decided to write the book "because of an intense love of St. Peter's ever since boyhood, because more than eight years' happy work as Senior Priest at the church provided a somewhat intimate knowledge of the place, and because no-one else appeared at the moment to be willing to undertake the task."

From inception to publication Leachman's history took only two and a half years at the most to prepare. When one considers how much time must have been spent in research, let alone in the actual writing, and what a busy life he led in the performance of his ordinary duties, it was a great achievement that he was able to produce the book so quickly. Printers and publishers were Messrs. Sydenham & Co. of the Pier Approach, Bournemouth. The Bishop of London, the Right Reverend Arthur Foley Winnington-Ingram, himself a prolific author and later a parishioner of St. Peter's after he retired, wrote the introduction in which he referred to the Church being "very strong in Bournemouth, under the sympathetic Rural Dean, Canon Daldy, who holds men of all schools of thought together, and working in entire charity with other Christian bodies."

By the time Leachman's book was printed, November 1915, its author had already left St. Peter's to be inducted as Vicar of Christchurch. Leachman's incumbency at the Priory was only of very short duration, for he left Christchurch at the end of 1916 on taking up an appointment as Assistant Secretary of the Church of England Men's Society, a position he held until 1925 when he went to another seaside town, this time as assistant curate at Holy Trinity, Hastings. He died at St. Leonards-on-Sea in 1945.

Leachman's *St. Peter's* was justifiably hailed as an excellent and most useful piece of work. It is indeed fortunate that so much of the parish history was recorded at a time when there were still people alive who could remember Morden Bennett and some of the early days. It is perhaps not surprising that a book produced so quickly should contain a few errors, but the present writer can only express here his deep sense of gratitude to Leachman whose book has been so very useful as a basis for the earlier chapters of the present work. The value of Leachman's history has, of course, diminished with the passing or time and is now so dated that it is high time another book was issued — hence the present work. Recent criticism of Leachman's *St. Peter's* by the Rev. Gordon Roe appeared in the Parish Magazine for August 1959. After referring to the fact that it contains much that is useful Roe pointed out that it is "sadly lacking in lively and relevant detail. There is, for example, practically nothing in it about the development of the worship at St. Peter's and scarcely a whisper about the life and work of assistant curates." Possibly Leachman was so modest that he mistakenly thought nobody would be interested in the activities of mere assistant clergy. Let us hope it will be considerably less than another half-century before this enthralling subject is tackled again.

CHAPTER XVII

War And Memorials

BY THE time the new organ and vestries were finished England was at war, but this did not dampen Daldy's enthusiasm for new buildings and improvements. The next thing he wanted was a mortuary chapel. "Year after year," he wrote, "I look forward to the time when there will be in Bournemouth some Chapel where the bodies of the Departed may rest in the interval between death and burial. There are others who feel the same. One, Mrs. Samuel Smith, has sent me £100 to open a Fund for building a small Chapel for the purpose. We have what I think would be an admirable site. With £1,000 I think we could do it well. Such a Chapel would, I think, be appreciated by the public and especially by the large and important class who keep hotels, boarding houses and lodging houses in the town. I hope the matter will not be allowed to drop." A number of subscriptions were given towards this project but it soon became clear that any building operations would have to be delayed until after the war.

For the time being St. Peter's contented itself with installing a War Shrine in the Church. This was completed in 1917 to Comper's design at a cost of £120. The purpose of the Shrine was to signify the simplest and deepest act of the faith, the Death of Our Saviour on the Cross, the hope and glory of the world. It was also intended as a reminder to pray for those who had offered their lives in the war.

By the end of the war £750 had been promised towards the cost of the mortuary chapel and in 1919 it was decided to proceed with the work and to dedicate the chapel as a memorial to those parishioners who had died in the recent conflict. In 1920 Comper's plans for the "War Memorial Chapel" were ready. He had designed a stone building, large enough to accommodate fifty people, to be built on an unconsecrated piece of the churchyard. Unfortunately, there had been an enormous rise in building costs in the immediate post-war years and the parish was quite unable at that stage to proceed with a project estimated to cost about £3,500, so for a second time it had to be postponed.

It was under Daldy's successor, Lumley Green-Wilkinson, that the subject of the memorial chapel was revived again in 1924. This time it was decided to abandon any question of providing a building large enough for general use and to erect a chapel big enough for the use of the parish. Comper accordingly re-designed his plans and produced drawings for a smaller building costing only about £2,600, of which £2,100 was already in hand or promised. In June 1924 a full-size skeleton framework of the chapel and its vestry was put up on the site so as to give the people a clearer idea of the size and general effect of how the building would look in the churchyard. Messrs. Jenkins & Sons gave a firm estimate in the sum of £2,523 plus 5% for contingencies and the plans were submitted to the Borough Council for approval.

Comper then had second thoughts about the site and a slightly different position was chosen, to the south of the Keble Chapel. By the end of January 1925 all the money was available and the necessary faculty obtained. The final contract, on the basis of which building operations started in May, 1925, was for £2,991 18s. 0d. to which would have to be added about £500 for furnishing, lighting, heating and path-making. At this stage it was decided to name the new building the Chapel of the Resurrection. To underline this theme Comper designed a very beautiful carving of the Resurrection to adorn the edifice. The dedication of the new chapel on 30th June 1926 was supposed to be performed by the Bishop of Winchester, but when he was unable to come Archdeacon Daldy returned to his old parish to dedicate it for him. At the same time was dedicated the inscription added to the War Shrine bearing the names of the men of St. Peter's congregation who had given their lives during the 1914-18 war.

As the Chapel of the Resurrection was not big enough to satisfy the need of the whole town for a mortuary chapel some limitation had to be placed on its use. It was agreed that it should be available for mortuary purposes in the case of all those on the electoral roll of the parish and for visitors who had been ministered to in sickness by the clergy of the parish. It might also be used for other churchpeople by arrangement with the vicar of any other parish in Bournemouth. In every case a minimum fee of one guinea would be charged towards the upkeep of the chapel. Green-Wilkinson expressed the hope that the chapel would be used by those who cared to pray and watch by the bodies of their loved ones and who might wish to have a Requiem Celebration before the body was removed for burial. "It must be clearly understood," the vicar reminded his people, "that the Chapel is intended for such use, and *not* merely as a mortuary, for which other provision already exists in the Borough. The name of the Chapel is intended to remind us of our Christian Faith in the Resurrection of the Body, and consequent reverence for the mortal remains of those who have passed over." It is a pity that the Chapel of the Resurrection is no longer used as frequently as it used to be, largely due to the increasingly common practice of funeral directors maintaining their own chapels of rest. When Daldy and Green-Wilkinson promoted the idea of the chapel difficulty was often experienced in finding a suitable place for a body to lie between death and burial where it might be in peace and accessibility, particularly in the case of those who died in hotels, lodgings and nursing homes, where a body was not ordinarily allowed to remain for more than one night.

In 1912 the parish started a Free Will Offering Scheme as a means by which members of the Church could readily make their offerings week by week and month by month. The object was to promote a systematic programme of almsgiving so that the work of the Church would be supported whether the giver actually came to a service or not. By 1915 there were 234 members in this scheme and all the money collected from it was sent out of the parish for diocesan or missionary work. Daldy pointed out that giving in this way was the scriptural method of making contributions and the most reasonable way for a parishioner to take his share in the work of the Church. By 1920 the parish was regularly and consistently supporting twenty-six different missions.

The three schools maintained by the parish were still doing very good work under Barker and had between them over three hundred pupils. In the report of the Inspector for February, 1915, the boys' school was said to be keeping up its reputation for sound and thorough work. "The written work on the whole was quite satisfactory and the singing very sweet." The girls' school also had a good report, the chief fault mentioned being over-eagerness by the pupils, some of whom were in the habit of giving wrong answers for lack of a moment's thought. In the infants department it was said that "an excellent foundation in religious knowledge is being laid." In that same year, 1915, Barker, the headmaster, had to resign due to ill-health and he was succeeded by Mr. G. C. Seeviour, an old boy of St. Michael's School in Bournemouth who was then headmaster of the West Street School at Sutton. Seeviour soon afterwards was appointed a diocesan lay reader.

In 1918 the local education authority decided to make St. Peter's Schools into a mixed school. The centre of the town was by now decreasing in population, especially among those who made use of the elementary schools, and attendances had been going down for some time. This reorganisation left the school in two departments, mixed and infants. Miss Firbank, who had been the headmistress of the girls' school for the previous seventeen years, was appointed head of the Council School for Girls at Boscombe.

The ordinary weekday services at St. Peter's during Daldy's later years as vicar consisted of daily Celebrations at 8 a.m. and on Wednesdays at 7 a.m. On Thursdays there was an additional Celebration for invalids at twelve o'clock. Matins was said on weekdays at 10 a.m. and the Litany sung on Wednesdays and Fridays at five minutes after noon. The weekday Evensong was sung at 5.30 p.m. In 1916 Daldy was complaining that he felt uncomfortable about having attendances of only twenty or thirty at the early Celebrations on weekdays.

Among the clerical staff Frederic Guy, priest-in-charge of St. Swithun's, retired in 1916 and was replaced by Maurice Bailey, who came from Otterbourne and was later vicar of East Coker, near Yeovil. Blyth went to Weymouth in 1919 as vicar of Holy Trinity and Arthur Sayer, who had been an assistant curate at St. Peter's since 1916, became Daldy's senior priest-in-charge of the Mother Church. One of the junior priests at this time was the Rev. J. L. B. James, uncle of the present vicar of St. Peter's. Despite the calls of war Daldy was able to maintain his usual large clerical staff without any difficulty until towards the end of 1917, when several of the younger priests volunteered to go as chaplains to the forces. Many were still serving in that capacity in 1919 when Daldy was trying to build up his staff again to its usual strength, but there was a national shortage of clergy and suitable men were hard to find. Changes in the value of money due to the war meant that more pay had to be found for the assistant priests. Up to 1919 the salaries paid at St. Peter's had been reasonably generous, with a minimum of £210 per annum, and the vicar remarked that when he was first ordained he considered himself fortunate to be paid £120 a year, when the usual salary for a young priest was only £80 or £100. But something now had to be done to make service at St. Peter's more attractive financially and a new scale for assistant curates was adopted, starting at £200 and rising by annual increments of £10 to £350 a year. The priest-in-charge at St. Swithun's was to receive a salary of £250 plus the Easter offering at that Church.

A major change in the position of the laity of the parish was brought in 1918 by the formation of a Church Council. This was hailed as a great advance well in keeping with the changing age which looked upon the work of the Church not merely as something to occupy the clergy but as the responsibility of the whole body. The new Council held its first meeting on 7th February, 1918; this was superceded in 1920 by the election of the first Parochial Church Council under the new laws which had then come into force. From the outset it was arranged that the Council members from each Church should also hold their own separate meetings but that any decisions made by these committees would only take effect after ratification by the full Council.

Daldy's sixteen years as vicar of St. Peter's came to an end in 1920 when it was announced in June that he had been appointed to succeed Dr. Fearon as Archdeacon of Winchester and Residentiary Canon of Winchester Cathedral. Arrangements were made for him to leave Bournemouth early in November. Though the new appointment was a great honour for the vicar, he felt some sadness at having to leave St. Peter's. "I have found such happiness here, in the Church, and in the people and the work," he wrote, "that I can hardly face leaving you all. But above and in everything I have seen the Grace of God guiding, helping, and strengthening me every day. It is the recollection of God's continuous blessing that makes it possible to face the future."

So departed from St. Peter's one of its greatest and most influential incumbents. It is hardly possible to compare the dispirited parish he inherited in 1904 with the spiritual richness which was now there for his successor to take over. On 16th December the Archdeacon and Mrs. Daldy returned to St. Peter's for their presentations from a grateful congregation:

> Proceedings began with a display of hand-bell ringing by our own team, after which Mr. Druitt took the chair, supported by Mr. Palmer. In his speech he emphasised the various aspects of the work done by our Vicar during the 16 years he has been living in Bournemouth, and pointed out how much the Parish and the whole Town owe to him for his labours, at the same time giving a resumé of what has been done in the Parish under his guidance and inspiration. He ended by handing him a framed illuminated Testimonial and cheque, and explained that among the contributors were Railway men and members of the Labour Party. In the name of the Ringers he gave him a silver inkstand in the shape of a bell, and to Mrs. Daldy he gave a leather dressing case.
>
> The Archdeacon in his reply expressed his deep gratitude for the gifts and for all the kindness he had received during his ministry at St. Peter's; he felt that what had just been given was the culmination and expression of what had been so wonderful a feature all along — the good-will and kindness of the people; one of the most difficult speeches he had ever had to make in that hall was to express his thanks adequately that day. He also referred with

real pleasure to the presence of Dr. J. D. Jones, and his friends on the Railway and amongst the Labour Party.

After Mrs. Daldy had also returned thanks and a song from the Rev. E. Heriz-Smith, an excellent tea was served.

Daldy's resignation from St. Peter's coincided with the need for making more satisfactory permanent arrangements for the separated part of the parish in which the Churches of St. Ambrose and Christ Church functioned. The people of St. Ambrose wanted to be formed into a separate parish and their Church Council representatives had unanimously passed a resolution to that effect. Patterson, who had been in charge of the district since 1888, considered that the paramount spiritual interests of St. Ambrose demanded that it should immediately be made separate and independent. The Bishop of Winchester consented to the raising of an endowment fund and Patterson and his helpers set about collecting the money. The trustees of Christ Church, who were anxious to preserve the evangelical traditions of that place, asked either to be constituted as a separate parish or to become a Proprietary Chapel. They pointed out that the agreement with Daldy had operated most satisfactorily since 1908, but they did not want to be placed under St. Ambrose and were fearful for the security of their status under whoever might be appointed as the new vicar of St. Peter's.

In November 1920 the Bishop appointed seven Commissioners "to enquire into the spiritual needs of the Parish of St. Peter's Bournemouth" and to submit a report. The Commissioners, who had among their number Archdeacon Daldy and James Druitt, were ready with their recommendations in March, 1921. In their opinion St. Ambrose district should be formed into an independent parish as soon as possible and that all the sittings in the Church should be free and unappropriated. They felt that this would be for the spiritual benefit of both St. Peter's and St. Ambrose. The new parish would contain between 4,000 and 5,000 people and its vicar would have the spiritual oversight of the Royal Victoria Hospital and the Herbert Convalescent Home. The Church had a "non-provided" Elementary School and an excellent Parish Hall. Christ Church would remain in the area of St. Ambrose with its status secured as far as possible, but the Commissioners did not think it appropriate to recommend Christ Church being formed into a new parish.

The Patron, Sir George Meyrick, gave his consent to the scheme proposed by the Commissioners. The separation of St. Ambrose would reduce the income of the vicar of St. Peter's by about £120 a year from seat rents and also mean the loss of some fees. There was some anxiety about Patterson's position because, although he intended to retire in about two years, the immediate separation of the St. Ambrose district would mean his having to leave sooner than he had anticipated. Patterson, however, was so keen on St. Ambrose becoming a separate parish that he gladly agreed to make the sacrifice. The Bishop wrote to the Archdeacon praising Patterson's unselfish conduct:

> I fully appreciate the anxiety of the Commissioners lest by action now taken any kind of slight should seem to be passed upon the Rev. J. I. Patterson. To his labours for all the long period of 31 years the District now to be made a Parish owes a very special debt: and it may well seem a matter of regret that the act of at last fulfilling its hopes of becoming a Parish should have the effect of hastening, as it will do, by two or three years, the end of his connexion with it. Mr. Patterson himself . . . is generous enough to wish that this difficulty should not be allowed to retard the separation of the District, to which he attaches great importance. And we should not really be consulting either his feelings or his interests if on his personal account we postponed what is parochially so desirable. As it is, Mr. Patterson's connexion with the District will end in universal respect.

Patterson will aways be remembered as the founder of St. Ambrose as we now know it. During his later years he organised many improvements to the fittings of the Church and arranged for the building of the Church Hall. Largely through his efforts he freed St. Ambrose of debt and in the space of just one year collected no less than £2,373 towards the endowment fund. After the Order in Council of 14th October 1921 constituting St. Ambrose a new parish Patterson stayed on in temporary charge until the arrival of the first incumbent. When he did eventually retire he remarked that he had served under five Bishops of Winchester, four vicars of St. Peter's and had worked with more assistant priests than he could number. The wishes of the people of Christ Church were not forgotten; the Bishop made Christ Church a Conventional District, with a separate Parochial Church Council.

The name of Daldy's successor at St. Peter's was announced in October 1920, before the new Archdeacon had left Bournemouth. This nominee was the Rev. Basil Sidney Phillips, M.A., a graduate of Keble College, Oxford, who had been ordained in 1900. Phillips had served in only two parishes, as assistant curate of Dorking until 1911 and, since then, as vicar of South Farnborough. In addition to his parochial responsibilities he had been Rural Dean of Aldershot since 1919. The institution of the new vicar was arranged for 11th January 1921. The Church Council passed a resolution welcoming his appointment and inviting him to a social gathering on the day of his institution and induction. Then, in November, Phillips withdrew his acceptance of the living and decided to remain at South Farnborough. He was not a very fit man and appears to have thought that the work of running St. Peter's would be more than he could manage. When his health failed to improve Phillips resigned his benefice and deanery in 1923. St. Peter's nearly saw him on Good Friday, 1924, when he was engaged to conduct the Three Hours Devotion, but at the last minute, upon his doctor's instructions, he had to withdraw.

Sayer took charge of the parish during the vacancy and the people of St. Peter's waited hopefully for news of who would be their next vicar.

CHAPTER XVIII

The Archbishop's Confidant

WHEN PHILLIPS announced that he would not, after all, be coming to St. Peter's the quest for a new vicar had to begin all over again and, early in 1921, the choice fell on the Rev. Lumley Cecil Green-Wilkinson, then rector of Ascot Heath, who was having to leave that parish because his house had been sold. As he was unable to come to Bournemouth until after Easter, Thursday, 7th April was fixed as the date for his institution and induction. So there came to St. Peter's, albeit as second choice, a true Christian gentleman in the highest traditions of the Church who became one of the most respected and beloved incumbents of all time.

Green-Wilkinson was a priest of most varied experience. A graduate of Magdalen College, Oxford, he had, during his varsity days, enlisted for the Boer War as a private soldier. Then, after his ordination in 1903 he spent five years as assistant curate of Holy Innocents, Hammersmith, where he was noticed by the young Bishop of Stepney, Cosmo Gordon Lang, who took him onto his staff as personal chaplain. From 1908 until 1912 Green-Wilkinson worked in Somers Town as Head of the Magdalen College Mission, after which he became successively rector of Aston Tirrold and Ascot Heath. In the early part of the First World War he took time off from his parish duties to serve as a chaplain with the armed forces on the Western Front.

Green-Wilkinson's close association with Archbishop Lang continued long after his chaplaincy at Stepney had come to an end and the two men remained firm friends. Lockhart, in his biography of the Archbishop, frequently mentions this long friendship. During the Stepney period Lang referred to Green-Wilkinson as "an unfailingly cheerful and unselfish companion" who, returning home with Lang after midnight following the Bishop's speaking engagements, would fry him eggs and bacon over the study fire. Lockhart also tells the story, related to him by Green-Wilkinson himself, of Lang's first motoring adventure.

> A few of the Bishop's friends wished to provide him with a motor car, but Lang, although touched by their kindness, refused the offer. Then one night in Poplar, happening to meet George Lansbury and some fellow Socialists, he told them of his decision and discovered, much to his surprise, that they thought he had made a mistake.

He withdrew his refusal, and presently a Belsize coupe turned up, complete with chauffeur. The first journey, however, was nearly a disaster. The Bishop had a Confirmation at Stoke Newington and, thanks to the Belsize, the time of departure was later than it would have been for a journey by bus or train. At last the moment arrived. Lang and his chaplain got into the car. The chauffeur began to operate the starting handle. Nothing happened. Lang, who never liked mechanical novelties, felt that his first suspicions were being amply confirmed. "This car of yours will make me late," he said reproachfully to his chaplain and, seizing his bag, hurried off to catch a bus in St. Paul's Churchyard. With his departure the car at once started. The Bishop was retrieved and off he went, to collide a few minutes later with a whisky van. Out jumped the chaplain to take the names and addresses that would be required by the insurance company, and presently returned to find an irate Bishop, shrinking back in his seat in the car, which had become the centre of a large and critical crowd. As a result of this mishap Lang, for the first time, he claimed, was late arriving at the Church, and Mr. Green-Wilkinson was told it was all his fault for insisting upon a car.

After Green-Wilkinson's induction to St. Peter's Sayer was invited to remain as senior priest, but there was a change at St. Swithun's where Bailey was replaced as priest-in-charge by Ernest Holden. Holden stayed until 1925, when he went to Southampton to serve under Daldy at St. Mary's. Another new assistant curate in 1921 was Charles Rockett, who had been persuaded by Green-Wilkinson to resign as rector of Shaftesbury so that he could join the staff of St. Peter's. Rockett succeeded Sayer as senior priest in 1923 when the latter became vicar of Westend, Southampton. Sayer exerted a great influence at St. Peter's; he was very highly thought of and, in addition to his clerical functions, acted as assistant organist.

When Sayer left, Green-Wilkinson encountered considerable difficulty in filling the vacancy on the staff owing to the shortage of available living accommodation. Sayer had had to move twice in the seven months following his marriage in 1922 and two excellent priests gave up the idea of coming to St. Peter's because they found it impossible to rent a small unfurnished house within a reasonable distance from the Church. The vicar appealed for somebody to come forward who was willing to invest some money in buying or building a house which could be let to the clergy; otherwise he would be limited in his search for a priest to one who was prepared to live permanently in lodgings.

While the problems of housing were considered Green-Wilkinson engaged as temporary assistant curate George Cuthbert Scarlin, who had recently returned to England from mission work in Costa

Rica, and gave him special responsibility for the Mission Room and district. At the beginning of 1924 Scarlin suggested a New Year's resolution to keep the Fourth Commandment:

> There are many opinions as to the observance of the Holy Day, he wrote. The meaning of the word 'holy' means to 'keep separate,' that is, Sunday is to be a different day to the weekdays. As on weekdays our minds are occupied chiefly about *material* matters, so on Sunday they should be occupied more on *spiritual* matters. We know that God is ever-present to each one of us, day by day, but when we kneel in that Presence we *realise* more fully the nearness of that Presence. Many in the Mission district could regain the assurance of the presence of God if only they would rouse themselves out of the habits of neglect or carelessness.

When Scarlin left St. Peter's for a regular curacy at Basingstoke later in 1924 the problems of housing the parish clergy were still unsolved. When Holden left St. Swithun's in 1925 the accommodation difficulties became even more acute and this time a house had to be purchased for the new priest-in-charge, Rupert Pitter, a former vicar of East Cowes, who arrived in 1926. To this end, with the aid of a loan from the bank, the parish bought a leasehold house at 15 Knyveton Road for £2,500 and the Pitter family moved in to the first *St. Swithun's House.* The vicar appealed for donations towards the purchase and also the cost of acquiring the freehold reversion from Sir George Meyrick. One fund-raising method was the issue of special collecting cards. These contained ten spaces for shilling contributions, ten for sixpenny, and sixty for penny contributions. A filled card therefore amounted to £1.

Apart from meeting large capital items like housing, the finances of the parish were still in quite a healthy state. The freehold of St. Peter's Hall was bought from Sir George Meyrick for £500 in 1921 and cleared within two years, the debts left outstanding when Daldy resigned were all paid and money was coming in steadily towards the cost of the Chapel of the Resurrection. Green-Wilkinson justifiably took some pride in the encouraging financial position, which was largely due to the Duplex Free Will Offering Scheme and the hard work in organising it that had been done by William Danby, who replaced Druitt as vicar's warden in 1922. The Duplex scheme was started in the parish on 2nd July, 1922, with the immediate result of greatly increased receipts. In the first twelve months of operation over £622 was collected in the envelopes, part of which was earmarked for the Church overseas and part for the Church at home. Nevertheless, Green-Wilkinson had some difficulty in persuading many of his congregation to join the Duplex scheme and had to continue praying for fine weather on Sundays so as to be sure of keeping up the Church collections. "Oh why," he pleaded, "won't *more* of you join such an obviously successful scheme?" It seemed strange to the vicar that out of an electoral roll of nine hundred names there should be only 210 regular contributors to the Church funds. The backbone of the parish finances was still the vicar's New Year Appeal.

One of the Church Council's activities in 1921 was to form a Budget Committee, to estimate the parish's financial requirements for the following year. The estimate for 1922 came to £4,310, made up as follows:

St. Peter's Church Expenses	£500
St. Peter's Choir Home	£350
St. Peter's Choir, Organ, Organist	£290
St. Swithun's Church Expenses, Choir, etc.	£450
Parochial Clergy Fund and Vicarage Rates and Taxes	£1,350
Poor Fund	£250
St. Peter's Churchyard	£100
Parish Magazine	£30
St. Peter's Mission Room	£60
Day Schools	£50
St. Peter's and St. Swithun's Sunday Schools	£50
Winchester Diocesan Fund, towards quota	£450
Central Church Fund Quota	£180
Parochial Missionary Association Ordination Candidates	£100
Cleaning of St. Peter's Church (Special)	£100
	£4,310

A note added at the end of the budget asked that cheques should be made out to the Rev. L. C. Green-Wilkinson, and crossed "Lloyd's Bank, Bournemouth."

One particular financial worry in the early nineteen-twenties was the cost of keeping the Choir Home going. The funds in this account had got so short that there even had to be an appeal for someone to "help with gifts of 6 pairs of sheets, 12 pillow cases, 6 bath towels and a table cloth." In 1924 it was decided by the Church Council that the money spent on food and lodging for the Choir Home boys would be more profitably expended in providing free secondary education for all the St. Peter's choirboys, who might in future be drawn from Bournemouth homes. The Choir Home was accordingly closed permanently at the end of July 1924 and the premises sub-let until the expiry of the lease in 1926. The three Home boys who were still there were boarded out at the expense of the Choir Home Fund for so long as they remained in the choir.

By 1927 only one former Home boy was still being maintained by the parish.

The Choir Home Fund was kept going with the object of trying to start a Church Secondary School when possible to do so. This idea, however, came to nought, for Green-Wilkinson's successor would have none of it and refused to become involved in matters of secondary education. Marsh wrote:

> We ought to be spending more money on beautifying the worship of the Church by improving the music. I hope you will not subscribe any further to such a problematical object as a Secondary School, but that you will subscribe largely to the beauty of our Services in supporting our Choir itself, and supplying more inspiring music. We hope to divert your generosity into a more practical and immediate channel for the Choir and the musical portion of the services.

After six months in the parish Green-Wilkinson decided to introduce a few slight changes in the services at St. Peter's. Firstly, he resolved to have a Children's Service every Sunday afternoon and to combine this with the First Evensong. This would begin at three o'clock, while the children were at Sunday School, but after the third collect the children would come across to the Church and occupy the front seats in the nave. Then, in place of the sermon, the children would be catechised and examined on their lessons, thus following the principle of the first rubric at the end of the Catechism in the Prayer Book. The vicar apologised to those adult members of the congregation who had grown used to having a sermon on Sunday afternoons, but he considered there was insufficient time to hold two completely separate services.

The large number of communicants at the Sung Eucharist on Sunday mornings worried him, so he instituted a system whereby only those who had given notice beforehand or marked the slate on arrival at Church should receive Communion. The vicar wrote:

> You will all see the practical difficulty with 300 or more persons in Church for the Celebrant to know how many communicants to prepare for. The numbers vary so much that on one occasion I had over-estimated the number by 22, and every reverent minded person will agree that this should not be.
>
> Again with such limited time at our disposal the number of communicants is partly responsible for the omission of the sermon from the only place (except for the Ordination Service and Marriage Service) where a sermon is ordered by the Prayer Book.
>
> Apart from these difficulties there is the more serious danger that with our present lack of system the 'stewards of the Mysteries' should make it easy for casual visitors to communicate without the due preparation taught in the Catechism. Many of us have known

> cases where people have only decided to communicate when others in the same seat did so. Besides this we seem to be encouraging people young enough and strong enough to come early to break the ancient custom of the Catholic Church that the Blessed Sacrament should be received before we break our fast.
> There will, in such a parish as ours, always be a number of old and delicate people whom one will expect to communicate at that service, and I shall be grateful if they will kindly send me, once for all, notice, as required by the Rubric, of their desire to do so. Where there are so many visitors, it would perhaps be rather drastic to enforce the Rubric requiring similar notice from them, but they will be requested at least to mark a slate at the doors on coming into Church.

It took a little time for the new system to be understood; only a few weeks later Green-Wilkinson was complaining that twelve people had omitted to give notice on the slates. Despite these little problems the vicar was very pleased to note a decided increase in the number of worshippers at the Sung Eucharist.

It had been the custom in Daldy's time for the parish to hold a quiet day towards the end of Lent each year. Green-Wilkinson continued this practice and was careful to tell his congregation how they should behave:

> I want to remind you that you cannot spend the 'Quiet Day' *properly* unless you take advantage of the special meals in St. Peter's Hall. If you go home you cannot help your thoughts being disturbed by letters, newspapers, and those you meet; you also lose the sense of fellowship and common aim of those taking part in such a day, and incidentally you make the expenses greater by not sharing in the cost of the meals. The 'Quiet Days' at St. Peter's have always been real ones, thanks to the convenience of St. Peter's Hall, and we must resist their becoming just a series of addresses to be attended between times on an ordinary day, as has to happen in the case of some Parishes, one has known, not so favourably placed. The 56 places in the Keble Chapel are reserved for those who have entered their names for the whole day, and it is suggested that they occupy the same seats throughout.

In June 1923 Crumpler completed fifty years as sacristan of St. Peter's; he had originally been appointed by Morden Bennett on 9th June, 1873, when still a very young man. On St. Peter's Day, which also most appropriately happened to be Crumpler's birthday, the customary parish party was held on the vicarage lawns, and this was made the occasion of a series of presentations to mark the sacristan's jubilee. The Archbiship of Wales, who was visiting the parish at that time, presented Crumpler with an illuminated address and the people's warden, W. J. Palmer, handed over the parish's gift of a cheque for £200. Crumpler was also given a

c. 1840.

THE TEMPORARY CHURCH. Two cottages, near The Square, converted into a combined Church and schoolroom.

1849.

THE PARSONAGE. The first Parsonage at Bournemouth from a lithograph by Harriet Daniell. It stood above the churchyard and was built in 1846 by Morden Bennett.

c. 1850.

ST. PETER'S CHURCH, built 1844, from the frontispiece to "The Visitor's Guide to Bournemouth."

1860.

THE PROPOSED DESIGN [above] as depicted in Brannon's "Illustrated, Historical and Picturesque Guide to Bournemouth." The engraving was presumably prepared from Street's drawings of about 1855 and show the Church as it was then intended to be built. No provision was being made, at that time, for the eastern transepts, nor for the western transepts or vestibules. Major changes were also to be made in the design of the porch, clerestory, tower and spire.

1862.

'ALL HEIGHT AND NO LENGTH.' [Opposite] The Church after the addition of the aisles and clerestory.

1865.

FROM THE NORTH-EAST. Showing the recently completed chancel and the original vestry block with its spiral staircase.

1871.

BOURNEMOUTH'S TOWN CENTRE. A view of the growing town from Richmond Gardens. The tower of the Church has still to be joined to the nave.

c. 1871.

GERVIS PLACE. The immediate surroundings of the Church showing Gervis Place and No. 1 Westover Villas.

1874.

THE SEPARATED TOWER. The tower was built some distance away from the nave, so that the western transepts, or vestibules, could be erected to fill the gap. The heap of building material on the left of the picture is for the construction of the vestibules, which were completed in December 1874. The building in the distance is Adelaide Villas on the corner of Yelverton Road.

1880.

FROM THE SOUTH-EAST. [Above] Showing Alexander Morden Bennett's grave (centre foreground) and the doorway which was blocked up when the sacristy was added in 1906. At the extreme right of the picture is one of the school buildings.

1879.

THE SPIRE COMPLETED. [Opposite] Through the scaffolding can be seen the cross and weathercock which blew down in 1880. to be replaced by the present cross, without the cock, in 1882.

1907.

ST. PETER'S HALL. [Above] Architect's drawing of the hall, then in course of erection.

1904.

THE REV. A. E. DALDY. [Opposite] One of a series of portraits of Bournemouth personalities published in "The Bournemouth Graphic." Its caption is headed: "The new Vicar of St. Peter's."

c. 1910.

THE SCHOOLHOUSE. [Above] From a picture postcard: Mr. C. T. Barker was the headmaster at this time. The schools were pulled down in 1937.

1919.

AERIAL VIEW. [Opposite] St. Peter's Church and Schools, being one of a series of Bournemouth views photographed from an aeroplane.

1938.

ST. PETER'S CLERGY. Left to right, the Rev. F. A. Sanders, the Rev. Canon Hedley R. Burrows and the Rev. H. W. M. Hearsey.

1956.

THE BISHOP OF BERMUDA. The Right Rev. A. L. E. Williams (Vicar of St. Peter's, 1946-56) just after his consecration as Bishop of Bermuda.

1962.

ST. PETER'S CLERGY. A photograph taken by the author at a garden party at the Vicarage, 18 Wimborne Road, showing (left to right) the Rev. W. H. Fox Robinson, the Rev. C. G. Sykes and the Rev. T. E. Evans.

1964.

'THE VICAR GOES ALOFT.' The re-roofing of the nave of St. Peter's.

1967.

THE REV. COLIN JAMES. Vicar of St. Peter's since 1967; the photograph was taken in 1959, while Mr. James was employed by the Religious Broadcasting Department of the B.B.C.

framed portrait of himself and an album in which was inscribed the names of all the subscribers. The vicar congratulated him upon the brave way in which he overcame his emotion and got on with his reminiscences and thanks. The formal address recorded the cordial affection and esteem in which Crumpler was held by all the clergy and parishioners "not only for the way in which you have for fifty years performed the important duties of your office, but also as a personal token of esteem and respect to you as a devout and consistent member of the Catholic Church of England." Reference was then made to Crumpler having served faithfully under six vicars, and that these times had not always been easy: "During the troubles and uncertainties that prevailed after Mr. Bennett's death you remained faithful and true in your allegiance to St. Peter's and its traditions, and to his immediate successor you proved a very friend in need, and when in God's great providence St. Peter's became itself again, no one felt the joy and happiness more than you." It was indeed a happy occasion, for, as was well known, Crumpler was a friend of everyone who had been connected with St. Peter's during those fifty years.

Green-Wilkinson recalled many years later that when he came to St. Peter's he was naturally anxious about attempting to satisfy the high standards to which Crumpler had been accustomed during forty-eight years, under six vicars. After some weeks the new incumbent ventured to suggest a slight change of custom and was touched by the readiness with which Harry fell in with his request. He just said, "You must forgive me if at first I sometimes forget; after so many years I get forgetful about any change." Crumpler was a venerable-looking old man with a charming personality and completely identified with the Church. The story is told of the small boy sent to the Church with a note for the vicar who said he could not find the vicar but had given the message to St. Peter!

When Green-Wilkinson went away for his summer holiday in August 1925 the Rev. P. Oakley Hill, vicar of Christ Church, Hoxton, came to Bournemouth where he stayed at the vicarage and helped with the services at St. Peter's. Hill has left us some interesting impressions of St. Peter's at this time. Under the heading *Beautiful Bournemouth* he wrote about his working holiday:- "My previous knowledge of Bournemouth had been the little one gains on fleeting visits to preach, as an East London priest, for the East London Church Fund. Now one has had the privilege of getting to know Bournemouth in its beauteous summer garb, and filled with holiday visitors, and, best of all, to get into heart-to-heart touch with the St. Peter's and St. Swithun's congregations as a temporary member of the staff. Coming from the poor surroundings of a Hoxton Parish, one much appreciates the physical and spiritual beauties of St. Peter's; its great number of devout woshippers; their generous giving; the service of praise so well rendered by Organist and Choir; the very lovely and dignified Sung Eucharist; the due order of daily celebrations and choir offices, most of them in the delightful Keble Chapel; the devoted band of men, officials and servers; and, last, but not least, the keen and 'live' type of priest you have on the clerical staff. I have not had the pleasure of meeting your Vicar face to face, but all that I have seen at St. Peter's is a reflection of what he must be, and I know him through knowing his Church. I go back to 'the daily round, the common task' of strenuous East London work, reinvigorated in mind and body, and thankful to know that St. Peter's is interpreting to its own large congregation, and to thousands of visitors, the same Catholic teaching of our beloved Anglican Church."

A very important and far-reaching reform carried out at St. Peter's under Green-Wilkinson was the abolition of the antiquated system of pew rents, which had been in operation since the earliest days and provided the vicar with the bulk of his income. But it was a system not in accordance with modern thought that all seats in Church should be free. Pew rents meant that barriers were set up in Church between residents and visitors and between the rich members of the congregation who could afford to reserve the best seats and the poorer members who could not. Furthermore, the scramble for such vacant seats as there were involved an undignified disturbance to the worship of the Church because people without rented seats were not permitted to take the vacant places until the choir entered for the commencement of the service. Green-Wilkinson rightly complained about these disturbances, as a result of which the churchwardens wrote to all the seatholders asking for their help in getting others into any empty places at an earlier time.

During Daldy's incumbency, when the vicar was able to collect pew rents from three Churches, the income from that source was over £500 a year, compared with little more than £150 from the endowment. The financial implications of any reform of the system could not therefore be ignored, and if the seats were to be made free some provision would have to be made to augment the vicar's stipend.

The first approach towards reform was made in 1924 when the Seat Rent Committee sent a circular to all the 148 seatholders asking them to express their opinion of the existing system. Of these, 108 replied and their answers were so evenly divided (forty-eight for retention of pew rents and sixty in favour of free seats) that the Committee felt itself in some difficulty in framing a definite recommendation to the Church Council. It was, however, decided that an endowment fund should be opened before doing away with seat rents and that everyone on the electoral roll of the parish who was not a seatholder should be asked how much they would guarantee to an endowment fund if all the seats were made free. The Church Council hoped to be able to raise enough money to provide £500 annually for the vicar's stipend in lieu of the seat rents. For this to be realised it was estimated that a capital sum of at least £8,000 would be required.

At this same time the Church Council also resolved that the churchwardens should be requested to entertain no new applications for the renting of seats. The situation was not entirely satisfactory to the vicar because although he felt it was a wise decision to make the seats free there was as yet no certainty that the loss of the rents from his stipend would be made up from other sources. He feared that his income would become steadily less, as seatholders died or moved, until it disappeared altogether.

Fifty-four seatholders who agreed to give up their seats promised to give £118 a year to a Vicar's Stipend Fund and ninety-two people who did not rent seats promised £94 a year upon condition that the pew rent system was abolished.

> I cannot but believe, wrote the vicar, that once the step is taken, subscriptions will be forthcoming to make up the £400 per annum which used to be derived from seat rents in the two Churches before boarding-houses began to swallow up the private residences. The Vicar of St. Peter's will always be dependent upon the congregation for his stipend, and if the seats are empty he will be starved out, whether there be seat rents or subscriptions to the Vicar's Stipend Fund, but in the latter case he will at least have reason to hope that it will be someone's business to see that his stipend is not annually decreased by about £40, as happens at present!

Green-Wilkinson was quite correct in saying that his income from the pew rents was being steadily eroded. When St. Ambrose became independent about £120 annually was lost from that Church and the figures for St. Peter's and St. Swithun's were showing a marked decline, £440 in 1922, £400 in 1923, and £360 in 1924. The final decision was taken in January, 1925 when the Annual Church Meeting approved, with only two dissentients, the abolition of seat rents in both Churches as from Low Sunday, 19th April, 1925; since that date all the seats have been free. More contributions to the endowment fund were collected and many of the former seatholders kept up payment of their rents by transferring the money to the Vicar's Stipend Fund. Green-Wilkinson's confidence was not misplaced, for in the year ended Easter, 1926 he received a greater income from the Stipend Fund than he had got from seat rents in the previous year. By 1926 the Church Council was so encouraged by the response that it decided to guarantee a fixed sum annually towards the vicar's stipend.

The freeing of the seats was a great thing for the parish, ridding it of an outmoded system with which progressive elements in the Church could hold no sympathy and enhancing the dignity of the worship by avoiding the waiting queues and the rush for spare seats before Matins.

Another change in the seating arrangements at St. Peter's which was made at this time was the fixing of the chairs in the Keble Chapel. It had been the custom to place these chairs facing east for the weekday services and to turn them around for Sundays so that they faced north. Green-Wilkinson found this practice rather inconvenient and furthermore it gave the elderly sacristan a great deal of unnecessary work in having to move all the chairs every Saturday and Sunday night; so in 1926 all the Keble Chapel seats were fixed facing east.

The last important change introduced by Green-Wilkinson into the worship of St. Peter's was to substitute *The English Hymnal* for *Hymns Ancient and Modern*. By the end of 1926 the Church's stock of hymn books had become very low, due to what the vicar described as the shocking way in which people had been taking them from the Church. As examples of this, the vicar instanced that stamped copies of these books had recently been returned from a second-hand bookshop in Swansea and from Basingstoke Parish Church. As a new stock of hymnals had to be purchased in any case, Green-Wilkinson felt that the time was ripe for the adoption of the newer English Hymnal, which was already being used in over a thousand Churches and in many Cathedrals. It was pointed out that the English Hymnal contained all the best of the hymns in the older book, together with a number of beautiful translations of old hymns, and some new ones. The vicar promised that the old favourite hymns would still be sung and that the new hymns and tunes in the English Hymnal would be introduced with tact and consideration. Five hundred copies of the new book would be needed and of these Danby, the vicar's warden, promised to give one hundred. The congregation were encouraged to contribute towards the cost, or better still to buy their own copies, which were available at prices from a shilling upwards.

St. Peter's and St. Swithun's started using the new hymn book at the beginning of February 1927, and for several Sundays congregational practices were held at 6.15 p.m. before Evensong so that the people could begin learning some of the new music. The change was soon found to be a great improvement and the English Hymnal has been used in the parish ever since. However, as it turned out, the new book was only introduced in the nick of time; for by the end of 1927 there was a new incumbent who made it clear that, apart from the Eucharist hymns, he much preferred the Ancient and Modern with Second Appendix. A later organist of St. Peter's, Michael Peterson, writing in 1958, referred to the reasons for the change of hymnal with obvious approval:

> By about 1900 Hymns Ancient & Modern had become the standard book for the Anglican Church. A. & M. was a landmark in the history of hymnology and was a fine tribute to the high ideals of the Victorian age, but on the musical side the compilers were, perhaps understandably, influenced by some of the less desirable features of the period. . . . In 1906 appeared the English Hymnal, of which the musical editor was Vaughan Williams. In this hymnal, treasures from the past were recovered and included, and folk music which had been edited was restored to their original forms; melodies were pressed into service.

He noted that A. & M. contained:

> many tunes, edited to conform to Victorian ideas of churchiness and music often included which was trivial and frankly sentimental.

Throughout his ministry at St. Peter's Green-Wilkinson was trying to preserve and extend the sense of social fellowship among his congregation, and particularly among the younger people. A firm step in this direction was the formation in May, 1926 of the St. Peter's Players Dramatic Club, which has functioned as a very active parish organisation ever since. The vicar became the first president of the Players, with Rockett as vice-president. Miss B. E. Dean of 46 Old Christchurch Road was the original secretary. The first performance by the Players took place in St. Peter's Hall on Saturday, 13th November, 1926. There was a matinee at three o'clock, followed by an evening performance at eight o'clock. Tickets, at 3s., 2s., and 1s., could be obtained from members of the club or from the Dousona Gramophone Company at 108 Old Christchurch Road. The plays presented were *Always Polite,* a short sketch by Herbert C. Sergent, and *My Lord in Livery,* by S. Theyre Smith. The proceeds were given in support of the St. Peter's Rangers and Girl Guides. Unfortunately, 13th November was a very wet day and the audience not as large as had been hoped. However, it was a most enjoyable entertainment; the Players had made a good beginning. The second effort, and the first full-length play, was a three-act farce called *Jane* which was presented on Saturday, 23rd April, 1927. This play was repeated in the autumn in honour of the Prince of Wales' visit to Bournemouth. In their early days, in addition to their dramatic activities, the Players were starting to form an orchestra; they also had an enthusiastic lawn tennis section.

The last two years of Green-Wilkinson's incumbency at St. Peter's saw the parish concerned with two very different matters of national importance. In 1926, at the time of the General Strike, the railwaymen used St. Peter's Hall as their headquarters and two special Church services were held at the men's request. St. Peter's had been associated with the Trade Unions over a long period since for many years the National Union of Railwaymen and other unions had held their regular executive committee meetings in the hall, the railwaymen meeting there every Friday night. When the strike came, the tructees, with the approval of the police, made the hall available to the men whenever it was not otherwise booked, a step which helped considerably in the avoidance of any public disorder. Green-Wilkinson was delighted to have this opportunity for the Church to play a practical part in trying to maintain Christian ideals in the minds of those engaged in these industrial disputes. Then, in 1927, came arguments of another kind, this time over the proposed new Anglican Prayer Book, which Parliament eventually refused to accept. The people of St. Peter's studied the new book and welcomed it, for it would have authorised a number of practices to which St. Peter's was already accustomed and represented a distinct advance in a Catholic-minded direction. Both Green-Wilkinson and his successor advocated support for the new book and hoped that its use would become lawful; both were disappointed when the measure was defeated.

The end of Green-Wilkinson's incumbency at St. Peter's came fairly suddenly. For some years the vicar had been troubled by an increasingly croaky voice which got worse during the winter months and had become particularly bad since Steptember, 1926. He sought the opinion of several throat specialists who reached the decision that his tonsils would have to be removed, and that after the operation he would have to undergo further treatment for his throat and for arthritis in his knees. The doctors were unable to say how long the vicar's incapacity was likely to last and strongly advised him to resign. This advice Green-Wilkinson felt bound to accept, and explained the position at the Annual Church Meeting on 22nd February, 1927. "The indefinite absence of a vicar from such a parish as this," said Green-Wilkinson, "cannot but harm the life of the parish, unless he intends to remain for a really considerable time after his return, and this for various reasons I do not feel able to contemplate, though I had hoped to remain for a year or two more. So, after consulting the Bishop and others who know all the circumstances and have read the medical reports, I have decided to resign the benefice after Easter. The sooner this decision is made known the better chance there is of a new vicar taking up the work when I lay it down, and above all things, a long vacancy should be avoided."

In his address to the Annual Church Meeting Green-Wilkinson explained that the decision to resign had not been come to lightly. He had spent six years in one of the best appointed parishes in the country with a beautiful Church and many material advantages, but he felt God was calling him to leave and that perhaps it was not good for any priest to enjoy such material and spiritual luxury as St. Peter's provided for too long.

The people of the parish received the news with profound regret, for both the vicar and Mrs. Green-Wilkinson had earned the deep affection of everyone connected with the two Churches. It was said that no priest could have dedicated himself more thoroughly to his parish. Green-Wilkinson's departure was marked by a record Easter offering and the presentation to him of an eighteenth century mahogany bookcase by Hepplewhite. The operation on the vicar's tonsils was performed on the very day that his resignation took effect, 30th April, 1927, and soon afterwards he was able to go abroad to commence his recuperation.

The practical results of the six years of Green-Wilkinson's incumbency were by no means inconsiderable. He had got to grips with the changed values of money and political attitudes which had followed the war, he had freed the parish of the antiquated system of pew rents, he had brought into use a more up-to-date hymnal, and had arranged for the building and furnishing of the much-needed Chapel of the Resurrection.

Though Green-Wilkinson himself died in 1949, the family name remained an honoured one in the Anglican Church. His son Oliver, who was a schoolboy in the twenties, took Holy Orders after the Second World War and became Archbishop of Central Africa.

The Archbishop, whose untimely death in a motor accident in 1970 brought sadness to his many friends, disclosed on a recent visit to Bournemouth that it was at St. Peter's that he found his vocation for the sacred ministry; it was also the Church at which he made his first Communion after being confirmed. And if you look at the subscription list for the building of the Chapel of the Resurrection you will see that the young Oliver contributed ten shillings.

After retiring from St. Peter's and regaining his health, Lumley Green-Wilkinson went back to the service of his old friend Archbishop Lang, who had just been translated from York to Canterbury, and they remained constant companions for many years. Lang was full of gratitude for Green-Wilkinson's devotion, referring to him as his "invaluable controller of the household" and even going so far as to say that he ought to have been either a valet or a nurse. Green-Wilkinson's duties at this time have been described by the Archbishop in the following words:

> True, he was only an extra-non-resident chaplain; but he was very often an acting chaplain on all sorts of occasions, Consecrations, etc., including the Coronation; and his ever cheery presence came constantly like sunshine into Lambeth. He took over all my financial affairs, paid the wages, kept the accounts . . . and so took off by shoulders a burden which by nature I am very incapable of bearing. I can never express what I owe to his service, then and ever since.

After attending the elderly Archbishop at the Coronation of King George VI, Green-Wilkinson was heard to remark, "Thank God that is over!"

CHAPTER XIX

Financial Crisis

GREEN-WILKINSON'S successor as vicar was an older man, the Rev. Hubert Henry Lovatt Lloyd Marsh, M.A. (Oxon.), who had been ordained in 1897 and had spent the whole of his clerical career in the northern part of England. From 1904 to 1909 he was Precentor of Manchester Cathedral and thereafter successively vicar of Sutton-on-Trent (1909-12), St. Andrew's, Derby (1912-18) and St. Peter's, Mansfield (1918-27). Since 1922 he had been Rural Dean of Mansfield and since 1924 Honorary Canon of Dunham in Southwell Minster. Instituted and inducted at St. Peter's on Whitsun Eve, Saturday, 4th June, 1927, Marsh noted that the great difference among the congregation between Bournemouth and Mansfield was that at St. Peter's there were fewer Dukes, Duchesses and Miners.

In his first message to the people of St. Peter's Marsh said that the pleasure he anticipated in sharing in the beauty of the worship of his new Church was "closely mingled with a sense of unworthiness and timidity." Marsh's incumbency was not one of the happier nor more progressive episodes in the history of St. Peter's, for he lacked some of the friendliness and kindness of his predecessors. Those who dared to hold opinions contrary to his own were wrong, so confident was he of the infallibility of his own views. If something was not to his liking it was not his usual way to mention it quietly behind the scenes; a public rebuke was far more likely. He issued instructions to his people on how to behave in Church in a way which even young confirmation candidates would have found insulting, and on one occasion he tried to teach his congregation how to recite the Lord's Prayer *his* way. The unfortunate result of this behaviour was the division of his congregation into those who supported him and those who did not.

He had hardly arrived in the parish before broadcasting severely critical views about the Church music, especially the psalter and the "unknown, cold and severe hymns" of the English Hymnal. Marsh was himself an expert musician and clearly in a position to be helpful in bringing about some improvements, but the manner of his approach was tactless in creating serious issues out of a number of minor problems which could have been solved easily in other ways.

But the new incumbent wanted everything changed at once, and the dictatorial tones he adopted in expressing his opinions made it seem as if he was being unreasonably critical of previous vicars and the musical traditions of St. Peters. If he had troubled first of all to gain the confidence of his congregation he might well have found a ready acceptance of his ideas. He spoke of the Briggs & Frere psalter as harassing and distressing those who would seek God and His Love and demanded its abolition. The English Hymnal he thought frigid and anaemic, and many people believed he meant to revert to Hymns Ancient and Modern.

Throughout all this the vicar had some excellent suggestions to make about the music, on which he was an undoubted authority, and was at pains to explain that his proposals were made with the object of keeping up to date and making the worship acceptable to the congregation, many of whom were far from satisfied with the chants and hymns then in use. Aestheticism was all very well for the St. Peter's Sung Eucharist, which Marsh believed was "the most perfect in England (provided we could get one more tenor)," but for Matins and Evensong it was "entirely contrary to the spirit of England." There should be a repertoire of at least sixty grand anthems and preferably no settings for the canticles. If only Marsh had made his proposals more tactfully and used more amicable terms in expressing his views he would probably have commanded universal support and respect; as it was he quickly marked himself out as a vicar who was likely to be "difficult"—and so it proved.

But there were some mitigating features. It was Marsh who urged the women of St. Peter's to start a Mother's Union branch in the parish:—

> First, it is the greatest Union of Christian women the world has ever known, numbering over 500,000 women. Secondly, the members are pledged to uphold the sanctity and indissolubility of the marriage tie. Thirdly, members are pledged to encourage parents to feel their responsibility in training their children, who are the future fathers and mothers, to live pure and Christ-like lives. Fourthly, they are pledged to organise in every place a Branch of the Mothers Union, which will unite in Prayer, and by their own example lead the homes of that place to maintain that happiness which has been the strength of English family life in the past, and which it should be the object of every Englishwoman to hand on as a tradition for future generations.

The challenge was accepted, and by the early part of 1928 the St. Peter's Branch of the Mother's Union was fully established, with Mrs. Marsh as the first Enrolling Member.

Ready for any opportunity to show off his musical prowess,

Marsh played the piano at a United Parochial Concert at the old Winter Gardens on 14th January, 1928. He gave four solos and accompanied the Bournemouth Municipal Orchestra in Mendlessohn's *Capriccio Brilliante.* The vocalist at this concert was Mrs. Eric Southam, wife of the vicar of St. James, Pokesdown, and better known in musical circles as Miss Margaret Champneys. The proceeds of the performance were divided between the two Churches. In February the vicar played at a benefit concert for the orchestra and repeated the Mendlessohn Capriccio by special request.

There were many changes among the assistant clergy and principal parish officers during Marsh's early years; even some of the new curates only stayed a few months. Among the newcomers was Henry Lewin, from Australia. Rockett, the senior priest whose young wife died in 1929, left in 1930 to work with Daldy at St. Cross, Winchester. At the end of the same year the Mission Room was closed and its altar and equipment given to Wool Church in Dorset which was ministering to the soldiers in the Tank Corps. A notable arrival in 1928 was the young Leonard South, appointed to work under the elderly Crumpler. South thus began his long and honourable association with St. Peter's as assistant sacristan and, later, sacristan, which lasted, broken only by service in the armed forces during the war years, until 1963. There were also changes among the churchwardens. Palmer, after twenty years as people's warden, contracted a very serious illness in 1928 which compelled him to resign; and when he died in 1930 he had completed forty-five years continuous service as an official of the Church. The silver tea-service which the parishioners presented to him as a token of their thanks for all he had done is still a treasured and regularly used possession of the writer's family. A special vestry meeting was held for the purpose of appointing a new people's warden in place of Palmer and the parish was treated to the spectacle of the first contested election since the time of Morden Bennett, George Cookman being successful with 62 votes against twelve cast for F. T. Hawker. Cookman continued to hold office until 1935 when he was succeeded by his predecessor's son, Colonel Charles Palmer. Another Charles Palmer, formerly a vicar in New Zealand, became one of the assistant curates of St. Peter's in 1929. Soon after Marsh was inducted Danby, the vicar's warden, died and was succeeded by Admiral Francis Miller, who also took over responsibility for running the Duplex Free Will Offering Scheme. In 1929 Miller refused re-appointment and Colonel R. J. Malet became vicar's warden in his place, followed in 1932 by Allan Webber.

In his determination to beautify the worship of St. Peter's Marsh decided that the reredos needed restoring with paint and gilt, so that the figure of Our Lord in Glory and the Angels might "flash down the Church and attract worshippers to the symbol of the perfect worship in Heaven." Messrs. F. de Jong & Co. of Camden Town gave an estimate for £85, but fortunately it was found possible to engage a local artist, H. J. Harding, who carried out the work for £53 10s. 0d. Mrs. Byass kindly met the expense of the restoration as part of a memorial to her late husband. The work was completed in 1929.

The vicar and Archdeacon Daldy would have liked to see the roof and all the painted portions of the chancel and sanctuary renovated at the same time, but this would have been a very costly business and more than the state of the Church's finances would allow, though it was found possible to restore some of the murals. Finance was now becoming a troublesome feature of Church life and there was a growing anxiety about money matters. In 1927 the Church Council had guaranteed £500 a year towards the vicar's stipend in lieu of seat rents and Chandler's salary was raised from £175 to £200. But despite cutting down expenses wherever possible the accounts for 1928 ended with large deficits and the parish was only able to meet a very small part of its diocesan obligations. In 1929 the position got worse and the outlook for 1930 seemed very grim indeed, though several prominent parishioners gave what help they could. One of these was Mrs. Evelyn Newman, assistant organist since before her marriage, who gave up her salary and provided her services gratis. Her duties as assistant organist involved her in carrying the whole burden of the St. Peter's music for a period of five months in 1932 while Chandler was very ill. Mrs. Newman is, of course, well-known as one of the great stalwarts of St. Peter's; the contributions she has made over the years to both the spiritual and material sides of parish life are immeasurable.

It was at about this time that another lady, Miss Jeannie Deane, began her long and unbroken record of service to St. Peter's in making contributions of a different kind, book reviews for the *Parish Magazine*. Soon after passing the Lambeth Diploma Exam in 1931 Miss Deane published her first review—of a book called *In the Heart of South London*. She recalls:— "I thought Canon Marsh had a mind more social than theological, and picked the book accordingly, and sent the review offering to do others if he thought it might be a worthwhile 'feature' in the Magazine for visitors and others. I don't remember whether he accepted orally or in writing, but anyhow he seemed quite pleased, and that was that." Thereafter, month after month, Miss Deane has enlivened and enriched the parish records by a long series of reviews and book lists. Throughout this painstaking enterprise she has concentrated on books which the lay churchgoer may find interesting or useful, dealing with them in a straightforward way that does not presuppose knowledge which the layman does not possess, and has neither time nor inclination to acquire. There can be few parishes which have been so comprehensively and entertainingly kept abreast of religious literature.

The most far-reaching change for the parish carried through during Marsh's incumbency was the sale of the vicarage, most of the proceeds of which were used to establish an endowment for the living. The value of the benefice during the early years of St. Peter's was very small. The endowment provided by the Gervis trustees in 1845 was £50 per annum and, apart from the free use of the parsonage which had been built at his personal expense, this is all Morden Bennett regularly received. By 1890, when Fisher was inducted, the net income, according to *Crockford's Clerical Directory* for that year, was £150. By 1930 Marsh was receiving an income of about £800, most of which had to be raised within the parish, including the sum of £500 guaranteed by the Parochial Church Council. *Crockford's* for 1929 gives:— "Tithe Rent Charge £50; Queen Anne's Bounty £29; Ecclesiastical Commissioners £64; Fees £50; Easter Offering £288; Stipend Fund in lieu of Pew Rents £322; Gross and Net Income £805 and house." The effects of the situation were firstly that the resources of the parish were being severely taxed in providing a stipend, and secondly that, in spite of the guarantee, the living could only be accepted by a priest who had some private means at his disposal which he was prepared to spend in the course of his work.

As early as 1913, in Daldy's time, the vicar had decided that steps should if possible be taken to secure an adequate endowment of the living. One of Daldy's suggestions was to sell the vicarage and buy a cheaper one, but his efforts met with no success because the patron refused his consent and there were other legal complications. In 1930, a year of financial anxiety both for the nation and for the parish, Marsh resolved to try again. The Parsonages Measure, 1930, an enactment of the Church Assembly, had simplified the legal procedure, and the patron had indicated his willingness to co-operate. The timing of the scheme coincided with a report of structural defects which had become apparent in the fabric of the vicarage, and Marsh knew that heavy expenditure would soon have to be laid out in repairs if the house was to be retained.

Accordingly, in October, 1930, the Church Council passed a resolution "that in order to relieve the parish from the necessity of providing the Vicar's stipend it is desirable that the vicarage should be sold and the proceeds placed with Queen Anne's Bounty for the benefit of the living." Marsh felt that the people of the parish would be grateful if the sale of the vicarage meant abolishing the great burden to the congregation of providing a stipend whilst money was so sorely needed for assistant clergy and the maintenance of both Churches. Approval of the projected sale was obtained from the Bishop of Winchester and all other interested parties, including Daldy in his capacity of Archdeacon. Then the troubles began.

It is not intended here to praise or condemn either side in the disputes which followed. The unfortunate fact is that the vicar, supported by the churchwardens and a small majority of his congregation, was actively opposed at almost every turn by a substantial minority of the people. It is probably fair to say that, with his customary want of tact, the vicar failed adequately to explain his true intentions and the reasons for them until the transaction was well advanced. He seems entirely to have discounted the possibility that he might have been mistaken or that other people might hold differing views. The opposition party felt that the vicar was forcing his own opinions upon the parish and had been panicked by the pressures of financial urgency into taking precipitate action which would eventually prove to have been unjustified. Mounting criticism of the vicar, particularly of his proposal to buy *Inglethorpe,* 24 Manor Road, as the new vicarage, created a rift within the parish just at the very time when it ought to have been closing its ranks in the face of its difficulties.

The sale of the old vicarage was arranged by Messrs. Rebbeck Brothers towards the end of 1930. The price agreed was £31,000, part of which would have to be spent on the new house. Marsh undertook to vacate the vicarage by Midsummer 1931 and announced that he wanted to buy Inglethorpe. The vicar said he thought he should live among the majority of the residents in that part of the parish and this particular house was the only suitable one available. When consideration of the purchase came before the Church Council on 5th January, 1931 the vicar and Mrs. Marsh deliberately stayed away so as to allow members to express their views openly without embarrassment. However, in view of much criticism and as a compromise, it was resolved to defer the question of purchasing Inglethorpe for the time being in order to see whether any other house became available. Marsh was naturally very disappointed at the delay, fearing that he might lose the house to another buyer. He increased his efforts to have his proposal approved and on 9th February a sub-committee was appointed to report to the Church Council. The Council met the following week to consider the sub-committee's report and decided, by the narrow majority of 21 votes to 17, to proceed with the purchase.

This rather grudging approval by the parishioners enabled the vicar to go ahead with his plans, but other complications then arose. In the first place, Marsh wanted to take possession of Inglethorpe before the sale of the old vicarage was completed, but Queen Anne's Bounty refused to advance the money, so the vicar had to borrow it personally. Furthermore, the Bishop had second thoughts about the wisdom of the transaction and, in an effort to avoid any difficulty with the diocesan authorities, extracted an undertaking from the vicar that, in the event of his successor not wanting to live at the new vicarage, he would be personally responsible for any loss on re-sale up to the figure of £500. Considering that Marsh had persuaded Sir George Meyrick, the patron of the living and the ground landlord of the estate on which the house stood, to part with the freehold reversion of the property, the demand for the undertaking must have seemed a rather harsh proviso.

During the negotiations the vicar complained that he had "got more kicks than ha'pence" but, having moved into Inglethorpe in June, 1931, he went to great pains to explain why he had insisted on making the change. "The parish," he wrote, "could no longer afford to maintain a vicar, and the only way to secure a vicar for all time was for the present vicar to sacrifice his home, and sell up the one available asset and establish the parish for the future." He was very proud of the congratulations he received from Archdeacon Daldy for "having accomplished a great thing for St. Peter's." Looking back at the troubled negotiations, Marsh recalled, "Every conceivable difficulty has been placed in the way from the beginning, and if it were a private matter one would be inclined to have nothing further to do with it . . . it is the work for a man of thirty to have tackled at the beginning of his career . . ." Marsh himself was exactly twice that age. Even when the proceeds from the sale of the old vicarage were received the incumbent was not allowed to settle down in complete peace, for the new vicarage was besieged with begging letters seeking donations for charity out of the riches which some people believed had found their way into the vicar's pocket.

When Marsh left St. Peter's in the summer of 1935 he had the pleasure of knowing that his successor would have an assured income of £1,300 a year. He wrote at the time: —

> With great difficulty, with opposition from those less gifted with vision, with eighteen months serious anxiety and with considerable personal expense I made use of the one asset which St. Peter's possessed in the material world, the former vicarage. It was not old enough to have any traditions, and very few parishioners made use of it. I sold it and created a possible income which should relieve the parishioners of the burden of providing for a vicar. The vicar's stipend was established for ever. Otherwise there would now be no vicar at all.

On 20th February, 1932 an article highly appreciative of Marsh's work in endowing the benefice and meeting the changed conditions of the parish appeared in the *Bournemouth Daily Echo*. After referring to the fact that the central area of Bournemouth had been denuded of its residential population, the writer continued: —

> The Vicar and Congregation of St. Peter's Church, the Mother Church of Bournemouth, faced up to the financial consequences of the transformation in the character of the parish. . . . Canon Marsh has set what can only be described as a noble example. He is making a sacrifice amounting to £700 a year as part of a re-arrangement which will provide a permanent endowment of the benefice by which an incumbent is for all time assured to the parish. By relinquishing £500 hitherto subscribed by the congregation for his stipend, and taking upon himself the payment of rates and taxes and dilapidations hitherto paid by the Church Council, amounting to £200, the Vicar is making a sacrifice of what many men of his years and attainments would regard as a comfortable competence. And it is all the more worthy when certain facts are recalled, for neither length of association nor gratitude for a care-free incumbency can have occasioned it.

Any financial sacrifice on the vicar's part was, of course, temporary, for during the remainder of his tenure of the living Marsh was able to draw the increased stipend now produced from the income arising from the net proceeds of the sale and purchase. Soon after the sale the old vicarage was pulled down and the Bath Hill Court flats now stand on the site.

It will probably remain a matter of some controversy as to whether Marsh should be regarded as a benefactor to the parish or as a man who panicked himself into forcing wrong ideas upon his congregation. There can be no dispute that selling the old Parsonage resulted in providing a generous endowment of the living which St. Peter's had previously lacked, but nevertheless he insisted on selling one of the town's most valuable sites at a time when the Church's financial troubles were not really as bad as he believed they were, and when property prices were low. What would the site be worth today?

Though the traditional June garden parties were given up after the sale of the old vicarage Marsh was always trying to do what he could to preserve and extend the social side of parish life. The following is an example of this sort of activity, an account of the 1934 New Year parties:

> By the kind invitation of the Vicar and Mrs. Marsh two delightful parties were held at the Hall on Wednesday, January 3rd. In the afternoon from 3.30 p.m. to 6 p.m. the Vicar and Mrs. Marsh greeted nearly two hundred friends, who afterwards were afforded the opportunity of social intercourse whilst tea was served. The Mayor and Mayoress of Bournemouth were present during the afternoon, and music was supplied by Miss Helen Boyd's Trio, and in addition, to the delight of all present, the Vicar played three pianoforte solos with a charm greatly appreciated by all.
>
> In the evening the Vicar and Mrs. Marsh entertained a further company of about three hundred from 8 p.m. till midnight. The first portion of the evening was devoted to the production of two one-act plays, produced by Mr. Thos. Marsh; the casts included Mrs. Barry, Mrs. George Parsons, Miss de Horsey, Miss Dyson, Miss Colville, Col. Stenhouse, Mr. Hilary Watts, Mr. Rupert Widsen, and Mr. Thos. Marsh; both plays were extremely well presented, and gave great delight to the audience, who showed their appreciation by loud and continued applause. In connection with their production Mr. Marsh is anxious to express his great appreciation to Mr. Arthur Davis and Mr. R. Dear for all the help they afforded him in the setting and management of the stage. During the interval refreshments were served by the Misses Tuck, Mrs. Coward, and their ever-willing band of helpers, and the Players' Orchestra under Mr. Arthur Searle played a delightful selection of music.
>
> Following refreshments, the floor was cleared, and to the accompaniment of Miss Boyd's Dance Band, dancing was indulged in and much enjoyed till midnight.
>
> Both parties were a great success, the Host and Hostess gave themselves up unsparingly to ensure the enjoyment and comfort of all their guests. The parties were just happy family gatherings enjoyed in a family spirit by all, and all present were deeply grateful to the Vicar and Mrs. Marsh for affording them such an opportunity of meeting so many of the parochial family under such happy conditions.

Marsh did not always find it easy to carry out his pastoral visits. He complained that "rest" and "bridge" were almost insuperable barriers set between priest and people by the laity in Bournemouth.

The sale of the vicarage did not immediately affect the parish's financial troubles. Throughout the early thirties most of the Church accounts remained in debit and it was a constant struggle to keep things from getting any worse. In 1931 Pitter resigned as priest-in-charge of St. Swithun's and became incumbent at Laverstoke. This gave Marsh the opportunity to review the staffing arrangements and try to make some effective economies. He decided that from 1932 the clerical staff should consist of three priests (including himself) and one deacon, all working full-time, which would save £300 a year in wages. Nobody was appointed specifically to take charge of St. Swithun's. After Pitter left there was still £1,700 owing on St. Swithun's House and the rise in bank rate made it impossible for the Church to let it at a rent which would be high enough to cover the expenses of retaining it. So the Church Council resolved to sell the property. When the next vacancy in the clerical staff occurred in 1933 Marsh did appoint another priest for St. Swithun's. However, by this time the house at 15 Knyveton Road had been sold and the new priest-in-charge was forced to reside in rented accommodation. This was the Rev. William Richard Spalding Wray, M.A., who had been assistant curate at Ely and at Wisbech. Unfortunately for him, the parish's finances failed to improve significantly and in 1935 the staff had to be reduced still further. Wray, as the latest comer, was the man who had to go. The Archdeacon's advice was sought and a special committee set up to investigate all the Church finances. Marsh gave up his Easter offering and donated £100 of his private means in an effort to assist the parish.

Throughout all this time the vicar still wanted to proceed with his schemes for restoring the Church fabric. The frescoes needed renovation, the chancel roof was so worn and dirty as to be unrecognisable, the heating apparatus was worn out, the lighting ineffective and the heating accommodation questionable. Marsh thought it would be worthwhile trying to raise support for these projects from the townsfolk of Bournemouth and not merely from the Church members, so a public meeting was held on the afternoon of Thursday, 8th November, 1934, at St. Peter's Hall, to consider the means whereby funds might be raised for the restoration of the fabric and the improvement of the Church:

> In opening the meeting, the Vicar explained that it was informal and had been very little advertised. He pointed out that the Mother Church of the town had, in the past, given generously towards the establishment and support of parishes in all parts of the town, and now, being left as a city church with fewer residents each year, she must appeal to the whole town to come to her assistance. The aim of the appeal should be to raise not less than £5,000, to make good the inroads of time and weather, and to clean and restore the interior. The lighting and heating were both inadequate, and should

be revised. The heating accommodation, only intended to be temporary, compared unfavourably with that of other churches. Two great conferences were to be held during the coming year, and efforts should be made at once if work was to be done before they met. The present generation had the duty of sharing in the restoration and upkeep of the glorious heritage handed down from the past, keeping St. Peter's a worthy mother to the town.

Mr. Webber emphasised the necessity of the work outlined. Since the addition of the vestries and sacristy, no work of importance had been undertaken, and it was time efforts were made to arrest deterioration from time and weather. As St. Peter's was the centre of civic and corporate life of the town, a wide appeal should be made for the Mother Church. For many years she had given to the younger parishes, who are now in better circumstances, and should be willing to give her assistance. It was time a definite start was made in doing and not only talking of what should be done. It was essential the building should be made water-tight and clean. He suggested that small individual efforts at raising money would be welcomed, but that a large effort, such as Garden Fête at the Winter Gardens would give the whole town the opportunity of assisting. If a large Fête was contemplated, preparations should start at once, and it was suggested that it might include a Pageant of the history of the town.

Mr. Cookman strongly supported the proposal that a subscription list should be opened at once, and that a Gift Day should be organised for January 1st, when it was hoped a sufficient sum would be received to justify starting the most essential work and promise of further help over a longer period might be made.

£641 was raised at the Gift Day and by March 1935 a total of £948 was in hand; a fair start, but still rather a long way from the £5,000 asked for. However, it was enough to enable the renovations and cleaning of the fabric and murals to be done, thus revealing what Marsh described as "the hidden glories of the sanctuary and chancel."

There were also money worries concerning the schools, and the situation was not improved in having as vicar a man who, as we have seen, did not really want to be bothered with schools. Upkeep of the school buildings was becoming increasingly costly and there could be little encouragement in observing that, with the changed character of central Bournemouth, the number of pupils got fewer every year. Colonel Palmer, the correspondent to the School Managers, appealed for more donations in 1931:—

Contrary to popular opinion, the Education Committee does not meet all the charges. We, as Church people, have to keep the buildings in repair, to keep the playgrounds, fences and hedges in order, and to do certain limewashing every year. Some of the school buildings were erected in 1850—80 years ago—and in consequence

> the roofs are a continual source of expense. Every gale of wind, and every frost, means the slipping out of tiles, and the replacement of battens and tiles. As the only regular sources of income are the rents received from Mr. G. C. Seeviour and Mr. Crumpler, out of which the rates have to be paid, you can imagine how little is left, and how much remains to be done. A few old friends continue to send donations to the Day Schools Fund, but so many others have passed away.

So the schools struggled on for a few more years, though, in common with other Church activities, their accounts were in a most unhealthy state. Then, in 1934, Seeviour, headmaster for the last nineteen years, resigned. It seemed clear by then that no school in that peculiar situation could continue and at the end of March 1935 the Day Schools were closed.

At this stage a long dispute began about what was to happen to the immensely valuable site. The Church could certainly have made use of it for a number of purposes and if St. Peter's had been allowed to keep it a wide variety of activities could have been carried on there. But this was not to be. Under the original arrangements made when the schools were established the Meyrick Estate was entitled to reclaim the property when the schools were closed, and this it did. Then there transpired considerable argument as to what sort of re-development should be approved. A car park was suggested, but the Meyrick Trustees wanted to use the site for a commercial development.

It was thought in some quarters that the Meyrick Estate and St. Peter's had made some kind of bargain between themselves over the closure of the schools. This was quite untrue, but in 1937 the new vicar and churchwardens thought it necessary to explain that the patron of a living in the Church of England has no control whatsoever over the policy of a vicar or church council and that the St. Peter's patron had never once attempted to exert undue influence. This statement by the vicar and churchwardens of the time was made in August 1937 and put the Church's position beyond any doubt:

> First, the governing objective of our policy has been to act consistently with the original decisions made. A decision was made in 1935 to close the Schools. The Church then had no option but to admit the right of the Meyrick Trustees over the site; a right which was specifically claimed. It was a legal right which admitted of no challenge as far as the Church was concerned, though the Church Managers had their own scheme for the subsequent use of the Schools. In the light of the right claimed, and the admissions made, we have held that it would have been inconsistent to indulge in

agitation. Our second object was to preserve the unity of the Parish in the face of two rival schemes for the use of the site, in neither of which we had any interest.

The statement concluded with the suggestion that the public differences over what kind of development ought to be permitted should be settled at an independent inquiry by the Ministry of Health.

In the end the site was re-developed by the erection of Maples shop and a block of flats, but the Church was unable to make any profit out of the transaction, as it had a few years earlier when the original vicarage was sold. By the end of 1937 the school buildings had been demolished and the ground was being excavated and prepared for the building which was being erected by the Meyrick Trustees. The new vicar regretted that the school had to be pulled down, as it involved the Church in very great inconvenience, but he recorded that one pleasing feature in a troublesome business was that careful provision had been made by the Meyrick Trustees for the comfort of the retired sacristan, Harry Crumpler, who lived there.

On 13th July 1935 Marsh accepted the Bishop of Winchester's offer of Chilbolton Rectory and prepared to leave Bournemouth. He explained that he wished, for the sake of the living of St. Peter's, to resign before having to take a pension which he thought would cripple the work of his successor. When he left the parish he reviewed his eight years at St. Peter's and described them as "an uphill fight." He wrote, "We have passed together through a critical transition of conditions, and we may say we have reached the climax, where the old tradition has served its purpose and an entirely new tradition must be inaugurated. . . . We have become a parish of boarding-houses and hotels."

Marsh was instituted and inducted at Chilbolton on 29th October, 1935, the very same day as that on which his great predecessor Archdeacon Daldy breathed his last. Daldy's body was brought back to St. Peter's and interred in the churchyard next to the grave of Morden Bennett. At the graveside ceremony the tribute to Daldy's life and work concluded with these words:— "So passed a great man, a great Priest, and a great friend; a great man with great ability, keen, far-seeing business acumen, and a wonderful grasp of details; a great Priest with a pastoral heart, never sparing himself if he could bring comfort and help to a soul in need; a great friend whose loyalty and sympathy were at all times to be relied upon. God give him rest."

During the vacancy after Marsh's resignation the churchwardens were appointed sequestrators of the living in the usual way. Cookman then had to give up office (he died soon afterwards) and Colonel Palmer was appointed by the Bishop to be sequestrator in Cookman's place. It seems to have been tacitly assumed that the office of sequestrator in those circumstances carried the churchwardenship with it and the Church Council promptly welcomed Palmer to membership of that body as churchwarden. Palmer was properly elected as people's warden at the next Annual Vestry Meeting and continued to hold that office until 1944 when he became vicar's warden.

Marsh lived to a great age (perhaps it *was* just as well that he never took a pension out of the St. Peter's endowment) and died in retirement on 12th January, 1959. A later vicar of St. Peter's, Wilfred Fox Robinson, commenting on Marsh's death, recalled that he had been incumbent during a period of great change in the parish, adding, "The Church School went, as did original Vicarage; the former is a disaster, the latter a blessing." In 1935 there were a good many parishioners who felt that Marsh's going was a blessing. The next vicar would need to be really good.

CHAPTER XX

The Parish At War

A PARISH dispirited, torn by controversy and in debt; this was the legacy of St. Peter's awaiting Marsh's successor. The new vicar would need to be a man of great energy and purpose, someone who could deal sympathetically yet firmly with the many problems facing the parish, sustaining and extending its spiritual life and influence. As had happened in 1904 in somewhat similar circumstances, the need was met, this time in the person of Canon Hedley Robert Burrows, vicar and Rural Dean of Great Grimsby. Though still in early middle age, Burrows came to St. Peter's with perhaps a wider experience of the life of the Church as a whole than any previous incumbent, for he had served in a great variety of parishes, with their different liturgical uses, in both rural and large urban areas. Furthermore, he was closely associated with several leaders of the Anglican Church; both his father and his father-in-law were Diocesan Bishops (the Right Rev. Leonard Hedley Burrows at Sheffield and the Right Rev. Ernest Neville Lovett at Portsmouth, soon to be translated to Salisbury) and he had spent a period of his life as domestic chaplain to Green-Wilkinson's old friend, Archbishop Lang.

Burrows was ordained in Winchester Diocese to an assistant curacy at Petersfield in 1911. Then, in 1914, he went to the Western Front as an Army chaplain. After being invalided out of the service in 1916 he held a chaplaincy in Scotland and then joined Archbishop Lang at York. From 1919 he was assistant curate at St. Mary's, Southampton, where he was in charge of the Dock Street Mission and married his rector's daughter, Joan Lovett. His first incumbency was as rector of Stoke Abbott, Dorset, from 1921 to 1925, when he became vicar of St. Stephen's, Portsea. In 1928 he was appointed to the large and important vicarage of Great Grimsby, being also Rural Dean of Grimsby and Cleethorpes, and, from 1933, an Honorary Canon of Lincoln Cathedral.

The stir of the vigorous population of Grimsby, and all the thriving activities of that famous fishing port, at first disinclined Burrows to accept the offer of St. Peter's, but his wife had just been seriously ill in connection with the birth of their youngest child and a move seemed desirable. Accordingly, Burrows decided to come to Bournemouth and was instituted and inducted at St. Peter's on 16th January, 1936. Soon after his arrival in Bournemouth Burrows spoke of the possibilities and challenges which presented themselves in his new cure: —

> The opportunities in this parish are of a peculiar kind. They are quite unlike anything I have so far experienced. At times I have a feeling of blank misgiving, for there is no mass of people in roads and streets and houses whom I can call my parishioners. At other times I feel that the most wonderful opportunities may appear quickly and unexpectedly, for many find their way to St. Peter's and St. Swithun's.

Burrows threw himself enthusiastically into the life of Bournemouth and with truly amazing energy busied himself in vast numbers of activities, secular as well as religious. The importance of this was not to get people to come to St. Peter's, but rather to show the public that the Church was vitally interested in all their concerns. In the manner of Morden Bennett and Daldy, Burrows sought to re-establish the mother-Church as fulfilling a major role in the life of the town. The results were excellent, but the constant round of activity made the vicar tired. After his first year he greeted the coming of Lent with a feeling of relief. "Perhaps it is wrong," he wrote, "to say that one is looking forward to the season of Lent, because it must be a time of chastening, but a certain sense of peace comes over me when I think of Lent and the cessation of the continuous round of functions and meetings."

Of the worship of the Church at this time Burrows has written:

> I do not hesitate to say that in my whole ministry I have never found any life of worship nor any opportunity for evangelism to equal St. Peter's. I still feel that the services were exactly adapted to meet the needs not merely of a parish (for St. Peter's was very unlike an ordinary English parish) but of the very large cosmopolitan society that flowed into Bournemouth and incidentally filled the Church.
>
> There was the quiet and peace of the 8 a.m. Holy Communion. At 10 a.m., at the most beautiful Sung Eucharist, with all the proper appointments but no sermon, the sense of corporate worship was most marked. The choir was accustomed to stay for both the 10 a.m. and 11.15 a.m. services, and Mr. Chandler, the organist and choirmaster, trained by Sir George Martin of St. Paul's, had an unrivalled gift for enabling music to lift the soul and express worship. Then at 11.15 a.m. the Church full for Matins. Bournemouth was then, and I suppose it still is, an all-seasons place, and Sunday after Sunday the Church was well filled at 11.15 with people from all parts of England and beyond. At the great festivals and on special occasions it was sometimes not possible to find even standing room for persons inside.
>
> From the pulpit every Sunday morning at 11.15 the Church looked

full; but of course there was room for everyone. The churchwardens and sidesmen grappled splendidly, and the choir responded at 11.15 never tired by the previous service. But the most wonderful thing of all was the atmosphere of prayer.
When it came to Evensong at 6.30 p.m., with the choir again in full force, the situation was ripe for the mission appeal. Evensong was not so largely attended when I first came, but it steadily grew, and in the war years the Church was packed. I suppose the morning sermon tended to have a more intellectual appeal, the evening address a more personal touch. This is the point I want to emphasise, that coming from a fairly wide experience, I came to feel that St. Peter's had a tremendous opportunity to reach people. There were a large number of the regular congregations at St. Peter's who seemed to know how to pray, and this affected the visitors. These, often uncommitted Christians, found they were able to worship. This atmosphere remained during the war years, and so in this way a number of our 'regulars' fulfilled a great vocation. They were messengers of a high order in the Kingdom of God. At all times of the day in the week men and women came in and found they could say their prayers.

To his clerical staff Burrows appointed two excellent priests. The senior, who took charge of St. Swithun's, was Percy Steed, from Bexhill, who had already gained a thorough and most varied experience in Canada and Jamaica as well as England. The junior assistant curate was Frederick Alexander (Eric) Sanders, who came to St. Peter's from Pear Tree, Southampton. Sanders succeeded Steed as priest-in-charge of St. Swithun's in 1938 when the latter was instituted vicar of Upperby, near Carlisle. Marsh's remaining assistant curates had by this time left the parish, Lewin as vicar of Burton, near Christchurch, and Freeman to the staff of Margate Parish Church.

At his first Annual Church Meeting, in 1936, Burrows reappointed Allen Webber as vicar's warden, but Webber died that summer and to replace him the vicar secured the services of Colonel Vivian Stenhouse, one of Bournemouth's most colourful characters and an assiduous worker for the cause of St. Peter's. Stenhouse and Palmer remained the churchwardens during the rest of Burrows' incumbency, livening the social side of their office with a series of convivial hot-pot supper parties in St. Peter's Hall which they gave for the sidesmen and clergy. Stenhouse, a talented amateur actor, achieved some notoriety for the ventriloqual performances which he gave to the assembled company on these occasions.

At the end of 1936 the Church's last direct link with its first incumbent was severed with the retirement, following a long illness, of the elderly Harry Crumpler. He had been sacristan for over sixty years. Even in his retirement, however, Crumpler continued to assist at St. Peter's whenever he could and retained his close connection with the parish until his death on 3rd March, 1942. John Husband, vicar of Hursley, who, as an assistant curate under Ram, had known Crumpler in his early days at St. Peter's, recalled that he was all that a sacristan should be. In an obituary tribute Husband wrote, "His intense love for the Church which he so faithfully served must be well known to all, but his loving service was the reflection of his true love for his Lord. None that had the privilege of witnessing his devout worship in the Sanctuary can doubt it." Leonard South, who had been assistant to Crumpler for several years, succeeded him as sacristan on 1st January, 1937.

The year of Crumpler's retirement is also remembered for the distinction gained by the St. Peter's cricket team, under the captaincy of Arthur Davis, which reached the final of the De Zoete Cup competition. Burrows, himself a keen cricketer, turned out several times for the Church side.

Only four days after the new vicar's institution the whole country was saddened at the death of King George V. This gave Burrows the opportunity to speak for the whole community. There was a most impressive Memorial Service at St. Peter's, Richard Austin and the Bournemouth Municipal Orchestra providing additional interest and strength so far as the music was concerned. Austin was the conductor who had succeeded Sir Dan Godfrey as the Bournemouth Corporation's Musical Director when the latter retired in 1934. Five years later when Godfrey died so many people attended the funeral that a large number of the mourners had to stand in the churchyard while the Church service was in progress. Sir Dan's grave is at the edge of the churchyard near the Lych Gate. The tombstone is inscribed "In loving memory of Dan Godfrey, Knight Bachelor, For 41 years Director of Music to the Corporation of Bournemouth, who died on the 20th July, 1939, Aged 71 years. Music begins where words end." Godfrey was a man of great genius, not only for music itself, but for his manner of presenting it to the public and making ordinary people interested in what he was doing. But, beyond all this, he was a Christian gentleman, loving and loyal, ever willing to serve the causes of the Spirit. As the father of municipal music in Bournemouth and founder of the Bournemouth Symphony Orchestra Godfrey probably did more than any other man to spread the fame of Bournemouth throughout the world.

One of the first matters which the parish had to consider after the arrival of Burrows as its new vicar was the provision of a memorial to its former incumbent Archdeacon Daldy. Three ideas were proposed, re-seating the Church with chairs on a wood-block floor, providing new altar furnishings, or re-hanging and re-tuning the bells and installing a Sanctus bell to be rung from the chancel. The suggestion of a new 10 cwt. Sanctus bell, to be sounded in the tower by a switch placed in the Sanctuary, gained the greatest measure of approval and a preliminary estimate for £145 was obtained. It was intended that the new bell should be "a distinct and beautiful memorial to one of the greatest parish priests in this Diocese of Winchester. Every time it sounds it will remind us of the Living Presence of Christ and of them who worship continually before His Face in the Heavenly Life."

Before any definite decision had been made over the new Sanctus bell it was found that the existing peal was in a rather poor state and complete reconditioning was advised. Taylor's of Loughborough, who had manufactured the bells originally, suggested that, before re-hanging them, all the bells should be recast. They pointed out that the bells dated from 1871, a transitional period, and that many improvements had since been made in the casting of bells. The total cost of recasting would be about £370, but Mr. Dennison Taylor, the bell-founder, offered to meet half the expense himself. In addition there would be the cost of re-hanging. The Church Council resolved to make an appeal to the town and to have the work carried out as a commemoration of Coronation Year, 1937. Burrows asked for generous support:

> I do most earnestly hope the money will be forthcoming as the restoration of the Bells is a matter of real urgency. This is the only peal in the Borough of Bournemouth. The Bells have played their part in every phase of the life of the town, whether of joy or sorrow. It is wonderful what a sense of depth and uplift the Bells give at times to the whole community and their message reaches all.

The original estimates had to be raised quite considerably due to increases in the cost of metal, but when Captain Harry Norton, J.P., came forward with a cheque for £400 towards the expenses there was no doubt that the whole scheme could go ahead. Taylor's were given instructions to proceed with the work and the bells were dismantled from the tower and transported to Loughborough. Arthur Davis, the indefatigable leader of the St. Peter's ringers, witnessed the casting of the new bells and wrote a most interesting report of what he saw. Davis "entered the foundry just in time to see the tin being added to the molten metal. The heat was terrific, and there was something awe-inspiring in seeing and hearing the metal that was once our bells being stirred around like water. In such heat it seemed ridiculous to the layman to bother about taking the temperature of the metal, yet this was done several times during the casting operation. Finally the furnace was 'tapped' and the half-buried moulds each received their quota of the white-hot molten metal. So quietly and easily did the seventy-year-old foreman handle the job that one felt as if one was witnessing a very important and dignified ceremony."

On 20th November, 1937, after the re-hanging had been completed, the Bishop of Winchester, Dr. Cyril Garbett, came to St. Peter's to re-dedicate the recast peal and to dedicate the new Daldy Memorial Sanctus bell.

There were some other new additions to the fabric and property of the Church at this time. In St. Peter's Church was installed a sound amplification system, given by Mrs. Percy Callaghan in memory of her late husband. The equipment was so arranged that the volume of the loud-speakers could be increased or decreased as desired. This new apparatus, old-fashioned as it was judging by the more modern standards of today, gave excellent service for nearly a quarter of a century until it was replaced by an improved system during Fox Robinson's incumbency. Also in 1937, the flag pole on the tower of St. Peter's was taken down and a new one set up in a more satisfactory position in the churchyard.

The first St. Swithun's House having been sold following Pitter's departure from the parish, it was decided soon after Burrows' arrival to purchase another property to accommodate the priest-in-charge of the daughter-Church. Mrs. Bennett donated £500 towards the projected purchase and further generous gifts were made by Lord Magheramorne, his brother Mr. McGarel-Hogg and other parishioners. This enabled the vicar to buy, in his own name as sole trustee, a freehold house at 22 Frances Road. The price paid for it was £1,600 and the new acquisition was dedicated on 12th December, 1937. Soon afterwards, Steed and his family took up residence there. Through the efforts of St. Swithun's congregation the balance of the purchase money was soon raised, and the property was occupied by a succession of assistant priests until it was eventually replaced in 1966 by a property closer to the Church.

Money, which had been such a serious problem in Marsh's time, was no longer a great worry after the induction of Burrows. Under its new vicar, a popular and energetic leader, the congregation rallied nobly to the material support of its Church and a totally different atmosphere prevailed throughout the parish. Burrows modestly says that it always astonished him how rapidly the financial situation righted itself, "due to the fact that there was at St.

Peter's a core of devotion to Our Lord and His Church which was bound to prevail over trials as they arose." The vicar's appeals which Burrows made to his flock were generously supported and there is no doubt that his own personality and godly enthusiasm for his work had a great deal to do with the response he obtained. The people had taken to him at once giving him on his first Easter an offering of over £165 at St. Peter's Church alone, which Burrows rightly interpreted as a sign that, although he had only been in Bournemouth for a few weeks, he was already counted as a friend.

In fact every sort of realistic appeal was enthusiastically supported from St. Peter's and St. Swithun's. Burrows has recalled the day when a chaplain from the Missions to Seamen arrived to preach. "He didn't even ask for a retiring collection. All he asked was that I should give out his name and address to which any contributions could be sent. He wrote to me later to say he had received £206."

"As I look back on the inter-war years," writes Burrows now, "I am conscious of the steadily growing support, increasing congregations and a joy in worship which I had never experienced to the same extent before. But I would stress the fact that the advance of the parish was due to the lovely co-operative service of clergy and laity alike." Burrows was enormously helped in his task by his wife, who entered fully into any of the parish activities, and by the splendid clergymen he attracted to the two Churches. When Sanders became senior assistant curate upon Steed's preferment to Upperby Harry Hearsey joined the staff from All Saints, Southbourne, at a salary of £300 a year. What the clerical staff of the parish at this time may have lacked in numbers was amply compensated for in the excellence of these men, the great work they did and the far-reaching spiritual influence which they spread among those to whom they ministered.

Perhaps the most outstanding innovation at St. Peter's under Burrows was the presentation of the Epiphany Tableaux, staged in St. Peter's by Mrs. Burrows with the assistance of Arthur Davis. First displayed in January 1937, the Tableaux constituted a vivid illustration of the Christmas story in nine scenes, accompanying a shortened service of Evensong. The Church was filled night after night with people drawn as by a magnet into the light of Christmas and the Epiphany. The beauty, holiness and joy of Christ's birth could be felt at each service and a wonderful sense of worship was called forth in the congregation and the performers. The season of Epiphany was enriched for the whole parish and souls stimulated to deeper understanding and devotion. The new enterprise was a great spiritual success and was repeated in subsequent years until, with the war, the series had to be abandoned.

At Christmas during these years, and also in the wartime, the tree in St. Peter's, regularly given by Sir George Meyrick, was the collecting centre for money and presents to be sent as the Church's gift to some less fortunate parish. The account which Mrs. Burrows wrote of one of these valuable efforts during the war is typical:

> Sorting and packing all the lovely gifts brought to the Tree, was, again this year, a most exciting business. There were *hundreds* of parcels, and they were chosen with wonderful thought and consideration to meet the needs of all ages. A lot of sacrifice must have surrounded the gifts of sugar, tea, jam, chocolate and tinned fruit; and there were lovely new garments of every kind — jumpers, scarves, socks, warm vests, shoes and slippers. There was, too, a blanket, many woollen covers, more than half-a-dozen hot water bottles, and even a fur coat! We sent off three cases of groceries—there were tins and tins of Ovaltine—lots of Oxo and Bovril, rice, cocoa, soap, biscuits, nuts and sweets. The children were wonderfully provided for. Everything that we had asked for, to send to them, was brought in quantities. There were many enchanting toys, stuffed animals, lovely dolls, books and games. New babies had complete woolly outfits and woolly balls to pat and toss. All the loving messages attached to the presents added a lot to the assurance of love that went out to the people of S. Mary's, Southampton, from the people of S. Peter's. In all, eleven bales were despatched; it was impossible to count the exact number of parcels, but it can be said quite certainly there were as many and more than in previous years, and their contents exceeded all expectations as to what was possible or likely this year.
>
> S. Mary's is to have one great parish party at which many of the gifts will be distributed—they expect 600. From the money brought to the tree, S. Peter's will be able to foot the bill for this also.
>
> It is a lovely thing that this great opportunity for service has been seized by so many people as a joy and privilege, and as a test of the friendship that believes in burden-sharing.

September 1939 found the nation, and with it the parish, at war. Dean Burrows has very kindly given the writer his reminiscences of the war years at St. Peter's and what follows is largely compiled from the vicar's memories of those strenuous, urgent years which, he writes:

> . . . constitute the greatest test Bournemouth has ever experienced, and I venture to think the greatest proof of the soundness, discipline and faith of the people. All the past work of a hundred years came to the proof and, as I look back, to me the answer was glorious. Any book on St. Peter's with St. Swithun's should really bring out the depth of courage and faith revealed throughout the

Christian community. Of course, this applies to many other cities and towns under pressure during the war. But some people would hardly have expected all that sacrificial quality from a comfortable pleasure resort like Bournemouth. Things worked out very much as might have been expected during the first phase, until June, 1940. Large numbers of people still made their way to Bournemouth. Nothing interfered with the holiday season as planned! Public opinion did not think that so unmilitary a place as Bournemouth could be the immediate object of attack. St. Peter's and St. Swithun's were filled to overflowing Sunday after Sunday. I remember warning the staff that this state of affairs could not last.

At the onset of the war, I was asked to be chaplain to the Bournemouth Fire Brigade, and when the National Fire Service was constituted under the Home Secretary I was made an Honorary Company Officer Padre. Till almost the end of the war I was the only one in the country. On every alarm I went to the Fire Service H.Q., and travelled with Chief Officer Barker to any spot of bother in the area. I visited all the fire stations and took services fairly regularly for the personnel.

It was at eleven o'clock on a Sunday morning that Neville Chamberlain made his famous announcement that England was at war with Germany. By the time this news reached St. Peter's Burrows was walking to the lectern to read the second lesson, whereupon he informed the congregation. That evening Burrows started his sermon by saying he hoped all the people had remembered to bring their gas masks with them, though he had to admit he had forgotten his own. Over thirty years later Burrows says, "I can still hear the delighted roar of laughter throughout the congregation."

With the commencement of hostilities the Sunday Evensong at St. Peter's was timed to begin at 5.30 instead of half past six; as the winter evenings drew in an even earlier start was made, at 3.15 p.m. A system of Air Raid Precautions for the Church was drawn up, which the vicar published in the *Parish Magazine*:

(1) You will notice that we have made special arrangements for the protection of St. Peter's from fire. We have sand in buckets at different places in the Church, and a big dump in addition.
(2) Arrangements have been made to inform us should the syrens sound while Divine Service is being held. In the event of warning—which, by the way, is quite a different thing to an air raid—there will be a pause in the service and it will be possible for people to leave the Church should they so desire. Those in the south aisles can find accommodation in the basement of St. Peter's Hall; those in the north aisles in the air raid shelter provided underneath Maple's Showrooms in St. Peter's Road. The basement of the Church has been cleared and those in the chapels and the chancel can find shelter there.

(3) Those who wish to remain in Church may do so should they so desire.
(4) After the dispersal I shall bring the service in the Church to a conclusion with a prayer and the Blessing.
(5) For the comfort of the old, who cannot move very fast, may I say that Bournemouth is considered to be a non-vulnerable area.

Entertainments, though curtailed, were by no means forgotten during the war. One such event, particularly connected with St. Peter's, was the performance on 8th February 1941 by the Canterbury Company of the Pilgrim Players who presented T. S. Eliot's *Murder in the Cathedral* in the church. The play was a real joy to all who saw it, Martin Browne playing the role of Becket with vigour and subtlety. Burrows commented that the play being performed in Church "helped to quicken our grasp of the eternal spiritual issues involved in Becket's conflict with his temptations." Also with the war came the Sunday opening of the cinemas, a departure from normal practice accepted by many at St. Peter's only with considerable misgiving. The story is told of a girl in domestic service who, on being asked by her mistress whether she went to Church, replied, "I always *used* to go to Church, but now the cinemas are open I go there because I get three hours entertainment instead of one!"

At the beginning of the war a very distinguised churchman came to Bournemouth. From October to April every year from 1939 after his retirement as Bishop of London the Right Reverend Arthur Foley Winnington-Ingram lived just opposite St. Peter's vicarage at the Crag Head Hotel. He already knew St. Peter's well, having preached there several times for the East London Church Fund. He also preached some remarkable sermons at St. Peter's during the years of his retirement. He could not be heard very well, but it made no difference. The Church would be filled to capacity if it was known that he was preaching. Burrows has recalled that Winnington-Ingram celebrated at 8 a.m. on the first Christmas of his retirement, 1939:

> There was a very large number of communicants, and it completely exhausted him. When he turned to give the Blessing, he collapsed and fell. I thought he had gone. My server and I carried him to the sacristy, set him in a chair, and life began to revive. I got a doctor, and together we took him back to his hotel. I asked the doctor to see that he went to bed, and I told him that I should preach in his place at 11.15. If you please, he turned up at 11.15, and greeted the Churchwardens with these words "See how the Church revives." He insisted on preaching in a crowded Church. The doctor watched him from one side and I from the other. It was a perfect Christ-

mas Sermon, well delivered, lasting ten minutes. Then at the end he gave the Blessing, which, as he said, he had failed to give at 8 a.m. I never let him celebrate at 8 o'clock on Festivals again.

Notwithstanding that little episode, Winnington-Ingram led a very active life for a man of over eighty. He assisted often at St. Peter's and also at many other Churches in the locality, including, one day in 1944, taking a confirmation of service personnel at St. Barnabas, East Parley, which was being used by the Hurn Air Station authorities as their garrison chapel. The Bishop was also a keen games player and played golf regularly.

There were several more changes in the clerical staff. In 1940 Hearsey left St. Peter's on being appointed an Army chaplain. Now Canon Hearsey, his name will reappear in this story in connection with his hospitality to the St. Peter's choir at his Church of Holy Trinity at Nice. Hearsey's successor at St. Peter's was Nevil Tucker, who arrived in February 1941 and for whom in the following year a flat was rented in St. Peter's Crescent, on the site of the old schools. Sanders left St. Swithun's in the summer of 1941 and was inducted as vicar of East Meon. He is now rector of Overton, Hants., Rural Dean of Whitechurch and an Honorary Canon of Winchester Cathedral. Replacing Sanders as senior curate of the parish and priest-in-charge of St. Swithun's came Robin Price, who had held a similar position at a district Church in the parish of Cheam, Surrey. When Learoyd resigned as Rural Dean of Bournemouth in November 1940 Burrows undertook that additional responsibility and so allied himself even more to the life and witness of the town as a whole. By this time Bournemouth and St. Peter's were experiencing the effects of war in a more direct way.

The Church hall found itself put to more useful service during the war years than at any time since its erection. Dean Burrows writes most feelingly on this subject:

The most significant event that I can remember at the start of the war is the fact that St. Peter's Hall was not commandeered. In this I was well supported by the municipality, which reveals the great value of the close contact of the mother-Church with Bournemouth as a whole. Several times I had to meet with government applications for the Hall, but each time a decision was given in favour of leaving St. Peter's Hall free under Church management. This had important consequences for the community. I cannot remember now all the occasions when the freedom given us proved to be invaluable, but I can mention certain examples.

For instance, there was the N.U.R. Secretaries Conference. The Town Hall was not available, so the Mayor and I welcomed the men from all over the country at St. Peter's Hall. The Pavilion was no longer available for the Bournemouth Municipal Orchestra, so I let them have St. Peter's Hall for their concerts at a purely nominal rent. The Hall was crammed whenever the Orchestra performed. Service men, civil servants evacuated to Bournemouth, and the general public came, but it seemed mostly to be a crowd of young people. Dr. Cameron, Sir Thomas Beecham, Sir Adrian Boult and Sir Malcolm Sargent came down to conduct, and this arrangement continued until it became possible for the Orchestra to return to the Pavilion.

I think of the dances held there, men from Bovington Camp and the girls of the Women's Services having a really splendid time. I can see Bishop Winnington Ingram now, enjoying it all, dressed in the full purple evening dress of a Bishop, and wearing the star of the Victorian Order and his other decorations. Then there was the Under-Thirty Club, which met after Evensong on Sunday nights. Altogether St. Peter's Hall proved itself to be a great social centre in the strain and stress of war. I can't say how much we owed to the skill, patience and love of Miss Marjorie Firth, then Secretary of the Hall, and Mr. Dear, the caretaker. How he coped I don't know. Incidentally, owing to the saving of St. Peter's Hall from "the claws of the Government" I was able in the basement to provide for the S.P.C.K. Shop, which had, and I believe still has, such a big service to give to Bournemouth.

The most moving of all the events at St. Peter's Hall was after Dunkirk, when the French troops in large numbers were evacuated to Bournemouth. We were holding the annual meeting of the Moral Welfare Organisation in the Hall when without any previous warning the French *poilus* appeared at the doors and entered the Hall! Four hundred of them were allotted to us, but the pressure on us was so great that 100 or 150 were posted on the third day to another billet. I rang up the Town Clerk and asked who was in command of these men. His reply was "You are!" The officers all went to the Royal Bath, but I had one or two excellent non-commissioned officers with me and, standing on a chair, having hastily dispersed the Moral Welfare, I gave instructions as to where the men were to sleep, etc., and how order was to be maintained. My wife and other ladies in next to no time fixed up a bar for soft drinks and a grocery, fruit and confectionery stall at the entrance. We had them altogether for six days, I think. Not a single unpleasant incident occurred. Interpreters who understood French appeared from nowhere. It was a most moving and wonderful occasion.

The French officer commanding these men wrote to the vicar afterwards, and a translation of his letter, with a couple of words prudently censored, was published in the Parish Magazine:

Canon Hedley Burrows has received at St. Peter's a detachment of four hundred French soldiers, amongst them being men of the . . . These latter will never forget the warm welcome and the unstinting service which was given to them. They warmly thank the Vicar, the ladies and everybody who so generously contributed to making them happy, and assure them of their deep gratitude.

St. Peter's also received the thanks of the French Ambassador in London and of the Vicomtesse de la Panousse, head of the French Red Cross.

After the fall of France the war entered a second, and much grimmer, phase for the people of Bournemouth. A German invasion was now a real possibility, and the locality became part of a Defence Area. Burrows writes of these days:

> Fighting forces were moved into and around Bournemouth. On September 8th, 1940, a Sunday, there was expectation of invasion, and the cliffs were manned with troops. On August 13th the Battle of Britain was right over Bournemouth, but there was a good deal of cloud. I was at H.Q. Fire Station and saw a plane (actually more than once I saw a plane hit and disappear in the water) coming down over Bournemouth. The Chief and I set out, as was our wont, and we found on the rising ground of North Bournemouth a Spitfire in the scrub—and no pilot. A few seconds later the police located the body of the pilot on the other side of Mr. and Mrs. Hoare's house, and I said a prayer for him—in the garden where he lay. Later I took his funeral in Boscombe Cemetery. He was a New Zealander, Cecil Hight, who had come over to fight with R.A.F. Fighter Command.
>
> On April 7th 1943 we held a wonderful Memorial Service for him at St. Peter's. It was very moving that a very large contingent of New Zealand airmen were in Bournemouth at the time. The Secretary for War in New Zealand, Mr. Jones, was there to inspect them, and he was there with the whole contingent at the Service. Mr. Jordan, the High Commissioner for New Zealand, unveiled the memorial erected to Cecil Hight on the north wall of St. Peter's Church—wings made of Kauri timber, hardest and most beautiful of New Zealand trees, and carved by the boys of the Stratford Technical High School where Cecil Hight was educated. An old boy of the School, an officer in the Royal New Zealand Air Force, asked the High Commissioner to unveil the memorial. It was a wonderful service, broadcast live to New Zealand and relayed in all the radio services there. Mrs. Hight and the boys of the School sat up all night to hear the broadcast live, and it was a great joy to me that in a subsequent letter Mrs. Hight wrote "Dear Vicar—Yes, now I understand." At last she was filled with pride; in her earlier letters she could not reconcile herself to the loss of her boy.

Dean Burrows also writes about a wartime enterprise of a very different kind. Within the parish boundaries of St. Peter's was set up the Queen Club at the Lansdowne.

> After trial and error and as a result of a firm and keen desire of the Churches to help, the club was opened on 5th December, 1940 following a generous gift by Sir Alexander Maclean, a resident on the West Cliff and a famous industrialist. Strictly speaking, the Queen Club at the Lansdowne belongs to the story of Bournemouth

as a whole. In connection with it the names of Six Alexander Maclean (its President), Sir James Marchant, Mr. H. S. Smart and Mr. E. E. Rigby (respectively Chairman, Hon. Secretary and Hon. Treasurer) should be remembered; above all, the Quartermaster-in-Chief, Miss M. E. Jewers.

When I succeeded Canon Learoyd as Rural Dean I became, with the President of the Free Church Council, a Vice-Chairman of the committee. My wife from the start was the Chairman of five hundred ladies from 41 churches who staffed the canteen at the Queen. In this work St. Peter's, with the other Churches, played a vital part. A booklet, *In the King's Service,* published in 1945, states that over four million service men and women were entertained in the club. That does not mean four million individuals: many men and women made constant use of the club.

I found this club a really magnificent opportunity of being with the men and women of the Forces. What a lot I learnt! I can see one night in the Chapel room, a group of men of the New Zealand Air Force, most devout in their behaviour. Suddenly we heard a row down below in the lobby. Out we went, a seething mass of men, language and fists! A Gordon Highlander with a bloody nose holding his fist against an Australian. My 'devout' crowd rushed into the fray. I got through to the combatants and was not listened to. "It's all right, Padre — leave it to us — we'll soon settle it," shouted the New Zealand fellows. I had to get the Army Police. Then things cooled down.

Every night there were prayers. There were many and sometimes heart-rendering private talks with the men. On 'Monday night at 8' I always held my women's class. I would never allow any men present. And I really had a class of some of the best-looking girls in the Women's Services!

The committee agreed that the large surplus funds should be spent wholly on Service Charities and on provision for servicemen after the war. The Churches gained not one penny except the joy of service. The Maclean Mobile Canteens were presented to London with a portion of the money, though two canteens were on service in Bournemouth and one in Poole. We gave away money all through the war, but I think we had £20,000 left at the end which built homes for disabled men.

The need for the Queen was of course immensely quickened by Bournemouth becoming the Reception Centre for airmen overseas. They were a splendid lot. The way our women worked was beyond all praise. I stand in homage now, as I think of them. My wife was not strong, but she took her full turns behind the bar. I think the strain and the long standing must have taken its toll, but the women never failed. Many who used the club found new faith in God. Some who worked in the club found new faith in the Church. What a time — what a world — to live in!

On Sunday, 23rd May, 1943, St. Peter's came very near to destruction. At lunchtime, soon after the end of Matins, German planes carried out a sudden air raid on the town, the worst which Bournemouth experienced in the whole of the war. Beales' store, just opposite the Church, was demolished, as were several other nearby buildings, including West's Cinema, the Central Hotel and Punshon Memorial Methodist Church. St. Peter's had a most remarkable escape, considering that bombs fell only a few yards from it. The large window over the west door was blown in and a smaller window on the north side, in an angle of the wall facing west, was also damaged, though much of the stained glass remained intact.

The greatest danger was to the belfry, owing to the sparks which blew in under the louvres from the fire at Beales. These came in continuously and settled on the bell frames, threatening the safety of the bells. Firemen, assisted by several of the ringers, were kept busy for some hours with stirrup pumps and hoses, protecting the woodwork. At one time the louvres themselves began to smoulder, necessitating attention from a hose. The edifice otherwise escaped practically unharmed.

The vicar organised a supply of water for the tower where the difficult and dangerous work of fighting the fire was led by Arthur Davis. At one time there were as many as six stirrup pumps in action. The water had to be obtained from a tap in the Church basement, so a human chain, composed of servicemen, members of the congregation and civilians, was formed to pass buckets from the crypt up the belfry stairs, while another chain worked in the north aisle sending the empty buckets back. What the St. Peter's people were doing to help save their Church enabled the men of the Fire Service to get on with the far more important job of containing the very serious fire at Beales.

St. Peter's was saved. In the midst of all the noise and confusion there was a baptism that afternoon, parents, godparents and baby all turning up as if nothing had happened.

Although some of the approaches to the Church were not easy to negotiate Hedley Burrows was determined to hold Evensong as usual, so many helpers were kept busy throughout the afternoon cleaning the Church in readiness for the service. Despite all the difficulties, some two hundred people turned up for Evensong that night, and while the service was going on firemen and rescue parties were still at work outside.

By this time Evensong had reverted to its usual time of 6.30 p.m. In the later winters of the war St. Peter's was the only Church with a complete set of black-out curtains, with the result that huge evening congregations came to worship and pray. When Punshon Memorial Methodist Church was bombed it was given a temporary home in St. Peter's Hall, and the Minister, the Rev. T. H. Kirkman, later wrote to the vicar:

> The Methodists of Bournemouth will never forget your great kindness and brotherly sympathy. What we should have done if you had not come so swiftly to our aid I do not know. Personally I am more grateful than words can express.

After a few months the Methodists were able to obtain other premises for their services, but it is interesting to note that St. Peter's Hall has not always been the exclusive preserve of Anglicans.

There were many great services and acts of worship during the war. The nation was called to prayer. Two services in 1942 were specially memorable. On New Year's Day, just a few weeks after the attack on Pearl Harbour, President Roosevelt called the United States to prayer and the Archbishop of Canterbury asked everyone in England to join in, but it was not for England a National Day of Prayer. Though it was a week-day a great crowd came to St. Peter's for the ordinary said Matins prior to the Eucharist on New Year's Day! The Vicar spoke a few impromptu words, and advised this unexpected congregation to stay for the Eucharist, which they did. Then, on the third anniversary of the outbreak of war, on 3rd September, 1942, the whole town of Bournemouth gave itself to prayer in answer to the King's Appeal. Services were held all day not only in Church but in several business houses such as Beales and Allens. The services at St. Peter's and St. Swithun's filled the Churches with praying people.

Burrows was afraid that the immense financial strides which the parish had taken since his induction would be held back on the account of the exodus of people from Bournemouth after the collapse of France. But this was not so. He writes that "a splendid core of regular attenders at St. Peter's remained. And the atmosphere of prayer in the Church was such that entirely on their own, for St. Peter's never had a parade service proper, hundreds of young men and women in the Services thronged the Church both in the morning and at night. I started the Midnight Mass at St. Peter's in these years at Christmas. I had to go to the door myself on the first occasion to keep out a drunken section. But after that there was no further trouble. The noisy crowd moved off on a word from me."

The vicar's financial appeals to his congregation were well supported throughout the war. Even in the dark days at the end of 1941 Burrows approached the financial side of his parochial activity with quiet confidence, sending out his appeal as usual. "I always have rather a bad turn," he wrote, "when the time comes for me to send this out to you. The war years are so exacting for everyone's finances. And yet something tells me that you will not fail once again to make provision for the carrying on of the work of this parish." The response was excellent, as it always was. At the end of 1942 the effect of further transport restrictions was to cut off all bus services on Sunday mornings, making it very difficult for people to come to Church from a distance. This meant smaller collections, but the money the Church needed was made up from other sources. The satisfactory financial position clearly mirrored the spiritual feeling of the congregations of both Churches. As the vicar pointed out in the *Parish Magazine* in 1942: "The Church is not a building, it is a fellowship, and we are all part of the central and original fellowship from which the spiritual influence and Christian witness in Bournemouth has been generated."

To let Dean Burrows continue in his own words: "I want here to stress the quality of prayer and service at St. Peter's and at St. Swithun's. It was most moving. It constituted an evangelistic attraction which was sustained. Those who came under the influence of it either gave their lives or are far away now from England and from Bournemouth.

"The phlegm of the people was also most remarkable. At the very place where Hight's spitfire fell, later on the house of Mr. and Mrs. Hoare was bombed. The dear old man died, but Mrs. Hoare was pinned under the debris. It was a glorious moonlight night, and I was there the whole time. A gang of Royal Engineers skilfully worked to get Mrs. Hoare out. At length we could hear her. I called to her 'Mrs. Hoare.' 'Who is that?' she said. 'I am Canon Burrows; keep still; they are going to get you out.' Mrs. Hoare: 'Canon Burrows, how kind of you to come and see me today!'

"The children were a great joy to me. My small Sarah, aged 10, going in the bus up to her little day-school, was asked by a lady who she was. *Sarah*: 'My name is Sarah Burrows. I am the daughter of Canon Burrows, Vicar of St. Peter's. Not that I am any the better for that!'

"I had one awful moment. I wrote an obituary notice of one little old lady, killed in a raid, who always came to the 10 o'clock

Eucharist. The next Sunday, to my amazement, I saw her sitting at her usual place. I went to apologise. However, she said, 'I quite understand, Canon Burrows, how you made the mistake; it was my sister, and she went to St. Stephen's."

Two months after the Church's narrow escape from destruction Burrows was asked by the Bishop of Winchester (Dr. Mervyn Haigh) to become Archdeacon of Winchester and a Residentiary Canon of the Cathedral. He was as sorry to go as the people of St. Peter's were to lose him. In his valedictory message to his people Burrows referred to his "nearly eight years of unadulterated happiness" in Bournemouth during which "real progress in our parish and Church life has been made." Parties were given in their honour and presentations made to Archdeacon and Mrs. Burrows on their departure by many individuals and by parish groups and organisations. Burrows expressed his appreciation of the happy time they had had at St. Peter's and St. Swithun's:

> My wife and I cannot ever thank God enough for our life here, for our friends, and for our home. There has been a marvellous consistency of friendship shown towards us and our children which inevitably has given us a happiness which we can never forget or ever repay.

So Burrows, like Daldy before him, moved to Winchester as Archdeacon. And, as are Daldy and Morden Bennett, he will be remembered as one of the great men of Bournemouth.

During his time at St. Peter's it had been one of his greatest endeavours to give, from the pulpit and in his *Magazine* letters, the message of God and his complete emphatic conviction that nothing except a realisation of the moral and intellectual supremacy of our Lord could bring into human life the love and happiness that the world hungers for. We end this chapter with a quotation from one of these letters, written for Whitsun during the dark days of the war in 1941:

> We have never seen Christ in the flesh. We were not witnesses of His actual Resurrection, but though we have not seen Him we love Him, and that love springs from the illumination that the Holy Spirit brings to our hearts and minds. I ask you just to pause and think of this love of Jesus in the human heart for over nineteen hundred years, and of the power that this love has brought to the human heart, and of the service that his love has given to humanity. There is only one explanation of it, and that is that an unseen yet vivid and personal Force has been moving in the lives of men and women ever since Christ came to earth. At all times in the history

of the Church there has been sloth and deadness. The opposition of men's self-will to God, and the conflict of motives in the human heart, have seemed to cloud this love of God in Christ, but always and often with startling suddenness and in unexpected quarters the flame of this love has burnt up bright again, and the world has been able to see the marvel of the Christian life. No man can take credit and pride to himself in the marvel of Christianity when it appears. What we do is to give thanks to God for His undying Presence manifested afresh to us through His Holy Spirit.

CHAPTER XXI

The Centenary

DURING THE short interregnum between Burrows' departure for Winchester and the induction of the next vicar Price took charge of the parish, assisted by several elderly clergymen. Among these were Winnington-Ingram, the retired Bishop of London, who had taken to spending his winters in Bournemouth and who drew large congregations to St. Peter's when he was down to preach. Though well into his eighties, Winnington-Ingram was an active and charming old man who loved doing what work he could for the Church. This included taking confirmations in the district in order to relieve the bishops of the diocese.

The vacancy at St. Peter's was not for long. In December, 1943 the announcement came of the appointment of a new vicar, Norman Robert Boyd, then vicar of Hendon and a Prebendary of St. Paul's Cathedral. The institution was fixed for his 55th birthday, 8th January, 1944. Though ordained as long ago as 1913 Prebendary Boyd had only served in two parishes; he had been successively assistant curate and vicar of St. James the Great, Bethnal Green, broken by war service as a naval chaplain, and then for the past fourteen years vicar of the important London parish of Hendon, where he had acquired a reputation as one of the leading priests in the London diocese. He was accompanied to Bournemouth by his wife and three young sons.

Boyd was heartily welcomed at St. Peter's, and it soon became apparent why the people of Hendon had been so loth to lose him. A man of great ability and spiritual power, he held strong and uncompromising convictions, hated unreality, and was quite fearless in speaking out when he felt that a principle was at stake. Yet he possessed a keen sense of humour and surrounded everything he did with an energy and purpose which would have astounded even those who knew Morden Bennett. But Boyd could never be called pompous; indeed he seemed surprised at the warmth of the welcome he received from the people of St. Peter's, especially as he knew how popular Burrows had been. "Speaking of the Archdeacon," he wrote, "he will not be an easy man to follow. You won't expect me to be just like him, will you? I might be able to match his energy, but I cannot hope to vie with his laugh."

After his induction Boyd lost no time in encouraging his people to take their responsibilities seriously and to support the weekday services:

> I would plead with all those who are physically able to do so, to make their communion fasting. I am not unaware of the difficulties, but in days when so many are enduring unspeakable hardships on our behalf it does not seem to be a time for shirking so small a discomfort in so good a cause. In the case of older people and invalids unable to make their communion early, some relaxation of the rule has always seemed to me to be justified, but, speaking generally, it is more, not less, discipline which we need in our Church life today. Similarly, I would urge upon you the importance of what some people call 'week-day' religion, that is, attendance at one or other of the Services provided during the week. It has been one of the greatest misfortunes that religion has been regarded so often as a Sunday affair.

The new incumbent disapproved of the Reserved Sacrament being kept in the sacristy. He felt that the Church was the proper place for it, and the Bishop agreed with him. With the approval of the Church Council arrangements were made for the removal of thc aumbry to the south-west wall of the Keble Chapel. Two members of the congregation defrayed the cost of the stonemasons' and painter's work in moving the aumbry to this more fitting place.

Prebendary and Mrs. Boyd both objected to the vicarage at 24 Manor Road. The severe rationing of petrol served as a constant reminder that it was such a long way from St. Peter's Church, and Mrs. Boyd found it a difficult house to run, because of its great size and old-fashioned appointments. The vicar complained that it absorbed too much of his wife's energy, which might have been more profitably spent to the advantage of the parish. However he despaired of getting anything done about it. "Every day which passes," he said, "makes one feel what an advantage it would be to the parish to have the Vicarage in a suitable place much nearer the church. But it is also clear that in the present state of the market any suitable house which was to fall vacant would be snapped up long before the cumbersome processes required by the ecclesiastical authorities could even be set in motion. Now this means that if ever the mistake of Manor Road is to be rectified it will only be through the initiative of some individual who will let St. Peter's know of any possible property which might come into the market." If Boyd's incumbency had lasted longer one wonders whether he would have succeeded in disposing of 24 Manor Road and acquiring a more convenient house. We shall see that a later vicar managed to do it, but only by firmly refusing from the outset to live there at all.

In 1944 the military partnership of the two colonels was severed when Stenhouse decided to retire as vicar's warden. Boyd appointed Palmer, the people's warden, to be his warden and the vestry meeting elected Lawrence Bell, a local businessman who had been a sidesman for over thirty years. Bell was an indefatigable worker for the Church, particularly in connection with the Free Will Offering scheme, which he ran for many years with increasing success.

Boyd did not immediately relinquish his London connections on coming to St. Peter's. On Easter Monday, 1944 he performed his prebendal duty by preaching at Evensong at St. Paul's Cathedral. However, the war had managed to deprive him of one of the perquisites. "In the good old days," he remarked, "I should have been given a bottle of sherry for my trouble!" In May he did resign his stall, in order to make room for a London man, but he continued to use the title of Prebendary which by this time had become so firmly established. Boyd realised he was no longer entitled to it, but felt no harm would be done in carrying on as before.

At this time the St. Peter's sacristan, Leonard South, was still away at the war on active service and Arthur Davis was acting as his deputy. South was not available to resume his duties until January, 1946. In 1945 James Chandler had completed forty years as organist of St. Peter's and, to mark the occasion, he was presented with an illuminated address and a cheque for £300. The new service introduced by Boyd, with Chandler's co-operation, was the Festival of the Nine Lessons and Carols, held on Christmas Eve, 1944. This was the first time St. Peter's had ever had this service. It was preceded by the blessing of the crib and the Christmas tree, the latter presented in this as in former years by the patron, Sir George Meyrick. Unfortunately, in recent times the Festival of the Nine Lessons and Carols has been held during January and not on the traditional day.

Boyd was not entirely happy at finding that St. Peter's held a Midnight Mass as the first Communion on Christmas Day. He wondered about the wisdom of it but eventually decided to carry on with the service as in the past. Admission was by ticket, obtainable beforehand, and the vicar exhorted his congregation to spend the hours before the service as quietly as possible and to take no food after having supper at the usual time.

The end of the war in Europe brought with it a service of

Thanksgiving at St. Peter's, but Boyd was not content to accept this as anything but a beginning. There was still a bitter war raging in the East and the eventual peace would bring just as many challenges to religion as the war had done. The Church must be ready to enter the post-war era with a practical message of peace and to play its part in re-shaping the war-torn world. Such is the tragedy of life that this energetic, purposeful man was not himself destined to live long enough to see the complete end of the war.

The great event of Boyd's incumbency was the St. Peter's centenary in 1945. Just a century earlier the Chuch had been consecrated by Bishop Sumner on Morden Bennett's appointment as first vicar. Even with a war on this was not an occasion to be forgotten. Though new to the parish, Boyd was determined not to lose the opportunity of celebrating the life and witness of St. Peter's during one hundred years. "And through these years," the vicar recorded, "St. Peter's has carried on its work, exercising among the people an influence which it is impossible to measure, and witnessing to man's primary duty to worship God, while affording him also a place and services of great beauty, in the tradition of the Church of England, in which that worship might find expression. The old order has greatly changed. St. Peter's is no longer surrounded by the pleasant dwellings of a residential parish, but it still raises its noble spire among the shops, hotels and cinemas which are now its environment; it still maintains its services at a high level, and in the old tradition; and it offers to an innumerable company of shoppers and holiday makers a place of quiet refreshment and prayer at all times of the day. There is hardly a moment of any day when a visitor entering St. Peter's will not find someone engaged in prayer. Let us thank God for that."

The centenary was celebrated at the patronal festival in June, on a Friday. It was a lovely day. The Bishop of Winchester, Mervyn Haigh, celebrated the Eucharist in the morning and preached a sermon which was a stirring call to renewed faith in the Church. A congregation like that of St. Peter's, said the Bishop, made it easier for people to believe in the Church as being of Divine origin and as having that vital and indispensable part to play in human life which it was part of a Christian's faith to believe that it had. The Oxford Movement a hundred years before had done much to recommend faith in the Church to the English people; but the effect, though great, was still limited indeed. The arguments urged by those who reverenced Christ as in some sense a revelation of God but refused their loyalty to the Church were familiar. Some of them were weighty, but none really justified refusal on the part of such folk to identify themselves with the Church which they not unreasonably criticised. The need of the world today for such a life-changing and unifying society as the Catholic Church was meant to be, was now so plain and desperate that he believed that many were much more inclined than they had been to recognise the Church's claim to their adhesion. The Christ had appealed to his disciples "Whom say ye that I am?" They all knew St. Peter's answer and the passionate recognition and favour which his response drew forth. No less surely today Christ in His Church was asking the same question and waiting for the same quality of response and self-committal from mankind. Let St. Peter's folk show forth their thanksgiving that day not least in this — by dedicating themselves to be still more ardent witnesses by word and deed to the claims of Christ in His Church.

At the lunch party Green-Wilkinson, as the senior past vicar present, proposed the toast to St. Peter's. Dr. Haigh drew the number for the lucky seat, selecting none other than the number which was on the back of his own chair.

The evening was a festive occasion and drew in all the townsfolk of Bournemouth, The town can have seen few more impressive sights than that presented by the long procession of Church choirs through the streets and pleasure gardens. Almost all the Churches of the Deanery took part and there were over 300 members of choirs and clergy taking part. In the Gardens the scene from the band-stand, with choirs and clergy close to the edge of the stream and a great crowd pressing in from every side, was very beautiful. The Mayor joined the procession, giving it that link with the secular life of the town which was just what was wanted. When the procession reached the Church there was a triumphal service at which the Bishop of Southampton preached and Stanford's *Te Deum* was sung. Amplifiers relayed the music to the crowd standing outside the packed Church on that warm June evening.

The festivities continued over the weekend. On the Sunday the Archdeacon of Winchester, the former vicar Hedley Burrows, the patron Sir George Meyrick, and the Member of Parliament Sir Leonard Lyle, all participated. Boyd and the St. Peter's people worked very hard to ensure the success of the centenary commemoration. The collections went to the Bishop's fund for the assistance of Christians in the liberated and distressed countries of Europe, to whom the Church of England had undertaken to give a quarter of a million pounds. With the restrictions of war starting to be lifted, the centenary could not have come at a better time. Boyd laboured tirelessly with his customary vivacity. The Church had taken full advantage of this ready-made opportunity of displaying itself in triumph and joy.

But the rejoicing was short-lived. Late at night on 10th July, 1945, his wife's birthday, the vicar suddenly died. It was a time of great sadness and a stunning blow to the parish. Strong men wept. Boyd had apparently been in such good health; and though his incumbency had only lasted a mere eighteen months his people had already become infected by his hearty good humour and bright and breezy manner. He was so greatly esteemed, not only among his own parishioners but the Bournemouth townspeople generally. He had worked so hard over the centenary, and enjoyed every moment of it.

Three days later the Bishop of Winchester came back to St. Peter's to conduct the funeral. The affection in which the deceased vicar was held was shown in the large gathering which filled the Church for the service. Dr. Haigh pointed out in his address that Boyd had for long been working without the support of a third member of the staff such as, at the least, he ought to have had. He had thrown himself into the observance of the centenary with great enthusiasm, but it had placed a considerable extra strain on him. There could be no better tribute to Boyd and the quality of his work than the fact that before coming to St. Peter's he had been associated with only two parishes in thirty years. He was buried in the churchyard in a grave next to his great predecessors Morden Bennett and Daldy. He could hardly lie in more fitting company. There can be little doubt that but for his untimely death at the age of only fifty-six Boyd would now be counted as one of the greatest vicars St Peter's has ever had. At the moment of victory in war and challenge in peace he had his parish poised for the religious leadership of the Bournemouth area in the post-war age. Now, in the twinkling of an eye, the promise had withered; another interregnum, and then other hands would have to take on the task.

But whose? Fate shows itself in many curious ways. The timing of Boyd's death might have come straight out of Thomas Hardy. The obvious choice as successor was no longer available, by just forty-eight hours. On 8th July, Price, priest-in-charge of St. Swithun's, announced that he had accepted the Bishop's offer of the living of Christchurch Priory. It seems probable that the patron would have appointed him to St. Peter's if it had been possible to do so. As it was, Price left for Christchurch in November. As a tribute of the congregation's affection and respect he took with him a testimonial of £400. Few St. Peter's clergy before or since have received a parting present of anything like as much. When the time came to say farewell the Mayor, Alderman Harry Brown, said, "If we had more clergymen like Mr. Price we should not be bothered about getting attendances at Church."

For the final war victory St. Peter's held one of the most impressive services ever seen during its 100 years' history, a great Act of Thanksgiving on the morning of 15th August, 1945. The vast congregation filling every corner of the Church and overflowing out of the doors, the deep silence during the times of prayer, the volume of sound in the hymns, and the Archdeacon's address, all combined to create an experience which none who were present are likely to forget. The pealing of the bells through the day carried the Church's joyous voice all over the town. A full peal of Grandsire Triples, 5,040 changes, was rung, lasting three hours and twenty-seven minutes. Many visitors came to the Church that day; some even climbed the belfry stairs to express their appreciation of the ringing.

When Burrows was vicar he had suggested that a portion of the churchyard at St. Peter's should be set aside for the burial or commemoration of those members of the congregations who had died whilst on active service in the war. In the first place twelve white crosses were erected, some marking actual burials and others commemorating those whose mortal remains lie overseas. It was proposed that after the war the Garden of Remembrance might be retained and that a permanent memorial should be erected there on which the names of the fallen could be inscribed. It was during the incumbency of Boyd's successor, in 1947, that the Garden of Memory was completed and dedicated. It was considered that the south side of the Church was thereby much improved in appearance. Lionel Youngman of Bournemouth, the Church's architect, supervised the work and also designed an inscription panel for the War Shrine in the Church on which to record the names of those parishioners who lost their lives in the 1939-45 war. It was not until 1949 that permanent memorials were erected in the Garden of Remembrance in accordance with designs approved by the War Graves Commission.

Boyd's memorial at St. Peter's is the carved oak font canopy in Victorian Gothic style, designed by Youngman and placed in the Church in 1947. It cost £200 and is a most tasteful design, blending well with the building to which it belongs. It was dedicated at Evensong on 9th March, 1947. The inscription is quite simple, "In Memoriam, Norman Robert Boyd, Vicar 1944-45. R. I. P."

The vacancy in the benefice after Boyd's death was a long one, lasting just over ten months. Price took charge of the parish for the short time he still had before taking up his new cure. He continued his distinguished career in the Church with a most successful incumbency at Christchurch, succeeding Hedley Burrows as Dean of Hereford in 1961 and returning to St. Swithun's in 1968. He was offered an English bishopric in 1959, but refused on health grounds.

When Price was inducted at Christchurch there were no full-time clergy left in the parish. However, the Rural Dean of Bournemouth, Canon Learoyd, former vicar of St. Luke's, Winton, came to the rescue by taking temporary charge and keeping both Churches going. There was a severe shortage of clergy at that particular time, but Learoyd was able to obtain help from Bishop Winnington-Ingram and a number of elderly priests who made themselves available. The Communion services at the greater festivals presented considerable problems of manpower. Learoyd begged those in good health to come to one of the early services and asked invalids to avail themselves of the Communion service after Matins. Nobody could communicate at ten o'clock unless his or her name had been sent in beforehand.

James Chandler had to resign on very definite medical advice and left the parish after forty-one years as organist. He had great gifts, musically and spiritually, and in his able hands the music of St. Peter's became a very real part of the worship of the Church, and became known over the length and breadth of the country. Chandler's unfailing good temper, and keen sense of humour, endeared him to the people of the parish. On his retirement the St. Peter's authorities gave him a pension of £80 per annum for life which he enjoyed until 1953, when he died following an operation.

During the winter of 1945-46 St. Peter's and St. Swithun's anxiously, and sometimes impatiently, awaited the appointment of their next vicar. Unfortunately it was just the wrong period for the parish to be marking time. How different it would have been if Boyd had still been alive. Nevertheless, it was important that the appointment should not be hurried. It seemed essential to be sure of getting as the new incumbent a man who would build on, rather than destroy, the excellent work which Burrows and Boyd had done. Fortunately, as it turned out, the long wait was well worthwhile.

CHAPTER XXII

From Banbury To Bermuda

THE NEXT vicar was Canon Anthony Lewis Elliott Williams, vicar of Banbury and Rural Dean of Deddington. He was then fifty-three years old. The son of a doctor, Williams had Church connections in Ireland, one of his grandfathers having been Dean of Connor and Rector of Ballymena. Williams was an M.A. of Exeter College, Oxford, an honorary Canon of Christ Church and a Deputy Priest-in-Ordinary to King George VI (and later to Queen Elizabeth II). He resigned his canonry on leaving the Oxford diocese, but in 1950 became an honorary Canon of Winchester Cathedral and a Proctor in Convocation for the diocese. He did a lot of work at the Church Assembly, and during his incumbency at St. Peter's was a chaplain of the Order of St. John of Jerusalem, the only chaplain of that order in the diocese of Winchester.

After the appointment was announced the parish still had a further wait until Williams could leave Banbury to assume his new duties in Bournemouth. He had his deanery to hand over as well as a large parish, and was determined not to move until he was sure that everything was in order for his successors. Colonel Palmer, presiding at the St. Peter's Annual Church Meeting in 1946, said that St. Peter's was indeed fortunate to have secured such an able priest and keen parochial worker as its next vicar.

On his arrival in the town Williams soon discovered that the old ladies of Bournemouth were quite something. The day before his institution as vicar one friendly old dame stopped him ouside the Church and accosted him thus: "You are to be our new vicar, are you not? I do hope that we will all be happy! I expect you must be very nervous about taking services and preaching in such a large and important Church as St. Peter's. Do you know it seats nearly fourteen hundred people?" To which Williams brightly replied — "Well, I shall try not to be too nervous; anyway I have just come from a Church which seats two thousand." Another time when the new vicar was arranging the annual service of one of the parochial guilds another elderly lady kindly said, "This, of course, is a very important occasion. Would you like me to choose the hymns for you? You see, I have attended St. Peter's all my life." Williams declined with grateful thanks!

The institution and induction took place on 16th May, 1946, and on the same day Williams took over from Learoyd as Rural Dean of Bournemouth. He found that his deanery duties occupied at least a third of his time. Having taken on these extra responsibilities from the very day of his institution, Williams had no time, as some of his predecessors who ultimately became Rural Dean had had, in his early years in which to devote all his energies to the parish alone. Nevertheless, this did not seem in any way to affect the worth or extent of his ministry at St. Peter's. He soon settled down happily in Bournemouth and became greatly beloved by his congregation.

Williams inherited a serious staff problem, for there was now no organist and no full-time assistant curates. Bishop Winnington-Ingram, one of the clergy who had been helping Learoyd during the vacancy, died that summer at the age of eighty-eight. His last words to Williams as he left the town that year were, "I hope to be back in Bournemouth in the autumn and to do anything I can to help."

Williams solved the staffing difficulties by bringing with him two assistant priests and an organist. As priest-in-charge of St. Swithun's came Keith Parkinson, a "double first" and winner of several University prizes. He had served under Williams at Banbury and was then assistant curate at Weeke, near Winchester. Parkinson seemed to share Boyd's reservation about the Christmas Midnight Eucharist at St. Peter's. "There may be a number of our communicants," he wrote, "who will go to the Midnight Mass at St. Peter's. I would ask these people, if they intend making their Communion at that Service, to see that the evening is spent in a quiet way as a preparation for that Service. It can, also, so easily degenerate into the lazy man's Service, insofar as many find it pleasanter to stay up than to get up."

John Coutts, a graduate of Exeter College, Oxford, like the vicar, and then assistant curate at Banbury, came to fill a similar position at St. Peter's. He was possibly the finest preacher to serve the parish in recent times. Banbury lost yet another member of its staff when the organist, Charles Palmer (not to be confused with his namesake the churchwarden), whose choir had won many competitions in Oxford diocese, also came to St. Peter's. It must have been quite an exodus from Banbury!

In 1948 there was publicity in the national press about St. Peter's when Williams was physically assaulted in Church while conducting a wedding service. The vicar has described the incident and the events leading up to it as follows:

> One day a very young couple came to put in their Banns of Marriage. As the girl was only sixteen and the young man nineteen I had to ask for written consents from both lots of parents. These were duly obtained. They wanted a fully choral wedding — organ, choir, bells, etc. The young man explained that he was doing very well in business and that he had bought a home and a car and many other things. Two weeks later the girl called to see me again: such a tragedy, Mother had had a stroke. They now wanted just a very quiet wedding, and there would only be two witnesses — the bridesmaid and the best man. Also could they have the service half-an-hour earlier than originally arranged. Everything just as quiet as possible on account of poor Mother. I expressed my sympathy and fresh arrangements were made.
>
> On the day of the ceremony we had got as far as the concluding prayer before the final blessing when, at the bottom of the nave, a very large stout man came into the Church storming and shouting. He rushed up the aisle and came straight to me. 'Stop all this,' he roared. I paused to point out that a Church was not the place for such noisy behaviour and that the ceremony was practically completed. I added, 'If you have anything to say come into the vestry; we are just finishing.' Before I knew where I was he had pushed past the waiting couple and struck me a violent blow on my mouth with his fist. 'How dare you!' I cried.
>
> However I concluded the service and as I turned to lead the shattered little group into the vestry I saw that my blood had splattered the marble floor of the Sanctuary. I had some such thoughts as — 'Now I know a little of what St. Thomas a Becket felt when his career was ended in violence at Canterbury Cathedral.'
>
> The girl's father followed us into the vestry looking a trifle abashed. Whilst our excellent verger rushed out to look for the police I ascertained what had happened to cause such a scene. Briefly, the girl's parents had discovered that the young man was highly unsuitable for matrimony. After forbidding the match, they had very foolishly sent the girl to tell me it was all off instead of coming themselves. The girl had told me a pack of lies and made the fresh arrangements for an earlier ceremony, determined to go through with it all. I pointed out that I still had the consent forms.
>
> At that moment the verger returned triumphantly with no less than three policemen. 'Give my Dad in charge, Vicar,' shouted the girl; 'it would do him good to go to gaol.' I refused, and in the meantime the father fled from the vestry. I told the police not to follow him. It turned out to be the bridegroom who went to prison. No wonder he had plenty of money. He was ultimately proved to have stolen and sold quite a number of cars.
>
> Later that same eventful afternoon I went up to London. The next day, a Sunday, I was on duty at the Chapel Royal at St. James's Palace and with a very stiff and swollen mouth took the service with Her Majesty Queen Mary amongst the distinguished congregation. I remember I had a severe headache for several days.

> On my return to Bournemouth on the Sunday afternoon I found four newspaper reporters awaiting me for full details. I also got the information that the girl's father was an ex-pugilist! Finally, the Daily Mail rang me up from head office at 2.30 a.m. the following night, for which attention I was not grateful. Both of us had our photographs in that great newspaper — such is fame!

Williams also tells another story about a disturbance during service, but this episode had less drastic consequences. At Evensong one Advent Sunday he was reading the second lesson when a man in the front pew jumped up and shouted "I am John the Baptist!" "Then sit down and hear what I have got to read about you in this lesson," rejoined the vicar. Quite satisfied, the man sunk quietly into his seat, and an anxious sidesman returned to his pew.

At St. Peter's Church the bomb-damaged windows, which had been just temporarily filled with plain glass, were properly repaired in 1947-48 by Messrs. James Clark & Co. The great west window under the tower is a fine piece of modern glazing and harmonises well with the Victorian Gothic Church. The war memorial was completed in 1949 and, when all the money had been found except the last £31, Williams resorted to one of Morden Bennett's tested methods of fund-raising: "I will gladly give three guineas myself if nine others will do the same."

Money was a worrying problem during the whole of Williams' incumbency, as it seemed to be in Churches everywhere. The cost of keeping St. Peter's and St. Swithun's going, and at the same time honouring the diocesan and missionary obligations, was ever increasing, but the congregation's response was most heartening. The parish kept out of debt, paid its quotas in full, and raised very considerable sums for the Bishop of Winchester's "My Call" and for essential repairs to the fabric of St. Peter's. The Bishop's call in 1947-49, for money needed for the reconstruction of the diocese after the war, demanded from the parish a total of £1,620 in addition to the usual quotas. In fact, this amount was exceeded and Dr. Haigh was very pleased about it. He wrote to the vicar: "I do congratulate you and your people with all my heart on completing your magnificent gift of £1,715 in response to My Call. St. Peter's folk are really splendid, and they have given the finest possible lead to the diocese. Their parochial target was by far the largest in the diocese, and their parochial gift has been yet larger still."

The methods used to raise the additional cash required to balance the Church's books were a Vicar's Appeal for £1,000 each year and the holding of an annual gift day. Before one of the gift days Williams told his people: "I always hate having to ask for money, but ever since I have been ordained or, at any rate, since I first became an incumbent at the age of twenty-eight it seems to have been my fate to be continually on the beg!" The days were gone when big items of expenditure could be met by gifts from a few wealthy individuals; instead, the parish now had to rely very largely on the regular giving of smaller sums by many members of the Church. Williams felt that "the situation of a parish is on the whole sounder when it depends upon the more modest support from the many than when everything is done by three or four wealthy and generous people."

The restoration appeal, launched in 1950, was for £6,000 for repairing the steeple and other parts of the Church fabric, and rebuilding the organ. Some of the most urgent work on the spire had to be done immediately, for it was found that much of the pointing and stonework on the south and west sides had perished, thus creating a risk of danger if further damage was done by the winter frosts. By the end of 1951 £4,278 6s. 0d. had been subscribed and all the essential work was completed by the end of 1952. The building restoration was supervised by Lionel Youngman. The organ was rebuilt by the original makers, Harrisons of Durham, at a cost of over £2,000. A proposal to discard Street's pews and to re-seat the nave of the Church with chairs was fortunately abandoned.

For a week in the May of Festival of Britain year, 1951, the chancel steps of St. Peter's became a theatre stage for performances of *A Sleep of Prisoners,* a play specially written for the Festival by Christopher Fry. This was presented by the Religious Drama Society and the Pilgrim Players in conjunction with the Arts Council of Great Britain. Fry himself mingled with the audience at one of the performances and met the vicar and churchwardens afterwards in the vestry. In the programme notes the Bishop of Chichester explained that:

> Religious Drama is an essential part of the Festival of Britain. The Christian religion is itself part of the patrimony which was left us by our forefathers; one great cause why (to use Burke's words) we may put in a claim to as ample and early a share in all the improvements in sciences, in arts, and in literature as any other nation in Europe. It is also the foundation of drama in England.

A Sleep of Prisoners is set in a Church where four prisoners of war are locked in for the night and their dreams are unfolded. It was a deeply moving play, though not lacking in moments of amusement. One trouble was that the audience was under the disadvantage of wondering whether it was in the best of taste to laugh in Church.

Over three thousand people came to St. Peter's to see this ambitious production before it moved on to London where it was presented as part of the Festival programme in the capital. Williams had to explain that St. Peter's would not be making a penny out of this theatrical venture:

> The Religious Drama Society asked us for the loan of the Church and we gladly lent it to them. Some people seem to think that the Church funds will get something out of it, but actually all we shall get out of it is the task of clearing up after the actors have gone.

One of the local theatre critics drew attention to the fact that a Church is not the most comfortable place for seeing a play, and he gave a few tips for the benefit of future audiences:

> Take a cushion of some sort with you, and a top coat if it is a cold day. Get there early to get a seat where you will not have to crane your neck to see what is going on.

On 17th July, 1952 thieves broke into St. Peter's Church and did considerable damage. The lower panel of a stained glass window in the east wall of the Keble Chapel was smashed, a ventilator opened and the Church collecting boxes, despite having been emptied by the sacristan the previous evening, all broken open. Very few things were stolen, among them the leather gloves and straps belonging to the various standards and flags carried at military parades, and a bottle of Communion wine. Keys were taken and thrown about and the outside doors jammed, so that when the celebrant and the sacristan arrived at 7.45 a.m. they could not get in and the congregation of nine for the Friday morning Eucharist had to be sent away.

At Ascensiontide, 1951, was held a mission to Bournemouth, a project led by the vicar in his capacity as Rural Dean and covering, with its preparation, nearly two years work. The object of this Mission was "to convert men and women to Christ and to recall them to the service of His Church." It aimed to seek to convert those outside the Church from unbelief to faith in Christ and at the same time to strengthen the faith of those inside. Bishop Haigh explained why Bournemouth had been the place chosen for this enterprise:

> It is not, in my judgment, that Bournemouth needs a Mission more than other places. Rather, it is that the Church in Bournemouth is sufficienly strong and vigorous to desire to be made stronger and more vigorous still, and it is not unworthy of the best which many

at present unassociated with it will be asked to bring into its life and work.

Canon Roger Lloyd, the Diocesan Missioner, was assigned to St. Peter's and Holy Trinity Churches for the Mission campaign. The whole of the geographical parish was systematically visited by members of the congregation. In consequence of these endeavours a Women's Fellowship was set up and a panel of parish visitors formed to maintain the Church's contacts with those who remained outside. Also arising out of the Bournemouth Mission was the parish prayer group which proved very helpful to the life of St. Peter's in many ways. The primary object of this group "is to come closer to God and so in time to learn more of His Will for us and to become of more service to Him."

Williams was particularly anxious to keep his parishioners together as a social unit, and he carefully fostered all kinds of bazaars, garden parties, coffee mornings, whist and beetle drives, and many other events which enabled the congregations of both Churches to get to know one another better. The residents who came regularly to services were as often as not living outside the parish boundaries, and the vicar made continuous efforts to develop a sense of community and fellowship among them. He found his work teeming with interest and challenge and was horrified to discover about the middle of his time as vicar that he was a member of over forty committees of one sort or another and chairman of at least half. "It was all rather like living on a moving staircase," he remarked. Every year he wrote between 2,500 and 3,000 letters. He was the first vicar to take a major acting role in a production by the St. Peter's Players when, in May, 1948, he appeared as the Inquisitor in Bernard Shaw's *St. Joan.* A theatre critic commented that the Inquisitor was "played with literary and histrionic skill, and an attractive performance."

Williams was a man of great personal charm who possessed that wonderful gift of being able to get on well with all kinds of people. His pastoral ministry to the old and sick folk in his parish and among his congregation was of immense value. Williams himself was particularly conscious of the great need for visiting and looking after the spiritual needs of the sick; he wrote that "In such a town as Bournemouth, with its numerous elderly and invalid people, this responsibility is a very vital part of the work of the clergy." The time and careful attention which he gave to it were tremendous. His views on the reserved sacrament are specially interesting:

Reservation, although mainly abandoned in the Anglican Church in

England for some hundreds of years, owing to political history, has become quite common again. There is Reservation in about half the parishes in Bournemouth, for instance. Reservation is a thoroughly primitive practice of the Christian Church and is alluded to in the Early Church as a normal practice as early as the year 150 A.D. in the writing of Justin Martyr. . . . When the Sick receive the Reserved Sacrament they are receiving the Bread and Wine which were consecrated in church in the presence of the worshipping community. There is thus an emphasis on the union of the isolated individual with the fellowship of the whole Body of the Church which should undoubtedly mean to him or her additional strength and comfort, and is indeed an instance of the realisation of the Community of Saints.

There were several changes in parish personnel during the incumbency of Canon Williams. In 1949, due to the death of Lawrence Bell and the resignation through ill-health of Colonel Palmer, two new churchwardens took office. W. J. Lewis, the manager of the local trustee department of Barclays Bank, was appointed vicar's warden, and Gilbert Marshall, a diocesan lay-reader and secretary of the Bournemouth Y.M.C.A., was elected people's warden. T. H. Ringrose replaced Lewis in 1950. There were two noteworthy celebration parties, one in 1947 to mark Colonel Palmer's fifty years of office as sidesman and churchwarden and the other in 1951 to celebrate George Head's similar period of service at St. Swithun's.

Coutts left in 1951 and was appointed vicar of Holybourne. He was replaced as senior priest by the rector of Dursley, Canon Helm, M.C., M.A., T.D., who, like the vicar, was also a chaplain to the King. Parkinson was instituted as vicar of St. Augustine's, Bournemouth, and left St. Swithun's in 1952. His successor there as priest-in-charge was a bachelor from Leicestershire, Peter Chandler. In 1955, on a reorganisation within the parish, Chandler transferred his main duties to St. Peter's and Percy Steed, the erstwhile priest-in-charge who had just resigned as rector of Barnes, returned to St. Swithun's. Soon afterwards, Chandler was appointed vicar of North Baddesley. Thomas McKee, an Ulsterman and former naval chaplain, joined the St. Peter's clerical staff in 1953 from St. James', Pokesdown, where he had been serving for a year under Wilfred Fox Robinson, who was later to succeed Williams as vicar of St. Peter's. Canon Helm retired in 1955, and he was replaced during the following year by Canon Leslie Brasnett, who had then just retired as vicar and Rural Dean of Runcorn in Cheshire. Brasnett, a former scholar of Christ Church, Oxford, was a distinguished cleric, still in the full vigour of life, who had moved to Bournemouth on account of his wife's health. The learning, humanity and experience which Helm and Brasnett successively brought to St. Peter's deepened the spiritual life of the parish and enabled the vicar to leave a senior man in charge when he was away performing his many outside duties.

There was another change of organist in 1953 when Palmer resigned. On accompanying Williams from Banbury, Palmer had been appointed to St. Peter's for five years, but after his recovery from a serious illness at the end of that period, during which his wife, also an accomplished musician, had carried on in his place, the vicar had asked him to stay for a little longer. Williams advertised the vacancy and received no less than seventy-two applications for the post. These he considered with great care, for he felt it was most important to secure the services of someone who was not only a talented musician but also a convinced Christian. He chose a twenty-eight-year-old graduate of Christ Church, Oxford, Michael Peterson, who was then assistant organist of Wells Cathedral and organist of Wells Parish Church. He came to St. Peter's in April, 1953 and immediately entered very fully into the life of the Church, spiritually and socially as well as musically.

By this time there was another vicar's warden, following Ringrose's sudden death in 1952. Williams this time appointed another official of Barclays Bank, Ronald Hines. Through the next eight years the new warden set a fine example to the parish by the most conscientious attention to duty and skilful handling of the Church's finances. In the Hines-Marshall partnership, which lasted into the next incumbency, St. Peter's was served by men of great humanity and spiritual power. The progress of the parish during those years was due in no small measure to their efforts.

When his fruitful and happy incumbency had lasted just over ten years Williams received the honour of being named as bishop-designate of Bermuda. His consecration was fixed to take place in Westminster Abbey on 21st September, 1956. The vicar discovered that a somewhat curious legal position would arise upon his elevation to the episcopate. He explained, "My consecration as Bishop on 21st September automatically vacates this benefice! As we do not leave England until November, the churchwardens would like me to stay on and carry on until the end of October, which I will be very happy to do, although I will technically no longer be your Vicar, but their employee!"

It was, of course, a great honour for Williams, the first vicar of St. Peter's ever to be made a bishop. It was a well deserved recognition of a most successful career, and Bournemouth was very proud of him. Williams enjoyed the proceedings immensely, though he found that the number of garments he had to procure for his new dignity, and the length of time spent in having them fitted, "must rival what many brides have to endure, whilst the expense is rather breathtaking." The Consecration at Westminster Abbey, conducted by the Archbishop of Canterbury, was a most impressive occasion. A huge crowd of St. Peter's people went to London to support their vicar with their prayers and good wishes. With the exception of Brasnett, who took charge of the parish during the vacancy, all the St. Peter's clergy set off for different parts of the Commonwealth, the Bishop to Bermuda, McKee to Central Africa and Steed to Jamaica.

Williams summed up his ministry at St. Peter's thus:

> As I look back I realise what a lot has been done for the Church—the £6,000 Appeal which saw the restoration of the spire, the roof and the organs at both St. Peter's and St. Swithun's; the re-decoration of the interior of both churches; the renewal of frontals and vestments at St. Peter's, so that we now have two beautiful and complete sets of vestments for each of the four liturgical colours. Then there has been the rebuilding of the Church wall on the north side of the churchyard in beautiful stone, and the new steps up to the west door. On the spiritual side and more important still there has been the Mission to Bournemouth and all that preceded and followed it, including the birth of our Parochial Prayer Group. How happy I am to be able to note that the congregations of St. Peter's have been at their largest during the last three years of my time amongst you. The very considerable growth of members attending the 10 a.m. Sung Eucharist on Sundays has perhaps been my greatest joy.

When he left St. Peter's prior to his departure for Bermuda the parish presented him with a silver and ebony pastoral staff, suitably inscribed, and gave Mrs. Williams a travelling clock. On his last Sunday huge congregations filled the Church, over two thousand people altogether. The hall was so packed for the farewell party that it was impossible for Bishop and Mrs. Williams to walk around or even see everyone who was there. So departed one of the most beloved vicars St. Peter's has ever had.

It is probably too soon to assess the practical results of Williams' ministry at St. Peter's, but unquestionably he succeeded, without sacrificing any principles, in bringing his Church to terms with the outlook of the modern, post-war age. He entered fully into the life of the town and its municipal affairs, serving on two committees of the Borough Council and acting as Mayor's Chaplain six times. Under his leadership St. Peter's began to realise the role it had to play in post-war Bournemouth, a role different, but no less important, than that which had been required in the old days. The changes in the character of the parish, which had started between the wars, were now more obvious than ever. Williams perceived how the spiritual life and witness of St. Peter's were likely to develop and, with that tactful wisdom and loving concern which characterised his whole self, carefully set his parish on the path towards its new destiny. Like Morden Bennett a century earlier, he gently shepherded his people along the way they had to go. The great humanity of the man, his love for all kinds of people, and the deep spiritual strength inside him, made him a natural Church leader; it is not surprising that persons in high places selected him for a bishop.

CHAPTER XXIII

Fox Robinson Arrives

THE PATRON'S choice as the new vicar fell on the Rev. Wilfred Henry Fox Robinson, vicar of Friskney, Lincolnshire, who had previously held the Bournemouth incumbency of St. James, Pokesdown, from 1947 to 1953. A clergyman of the younger generation, Fox Robinson had been ordained in 1935. After two assistant curacies in Derbyshire he served during the war as a chaplain in the R.N.V.R. and held a series of naval appointments until his induction at Pokesdown. It has been said that about the sum total of information about him which the average parishioner had when Fox Robinson's name was announced was "A large man—a large family—did a lot for Church Schools or something when he was at St. James, Pokesdown."

The new vicar recorded that his first reaction on being offered the living was to turn it down on measuring his incapacity against the abilities of the great clergy St. Peter's had had. He was already in a quite comfortable position, enjoying the life of a pleasant country vicarage with glebe and animals. It would mean some considerable readjustment for his family to leave their rural surroundings and return to a large town parish. Nevertheless, Fox Robinson decided upon reflection to accept the offer of St. Peter's "as a very serious personal challenge."

One of the first announcements by Fox Robinson after his appointment to St. Peter's but before his arrival to live in Bournemouth was that he preferred not to reside in the vicarage. He felt that 24 Manor Road was too far away from St. Peter's Church and suggested that another house should be bought which was more conveniently situated. When Williams vacated the vicarage on leaving for Bermuda the opportunity was taken of making a full and careful inspection of the premises. The Diocesan Architect found that many repairs and improvements were needed and gave an estimate of £1,680 as the probable cost. This report served to reinforce Fox Robinson's plea for a change. Would the parish be justified in spending so large a sum in altering and repairing a house which was not entirely suitable for its purpose?

Fox Robinson's opinion was fully supported by the diocesan authorities at Winchester, except that they suggested he should move into the vicarage and live there while a sale was being arranged. The vicar refused to do this, presumably thinking that if he complied with the suggestion his proposal for a change of vicarage might become shelved, and instead when he came to Bournemouth in February 1957 he and his family moved into the vacant curate's flat in St. Peter's Crescent. It remains a matter of wonder to many parishioners that after leaving his large old Queen Anne period vicarage in the Lincolnshire countryside (where he had to leave behind his pigs, cows and poultry) Fox Robinson was able to fit himself, his wife and seven children into a tiny flat, the sole merit of which was that it was within easy reach of the parish Church.

The vicar wrote at this time:

> I ought to say at this point why we are not living in 24 Manor Road. Even though a fairly large sum will be required to bring the house up to date it will still be an increasingly expensive house to live in. In the interval between accepting the living and the time when petrol was rationed although I myself covered just under 5,000 miles travelling backwards and forwards in an attempt to match the incomparable efforts of the Churchwardens and Mr. R. Phillips, the diocesan architect, we have so far failed to find an alternative Vicarage to 24 Manor Road. My wife and family, therefore, are having to squeeze themselves into the Assistant Priest's flat. This is obviously going to be a stumbling-block in ever looking for a much-needed second curate for St. Peter's. Will you therefore please urgently commend these needs in your prayers.

The Church Council resolved to sell the vicarage, but the Church Commissioners refused to allow the sale to take place until a suitable new house had been secured. The search for a new property then began in earnest, somewhat hampered by the lack of any definite knowledge of what sum of money the existing vicarage would fetch, opinions varying from £7,500 to £10,000. Several houses were seen and inspected and the most desirable proposition was *Hillbrow,* at the top of Richmond Hill, which could be bought for £14,500 (plus £1,500 for carpets and curtains) against the vendor purchasing 24 Manor Road for £10,000. At a long meeting on 3rd June the Church Council debated the proposal and eventually, by the small majority of 14 votes to 10 with a large number of abstentions, authorised the vicar to proceed, "a decision," wrote Fox Robinson, "involving both us and the parish in heavy cost, but, I believe, a Godsend for St. Peter's."

Unfortunately, by the end of July, certain difficulties had arisen over the transaction which resulted in the vicar having to report that "we are back where we started nine months ago, despite superhuman effort and much prayer. It is obvious that a Vicarage in the vicinity of St. Peter's is just as essential now as it was 120 years ago when the first Vicarage was built. The cost has been found to be crippling." The renewed quest for a suitable property was soon over, for in August it was found that Alderman Bennett Beale's residence at 18 Wimborne Road was in the market for sale at £6,350. The vicar interrupted his holiday to make a fleeting visit to Bournemouth to see it and was delighted. Built in 1933, this house had ample living accommodation with five bedrooms, all in first-class condition, and in the garden there was even a conker tree for the children. As soon as permission was forthcoming from the Church authorities the purchase was completed and Fox Robinson moved in with his family. The new vicarage was dedicated on 8th December, 1957 by the Bishop of Winchester, Dr. Alwyn Williams, in the presence of the patron, Sir George Meyrick.

It was now possible to dispose of the old vicarage in Manor Road which Messrs. Fox & Sons agreed to sell by auction on 27th February 1958, unless an offer in excess of £10,000 was received meanwhile. In the auctioneers' brochure the premises were described as occupying a premier position on the East Cliff and Freehold, "which is most unusual and unique in this part of the town." The sale room at St. Peter's Hall was packed out for the sale when the old vicarage went under the hammer for £9,050. This satisfactory realisation meant that a surplus would arise after repaying the loan on 18 Wimborne Road and settling all the expenses. The balance was partly used in 1959 to extend the dining-room of the new vicarage, the remainder being transferred to the endowment capital of the benefice so that the income of the living would be slightly increased. The buildings at 24 Manor Road were pulled down by their new owners and the site used, as had been that of the original parsonage, for the erection of a block of flats.

Fox Robinson introduced few changes in the services at St. Peter's. One new service was Compline, which he began holding on Wednesday evenings during Lent, 1957, and this was continued, with a short preparation for Holy Communion, on Saturdays at 7.30 p.m. The Compline service was dropped when the vicar resigned in 1966. As an encouragement to the younger members of the congregation who wanted to come to the Sung Eucharist on Sunday mornings a creche for babies and very young children was set up in the vestry from September, 1958, staffed by Mrs. Diggle and other ladies of the Church. At the Sung Eucharist itself Fox Robinson, undeterred by the failure of Daldy in this respect, insisted on having a sermon as directed by the rubric. To compensate for the extra length of the service and enable it to be over in time for Matins at 11.15 the Introit was omitted. Morden Bennett would surely have disapproved of leaving out the Introit; his views were clearly stated in 1869:

> In our present Book of Common Prayer the Introits are omitted; that is to say, there are no directions given for introducing them. But we feel at liberty to introduce hymns into the other services without any positive command for so doing, because we consider that it tends to edification, so we feel that we are permitted to sing a few verses from the Psalms at the commencement of this Eucharistical office. And if this practice were restored, we should find that it would give a special meaning to certain passages of Holy Scripture, which we had not perceived before. Take, for instance, the first two verses of Psalm xlii: 'Like as the hart desireth the water brooks, so longeth my soul after thee, O God. My soul is athirst for God, yea, even for the living God: when shall I appear before the presence of God?' Consider how suitable these words are as an introduction to the Communion Service. Observe how they seem to bring us once into the presence of our dear Lord and Saviour, and prepare our minds for the spiritual gifts which we hope to partake of.

Fox Robinson made the Sung Eucharist more of a family service, though he was always most anxious not to disturb the St. Peter's traditions of a choral celebration of praise and thanksgiving. He introduced the blessing of all the children, and later made the congregation participate in the offertory and join in the prayer of humble access. But in no sense did he transform the service into the "parish communion" which has become so popular in many places during recent years. In his preaching he laid greater stress on the sacrificial aspects of the Holy Eucharist and less on the aspects of worship and praise.

During Lent, 1964, beginning on Ash Wednesday, an evening Eucharist was held at St. Peter's at 7.30 p.m. This departure from previous practice was designed to enable members of the congregation who could not come to Church at eight o'clock in the morning to attend a weekday celebration during the Lenten period. Fox Robinson always indicated his willingness to hold services at any time which was convenient to a sufficiently large group of parishioners. At the greater festivals there was often an early celebration at 6.15 a.m., and on one occasion his assistant curates were dismayed to hear that the vicar was considering the possibility of holding a service at three o'clock in the morning for the benefit of newspaper employees who left work at that time.

In January, 1965, there was introduced an evening Eucharist to be held on Thursday at seven o'clock, except when a red-letter day fell during any week when the service was transferred to that day. Peter Brett, who had then recently arrived in the parish as assistant curate, wrote about the Weekday Evening Communion in the *Parish Magazine*:

> Recently the practice of holding Holy Communion in the evening has been growing. There are many difficulties for some people in attending the usual daily celebration in the morning, and our parish is no exception. Our congregation is so wide-flung, and many go to work quite early; mothers are involved in getting children off to school; and so on. And we have been asked to provide a Holy Communion on an evening during the week.
> Some of us, brought up in the tradition of morning Communion, have felt uneasy about the whole idea of the Sacrament taking place in the evening; but the first concern must be that this central activity of the faith should be readily available. There is the condition, however, that it should be approached with the reverence and recollection that must attend it.
> The Vicar has agreed that we should begin a weekday evening celebration, and it would seem sensible that we should adopt the new Roman Catholic rule of fasting. This rule has been moderated, with the evening Communion in view; and it is that for one hour before the service we should abstain from food. This does mean that due importance is given to the event, and that we are reminded of the preparation that should always be made before our Communions.

The 7 p.m. celebrations on weekdays were stopped after exactly one year. By January, 1966 it was noticed that there were no less than forty-six regular services between the two Churches in each week. The time had come for some of the less well attended services to be discontinued. The evening Eucharist communicants had become so few that this service was one of those which came to an end.

In September, 1957 the St. Peter's Fellowship was inaugurated, a social gathering in the Hall after Evensong on Sunday nights. Here, for some time, were held meetings, talks, discussion-groups, games and pantomime rehearsals, in fact all kinds of activities of interest to people of all ages and all types. The pantomime in January, 1958 was *Robinson Crusoe,* produced by Mrs. Nellie Pearmain. Though performed for one night only, it was a great success and the forerunner of many other witty productions which became particularly noted for the verse parodies of Michael Peterson and the clownish antics of the assistant curates.

Suitable assistant priests for St. Peter's were not easy to find. Throughout the early period of his incumbency Fox Robinson pursued a relentless quest for two young men who could help him run the parish and "restore the staffing position at St. Peter's to what it ought to be for a Church of this size and type." That the vacancies were so long being filled was due to the vicar's particular insistence that he would make no appointment until he was absolutely sure that he had found the right man. And it is a great tribute to his judgement in the matter that all the young assistant curates he brought to St. Peter's were most highly regarded and played very positive parts in improving the life of the parish. All of them secured well-merited advancement in the Church when they left Bournemouth. It is perhaps not generally known how tireless and painstaking Fox Robinson was in the investigations and interviews he held when these appointments were under consideration. Many vicars would have settled the difficulty by taking the first or second young man who came along, but not Fox Robinson, even though it involved him in a lot of additional work. We shall see something later on of the great influence which his assistant curates had upon the parish and in the town of Bournemouth.

First to be appointed was a newly-ordained deacon, Gordon Roe, who came from Oxford where he had been reading for a Ph.D. degree. He arrived in Bournemouth with his wife and children in June, 1958, taking up residence in St. Swithun's House at 22 Frances Road. As befitted a scholar of his attainments Roe soon busied himself with reorganising the records and archives of St. Peter's, and appealed for a new and up-to-date parish history which could include some material about the worship of the Church and the doings of the assistant curates, subjects which Leachman had neglected. Roe's persuasive arguments were largely responsible for a start being made on the present volume. Setting a good example himself, Roe published a series of most interesting articles on *St. Peter's Worthies,* among whom he counted William Godwin, Mary Wollstonecraft, Mary Shelley, Morden Bennett, Sir Henry Taylor and John Keble.

Fox Robinson's second clerical appointee was Eric Evans who came from Margate Parish Church as senior curate. Evans arrived in August, 1958 with his young wife and moved into a rented flat at Harewood, St. Valerie Road. Evans' persuasiveness upon the present writer and many other St. Peter's people took a different form, for he is now best remembered in the town as the founder and first director of the Bournemouth Samaritans. His wife Linda revived the Sunday School in 1959 (St. Peter's had been nearly thirty years without a Sunday School because it was thought there were no children in the parish) and within a very short time there was such a demand for places that the children had outgrown the vestries and taken over the Hall for their Sunday morning lessons. The appointment of Evans involved the Church in being no longer able to afford the part-time help of Canon Brasnett who then severed his connection with St. Peter's and moved to St. Augustine's as assistant priest under Keith Parkinson, the former priest-in-charge of St. Swithun's.

So far as St. Swithun's Church was concerned Fox Robinson and his churchwardens took a bold line, tackling a problem which even Daldy had failed to solve in a lasting way, the virtual independence of St. Swithun's within the parish. Almost at once after his induction the new vicar announced that he was making arrangements to give St. Swithun's a wider measure of control over its own affairs through its elected representatives, with the object of contributing to the dignity and standing of the daughter-Church in a way which was nevertheless compatible with the traditional relationship between the Churches. Fox Robinson made it clear, however, that to regard his scheme as a stepping-stone to dividing the two Churches into separate parishes would be a mistake, as this was not his intention. A St. Swithun's Committee was set up, consisting of the vicar, the priest-in-charge, the St. Swithun's wardens and other members of the Church Council representing St. Swithun's. This committee had to deal with all the expenses of St. Swithun's Church and churchyard, the stipend and housing of the priest-in-charge, the management of St. Swithun's Hall and one-third of all quotas and general administrative expenses incurred by the parish as a whole.

In this enterprise Fox Robinson was staunchly supported by the remarkable man who was then the priest-in-charge, Canon Gordon Clinch. When he came to Bournemouth to retire in 1956, after being incapacitated by a long and serious illness, Clinch had already, as he thought, completed two careers. To begin with, he had served in the Indian police, and latterly he had been a distinguished Worcestershire parson, Rural Dean and Honorary Canon. During the vacancy he had helped Brasnett at St. Swithun's and fully expected to resume his retirement when the new vicar of St. Peter's was appointed. However, at Fox Robinson's request and while the vicar was looking out for suitable young assistant curates, Clinch agreed to join the permanent staff for twelve months, though in fact he stayed much longer.

Clinch enthusiastically approved of the arrangements for greater independence at St. Swithun's, pointing out that they were "a step in the right direction and would provide the people of St. Swithun's with the necessary incentive for keeping their own house in order and raising the funds necessary to meet their obligations." The St. Swithun's Committee launched a new Free Will Offering Envelope Scheme which was an immediate spiritual and financial success. The leading laymen responsible for all this purposeful activity were the wardens, George Head and Ronald Phillips, and the treasurer, Sidney Bell, J.P. Despite the legal requirement that the churchwardens of St. Peter's, Ronald Hines and Gilbert Marshall, had to act officially as wardens for the whole parish they wisely and tactfully left the St. Swithun's people to manage their own affairs without interference and only tendered advice when requested to do so.

There was a change of churchwarden at St. Peter's in 1958 when Marshall retired as people's warden and did not seek re-election. It was one of the few contested elections of modern times. Four candidates were proposed, George Burr being elected. The election proved to be a slight rebuff for the outgoing warden who had tried to ensure that his own nominee, whose name he had already given to the Church Council, would succeed him. As it turned out Burr's election was a very wise choice, for it secured as churchwarden a man who served in that office for seven years with great distinction. He possessed the gift of knowing when to use his firm restraining influence and when to press forward with enterprises which he realised were in the best interests of the parish. Looking back on four years of happy partnership with him the present writer has pleasure in recording here his sincere appreciation of Burr's wise counsel in so many things and the great debt of gratitude St. Peter's owes to him.

The summer of 1957 saw the founding by Stanley Tigar and Canon Brasnett of a St. Peter's Football Club. The idea was for the team to compete in a cup competition during the winter with other Church sides in the locality. Though it sometimes had to go on to the field with only ten men available the St. Peter's team enjoyed considerable success from the outset and in a few years had grown strong enough to win the cup and become champions of the league. Percy Cole was the first president of the club, Michael Bazeley, captain and Stanley Tigar, secretary and manager.

The winter of 1956-57 had shown that the solid fuel heating system of St. Peter's Church was both inadequate and expensive. Accordingly a new oil heating apparatus was installed to replace it, being first used in November, 1957. Not only was the new system more economical, but, as the vicar explained with no little enthusiasm, it is "almost entirely automatic, with a clock that almost thinks, photo-electric cells, electronic switchgear and other marvels." One of the parish wags remarked that the heating at St. Peter's "is now so sensitive that when the preacher warms up the heating cuts itself off!"

CHAPTER XXIV

Stewardship And Samaritans

THERE CAN be no doubt that the most important spiritual and financial development at St. Peter's during the years of Fox Robinson's incumbency was the parish's participation in Christian Stewardship. This has been defined as "the practice of systematic and proportionate giving of time, abilities and material possessions based on the conviction that these are a trust from God, to be used in his service for the benefit of all mankind in grateful acknowledgement of Christ's redeeming love."

First whispers of the aims and ideals of Stewardship were heard in connection with money matters soon after Fox Robinson's arrival. He discovered that although £120 per week was needed to keep the parish going only £65 was coming in from collections. But it was not just a matter of finance; there were deeper and more fundamental spiritual problems to be faced, for which the congregation needed, and got, careful preparation. Brasnett began to set the tone in the summer of 1957 when it was estimated that the Church accounts would be in deficit to the extent of £1,000 by the end of the year: "The work of our Church, God's work, must never be hindered by lack of material resources. May I put it quite bluntly? If the money is not forthcoming, there is something wrong about the depth or sincerity of our gratitude, of our love in response to His."

Hard work, effective preaching and a successful vicar's appeal had their beneficial results. The accounts were closed at the year's end without deficit, despite the fact that there had been no bazaar or gift day for parish funds. True to the traditions of Morden Bennett, Fox Robinson cast the most disapproving eye on such functions unless the proceeds were intended for some worthy object outside the parish, such as missions.

The idea of Stewardship was nothing new (for instance, thirty years before, Marsh was expressing his hope "that all members of the congregation will endeavour to support the Church in proportion to their income, so that they may become good stewards of the sums entrusted to them"), but the principles and practice of Stewardship gained ground at the time of the Lambeth Conference in 1958 which declared that "A parish without a sense of stewardship has within it the seeds of decay. A man who refuses to be a steward of his time, talent and money is unworthy of being in the Father's House." The Church Council was lectured on "planned giving" and the vicar's appeal of that year invited a response based on the Stewardship ideals.

The period of the Lambeth Conference was marked at St. Peter's by a constant stream of Bishops from all over the world visiting the parish and preaching at services. These included the former vicar, Bishop Williams of Bermuda, a former vicar's son, Oliver Green-Wilkinson, Bishop of Northern Rhodesia, who recorded his pleasure in being "able to celebrate for the first time at the Altar where I made my first Communion and in the Church where I found my vocation for the Priesthood and the Mission Field," and Bishop Gower of New Westminster, British Columbia, who celebrated the centenary of that Canadian province with a service in honour of Richard Clement Moody, whose grave is in St. Peter's churchyard.

In the town of Bournemouth the Lambeth Conference was marked by a procession of witness on Monday evening, 23rd June, 1958, in which all the local Churches joined, to awaken in churchpeople a clearer understanding of the world-wide scope of the Anglican communion and to demonstrate to the community at large something of the vigour and missionary enterprise of the Church. Led by the Bishops of Delhi and Kalgoorlie, two processions, comprising in all over two thousand people, marched through the central part of the town, both headed by the Cross and a band. Traffic was stopped and the townspeople noticed the banners of the different parishes leading their contingents to services at St. Peter's and Holy Trinity.

It seemed as if the Church was making some impact upon the community it sought to serve. Fox Robinson maintained the tradition of his predecessors by being chosen as Mayor's Chaplain on several occasions. St. Peter's, the mother-Church in the centre of the town, tended to become more outward-looking towards its geographical parish, though it was not the first Church in the Bournemouth Deanery to promote a Christian Stewardship campaign. This came for St. Peter's in the autumn of 1959.

Fox Robinson explained that in North America the Stewardship movement had resulted in a great increase in churchgoing and he thought this could be echoed in Bournemouth. Stewardship would bring blessing to human lives as it gave Glory to God. It taught Christians to acknowledge their responsibility to God for the use of their time, talents and treasure. Although the vicar was not yet able to convince the whole of his congregation that the particular campaign method which he proposed to adopt for St. Peter's was a good thing, the Church Council resolved to proceed. There would be a campaign with a parish supper and every-member canvass, seeking commitments for increased giving of abilities and money. Fox Robinson recalled the St. Peter's traditions in urging support for this policy:

> In the past God has called this parish to do great things for Him. By faithful response a hundred years ago the basic pattern of Bournemouth church life was established. Church Schools were built throughout the town on the faith and faithfulness of our forebears in this parish. Many have gone from our congregation to the Priesthood, to the Mission field, to the Religious life. Today countless souls look to this parish for a lead in Christian Stewardship.

Thus it was that St. Peter's participated in the first united Deanery canvass ever held in England. The parish's financial targets were £7,860 for St. Peter's and £2,826 for St. Swithun's, as greatly increased incomes were required by both Churches for 1960. The campaign was launched with a parish supper at the Pavilion; a delightful report of this gathering written by Eric Evans brings to mind the account of the East Parley festivities of nearly a century before.

> To call this splendid occasion a supper is really a misnomer, for it was actually a dinner in the grand manner. Those of us who arrived early at the Pavilion were thrilled by the sight of a sea of gleaming white linen tablecloths and napkins, glittering with glass and silverware; each table also being tastefully decorated with flowers. Places were laid for about three hundred and twenty people, but our actual numbers were around three hundred. Unfortunately it was a very wet and stormy night which doubtless prevented some folk from coming as intended. The meal itself was superb and from the soup to the coffee every dish was admirably prepared and beautifully served.

After describing the speeches made and resolution passed in support of the Stewardship programme Evans ended his report with these words:

> Thus concluded a memorable evening in the history of the parish. Those present will not easily forget it. We have committed ourselves not only to a great task but to a new way of life, and must ever remember our Lord's words when he said that no man having put his hand to the plough and looking back is worthy of the Kingdom of God. Would to Heaven that every single one of our Church people had been there to join us in our venture, but what the pioneers do today, the many may do tomorrow.

On the first Stewardship Sunday, 15th November, 1959, seventy-eight Church members were commissioned to go out and visit the congregations of both St. Peter's and St. Swithun's in their homes. It was difficult at the time accurately to assess the spiritual implications of this campaign, but, as one visitor commented, "the Parish will never be the same again." The financial results of the early returns (it was rather like an election night as the visitors came back with their envelopes of completed commitment cards) were remarkable and the vicar was soon able to report that over one-half of the amounts needed had been given or promised.

Christian Stewardship gained a far greater hold on the parish during succeeding years when full-scale campaigns were also mounted upon similar lines. However, within a few years it was realised that the every-member canvass by personal visits annually no longer held the same impact as it had done in the first campaigns; and there seemed to be nothing new which could rekindle the freshness and enthusiasm that had characterised the early efforts. By this time Stewardship had gained an impregnable foothold on the parish and its results were apparent in other directions than money, the finance being left to circularisation by post rather than personal call.

A cub pack, a youth club, new prayer and Bible-reading groups and retreat weekends were all activities mainly derived from the congregation's new awareness of Stewardship and the spiritual stimulation which urged a great many parishioners to endeavour to live their lives closer to God. The outward result of this awareness and stimulation which gained the greatest publicity and soon acquired an influence far beyond the parish boundaries was the establishment of the Bournemouth Samaritans, founded by the senior priest at St. Peter's, Eric Evans.

To put it in its briefest terms the Samaritans exist to help any people that come to them who are tempted to commit suicide or are in great despair. The organisation had originated in London only a few years previously under the leadership and inspiration of the Rev. Chad Varah, vicar of St. Stephen's Walbrook, and had just begun to spread to other centres in the provinces. Evans saw the need for a branch of this organisation to function in Bournemouth and the surrounding area and determined to start it. The Bournemouth Samaritans thus began under the auspices of St. Peter's Church with its headquarters in St. Peter's Hall, though it was soon embracing a membership of people from all denominations working together towards the object of helping those in acute despair or with suicidal tendencies in their times of greatest trouble.

Evans summed up the spiritual implications in an address to the Bournemouth Ruri-Decanal Conference soon after the local Samaritans service opened:

> We are often reminded that the Church is the Body of Christ on earth; and therefore called to be His voice, His feet and His hands. The Church has tried to be just this, but changing circumstances and social conditions mean that the Church, too, has to adapt itself to meet the needs of each succeeding age. There are many of us who feel that Our Lord, if He were here on earth in person today, could not, and would not, sit down and witness with equanimity the sufferings which many folk undergo. It is, I think, to anyone who has eyes to see, that many people are spiritually sick; perhaps through sin, or perhaps because they have been victims of circumstances, or through ill-health and no fault of their own; but they are people who feel they are farthest away from the love of God. Perhaps they have never known that love, and because of this, when things go wrong see no purpose in life at all, and are tempted to put an end to everything; in other words, people who may well die through lack of that love. The purpose of the Samaritans is to help such people.

Evans was most energetic and purposeful in getting the Samaritans started. If his approach on the subject to the present writer is any guide to his normal practice his method was to thrust into the hands of his intended recruit a copy of the *Readers Digest* which contained an article about Chad Varah and the Samaritans and say, "Go home and and read that; then come along on Tuesday evening to the preparation class." The training sessions for the first "volunteers" went on through the winter of 1960-61, guided by Evans himself, Chad Varah and his assistant Eric Reed from London, and Drs. Doris Odlum and James Fisher who generously gave their time and imparted their professional knowledge as honorary psychiatrist and medical adviser respectively. Then, on 6th March, 1961, the Bournemouth Samaritans was inaugurated at a public meeting in St. Peter's Hall presided over by the enthusiastic Mayor, Mrs. Bessie Bicknell. Evans was appointed first Director, with Canon Clinch as his deputy, who took over the directorship after Evans left Bournemouth in 1962.

The telephone line of Bournemouth 21999 became one of the busiest in the district as calls came in from despairing people seeking that friendship and loving concern which the Samaritans offer. Although the Bournemouth Samaritans is now quite independent of St. Peter's, it still derives substantial support from the parish, by prayer, service and money, and continues to do its work in the tradition of that first Samaritan who helped the man on the Jericho road. As Evans explained when forming the Bournemouth branch, "He merely gave help when it was most needed—so, I hope, shall we."

Another direct result of the Stewardship visiting to the known members of St. Peter's and St. Swithun's was the parish survey, carried out in February and March, 1961, which involved visiting the homes of all the residents within the parochial boundaries, in order to discover their church affiliations, if any, and to invite them to join in the activities of the parish. Fox Robinson sent a special message to all those visited:

> For 115 years, since it began, your Parish Church has been outward as well as upward looking. Worship of God in Christ matters above all, and in and with our worship goes, and comes, Christ's love for souls—*all* souls. Your Parish Church cares for God and for the things of God. It also cares for God's children, and tries to reflect the Gospel truth that He loves them one by one. Jesus saves us, one by one. Jesus feeds us (in Holy Communion), one by one. Jesus forgives us, one by one. Jesus cares for each, as a Shepherd for the last sheep.
>
> Our visit to your home is meant to *show* you just this, and our prayer is that you may see it, and rejoice to God's Glory and your own salvation. But remember, too, that your Parish Church is your spiritual home. It is where God's family gathers, where *you* have a place. If that place is empty our family life and worship is incomplete; and the work of God's family suffers. So do you.

Three thousand households were visited, representing about 90% of the population of the parish; and once again the people in the centre of the town were reminded that their Church wanted them and cared about them. When David Haslam came to St. Peter's as assistant curate in 1962 it was supposed to be his chief duty to work on the results of the parish survey and conduct a special mission towards the geographical parish. This he did, so far as his other duties allowed, with an encouraging measure of success, but his work was hampered by the fact that the appointment of a new senior priest to replace Evans, as Fox Robinson intended, was never made, and so Haslam had to perform those duties as well as the ones for which he had been given special responsibility. In the St. Peter's ministry to the parish itself, the honorary assistant priest, the Rev. Eric Norton, commenced most valuable service, particularly among the Jews in the town, for which his Old Testament scholarship and sympathetic personality particularly fitted him and which he still continues with great distinction. In the summer of 1965 another parish survey was carried out, when further visits were made to the homes of the parishioners.

The vicar summed up the achievements and spiritual progress which had emanated from the Christian Stewardship inspiration as "a partnership of clergy and laity seeking jointly God's purpose in our parish and each in our own lives. The Church advances as God's people *seek first* His Kingdom and His Righteousness."

CHAPTER XXV

"The Time Of The Plough"

IN ADDITION to acquiring for St. Peter's a vicarage nearer the Church Fox Robinson set himself the task of equipping the parish with a number of properties for use as residences by the permanent staff, both clerical and lay. The first of these ventures, carried out in 1961, was the erection of two new flats on the second floor of St. Peter's Hall to the plans of Mr. Ronald Phillips, who was then both diocesan architect and vicar's warden at St. Swithun's. One suite of rooms was intended for an assistant curate, the other for a resident caretaker. The Church Council agreed that this proposal was long overdue and that its implementation would make a great difference to the efficient running of the parish. Messrs. W. Hayward & Sons were awarded the building contract on a tender of £6,958, and the work went ahead during the summer months. Realisable securities held by the Church were cashed to provide over half the cost, in addition to which were put gifts of nearly £1,000 and interest-free loans of £1,500. The rest of the money was borrowed from the bank, several of the loans were converted into gifts, and everything was finally paid off by 1966. The builders got on with the work so quickly that the new flats were ready in advance of the stipulated contract date and were opened by Lady Meyrick on 1st October, 1961. Dean Hedley Burrows, the erstwhile vicar, performed the dedication ceremony. First residents in the new accommodation were Mr. and Mrs. Philip Davis, the new hall caretakers, and the Reverend David Haslam, who joined the clerical staff in 1962 when Evans left Bournemouth to become Youth Chaplain to Gloucester Diocese.

Gordon Roe, the lively and popular junior priest, left the parish in the spring of 1961 to become priest-in-charge of St. Michael's, Abingdon. During his ministry there he became Dr. Roe upon being awarded the degree of D.Phil. at Oxford University. To replace Roe a newly ordained deacon named Colin Sykes, who had been a schoolmaster, joined the staff in September, 1961 and went, with his parents, to live at St. Swithun's House. All these assistant curates were of the highest calibre (indeed it has been deservedly said of Fox Robinson that few vicars can have displayed such unerring judgement in the choice of staff) and St. Peter's was most fortunate to have as its curates men who could both expound theology in a modern and helpful way and let their hair down as robbers and broker's men in the parish pantomimes. Their ministry to the local actors was a special feature of their work which was particularly valuable. It was not without its amusing side. Roe tells the story of his introduction as chaplain to the Aquabelles:

> The manager waved me towards a door marked in red paint, "Private—Keep Out—Ladies Dressing Room—Strictly No Admittance." As my hand reached for the handle my neck was fixed in a vice-like grip—or that was how I felt, though I was probably only grabbed by the elbow. "Where are you going?" asked a female attendant. "In there," I replied. "What for?" she asked suspiciously. "I am their chaplain," I declared. "I've heard that before," she rejoined!

Haslam had his sitting-room filled with signed photographs of celebrities in the theatrical profession and when he left St. Peter's at the end of 1965 to become vicar of East Worldham the local press called him "a 'hit' with the pop stars." Haslam replied modestly that several chorus girls had asked him to prepare them for confirmation and added:— "I have always been well received by those on the stage, who often find themselves travelling on a Sunday. It is because of this travel that we have taken the Church to them. I found that they seemed to want to talk about religion without my bringing the subject up." Sykes, who will long be remembered at St. Peter's for his straight talking from the pulpit and his sympathetic ministrations to the sick folk of the parish, had by this time left Bournemouth on taking up an appointment at Llandaff Cathedral.

There were also several temporary assistant priests from all over the world who joined the clerical staff of St. Peter's for short periods. Among them were Webster Nechironga from Salisbury, Southern Rhodesia, John Presswell, who took an appointment at St. John's College at York, Michael Corea, succentor of Singapore Cathedral who came from Ceylon with his Malayan wife before going on to St. Augustine's College at Canterbury, David Tsukada from Japan, who had been lecturing in Norway and also went on to St. Augustine's College, and Francis Msokosela from Archbishop Oliver Green-Wilkinson's diocese of Northern Rhodesia. Though these priests were at St. Peter's for so little time that it was difficult for members of the congregation to get to know them well, they did bring to the parish a much richer sense of the world-wide mission of the Church and were able to portray at first-hand some of the problems which still have to be overcome if true religion is ever to flourish in some of the more neglected areas of the world.

Canon Clinch maintained and extended the life of St. Swithun's Church for years longer than he had originally intended, eventually resigning in May, 1963. Thereafter Clinch devoted himself with great energy and ability to his duties as director of the Bournemouth Samaritans. Nobody was appointed to succeed him as priest-in-charge of St. Swithun's, much to the disappointment of members of that Church.

There was also a familiar face missing from St. Peter's. Early in 1963 the sacristan, Leonard South, who had served the parish for thirty-five years, resigned, to the great sorrow of many people at the Church. It was hard to get used to St. Peter's without him, for he had always taken great pride in the beautiful Church he loved and worked for. The new sacristan, appointed for duty at both St. Peter's and St. Swithun's, was Ronald Smith, formerly sub-verger at Lichfield Cathedral, for whom a flat was rented at 1 St. Peter's Crescent.

In 1964 further provision was made for staff accommodation with the purchase of *Normanhurst,* St. Peter's Road, a house converted into two flats. The congregation contributed generously towards the purchase, but most of the money was borrowed from the bank. The Smith family moved into one of these flats when the previous tenant vacated it. The vicar was most keen to secure a similar property for staff accommodation in the neighbourhood of St. Swithun's Church. The possibility of building in the grounds of St. Swithun's was considered, but that idea had to be discarded. Early in 1966 a very suitable house in two self-contained flats at 1 Gervis Road, just opposite St. Swithun's Church, came onto the market and was purchased for £9,100. At the same time the Church Council decided to sell 22 Frances Road as soon as a convenient opportunity arose. The acquisition of 1 Gervis Road involved the Church in considerable borrowing, but several gifts were received towards the cost, including one donation of £1,000.

The other very expensive project at this period was the re-roofing of St. Peter's Church. As early as December, 1962 the vicar was suggesting to his parishioners that they might "buy a slate." The appeal for funds was launched and by 1964 it was thought that sufficient money was in hand to justify a start being made. The roofing work was carried out during the autumn and winter of 1964, being finally completed in January, 1965. Messrs. W. Thompson & Sons Ltd. were the contractors. The cost, which had been estimated at about £5,000, came to a total of £4,661 15s. 6d., all of which was collected by the summer of 1965 as follows:

	£	s.	d.
Legacy from Major Reginald Spencer	1,000	0	0
Gifts and donations	3,092	18	1
Collections and boxes	269	4	10
Coffee mornings, etc.	252	19	2
Interest at bank	46	13	5
	£4,661	15	6

There were also some relatively minor, but nevertheless important, additions to the fabric. In 1958, as the result of an elderly lady falling down the west door steps as she left Church after a service, a pair of railings was offered, and these were erected early in 1959. In 1964 new gates for the churchyard were given in memory of two notable parishioners who had recently died; the west gates in memory of Thomas William Sutcliffe and the east gates in memory of William Vincent Robertson. In 1960 new sound amplification equipment was installed in St. Peter's to the design of Mr. H. J. W. Fowke, who took the most infinite pains and carried out frequent experiments to ensure that the best possible reproduction could be obtained all over the building. Halter microphones were introduced so that the clergy could use the new apparatus in many different parts of the Church. And the sanctuary lamps, which had hitherto been lit by wicks burning in oil, were electrified.

The years 1962 and 1963 saw the completion of two publications concerning St. Peter's. First in point of time, and a really excellent piece of work which has been most helpful in the compilation of this book, was the *Guide* to St. Peter's by Nicholas Taylor, of Sidney Sussex College, Cambridge, with photographs by Kenneth Hoskin of Bournemouth. Taylor's Guide is particularly valuable for its architectural notes, but it deals also with the history of the parish and the influences of Tractarianism and the Gothic Revival. It is far more than just a guide-book and was justly acclaimed by the *Church Times* as one of the best examples of this type of work which had been sent to them for review. The Guide was published by the Church Council which, in conjunction with the author, was careful to ensure that it was produced in a way that would do honour to the place it describes and the distinguished history of St. Peter's.

In 1963 the present writer, with assistance and encouragement from the authorities of Christchurch Priory, issued *The East Parley Mission* in celebration of the centenary of St. Barnabas school-chapel. On 21st July 1963 a special Sung Evensong was conducted by Fox Robinson at St. Barnabas Chapel to mark the centenary, and the little Church was packed. St. Peter's choir attended and the sermon was preached by the vicar of Christchurch, the Rev. Leslie Yorke.

There was a break with the past in 1963 when the Christopher Library, which had been housed in St. Peter's Hall for thirty years, was moved in its entirety to the new diocesan retreat and conference house at Old Alresford Place. The Library itself was a most remarkable collection of books, comprising over two thousand volumes on subjects connected with religion. Decreasing membership and increased expenses made the move from Bournemouth necessary.

A glance through the local newspaper files for these years reveals many odd items of interest to a St. Peter's historian. To take a few examples, there was a blaze in the churchyard which the Fire Brigade had to extinguish, an old age pensioner was fined £2 for being drunk and disorderly in Church, alms-boxes had to be replaced by safes because of frequent pilfering, the vicar's wife admitted keeping a dangerous dog and was ordered by the magistrates to keep it under control, a man convicted of attempted burglary at the vicarage was sentenced to twelve months imprisonment, the choirboys were borrowed by the Sadlers Wells Opera Company for performances of *Tosca* and by the Mayor to sing Christmas carols at his reception, a St. Peter's bell-ringer went to America to teach ringing at Washington Cathedral, and the vicar gave evidence at Court offering to look after a young parishioner who had pleaded guilty to fraud. On a previous occasion when the vicar had had to give evidence in Court he had commented in his diary, "Justice served, but the Lord's business not hastened."

In 1961 the choir made the first of three visits to Nice, on the French Riviera, where they sang at Holy Trinity Church, whose chaplain was Canon Hearsey, the erstwhile assistant curate of St. Peter's. The party, led by Eric and Linda Evans, Michael Peterson and Stanley Tigar, flew from Hurn to Paris on 5th April, just after Easter, and spent ten days abroad. A successful jumble sale at St. Swithun's Hall raised over £40 towards the expenses of the trip which, needless to say, was enjoyed immensely by everyone who went. Peterson wrote some most entertaining accounts of this and subsequent visits to Nice which were published in the *Parish Magazine* and are well worth re-reading.

Christmas 1960 saw the establishment of a new seasonal custom for St. Peter's, a joint effort with Bournemouth's Roman Catholics.

This was the live crib, presented in the churchyard on the evenings before Christmas. *The Daily Telegraph* reported the event and also carried a photograph of the scene. It was a historic occasion and understandably attracted wide notice, for it served to show that the essential truths which unite Christians are so much more important than the things which divide churchmen into different denominations. Hundreds of Bournemouth people came to watch the scene, enacted in front of the Chapel of the Resurrection, and so friendly and successful was it that the live crib presentation was repeated every Christmas afterwards while Fox Robinson was vicar.

On 3rd October 1965 St. Peter's marked the centenary of the daily Eucharist with a special service, and in 1965-66 the Church commemorated the centenary of its association with John Keble. A very successful Floral Festival was held in St. Peter's Church for three days in October 1965 in connection with the 120th anniversary of the parish when over £400 was raised for the fabric fund. There were over seventy floral arrangements, and the Church plate and vestments were laid out on exhibition.

The last two assistant curates of Fox Robinson's incumbency, Peter Brett and Brian Simmons, maintained the very high standards which had been set by their predecessors. Brett, who had been on the staff of Tewkesbury Abbey, came to Bournemouth in the summer of 1964. The flat which Evans had occupied being no longer available, Brett and his family resided in a flat which the Church rented for them at Dunholme Manor, Manor Road, close to where the old vicarage had been. In 1966 Brett was appointed to the chaplaincy of University and Hatfield Colleges at Durham University. After taking charge of the parish while the vicar was away on his extended leave during the summer of 1966 Brett left Bournemouth at the beginning of the university term to take up his new duties. Simmons came to St. Peter's immediately after his ordination as deacon at Trinity 1964, bringing to his ministry the unusual experience of a master mariner. His connection with the merchant navy was resumed in January 1967, when he became the Missions to Seamen chaplain at the newly established Seamen's Training School at Gravesend.

From 1964 to 1967 there were several changes among the parish churchwardens and also in the method of appointing them. In 1964 the writer, having served as vicar's warden for four years, asked to be released. In his place Fox Robinson appointed John Fawcett, a blind physiotherapist who has overcome his physical impairment in such a remarkable way that he carried out the duties of his office for five years with no less ability than a man of full capacity. By 1965 a new Measure of the Church Assembly had come into force which laid down an amended procedure for electing wardens. This new Measure provided that both churchwardens should be elected by the common consent of the minister and the people at a joint meeting of the local government electors for the parish and the Church members on the parish's electoral roll. If the minister and the people were unable to agree the minister was to appoint one churchwarden and the people the other. In 1965 the vicar decided, with the approval of the annual meeting, to continue with the old method of appointment, so he registered a technical objection to any names the people might submit. Fox Robinson then reappointed Fawcett as his warden and, with Burr declining to seek re-election as people's warden, the meeting unanimously elected John Gibbings in his place. The 1966 annual meeting resolved to act in accordance with the new Measure and, by common consent, Fawcett and Gibbings were reappointed.

Thus the old distinction between vicar's and people's wardens has now disappeared and become a part of history. The change in procedure, though a very real one in practice, should never have been necessary because, though the rule was more honoured in the breach than in observance, the old law had already provided for agreement between incumbent and people being reached if possible on both churchwardens. It is just curious to note that so strong were the traditions of separate appointments (in most other parishes as well as at St. Peter's) that until 1966 nobody seems to have troubled to make a real attempt to arrive at a common consent. In 1967, during the vacancy of the benefice, the task of choosing both wardens fell upon the people alone. Fawcett and Hines were the successful candidates. Both were re-elected the following year. Fawcett did not seek re-election in 1969 when that great stalwart of St. Peter's since pre-war days, T. I. ("Tip") Pearmain, was unanimously elected to succeed him. A very encouraging feature of recent times has been the tendency for churchwardens to serve for only a few years consecutively. In past years it had been the most usual practice for them to retain office almost indefinitely until retirement was forced upon them through death or infirmity.

In the summer of 1966 the vicar went away from Bournemouth on three months leave. Then, shortly before he was due back to resume his duties, Mrs. Fox Robinson was seriously injured in a motor accident in Lincolnshire, as a result of which the vicar announced on 24th September that he would be resigning the living at the end of November. He explained that, since his wife had an indispensable place in the day-to-day working of the parish, "neither she nor I would wish to ask the parish to accept an impeded ministry from me, particularly when there are so many signs of growth in the church life." Fortunately, by November, Mrs. Fox Robinson was sufficiently well recovered to enable her to return to Bournemouth. Early in December the Fox Robinson family vacated the vicarage and returned to their beloved Lincolnshire for rest and recuperation. In his last *Parish Magazine* was printed an appreciation of the previous ten years by a parishioner who was at St. Peter's before Fox Robinson Came. The article contained both an assessment of those times and a prophesy for the future which, in the few, short years that have since elapsed, has proved remarkably accurate, as the following extracts show:

> By 1957, the Church (in the wider sense) had realised that not only would things never again be as they were, but that it was no longer even desirable, or indeed right that they should be as they were. Though the phrase was not coined till some years later, "the wind of change" was already blowing. And for the future historian of St. Peter's the significance of the Fox Robinson incumbency will lie not in the happy, if often hazy memories of those who knew the parish before or after 1957, but in the extent to which St. Peter's was able to recreate itself to be the church in Bournemouth — a Bournemouth of which pre-war Vicars can have had no inkling.
>
> This is not the occasion to try to assess spiritual developments. Such things cannot be assessed in terms which would make sense in a magazine article, and in any case the growth of the spirit is generally "in secret." But since the spiritual often manifests itself in the material, the material growth of the parish may not be without significance. And of material growth and change there has probably been more than at any other time in the history of the parish, excepting possibly the days of the first Vicar.
>
> Problems still remain — the churchyard and the hall — but the next Vicar, though he will have to find curates and organist, will discover that many of the problems with which he might well have been faced have already been solved. The ground has been well ploughed and seed sown; some even now bearing fruit.
>
> Perhaps the last ten years will be seen to have been "the time of the plough." And although ploughing can sometimes be a painful process, William Blake wrote: "The cut worm forgives the plough." The worm will forgive, if needs be, not out of charity, but because it knows that in the long run the plough is followed by the harvest. And the harvest is as much the ploughman's as the reaper's.

CHAPTER XXVI

Up To Date

WHEN FOX ROBINSON departed Simmons was the only full-time assistant curate left in the parish, and he was due to leave in another five weeks. With two Churches to care for it was no easy matter. Fortunately, Norton and a group of very willing, retired clergymen undertook the maintenance of the services and as much of the general parochial work as could be managed. St. Peter's had already effectively been without a vicar for nearly six months, owing to the great deal of time that Fox Robinson had spent out of the parish between June and November. The number of regular services was curtailed and some others rearranged, so that the work could be conducted more conveniently. The congregation waited anxiously for news of Sir George Meyrick's selection of the new incumbent.

Another familiar face was also missing from St. Peter's, Michael Peterson the organist, who had left at the end of October 1966 on being appointed organist and choirmaster at Tewkesbury Abbey, an important position he richly deserved, though St. Peter's was very sorry to see him go after twelve happy years. Peterson had been to St. Peter's so much more than just an organist. He had played an important part in the furtherance of the spiritual life of the Church, had contributed a vast number of lively articles to the *Parish Magazine,* and had written some most witty words and appropriate music for parish entertainments. In the field of Church music he was renowned throughout the Bournemouth area as a brilliant performer, and he gave many excellent recitals on the organs of St. Peter's and other Churches. He was not afraid to introduce modern service settings and he kept his choir, despite difficulties sometimes in getting enough boys, well up to standard in the famous traditions of St. Peter's music. Peterson's humour over the matter of his own departure was typical:

> I thought at the time that it was my own decision to try and move, but now that the Vicar is going and the curates gone or going, I begin to wonder. It can't all be coincidence. And how often does a parish get the chance to redecorate all the rooms at once?

The last important thing done for the organ in Peterson's time was the installation of a new blower and humidifiers. By 1965 the need was urgent, for there had been a few occasions when the organ had been put out of action, sometimes just at the start of a service, and the trouble was always likely to recur in times of dry weather. A series of appeals was made towards raising the sum necessary for these renewals, which approached £1,200, and the work was completed in April, 1966.

The headmaster of Stoborough School at Wareham, Mr. Harry Sayles, a former assistant organist at Guildford Cathedral, was appointed to succeed Peterson on a temporary basis, pending permanent arrangements being made upon the induction of a new vicar. Sayles came to St. Peter's to join the choir at a most opportune moment, for Peterson was getting ready to leave and no other organist was readily available. Peterson has described how Sayles "arrived as a tenor and was rash enough after his first Evensong to ask if he could try the organ, thereby revealing himself as an organist as well. So convenient, as the 'Holiday-makers' were due to begin in about ten minutes. Just in time to get used to the organ!"

The vacancy in the benefice also coincided with some anxiety about money. Faced with a diocesan quota for the year of £2,959, nearly £60 a week, the parish was unable to meet the requirements. This was partly due to a changed formula for calculating the assessment which discriminated rather unfairly against the "down-town" type of parish which had to employ a comparatively large staff. The St. Peter's representative, David Preston, explained the parish's position to the diocesan conference at Winchester, but the majority decided to adhere to the new method of assessment. It was pointed out that the default by St. Peter's in paying the quota in full had not come about irresponsibly, but only after much heart-searching. Within a decade the demands of the diocese had approximately trebled.

Temporary charge of the parish after the departure of Simmons was taken by Norton, jointly with Canon Noel Yarrow, the former vicar of South Elmsall, near Pontefract, who had been assisting at St. Stephen's during his retirement. Writing during February, 1967, the editor of the *Parish Magazine* paid them and their helpers a well-deserved tribute:

> The inter-regnum continues, although, as many parishioners and visitors alike have commented, one is hardly conscious of it, such is the effective way in which Canon Yarrow, Father Norton and their retired (?) colleagues are carrying out their pastoral duties. We must not cease to thank God for the ministry of these priests, turning what could easily have been a most difficult period into a

smooth-running and, even more important, a spiritually fruitful time.

On 26th February the announcement came that Sir George Meyrick had appointed a new vicar and that his choice had met with the Bishop's approval. Designated as the new incumbent was the Rev. Colin Clement Walter James, the forty-year-old Organiser of Religious Broadcasting in the South and West for the B.B.C. at Bristol. The son of an Honorary Canon of Lincoln (observe the Lincolnshire connection which has been a common feature of so many St. Peter's vicars) and nephew of J. L. Beaumont James, assistant curate of St. Peter's under Daldy and later rector of Millbrook, James had already had a varied and interesting career.

Born in Cambridge, where his father was then vicar of St. Giles, James attended the King's College Choir School and then went to Aldenham School in Hertfordshire. After a spell in the Royal Navy at the end of the war, where he served in Hong Kong and there developed an interest in radio broadcasting, he returned to King's as an undergraduate to read history. Upon taking his degree he went on to Cuddesdon Theological College where he trained under Kenneth Riches, now Bishop of Lincoln. From there in 1952 he was ordained to a title at St. Dunstan's, Stepney, the mother-Church of East London and the parish Church of the High Seas. St. Dunstan's was a big parish in a working-class area, having a staff of six assistant curates, two Church schools, many clubs and organisations, and the chaplaincies of the London Hospital and Mile End Hospital.

In 1955 James moved to Stowe School in Buckinghamshire as chaplain and history master in the upper school. Four years later he joined the B.B.C. Religious Broadcasting Department in London and in 1960 succeeded the late Prebendary Martin Willson as Organiser in Bristol. The new vicar explained that this had meant a wide contact with many Churches of all denominations in the Region and scope for many studio programmes—plays, features, documentaries, talks and discussions—as well as radio and television outside broadcasts from Churches.

"Although it will be a great wrench to leave the B.B.C. after eight happy years," said James upon his appointment, "I am very much looking forward to returning to the parish ministry and to taking up new work at St. Peter's. This is one of the many Churches in the South and West that I have been associated with in religious broadcasting." He thought that at a time when the Church was developing a number of specialist ministries alongside the parish ministry it was a good thing that there should be an interchange between them, and hoped that the experience gained from the one could be fruitful in the other. His years with the B.B.C. have given James such knowledge and experience of religious broadcasting that he has written an authoritative and most valuable chapter on that subject for *A Manual for Holy Week,* published by S.P.C.K. in 1967.

Though it had become usual to hold the Annual Church Meeting in January or February, the 1967 meeting was delayed until after Easter in the hope that the new vicar would by then have arrived in Bournemouth. But James had several B.B.C. commitments to fulfil before he could be freed to take up his new duties and accordingly his institution and induction were arranged for the eve of the patronal festival, 28th June.

One of the most pressing tasks facing James after his induction was to engage new clerical staff. Two young assistant curates were appointed, and they arrived in August and September, 1967. The senior, Paul Iles, came to St. Peter's, wrote the vicar:

> . . . from Salisbury, where he was ordained in 1961 after graduating at Cambridge and training at the Salisbury Theological College. He served his title at St. Michael's in that city, while at the same time becoming Chaplain to the Bishop Wordsworth School. During the last three years he has doubled up his duties at the school with those of Minor Canon at the Cathedral. He brings many gifts to the ministry here, not least in music, since he is a Fellow of the Royal College of Organists. At the end of September he will be joined by Christopher Jones, who will live in the flat over St. Peter's Hall. Mr. Jones is no stranger to Bournemouth or to St. Peter's, since before his ordination he taught for a time on the staff of Ringwood Grammar School. It will be very good to welcome him back to our community. After reading English at King's College, London, he went to Wells Theological College for his training for the Priesthood. He was ordained in this Diocese in 1965 to a title at St. Luke's, Winchester, a large housing estate parish on the outskirts of the city. And now he comes to us to serve his second curacy.

Despite his busy life in parochial activities Iles has found time to play an active role in the life of the town as chairman of the Bournemouth committee for "Shelter," the organisation dedicated to the relief of the homeless. Jones, who numbered among his duties editing the *Parish Magazine,* set a precedent in August, 1968 by geting married at St. Peter's. So far as can be ascertained he was the only assistant curate ever to have been married in the Church during the tenure of his appointment.

James' third clerical appointment brought special joy to the parishioners when in October 1968 Robert (Robin) Price, now Dean Emeritus of Hereford, returned to Bournemouth to resume his old job as priest-in-charge of St. Swithun's, a position which had been vacant since Canon Clinch's departure in 1963. Though there are certainly valid arguments in favour of staffing the daughter-Church from St. Peter's it cannot be denied that this appointment to St. Swithun's brought renewed enthusiasm and optimism to the people there, enhanced as it has been by the return of their highly respected and much loved erstwhile pastor of the Hedley Burrows era.

A new organist, Frederick Hewitt, was engaged in September, 1967, who held office until the end of the following year. Hewitt came to St. Peter's from Walsall, where for six years he had been Director of Music at Queen Mary's Grammar School and deputy organist of the parish church. He is particularly remembered for his organ and harpsichord recitals. Hewitt bought the house at 22 Frances Road for £5,300 and the sale proceeds were put towards the money outstanding on 1 Gervis Road, which then took on the name of St. Swithun's House.

It was while Hewitt was organist that a new scheme of chorister bursaries was introduced. In May, 1968 the vicar and the P.C.C. agreed to offer annually six bursaries for competition to boys showing musical promise, the object being to benefit not only the successful candidates but also the standard of the singing and the life of St. Peter's. The announcement stipulated that:

> The successful candidates will be admitted to St. Peter's Choir, and will have remitted part of the fees for music lessons with an approved teacher. The competition is open to all boys between the ages of 8 and 11 (in the case of present choristers, up to 13). No previous musical training is necessary or expected, but where a candidate has already begun training, this will obviously be taken into consideration. The tests include reading of a psalm or hymn, musical ability tests, ear tests and voice trial.
> The awards will be subject to certain conditions, full details of which may be obtained from the Organist. There will be
> Two major awards: A half-hour lesson weekly with the Organist in any musical subject within his competence (Value £25). Should a boy already be learning one instrument, the award would be available only for training on a different instrument.
> Two minor awards: Bursaries of £15 for lessons with an approved teacher.
> Two exhibitions: Bursaries of £10.

Hewitt, with the assistance of Iles, achieved a great improvement in the standard of the choir and the number of boys, but problems arose about getting to practices and services the choristers who lived in the suburbs. A minibus was found which was available for purchase at £325 and at the Sunday services on 6th October 1968 the vicar asked the congregation to raise the money to buy it within five days. Not only was this sum forthcoming but also a sufficient surplus to pay for the insurance. "Gone are the days when parents need worry about their little ones loose in the town late at night," was a comment in the *Parish Magazine* afterwards. The bus is also used for the Choir Club outings and sports fixtures, thus enabling the boys to combine social activities with the disciplines of worship.

Cyril Knight, a well-known Bournemouth musician, succeeded Hewitt as organist in January 1969. Knight had held a similar appointment at St. Stephen's for nearly thirty years and is now upholding and strengthening the high musical traditions of St. Peter's. It was reported in the local press that he resigned from St. Stephen's because not enough choirboys could be recruited. While the minibus continues to function a similar fate should not befall St. Peter's.

At this period were two reminders of the connection between St. Peter's and the Bournemouth Symphony Orchestra. On 20th June 1968 a service of thanksgiving was held to mark the centenary of the birth of Sir Dan Godfrey. A happy occasion this, but followed on 28th February 1969 by a most moving service for the funeral of Constantin Silvestri, the orchestra's principal conductor in recent years.

Other staff changes took place at St. Peter's during 1968 consequent upon Smith, the sacristan and verger, leaving to take a position at Christchurch Priory. The property Normanhurst in St. Peter's Road, where he and his family resided in one of the flats, was sold at auction for £9,150 which almost entirely wiped off the remaining debts and mortgages on the parish properties. Godfrey French, who had been a server for many years, became the new sacristan and Dick Absalom combined the duties of St. Peter's verger with those of hall caretaker.

Populating the parish is another matter which the vicar and his charming wife have taken very serously since their arrival. Obviously the vicarage was too large for just the two of them, so in October 1967 they produced a son, William, followed by daughters in 1969 and 1970. The parish records for over a century, since Morden Bennett's time, bear witness to the congregation's love of having children at the vicarage!

James busied himself from the outset of his incumbency upon enlivening and enriching the social life of the parish and the worship of the Church. He stated his views on the former subject in the *Magazine* for November, 1967:

> Several months before I came here, someone asked me for my philosophy about Bazaars and Socials. At the time I confessed that I had not got one, but I am pretty certain that I have acquired one now! I am sure that they are important at several levels: we can work together and get to know each other, and we can create a neighbourly point of contact with non-Church members, and so on. In this way the time and talents of a good many people can be used creatively for the Church. Of course, it is important that we keep the right balance. The Christian life has to be a balanced life. We ought not to feel guilty about enjoying our leisure in a sociable and useful way, and yet no one suggests that we should become inward-looking and obsessed with our own activities. The Church exists to glorify God and to be a missionary force in our society. Everything that we do in recreation, money-raising, etc., is subordinate to this overall purpose.

It was on 8th November, the Feast of the Saints, Martyrs, Missionaries and Doctors of the Church of England, that a Grand Bazaar, with social evening afterwards, was held. This event was a huge success in every way, including the financial result of raising over £600 which was badly needed at the time to boost the parish finances. The vicar again referred to social events in his Planned Christian Giving appeal, saying that "the social side of our parish life is very important. The big social events of the year matter for two reasons. First, they give us opportunities of working together in Christian fellowship and service. Secondly, they enable us to make social contact with those outside our normal congregation."

Several new parish groups were formed. Monthly coffee mornings and afternoon "At Homes" were started, to which all were invited. Then there were the "Spearheads" to cater for the needs and interests of young married people and parents of school-age children. An "Under 35" group was started by Iles and Jones, the age demarcation chosen (according to James) to exclude the vicar but to include the curates within their own age group. This was later transformed into an "18-30" group. For the teenagers was created the "Topics," a post-Confirmation group and youth fellowship.

Probably the most interesting developments in recent years, changes which are still going on and under review, are those in the realm of liturgy and worship. In comparison with other churches in the locality St. Peter's has neither lagged behind nor been in the vanguard of so-called progress. James has very sensibly presented the new forms of worship to his congregation without recommending any fundamental departures or seeking change just for its own sake. Having allowed such developments to proceed in this way, always with the full approval of the Church Council at every step, he has cleverly contrived neither to anger the traditionalists, who find it difficult to accept any departures from practices to which they have grown used, nor to dismay the adherent of the more modern forms who may nevertheless be attempting to advance more quickly than is wise. In steering this middle course the result has been a balance to which no reasonable Christian could take exception, while at the same time ensuring that the services are not allowed to lapse into spiritual stagnation.

In July, 1967 the Church Council approved the use of the revised and much shorter Baptism service. Then, later in the year, a shortened confession was introduced into Matins:

> Almighty God, our Heavenly Father,
> We have sinned against thee,
> Through our own fault,
> In thought, in word, and deed,
> And in what we have left undone.
> Have mercy upon us,
> Grant us true repentance;
> And help us amend our lives,
> Through Jesus Christ, Our Saviour. Amen.

This and other changes were the subject of an article by the vicar in the *Parish Magazine* for December 1967. This sets out the details so well that it is here reprinted in full. Under the heading *Services at St. Peter's* James wrote:

> After discussion with the Parochial Church Council at the November meeting, it has been decided to make some minor alterations to Sunday Matins and Evensong at St. Peter's.
>
> At the Morning Service the Choir will enter singing the first seven verses of the *Venite* as an Introit. This will be followed by all or part of a hymn of praise, and the shortened Confession and Absolution set forth in the Series II service of Matins. The reason for these changes is twofold. First, it seems desirable to emphasise Adoration and Praise (in which the congregation can join) as the opening note of worship. Secondly, we can now meet the criticism that our present practice does not allow for the Confession, while at the same time the new form of confession (which will be printed in our prayer books) avoids the wordiness and top-heaviness of the one in the 1662 Prayer Book. I hope that these changes will enrich our worship and will be welcomed. At Evensong it has

been decided to open the service with a hymn and omit the office hymn.

Many people have asked what we are going to do about Series I or II services for Holy Communion. This was discussed at the November P.C.C., and it was decided to use the Series II service on weekdays in St. Peter's at 8 o'clock for a year, beginning at Advent. I think that this is the right way forward, and we shall be able to review the position next year in the light of experience gained and the considered comment of worshippers.

Change for the sake of change is as foolish as insisting on staying put because we have always done a thing in a certain way. We all known that our Church, like the Roman Church and some of the Free Churches, has reached the end of a liturgical ice-age. The new service, approved by Convocation and Church Assembly, has been carefully designed to meet a number of needs. First, the essential elements of the Ministry of the Word and Sacrament stand out more clearly. Secondly, the congregation can participate more fully. Thirdly, the service is more flexible, which allows it to be used in a style to suit our own tradition and the needs of our own people. Fourthly, the language is less wordy than that of 1662. Finally, the theology of the service is better balanced. The familiar emphasis on the Cross is balanced by a proper recognition of Our Lord's Resurrection and Ascension, His priestly intercession, and His final coming in Judgment.

All these are important matters which ought not to be ignored. They are of central concern to the whole nature of our corporate response to God as members of the Body of Christ. Just because they are important, the changes involved must not be rushed. We have to remember that for the great majority, particularly of our senior worshippers, our Christian character has been moulded by the 1662 service. In this way we have received Christ. We have to weigh this factor alongside the undoubted merits of the Series II service. The way we have chosen of using the new service at the 8 a.m. celebration on weekdays at St. Peter's allows for a real possibility of growth in worship without in any way pre-judging what should be the eventual form of our worship on Sunday. It is essential that such decisions should only be taken on the basis of practical experience and that there should be full discussion at every stage, and a general agreement secured. These are important matters and we want to avoid snap judgments of either enthusiastic praise or unyielding condemnation. What we shall need is a prayerful, considered and thoughtful answer to the question: Is the new way a better way, not only for us but also for the next generation of Church people, to worship, love and witness to Almighty God?

The Series II Communion service, which was adopted for use on weekdays for an experimental period of one year, gained general acceptance and seems likely now to remain in use indefinitely. On Advent Sunday 1967 a special morning service of dedication and renewal was held at 10.30, combining the Eucharist and Matins. Though difficult to follow and of almost interminable length it was a pleasant excursion in encouraging the ten o'clock and 11.15 congregations to worship together.

In September 1967 an altar was set up in the north transept of St. Peter's beneath the Crumpler window. More than half a century had elapsed since the old organ had been removed from this spot. It is surprising that this undoubted improvement was not achieved a long time previously. A pair of wooden kneeling-desks, designed by Ronald Phillips, was presented for the new north chapel in 1968 as a memorial to Mrs. Nellie Pearmain. And in 1969 was added a new altar table in memory of Mrs. Lilian Hines.

Possible changes in the Sunday morning Sung Eucharist were foreshadowed by James in his article quoted above. No hurried alterations were made, and for a time the only amendment was the reintroduction of an introit hymn at the commencement of the service. October 1968 saw the setting up of a congregational Worship Study Course at which the parishioners were asked to attend services according to the various alternative orders for Holy Communion permitted under the Prayer Book Measure of 1965 and to discuss them among themselves and with the clergy. The incumbent was impressed by "the free and friendly way in which questions were asked, information sought, and ideas exchanged and examined." In the result the Church Council authorised for an experimental period several minor changes in the Sung Eucharist celebration, acting on the vicar's advice to "take into account both the newly apprehended theological truths for which liturgy exists to give shape and form, and also the needs of the whole parish. Sacraments," James continued, "were instituted for men and women. The way in which we worship must be conditioned to the people we are. It must be related to the tradition in which we have been brought up, and to the spiritual experience we have been granted up to now. Our services must take a form in which we can naturally and gladly offer ourselves, our souls and bodies to God through our Lord Jesus Christ." Introducing the revised form of service, first held in January 1969, James wrote that:

> . . . the first part of the service will take place in the Nave, outside the Chancel gate. This part is the Ministry of the Word. And the natural focus is on the Lectern where the scriptures are read and the pulpit where the scriptures are expounded. The Epistle will be read from the Lectern, usually from the Prayer Book version, but when the meaning is not clear it will be from a more recent translation.
>
> The Gospel will be solemnly read (not sung) from the Chancel steps. The second part of the service (*i.e.* after the sermon) will naturally

take place at the Altar. The priest will face east, as is our present custom. The only changes here are small. The Prayer for the Church will be divided up into sections to allow a congregational response. The Prayer of Humble Access ("We do not presume . . .") will be said by everybody (as we do now) after the Absolution; the Comfortable Words will be dropped. This means that the penitential parts of the service are grouped together. They will be followed by prayers emphasising Adoration and Thanksgiving, *i.e.* Lift up your hearts, the Sanctus, the Prayer of Consecration and the shortened Prayer of Oblation. The rest of the Service remains the same. These changes are not made for the sake of change. There is no virtue in that. *The purpose of these very conservative changes in our well loved service is to bring out more clearly and deeply the treasure which we already have.*

Dean Burrows, who visited his old church in February 1969, was favourably impressed by the revised service, though he was not really happy about the omission of the Comfortable Words; he felt that they ought to be retained, if only for the strength they afforded to the priest as he prepared himself for the Consecration.

For Lent 1969, lunch-hour Holy Communion was held in St. Peter's, at 12.20 p.m. on Tuesdays and 1.10 p.m. on Thursdays, to cater for the needs of business people in the town centre, and the Thursday service has now become one of the regular Celebrations throughout the year. Choral Evensong was reintroduced as one of the regular services at St. Peter's from 1969 and is held on Wednesdays at six o'clock.

An additional pastoral responsibility recently undertaken by James is the chaplaincy of Boscombe Hospital, where he and the other clergy of the parish are doing such useful work among the sick. It is no sinecure; James has explained that one of the St. Peter's priests (they take it in turns) has to spend two-and-a-half or three hours at the Hospital every weekday in order to carry out the duties adequately.

It is also a pleasure to record that in 1970 the vicar was fittingly honoured by the Diocese of Winchester by being elected to serve as a Proctor in Convocation and as a diocesan representative in the House of Clergy in the new General Synod of the Anglican Church which was inaugurated at Westminster Abbey in the presence of Her Majesty the Queen in November of that year.

A current matter of great importance, which may have far-reaching effect and which is now under active consideration, is the question of possibly changing radically the parish structure within the centre of Bournemouth. For a long time now it has been felt by many that, with changed patterns of churchmanship and churchgoing, the basic organisation of the Church needs a careful rethinking, in the hope that a style of ministry and witness may be developed which is more in keeping with modern outlooks and a new awareness of the Church's role in the community.

In his pastoral letter for September, 1969 James considered these questions in a general way, writing not specifically about St. Peter's but about the dearth of vocations to the priesthood among young men. What, he asked, is the role of the clergy to be? It was too sweeping a condemnation, he thought, to write off the parish ministry as irrelevant to modern needs and problems. "But," he went on, "there are obviously too many parishes in the towns. We are over-churched. There is evidence that a lot of the younger clergy opt out of the parish ministry because they do not want to be condemned to maintain large, obsolescent buildings for dwindling congregations. Such a prospect may well deter young men from offering themselves for ordination. After all, few men would become schoolmasters if they thought that most of their energies would be spent maintaining, and raising money for, out-of-date school buildings, rather than teaching children, experimenting in new educational methods, and helping their charges grow to maturity."

Soon after this, the Bishop of Winchester, Dr. Falkner Allison, appointed a working party to consider the role and functions of the Bournemouth Town Centre Churches and to make recommendations to him and his Diocesan Pastoral Committee. The parishes under close review were St. Peter's, Holy Trinity and St. Stephen's. Then, at the end of 1969, while the working party was still in the course of carrying out its task, the benefice of St. Stephen's fell vacant. Presentation to St. Stephen's was accordingly suspended by the Bishop, who appointed James to act as priest-in-charge. Thus, the Bennett Memorial Church, which had been founded to honour the memory of the first vicar, became more closely linked to St. Peter's, though preserving its distinct and separate identity as a parish of its own. James wrote that, "The purpose of this change is that the two parishes, while keeping their distinctive traditions of worship, should not duplicate their activities unnecessarily, but rather do better *together* the things which up to now we have been doing separately."

Following the working party's report to the Bishop the Pastoral Committee of Winchester submitted proposals to the three parishes which were explained to the people personally by the Archdeacon and Bishop Cornwall. St. Peter's and St. Stephen's resolved to approve the proposals and any further action which may be taken on the matter is presently awaited. Writing in the *Parish Magazine*, James fully described and commented upon these recommendations:

> The first suggestion is that the three neighbouring parishes of Holy Trinity, St. Stephen and St. Peter with St. Swithun should be merged into what is called a Major Parish. This is a new category (under the Pastoral Re-organisation Measure) which allows existing parishes to create a new pattern of organisation without the smaller being absorbed or lost in the larger. Existing churches keep their status as parish churches with their own churchwardens and councils, etc. Why has a Major Parish been proposed in Central Bournemouth? The short answer is: to meet the changed conditions which affect all our present residential population (approximate figures: St. Peter with St. Swithun, 6,500; St. Stephen's, 2,400; Holy Trinity, 1,400), in a time when church attendance has declined, and the character of the town centre has altered. It is felt that if the three parishes came together, with their six priests functioning as a team ministry, we should be able to provide a comprehensive ministry to the whole area. In addition to serving our residential population and the members of our congregations, we should be able to minister to our "day-time parishioners" who work in the shops and offices in central Bournemouth, to the hoteliers, to the young people who flock into the town in the evening, and to the new element of 8,000 students at the language schools and at the College of Technology. At the moment we are hampered from this out-reach work by obsolete parish boundaries and by the restrictions of keeping three separate legal parishes going.
>
> What about the church buildings? As far as the two existing parishes of St. Peter and St. Swithun and St. Stephen's there will be no change. It is felt that St. Peter's should be retained because of its central position and its numerical strength; that St. Swithun's be retained because of its valuable siting in the midst of a growing residential neighbourhood and also because in this hilly town it enjoys the singular advantage of being on the level; and that St. Stephen's be retained to serve its existing congregation and because of its particular character it should also develop as a centre for liturgical, artistic and ecumenical activities for the benefit of the whole Church in the area, as well as maintain its most important ministry of spiritual direction and counsel.
>
> These kinds of proposals are being worked out and prepared in many parts of the country, not least in town centres which have changed their character since the time that local churches were first built. In our own situation in central Bournemouth I believe that a major parish served by a team ministry would be a great gain. It would ensure that the existing work of the Church is maintained and built up, it would also set us free to minister more effectively to people in their places of work, recreation and study as well as to people at home. The Church Catholic is always the Church Apostolic. And it is to further the Church's Mission that these proposals are submitted.

While the future of the Bournemouth Town Centre Churches was being prayed for and thoroughly discussed James appointed an assistant curate to act as resident priest at St. Stephen's and to have the day by day care of that parish. His choice fell upon the Rev. Anthony Caesar, a distinguished musician with a first class honours degree in music at Cambridge who also held a Fellowship of the Royal College of Organists. Before his ordination in 1961 to a title at St. Mary Abbots, Kensington, Caesar was Director of Music at Radley. He came to St. Stephen's from the Chapel Royal, where he was a Priest in Ordinary and also Chaplain to the Royal School of Church Music.

The year 1970 was celebrated by St. Peter's as the 125th anniversary of the opening of the Church. Early in 1969 the Parochial Church Council was debating how best to mark the occasion by some really worthwhile achievement, and it was decided to issue an appeal for £5,000 to be used for clearing and renovating the churchyard.

The task of maintaining the churchyard in good order had become increasingly difficult since the end of the war. Over fifteen hundred burials had taken place since 1846, the vast majority during the nineteenth century. In later years most of the graves had become neglected and in a great number of cases family links with Bournemouth had been broken. The rising cost of labour and the shrinking value of the yield of the churchyard's few endowments had made it impossible, and also unreasonable, for the present generation of churchgoers to restore the four-acre graveyard and the many forgotten graves to a decent state. As things were, there existed neither glory to God nor respect for the dead.

At the April, 1969 meeting of the Church Council it was agreed that there should be a large-scale clearance of headstones and kerbstones, the removal of dead and overgrown vegetation, the laying of new areas of grass and the planting of many new trees and shrubs. The fences, paths and steps would also be well repaired and the whole area laid out to the best advantage as a place of peace and repose in the centre of the town, though still retaining its character as "God's Acre." More than a hundred gravestones would be kept, including all those possessing historic, local or aesthetic interest.

A creative design for landscaping the site without detracting from its essential character was prepared by Miss Daphne Evans of the Hampshire County Architect's department at Winchester and this was approved and adopted by the Church and Diocese as a sound basis for carrying out the work. A faculty was obtained from the Chancellor and discussions opened with the Bournemouth Council, which indicated its willingness to undertake responsibility for the future upkeep of the churchyard, estimated at £1,750 annually, provided it was first put into an acceptable condition.

In October 1969 the appeal was launched, asking for funds to finance this worthwhile project and to enable an early start to be made on the first stage of operations. This appeal, for the creation of *St. Peter's Church Close,* was made not only to the parishioners and congregation but also, perhaps primarily, to the business community and populace of the whole town. Several local businessmen contributed most generously of their money and advice to ensure that the appeal was well formulated and widely advertised. The Mayor, Councillor David Beckett, and the Member of Parliament, Sir John Eden, were both most enthusiastic in their support and interest, which undoubtedly encouraged others to follow their example, and in a very few weeks there was enough money subscribed to allow a beginning to be made.

The Bournemouth Corporation played a greater part in the work than had been suggested originally, for they agreed that most of it could be done by their Parks Department, under the able leadership of Director Ross Young, provided the Church defrayed the expenses out of the appeal funds. And so, early in 1970, a start was made — as the vicar put it — "to turn a jungle into an amenity." Ross Young and his men had scarcely commenced their endeavours when the first signs of a wonderful transformation became apparent. Indeed, as early as July 1970, we find the Church Council passing a resolution congratulating the Parks Department on the high quality of their work. One stage followed another until the position has now been reached when final and successful completion of the work is confidently expected during 1971. With the aid of many contributions, large and small, and the proceeds of two Autumn Bazaars, the target of £5,000 was achieved before the end of the anniversary year.

In conjunction with the St. Peter's Church Close scheme the P.C.C. also resolved to renovate and repair the Chapel of the Resurrection and to convert it into a *columbarium* for the deposit of caskets of ashes and for use as occasion demanded for requiem Celebrations. The St. Peter's architect, Ronald Phillips, warden at St. Swithun's, designed the alterations and supervised the work, which was soon completed and the finished result hallowed by Bishop Cornwall on 7th July 1970. This redevelopment of the Chapel of the Resurrection is doubly welcome because not only does it enable the remains of departed parishioners to rest within the precincts of St. Peter's (which would otherwise be impossible now that the churchyard has been closed to further burials) but also the chapel itself has been restored to a new era of useful life, its original function having been only seldom required in recent years on account of the numerous chapels-of-rest which are now maintained by the funeral directors of the town.

The anniversary celebrations of 1970 did not consist only of tackling the problems of the churchyard. Throughout the summer there was a series of most enjoyable organ and piano recitals, concerts by the Bounrnemouth Sinfonietta and productions of T. S. Eliot's "Murder in the Cathedral" by St. Peter's Players, with music by St. Peter's Choir. Social highlight was the anniversary dinner at the Pavilion on St. Peter's Day, which was honoured by the Mayor, Alderman Edwin Lane, and other notables, including the Bishop of the Diocese, the Member of Parliament and the Town Clerk, the latter himself a regular worshipper at St. Peter's. Also in the 125th anniversary programme were an exhibition of modern Church vestments and ornaments and a Saturday afternoon garden party in the grounds of Mr. & Mrs. Hamblin's home in St. Valerie Road. It had been hoped that this volume would have been published in time to take its place as part of the anniversary, but circumstances, entirely beyond the control of the writer and all who have helped in its production, frustrated that hope, though the delay has allowed sufficient time to add these last few pages in order to complete the record of a century and a quarter.

The Church Council of 1970-71 is looking ahead towards streamlining itself and creating a more effective organisation, in the spirit of the synodical reform that has just started to transform the government of the Anglican Church at national, diocesan and deanery levels. Consideration by the laity of the worship and mission of the Church is to be extended, in the hope that the Council will not have to spend the bulk of its time on fabric and finance. Serious discussions are also being held about the future of the hall, in the hope that a more useful and realistic employment of the site may be achieved.

CHAPTER XXVII

"Upon This Rock"

AND NOW what of the future? This is the part of the book in which the writer may perhaps allow himself some relaxation from the strict rules which must always guide the historian who is doing justice to his subject and trying to be impartial in his presentation. There can be no real value in any study of the past unless it has some relevance for the present and the point of historical research is that it often enables future generations to assess those features of good and bad which are ever recurring in some contemporary form and to learn the right lessons from them. This book has been written primarily for the reader's entertainment, but the labours of compilation will have been in vain unless there is some message which may be of use when planning for the future.

We have seen how the Mother Church of Bournemouth was built up from the humblest of beginnings through the energy, far-sightedness and Godly wisdom of its first incumbent. But has it fulfilled the hopes and aspirations which Morden Bennett worked so hard to achieve? Are we Christians in danger of losing our way? Consider, for a moment, the position of St. Peter's in Morden Bennett's time. It was a rich man's Church, an upper-class Church, at a time when the divisions of the social classes within the community were so much more marked than they are today. Morden Bennett clearly found it difficult to make St. Peter's an acceptable place of worship for all his parishioners, as witness the pew rent system for the best seats or the Terrace Road Mission for poor people who felt they would not be accepted (and perhaps they were right) by the hard core of the St. Peter's congregation. Morden Bennett was lucky in having a nucleus of rich parishioners from whom to extract the funds he needed for his building projects and local missionary work. He himself, however, was a man of all the people; there is plenty of evidence that he was looked upon by the poor and uneducated members of his flock with the love and respect that only a true Christian who had their whole interests at heart could hope to enjoy.

But what of the other St. Peter's people? Were they all motivated by selfless considerations? One hopes it is not too unfair to suggest that many allied themselves to St. Peter's because it was the "right"

Church socially, that they paid for the missionary projects not because of any real concern but in gratitude to God that he had made them not as other men are. There is a feeling of the "All things bright and beautiful" atmosphere, that God not only made rich and poor but "ordered their estate." One cannot avoid getting the impression sometimes that Morden Bennett had to tread warily, keeping a balance between giving those who supported him financially what they liked and giving those who were almost cut off from religion what they needed. Even in Daldy's time it is possible to make the comparison between a single gift of nearly £3,000 for the St. Peter's organ and the postponement of building the much needed new class-room at the school for want of a few hundreds. Again, recall the financial pressure which Daldy had to contend with after his arrival at St. Peter's over the proposal to make St. Swithun's a separate parish; of people who wanted to control events during their life-time at a price which would cost them nothing because it would only be payable after they were dead. How far these comments are justified I leave for the reader to judge, but I do not think it irrelevant at least to question whether these things came about through true Christian enlightenment or for other reasons. If there is a message in this for today, and I believe there is, it should behove us carefully to examine ourselves and our motives.

The heated and uncompromising disputes over the ceremonials of public worship and the war between "high" and "low" Church are not just interesting historical records. They serve to show how far the different factions and denominations have progressed towards unity during the last fifty years and surely provide some background to the ecumenical campaigns of recent years. These days the divisions of Christendom are rightly held to be a shameful disgrace and the movement towards unity, evidenced at St. Peter's in recent times by a steadily increasing co-operation with Roman Catholics and Free Churchmen, most encouraging. Nevertheless, history only serves to underline how deep the divisions can be even within the Anglican Church itself; and relations with other denominations are unlikely to be improved by referring, as a St. Peter's clergyman once did, to St. Andrew's Presbyterian Church as "that Scotch Chapel in the Square." Bodies like the Bournemouth Council of Churches, organisations like the Samaritans and joint efforts like the Live Crib must surely be steps in the right direction even if, as yet, they only go to prove that our fellow Christians are pleasant enough people all seeking to do Christ's will and to serve Him faithfully. There is still a long way to go.

Arising out of these steps towards unity we are going to have to examine the case for now undoing much of Morden Bennett's work. For demolishing Churches rather than building them. In Victorian times the centre of Bournemouth was still largely a residential area and people mostly attended Church regularly. Nowadays the population in the central parts of the town has decreased and Church attendance generally is not what it was or should be. Is the time coming when all the Parishes of central Bournemouth should be joined together under one vicar and some of the Churches closed? The sites they occupy are valuable and this value could be turned to good account in furthering Christ's work in less favoured places where the need is greatest. Do we really need, can we really afford, more than two or three central Churches? Before you answer "no" too heartily, consider what your reaction would be if the serious suggestion was made of pulling down *your* Church. Questions like these will probably be posed quite soon. The Church must be ready with the right answer. The Christian answer.

It has been said that the Church should do more to encourage its nominal members, the "Christenings, Weddings and Funerals only" sort of people, to become more active in parish life and more regular in Church attendance. Perhaps it should, but one cannot expect the Clergy to do all the work. St. Peter's laymen have already done much in this direction. The Parish Survey is an example, for though its practical effect was very limited, there was possibly a spiritual effect which is not yet capable of assessment. Should the Church relax its standards and make itself more acceptable to the outsider? There are pressures in this direction at the present time. The traditions of St. Peter's recorded here all indicate that it should not lower its standards but should be jealous in maintaining the theological and moral principles it represents and the discipline Our Lord requires. Dean Hedley Burrows has written to the author most feelingly on this very matter, pointing out that St. Peter's has a great record in upholding the power and attraction of the Eternal and would be wrong to relax its standards merely in the interests of people who only love themselves. Theologians realise that there are some people who accept Our Lord's standards and others who do not. A Church cannot speak to both in the same words, but it must broadcast its message to both.

What of St. Peter's in its relationship to the town? St. Peter's is no longer Bournemouth in its spiritual aspect. It may have to work out its role as the servant. A priest who was assistant curate at St. Peter's a few years ago has said that in his time the clergy were rather uneasily straddled between the old triumphalism and the need to serve, without really reconciling or harmonising the two. Here is a challenge which deserves attention. The St. Peter's of Morden Bennett and Daldy was considered as representing the Church in Bournemouth, but its present spiritual influence on the town is not, perhaps cannot be, what it once was. It is no use looking back nostalgically and feeling self-satisfied because of past glories. Adaptations must be made to meet the changed circumstances. The Major and Corporation still traditionally attend St. Peter's for the annual Civic Service and on other important occasions. Our vicars have very often acted as Chaplains to the Mayor. But does this mean what it should?

The Church lives in a secular world. Either it must come to terms with this world or purposefully set about its conversion. St. Peter's, in the centre of the town with its traditions of faith and action, must surely be in a position to assume the leadership of a spiritual re-awakening. When the opportunity comes, or when we ourselves make the opportunity, shall we know what to do? The St. Peter's of the past can be a sure guide to the St. Peter's of the future if we correctly discern the way.

In the last fifty years particularly, the congregations of St. Peter's have mainly comprised people who reside outside the geographical parish, and in holiday time the visitors to Bournemouth. St. Peter's owes its main responsibility, of course, to the souls in its own parish, but there are so many places of worship close at hand that large numbers, even of the practising Christians, attend other Churches. The outsiders belong to St. Peter's for many different reasons. Some, like the writer, because of a continuous family tradition since the early days when St. Peter's was the only Church in Bournemouth. Maybe we ought to join actively in the life of the Churches near our homes and break with St. Peter's. Should we belong to a particular Church merely because our great-grandparents did and say no more than a polite "good morning" to the vicar round the corner? Some ally themselves to St. Peter's because it is a beautiful building, an impressive setting for weddings and special occasions; indeed many join the electoral roll just for the privilege of being married at St. Peter's which is convenient for their guests and close to the hotel where they are holding the reception. These may not be the best motives for seeking membership, but St. Peter's would not turn such people away provided they are sincere and fulfil the requirements of attendance. Better for the clergy and laity of St. Peter's to have the opportunity of conducting a pastoral ministry towards them than that nobody should. But it puts a strain on the resources of a parish when strangers come in just to take what they want and are prepared to give little or nothing in return.

There are some who come because they find at St. Peter's the spiritual atmosphere, the type of service, which suits them. Or they are friends of St. Peter's people, or they like the vicar, or don't like the vicar at the Church where they worshipped before. There are so many reasons. Some folk come to St. Peter's because they find they can remain almost unknown in a larger congregation and prefer it that way. Bishop Williams has said that when he was vicar, he found that some shy and diffident people, who shrank from divulging their troubles and problems in their own small parishes elsewhere, were more ready to come and open their hearts in the more anonymous setting of St. Peter's and there obtain a sympathetic pastoral ministration. These people may perhaps become members, perhaps not, but they keep the clergy busy and naturally the Church is always ready to welcome them and to see to their needs. The same is true of the holiday-makers who form so large a part of the congregation during the summer months and public holiday times like Christmas and Easter. To help meet their needs and at the same time to encourage visitors who might not be attracted to one of the regular services, special services have been arranged for them.

Holidaymakers are not always what they seem, and even week-end visitors can produce problems. Bishop Williams told me that one Monday morning while he was vicar his telephone rang and the following conversation ensued:

"Good morning. Are you the vicar?"

"Yes, I am."

"I am staying at an hotel and am in a little difficulty."

"Financial?"

"Well, yes. Only a *small* matter about my weekend bill. I have been doing a little entertaining and find that my account is for £28. I haven't any money left. Would you kindly lend me this little sum?"

"I am afraid that I have to confine my financial help to Charity and cases of need."

"I *thought* that you were a clergyman!"

"Quite; but not necessarily a fool," said Williams as he put down the receiver.

In the parochial life of St. Peter's there are other particular problems, especially that members of the congregation are apt to live so far apart that they do not know each other. Their paths may cross only on a Sunday if they attend the same service. Even

Church Council members are sometimes almost complete strangers to one another. There is very little community feeling or sense of fellowship unless these things are carefully fostered. Social activities, parish parties, coffee mornings, bazaars and similar functions help to fill this gap but they cannot provide the complete answer. The pastoral results of Christian Stewardship and the establishment of many and various parish organisations have done something towards solving the difficulty, which is a common one for any "down-town" Church in a large town or city. But the basic problem must remain until some new methods are devised of bringing the people still closer together. It is perhaps more difficult for a newcomer to become known and accepted in a large Church than in a small one. But, once the initial effort has been made, the large town Church does provide great opportunities for Christian service over a wide field. The progressive, forward-looking traditions of St. Peter's are forceful reminders that there is still plenty of scope for more service in many different ways.

We have seen in the history how St. Peter's started with such a small endowment that the early vicars had to be people of private means or they would have been unable to accept the cure. Morden Bennett even had to build the Parsonage as his own expense. Subsequently the vicar's stipend was slightly increased through pew rents and a guarantee from the Church Council but it still remained pitifully small. Then, by good fortune, it was found possible to sell the old Vicarage at a vast profit so as to provide an endowment for the incumbent's living more in keeping with the responsibilities of the office. The fall in the value of money through inflation means now that the stipend is no more than just about adequate and certainly bears no comparison with what a man would expect to earn in other professions when he has behind him the learning, experience and standing that are expected of vicars of St. Peter's. The parishioners have had an easy time in the past through not having to concern themselves unduly over this particular matter, but it is something which will have to engage their attention in the fairly near future if they expect to obtain or keep a vicar of suitable qualifications. Other parishes may be in a worse position, but this is no reason for St. Peter's people growing complacent when they ought to be setting an example. As fewer young men are offering themselves for ordination one cannot discount the fact that, although nobody would ever take Orders for financial advancement, the low pay of our Anglican clergy probably dissuades many good men from entering the sacred ministry. Here again the right answer must be found and action taken.

Despite Stewardship, or Planned Christian Giving (call it what you will), it does seem that the Church of England has got many of its financial priorities wrong. The maintenance of more Parish Churches than a modern large town really needs is an example of this. So is the tendency to spend so much on repairing old buildings and so little, by comparison, on extensions of the Church's pastoral work. A recent appeal by the Diocese for about half a million pounds for repair and restoration to Winchester Cathedral has raised doubts in some quarters as to whether the Church's money is wisely spent. In fact, whether the Church itself is a good Steward of its possessions. Churchmen of the future are going to have to consider these things carefully. Is it right to spend so large a sum on an old and out-dated building, whatever its historical associations, when a fraction of the amount required, intelligently employed in the missionfield or in providing Churches and clerical staff for new residential areas, would bring religion to neglected and often apathetic people who must sometimes wonder whether the Church really does care for them? Or does the Church just care about itself? Can the demands of self be reconciled with the outward-looking mission which the Church should represent?

What will be the result so far as St. Peter's is concerned? Bournemouth is more than a carefree holiday resort. It is a place where people have a certain leisure to think. It does not exist to cater for things that have little lasting interest. It must not give way to the enchantments of the sun and the sea-shore. There is more in Bournemouth than that, and its Churches have their role to play. We have seen something in this history of the spiritual significance of the great missionary activity which existed in earlier days and how the Church responded so magnificently to the challenge of the war years. These consequences, and others like them, are surely true expressions of God's glory and service in a place where the things of the Holy Spirit can, and do, come to the fore.

St. Peter's was built upon the foundation of Tractarianism whose strength lay in its refusal to accept time-honoured practices as permanent. It promoted change not for its own sake but because reforms were needed to bring about a renewal of life and health in the Church. The way of Christ is not stagnant. Surely there is today an even greater need to throw off some of the traditional restrictions and rigid organisation which bind our religion, so that the Church may achieve its proper development. The past is too apt to control the present; it will fetter the future unless something is done. The Church is a living thing; whilst its eternal truths remain unaltered its practical existence here on earth must continue to advance and expand. Old ideas, old buildings, old laws and old customs are a hindrance; when they no longer have a practical Christian significance in the modern world they must be discarded.

But we should never seek change just for the sake of change. As the spiritual strength of the Church is enshrined in the Eternal, the practical work of our religion must continue ever fortified by the achievements and foresight of past generations. It is probably not accidental that the dedication to St. Peter, the Rock of the Church, has come to represent the unchanging nature of God's truth and God's love in a town which itself has been continually changing. St. Peter's has borne outstanding witness to the faith. The prospects for the future, provided the opportunities are not wasted, are greater still. Perhaps this history only shows that, despite the greatness of the past, we are still just at the beginning.

Notes

Chapter One. For further information about the early development of Bournemouth the reader is referred to Mate & Riddle's *Bournemouth 1810-1910* (1910) and David S. Young's *The Story of Bournemouth* (1957), from which most of the background details in this and later chapters have been taken. An interesting account of the smuggling activities of the district is contained in E. Russell Oakley's *The Smugglers of Christchurch, Bourne Heath and the New Forest* (1944). The plot of ground "on the estate of Mistress Tregonwell" suggested by Dr. Granville as being the most favourable place for the Church, at the foot of what is now Richmond Hill, was later chosen for the old Scotch Presbyterian Church and is now the site of the National Westminster Bank. The reference to Talbot Village comes from Leachman's *St. Peter's* (1915), as does a great deal of other information throughout this book. See also *The Visitor's Guide to Bournemouth* (2nd Edition, 1842, & 3rd Edition, 1850) and Kathleen Chilver's *Holdenhurst, Mother of Bournemouth* (1956). Hugh Wyndham, who later held curacies at Toller Fratrum, Dorset, and All Saints', Portsea, is said to have come from Salisbury (see Leachman, p.7) and may have been related to the Tregonwell family through their connection with the Sydenhams of Somerset and Devon (see Young, p.55). There may also be a link with the Gervis family, for the priest-in-charge at Hinton Admiral in 1845 was the Rev. T. Wyndham, to whom he was possibly related. Young calls Hugh Wyndham "Bournemouth's first clergyman" and suggests (p.55) that he "doubtless continued to officiate even after St. Peter's Church was built in 1843." There is no evidence of this, and indeed it seems unlikely, since by 1845, according to the *Clergy List* for that year, Wyndham had become assistant curate of Toller Fratrum.

Chapter Two. Most of the details about John Tulloch come from Goodhart-Rendel's card index of architects in the R.I.B.A. library, and the writer is indebted to Mr. Nicholas Taylor for obtaining them, and also for other architectural notes which appear in this book. The inscribed foundation stone of the first St. Peter's does not seem to have been preserved when the present Church was built. A report of the stone-laying ceremony appeared in the *Hampshire Chronicle,* 4th October, 1841. Samuel Bayly died in 1864 and is buried in St. Peter's churchyard. The late Mr. G. E. Ellis refers to the deed of 14th June, 1845 in *The Parochial Development of Bournemouth* (1966).

John Tregonwell was the younger surviving son of Mrs. Henrietta Tregonwell. He later became one of the founders of Holy Trinity Church at Bournemouth and lies buried in St. Peter's churchyard. The Rev. William Rush Hallett Churchill, rector of Winterbourne Anderson, Dorset, from 1813 to 1847, was presented to that benefice by Lewis Tregonwell. According to the *Clergy List* for 1845 he also held the Rectory of Witherstone, near Melplash, Dorset, and resided at Colliton House, Dorchester. The organ is mentioned by David E. L. Salwey in an article about St. Peter's and its organs in *The Organ* for January 1938. Peter Tuck and Samuel Bayly were prominent freemasons and are mentioned in the *History of the Lodge of Hengist* (1897) by C. J. Whitting.

In 1846 the Gervis trustees obtained another private Act of Parliament

(9 & 10 Vict., cap. 29) giving them wide powers to develop and manage the estate during the minority of the heir. Rebbeck began as Parish Clerk at the old temporary Church in September 1840. When Sir George Gervis died he was owed two years' salary amounting to £10 and had to prove his debt before a Master in Chancery. He had to wait until 1847 before he was paid. The correspondence about this and the letters quoted in the text are preserved in St. Peter's archives. They were presented to the Church in 1942 by the family of the late Col. Thomas Victor Rebbeck, Mayor of Bournemouth in 1936-37 and grandson of the first Parish Clerk.

The District assigned to St. Peter's was constituted on 11th November 1845 by Her Majesty's Commissioners for building new Churches, with the consent of Bishop Sumner of Winchester. The deed of Assignment provided that the District should:

> *consist of parts of the said United Parishes of Christchurch and Holdenhurst and be bounded as follows that is to say on the South by Bourne Bay on the West and North West by the Bank which divides the County of Southampton from the County of Dorset as far as the North Bank of the Allotment No. 78 on the Christchurch Inclosure Award and the Map therein referred to then taking the North Bank of the Allotments in the said Award numbered respectively 78 and 79 also by part of the East Bank of the said two last mentioned Allotments by the North Bank of the Allotments numbered respectively 178, 103 and 30 in the same Award from the North East corner of the said Allotment numbered 30 in a straight line in a South easterly direction to the Eastern boundary of the Allotment numbered 210 in the same Award and then taking in the whole of the Allotment numbered 71 in the same Award and the West bank of the Road numbered 13 in the same Award being the Road leading from the last mentioned Allotment into the Christchurch Road then following the Christchurch Road aforesaid in a Westerly direction taking in the North Bank of the said Road as far as the East Bank of Allotment No. 77 in the same Award and then following and taking the East Bank of the Allotments numbered respectively 77 and 129 in the same Award which last mentioned allotment opens into Bourne Bay and Boscomb Chain.* (sic)

In terms of modern Bournemouth the District assigned to St. Peter's in 1845 extended from the sea west of Alum Chine along the County boundary to a point near the junction of Eldon Road and Boundary Road, from there to Wimborne Road near Jameson Road, southwards for a short distance along Wimborne Road and then west-south-west to Charminster Road near the Five Ways. The boundary then followed the "straight line in a South easterly direction" to Queen's Park South Drive near Soberton Road and from there to the junction of Holdenhurst and Ashley Roads. The District then included the land east of Ashley Road bounded on the north by Holdenhurst Road and on the east and south by King's Park, then following Ashley, Christchurch and Sea Roads to the sea at Boscombe Pier.

Chapter Three. Sumner was Bishop of Winchester from 1827 to 1869, the longest tenure of the see since the twelfth century. Morden Bennett's first wife was Maria Sarah, daughter of the Rev. Josiah Pike and Mrs. Pike of Upper Seymour Street, London. Edward Castleman, the first churchwarden appointed by Morden Bennett, is named in the inscription beneath the St. Peter window at the west end of the north aisle: *"This window is erected by Edward Castleman, Esq., of Chettle, Dorset, and Anne his wife, to the memory of their beloved daughter, Emily Anne, wife of T. B. Hanham, Esq., who died at this place and was buried at Chettle."* The original window was destroyed by bombing in May, 1943. The present window, also depicting scenes from the life of St. Peter, was inserted in 1951. An inscription similar to that quoted above is also painted on the glass. Morden Bennett's recollection of Bournemouth in 1845 comes from *The Bournemouth and Vale of Avon Parish Magazine* for October 1871. The quotation from Crumpler comes from a paper he read to the Church of England Working Men's Union Mutual Improvement Class in 1889.

The piece about the "High Church Colony" is quoted by the Rev. J. G. Forse in his article "The Catholic Revival in Bournemouth" in *The Church Union Gazette,* Autumn 1935. Alex. Bennett's reminiscences are reported in *The Bournemouth Guardian,* 27th October, 1904. The quotation about Morden Bennett's preaching is from an article by the Rev. Gordon Roe in the *Parish Magazine* for June 1959.

Chapter Four. For further details about Harriet Daniell and her pictures, see Young, op.cit., pp.56 & 57. A facsimile of Morden Bennett's notice about the Moordown school-chapel appears in *St. John's Moordown Parish History* (1924). Morden Bennett's own reminiscences of the founding of the East Parley Mission are reported in the *Bournemouth Visitors' Directory* for 5th January, 1878. Mrs. Bennett is buried in St. Peter's churchyard but the burial register does not mention their young daughter. The quotation about Sir Hubert Parry's father comes from the *D.N.B.* See also the *Bournemouth Evening Echo,* February 1964. The incumbent's views on Church schools are reprinted from *The Bournemouth and Vale of Avon Parish Magazine* for September 1871. Notes on the Shelleys and the Godwins can be found (inter alia) in the *D.N.B.* and the *Oxford Companion to English Literature.* The burial of the poet's heart is mentioned in Chapter Thirteen. An excellent article about William Godwin by the Rev. Gordon Roe appeared in the *Parish Magazine* for February 1959. This was followed by papers on Mary Godwin and Mary Shelley.

Chapter Five. Street started his architectural career as a pupil of Sir Gilbert Scott (Messrs. Scott & Moffatt of London). A list of his principal achievements is given by Leachman at pp. 107-109 at the end of a chapter of biographical details. The quotations about Christian Art and the North Aisle are taken from Leachman at pp. 95 and 24 respectively. The extract quoted from *Building News* (vol. ix, p.98) was kindly supplied by Miss Aslin of the Victoria & Albert Museum. The "village" church of Pokesdown is treated in *Bright's Illustrated Guide to Bournemouth* (1888), p.89. The quotation about the clerestory windows is from Nicholas Taylor's *Guide to St. Peter's* (1962).

Chapter Six. The details about East Parley have been taken from the writer's booklet *The East Parley Mission* which was written for the centenary of St. Barnabas' Chapel in 1963. An interesting booklet about the origin and development of *Bournemouth Fire Brigade* was published by the local fire authority in 1954. *The Story of Holy Trinity,* by the Rev. Frederick Bussby, 1953, is a source of much helpful information about the Church. The quotation from Crumpler comes from the paper already mentioned. Lord Wolverton's letter is in St. Peter's Archives. The altar candles are dealt with in Morden Bennett's *Pastoral Letter for Advent,* printed in the *Bournemouth Parish Magazine* for December 1865. See Chapter Eight as to trouble with the Bishop about the candles. The "handsome church" paragraph is from the *Magazine* for January 1866. In the *Magazine* for September 1865 under the heading "Answers to Correspondents" are questions about candles and vestments, the answers possibly having been written by Morden Bennett himself. These are reproduced here, upon the assumption that they express accurately the incumbent's views on these matters.

"A CATHOLIC enquires — Why the candles are lighted at the early celebration at St. Peter's Church on Sundays, and not at the late celebration?

"The rule established at the Reformation was that there should be two candles burning before the Sacrament, to signify that our Lord Jesus Christ, in His two-fold nature, is present in that Sacrament, and gives His blessing through that Sacrament. This rule has not been carefully observed of late years, and even now is not fully restored. The words of our Lord, Mat. IX, 17, seem to apply to this case.

"A CATHOLIC further enquires — Why the surplice is used at St. Peter's Church for sermons on week days, and not on Sundays?

"The surplice is the vestment prescribed by the Church of England to be used by Clergymen in their ministrations — See Canon 58, A.D.1603. The black gown is an academical dress prescribed by the Universities of Oxford and Cambridge to distinguish those members who have taken a degree, and who are on that account called graduates. This is consequently a dress that may be worn by a lay-man as well as by a clergyman, for it is well known that many of those who take a degree at the Universities do not enter into holy orders, but follow some other profession. So that the black gown, denoting the degree of master of arts, may be worn by a physician, or a barrister, or an officer in the army or navy, provided that he has taken that degree at one of the Universities, which is not uncommonly the case. Whenever a black gown is used for preaching it must be regarded as an unauthorised practice, whether it arise from ignorance of the church's rule, or from caprice on the part of the preacher, or whether it be adopted for the sake of expediency.

"Our readers will observe that the correspondent who puts these two last questions to us describes himself as a Catholic. We do not understand that he is a Romanist because he uses this term, but we regard him rather as a member of the Church of England. We are taught in our liturgy to pray for the good estate of the Catholic Church — that is, for the Church of Christ throughout the world, of which the Church of England is a branch."

Chapter Seven. Nicholas Taylor's *Guide to St. Peter's Church* (1962) contains a wonderful, detailed record of the artistic and architectural background, and having derived so much help from his work it seems almost churlish to question his preference for Street's 1860 design for the east window! Morden Bennett's explanation about the reredos comes from his *Pastoral Letter for Advent, 1865,* previously mentioned. The "No finer work . . ." paragraph about the pulpit is from *Building News,* vol. viii, p.444, and is quoted in full in *Bright's Illustrated Guide to Bournemouth* (1888) and in Leachman's *St. Peter's* (1915). The notes about the Exhibition were kindly supplied by Miss Elizabeth M. Aslin of The Victoria & Albert Museum. Street's design for the Church was exhibited in British Division, Architecture, No. 1811. The Octavius Curtis description of the east window is reprinted from pp.43-44 of *Bright's Illustrated Guide to Bournemouth.* The long description in *The Ecclesiologist* is contained in the October 1866 issue of that paper, vol. xxiv, pp. 260-264. The paragraph about seats is from the same *Pastoral Letter* mentioned above. The letters from Morden Bennett to Stephens and Webb are in St. Peter's Archives. Stephens was churchwarden from 1857 to 1859; Webb from 1868 to 1877.

Chapter Eight. Mention of the Bournemouth Amateur Musical Society is made by Mate & Riddle, *op.cit.,* p.213. As to the organs see the article already mentioned by David Salwey. The whole of Burton's contribution on the subject of music at St. Peter's during his time as organist is well worth reading and appears in Leachman's *St. Peter's,* pp. 153-156. The other quotations and much of the material used come from the early magazines, which are themselves treated in this chapter. As to the *Heather Bell,* see *Bournemouth 1810-1910,* pp. 145-146. The "Westover Pleasure Grounds" are now Bournemouth's Lower Pleasure Gardens. The "Cranborne Gardens" were the site of the Winter Gardens.

Chapter Nine. The quotation at the beginning of the chapter comes from *The Bournemouth Parish Magazine,* April 1869. An article about the Vestibules by the present writer, in collaboration with Nicholas Taylor, appeared in *St. Peter's Parish Magazine,* June 1962, and contains the quotation in which Taylor mentions the Law Courts. Sir George Gervis' letter to Mr. Stephens about the Bennett Testimonial, dated 16th February 1870, says "You could not have asked me anything that would give me so much pleasure as to join in a Testimonial to Mr. Bennett, and I think nothing could be so suitable or so pleasant to him as a peel (*sic*) of bells for the beautiful Church of St. Peter's which has been built entirely through his exertions and liberality. I shall be very glad to give £25 towards the Testimonial." This letter is preserved in St. Peter's Archives. Note also Lord Wolverton's letter on the same subject which is quoted in Chapter Six. Bishop Sumner's son wrote that he was "desired by my father to tell you that it will give him great pleasure to testify his appreciation of Mr. Bennett's zeal in the work of the Church at Bournemouth, and also his sympathy in his present weakened state." The reference to Col. Williams, in connection with the gift of the lectern, comes from Crumpler's paper previously mentioned. The nave frescoes were the subject of a paper by the present writer in *St. Peter's Parish Magazine, May 1962.* Details about the chancel arch fresco are from various numbers of *The Bournemouth & Vale of Avon Parish Magazine* published during the year 1873.

Chapter Ten. For the various parish boundaries see *The Parochial Development of Bournemouth* by the late Mr. G. E. Ellis (1966). The early history of St. John's Moordown is dealt with in *St. John's Moordown Parish History* by the Rev. Herbert Bloomfield (1924). The *Bournemouth Parish Magazine* for 1867, and the works already mentioned by Crumpler and Leachman, contain details about the Sanatorium Chapel, the Church Schools, St. Michael's and St. Clement's. The architectural notes in *Bright's Illustrated Guide to Bournemouth* (1888) are also useful. The District for St. Clement's was constituted by Order in Council of 19th August 1871. Parts of this area were taken in 1890 for St. John's Boscombe and in 1922 for St. Mary's. St. Clement's and St. Mary's became reunited in 1964. The quotation about Mr. Joy of Westbourne is from Crumpler. Towle's wife, Eleanor, was the eldest daughter of Sir Henry Taylor who is mentioned in Chapter Six. *The Churches of Bournemouth* by Alfred Webb (1910) contains much useful information about St. Ambrose. The account of the Branksome mission and St. Aldhelm's has been taken from an article contributed to *St. Peter's Magazine* for November 1965.

Chapter Eleven. See the *Parish Magazine* and the works already mentioned by Leachman, Crumpler, Forse and Nicholas Taylor. The intimate friend's appreciation of Morden Bennett, which extends to four pages in Leachman's *St. Peter's,* is well worth reading in full as an excellent contemporary tribute by someone who knew Morden Bennett well. The Bennett memorials are dealt with by Leachman and there is a good early account of St. Stephen's by Octavius Curtis in *Bright's Illustrated Guide to Bournemouth* (1888). The statues by Earp for St. Peter's tower are mentioned in the *Parish Magazine.* The statues by Redfern for Bristol Cathedral which were removed to East Heslerton are mentioned in *The Annals of Nineteenth Century Bristol* by John Latimer (1887). A photograph of Redfern's Latin Doctors, taken after they had been removed from the North Porch at Bristol, was published in the *Report of the Friends of Bristol Cathedral* (1969-70), page 18, accompanying an article by Mrs. Kathleen Sabin.

Chapter Twelve. Letters and opinions about the troubles described in this chapter may be found in the local newspapers of the time and in the *Parish Magazine*. Leachman does not give a very full account of the matter.

Chapter Thirteen. Most of the material used is from the works already noted by Leachman, Octavius Curtis and Nicholas Taylor, and from *The East Parley Mission* and the *Parish Magazine*. David Young's *The Story of Bournemouth* and an article published some years ago by "Richmond" in the *Bournemouth Daily Echo* were very useful for preparing the account of Shelley's heart burial. Burke's *Landed Gentry* and *The Landed Gentry of Ireland* contain details of the Rams and their family connections.

Chapter Fourteen. Mrs. K. M. Whitten, daughter of Mr. C. T. Barker, kindly supplied her reminiscences of life at St. Peter's. Phyllis Bottome's *Search for a Soul* was published by Faber & Faber in 1947. She died in 1963. The quotations of Fisher are from his contributions to the *Parish Magazine* and from the Vestry minutes. The quotation about G. F. Bodley is from Nicholas Taylor's *Guide*.

Chapter Fifteen. Most of the information about Daldy's arrival in Bournemouth and his early activities has come from the *Parish Magazine* and *The Bournemouth Graphic* for 1904 and 1905. Forse, in the article already mentioned, deals with the introduction of Confession and the Eucharistic vestments. The writer's great-aunt Miss Evelyn Keep, the schoolmaster's daughter Mrs. Whitten, and long-serving choirman Cyril Maynard, have kindly contributed their reminiscences. The quotations in tribute to Hume's reputation as an organist are from David Salwey's article previously noted. Daldy's remarks concerning the termination of Hume's appointment and his views about the proposed separation of St. Swithun's are in the *Parish Magazine*.

Chapter Sixteen. The main sources for this chapter are Leachman's *St. Peter's* and the *Parish Magazine*. On Scott Evans see *Bournemouth Daily Echo* for 10th, 14th & 15th January 1908. There are notes about St. Ambrose and Christ Church in Alfred Webb's *The Churches of Bournemouth* (1910). See Taylor's *Guide* for further details about the Keble Chapel. The quotation from David Salwey comes from the article in *The Organ* previously mentioned. Salwey and Taylor both comment on the organ case designed by Comper. In 1912 Daldy executed a Deed Poll constituting the trusteeship for the management of St. Peter's Hall. In 1960 the Parochial Church Council was appointed trustee by a Deed in the following terms:

"THE WINCHESTER DIOCESAN BOARD OF FINANCE the Trustees of the Winchester Diocesan Trust Deed of 1898 at the request of WILFRED HENRY FOX ROBINSON Vicar of the Parish and Church of St. Peter Bournemouth HEREBY APPOINT the Parochial Church Council of the Parish of St. Peter Bournemouth to be the Administrative Trustees of 'St. Peter's Hall Bournemouth Trust Deed' in place of Ronald Hines David Christopher Preston George Harry Robert Head the Reverend Canon Anthony Lewis Elliott Williams who have resigned and Gilbert Marshall Colonel Charles William Gustovus Palmer Colonel Vivian Dedman Stenhouse who have died AND

"IT IS HEREBY DECLARED that this Appointment shall continue during the remainder of the period during which the said WILFRED HENRY FOX ROBINSON is Vicar of the Parish and Church of St. Peter Bournemouth aforesaid and thereafter until any persons shall be nominated by any later Vicar of the Parish and Church of St. Peter Bournemouth aforesaid in accordance of the provisions of the Deed Poll dated the 12th day of January 1912 and made by Alfred Edward Daldy."

Chapter Seventeen. Dr. J. D. Jones was the famous local preacher and writer, minister of Richmond Hill Congregational Church. Heriz-Smith was assistant curate of St. Peter's from 1917 to 1921 when he was appointed vicar of Holy Trinity Church at Winchester. The connection between St. Peter's and the Railwaymen is mentioned in the next chapter with the account of parish activity during the General Strike. When Patterson left the parish upon St. Ambrose securing its independence he was given a testimonial cheque for £1,000, by far the largest presentation of this kind of which any record has been found. The quotations in this chapter are all from the *Parish Magazine*.

Chapter Eighteen. Up to the time when the Choir Home was run down and finally closed it had normally accommodated eight of the choir's eighteen boys, the other ten being Town boys. Once a month, when they were due to be paid, they had to go to W. J. Palmer's office in Albert Road, armed with a chit from the organist saying how much they were entitled to have, and there collect their pay, signing the churchwarden's register as a receipt. In Leachman's *St. Peter's* are two interesting photographs of Crumpler, one of him as a young man and the other when he had served forty years. The original handbill for the first production of St. Peter's Players is in the Church archives. Green-Wilkinson's recollections of Crumpler appeared in the *Parish Magazine* soon after the former sacristan's death in 1942. J. G. Lockhart's biography *Cosmo Gordon Lang* was published by Hodder & Stoughton. See the writer's *The East Parley Mission* for notes about Druitt and Sayer in connection with St. Barnabas Chapel. Sir Ninian Comper, the architect of the Chapel of the Resurrection, died in 1960.

Chapter Nineteen. Eric Southam became noted for his work on Church reorganisation in Bournemouth. Within the old parish of Pokesdown he separated St. James, St. Andrew's and All Saints, and founded St. Christopher's. He later became the first Provost of the new Guildford Cathedral. Mrs. R. N. Byass, who lived at Berry Court, St. Peter's Road, was one of the few remaining rich residents of central Bournemouth. She regularly paid for the choirboys to attend the Pantomime at Christmas time and gave £100 for the vicar's stipend at Easter. Miss Deane kindly supplied some notes about the book reviews she has written for the *Parish Magazine*. The clock presented by the congregation to the Rev. H. E. Lewin when he left St. Peter's in 1936 to become Vicar of Burton now stands in St. Peter's vestry. Colonel R. J. Malet, churchwarden from 1929 to 1932, was head of the Air Raid Precautions organisation in Bournemouth during the Second World War; he died in 1969.

Chapter Twenty. The account of Bishop Winnington-Ingram is from his biography by Dean Carpenter (Hodder & Stoughton, 1949) to which Dean Burrows contributed his reminiscences. The confirmation service at St. Barnabas is dealt with in *The East Parley Mission*. Dean Burrows has gone to the greatest trouble in recording his memories of Bournemouth and generously allowing the author to make full use of them. Without his help, enthusiasm and encouragement this chapter could never have come to life.

The inscriptions on the recast bells are quoted in Taylor's *Guide.* The quotations from Arthur Davis and Mrs. Joan Burrows are taken from the *Parish Magazine.* Hearsey's salary as junior assistant curate in 1938 is perhaps of interest as giving some indication of what the Church ought to be paying its staff today, taking into account the great difference in the value of money thirty years ago. The letter about the French soldiers is in the *Parish Magazine* for July 1940.

Chapter Twenty-two. The stories and much of the information for this chapter were kindly supplied by Bishop Williams himself. Several members of St. Peter's congregation have also been good enough to recall their memories of this time. In all these later chapters the *Parish Magazine* has been a major source of material.

Chapter Twenty-three. The quotation from Morden Bennett about the introit is from the *Parish Magazine* of 1869.

Chapter Twenty-four. Evans, the founder of the Bournemouth Samaritans, is now Canon Missioner for Gloucester Diocese. Since 1970 the Bournemouth Samaritans Director has been the Rev. Roslyn Aish, vicar of Hyde, near Fordingbridge, a priest who has close personal and family connections with Bournemouth and St. Peter's. Norton continues as Secretary of the Council of Christians and Jews in Bournemouth. The present vicar of St. Peter's, the Rev. Colin James, writing of Norton and his work in 1969, said: "He devotes much of his energies and skill to this most important work, which not only brings personal friendships, but deeper knowledge both of Judaism and Christianity itself. Here is a most valuable area of growth in understanding and reconciliation, and the evils of ignorance and prejudice are diminished."

Chapter Twenty-five. There is a close spiritual link between St. Peter's and the late Archbishop Oliver Green-Wilkinson's Diocese of Zambia (formerly Northern Rhodesia) in that the High Altar of Lusaka Cathedral, which Bishop Oliver built, was given to him by the people of St. Peter's.

Chapter Twenty-six. The details about the career of the new vicar, Colin James, were kindly supplied by him and by the Information Officer of the B.B.C. at Bristol. James has managed to do a small amount of broadcasting since coming to Bournemouth. For instance, in 1967 he presented a devotional study of Francis de Sales, written and narrated by himself, and in 1968 he preached at the Parish Communion service broadcast from St. Peter's on 27th October.

Chapter Twenty-seven. This is the chapter in which the author has allowed himself considerable freedom of personal expression, but he has been greatly helped in producing it by Bishop Williams, Dean Burrows and Dr. Roe. That is not to say that any of these three distinguished clerical gentlemen have any responsibility whatever for an opinion with which the reader may disagree.

List Of Vicars

1845-80	Alexander Morden Bennett.
1880-81	Vincent William Ryan.
1881-89	George Stopford Ram.
1890-1904	Cecil Edward Fisher.
1904-20	Alfred Edward Daldy.
1921-27	Lumley Cecil Green-Wilkinson.
1927-35	Hubert Henry Lovatt Lloyd Marsh.
1936-43	Hedley Robert Burrows.
1944-45	Norman Robert Boyd.
1946-56	Anthony Lewis Elliott Williams.
1957-66	Wilfred Henry Fox Robinson.
1967-	Colin Clement Walter James.

Vicars Designate who were not Inducted

1880	Edward Harland.
1920	Basil Sidney Phillips.

List of Priests-in-Charge of St. Swithun's

1876-80	Alexander Sykes Bennett.
1882-95	John Radclyffe Husband.
1895-1905	Duncan Woodroffe.
1905-09	Ernest Marling Roberts.
1909-13	Kenneth Hovil McMaster.
1914-16	Frederic Godfrey Guy.
1916-21	Maurice Roach Bailey.
1921-25	Ernest Harrington Holden.
1925-31	Rupert Russ Pitter.
1933-35	William Richard Spalding Wray.
1935-36	Walter Leonard Freeman.
1936-38	Percy Steed.
1938-41	Frederick Alexander Sanders.
1942-45	Robert Peel Price.
1946-51	Keith Edgar Hollyer Parkinson.
1952-54	Peter John Chandler.
1955-56	Percy Steed
1957-63	Arthur Harold Gordon Clinch.
1968-	Robert Peel Price.

List Of Churchwardens

1845-47	Edward Castleman.
1845-48	Samuel Bayly.
1847-55	Richard Elgie.
1848-53 & 1855-56	James Bell.
1853-54	E. V. Mainwaring.
1854-55	Peter Tuck.
1855-56	Henry Dickinson.
1856-57	Thomas Kingdon.
1856-57	Robert Kerley.
1857-59	Richard Stephens.
1857-65 & 1866-68	William Rogers.
1859-60	John Parkinson.
1860-64	Charles Allen King.
1864-66	Edmund Christy.
1865-66	Leadbetter Uppleby.
1866-68	Maj.-Gen. Crawley.
1868-77	Matthew Webb.
1868-69	William Mansfield Bill.
1869-70 & 1876-77	David Sydenham.
1870-76	Gustavus Lane.
1877-79	Charles Nixon.
1877-1908	Walter Scott Evans.
1879-87	Henry Salt.
1887-1902 & 1912-22	James Druitt.
1902-03	A. Kinsey Morgan.
1903-05	Charles William Keep.
1905-07	John Gregory White.
1907-12	W. M. Staniford.
1908-28	William John Palmer.
1922-27	William Francis Danby.
1927-29	Francis S. Miller.
1928-35	George Cookman.
1929-32	R. J. Malet.
1932-36	Allan Webber.
1935-49	Charles William Gustavus Palmer.
1936-44	Vivian D. Stenhouse.
1944-49	Lawrence Bell.
1949-50	W. J. Lewis.
1949-58	Gilbert Marshall.
1950-52	T. H. Ringrose.
1952-60 & 1967-	Ronald Hines.
1958-65	George Burr.
1960-64	Ian McQueen.
1964-69	John Fawcett.
1965-67	John Gibbings.
1969-	T. I. Pearmain.

List Of Organists

1843-?	J. Duncan.
?	Miss Pattison.
?	—. Baine.
1859-?	J. H. Caseley.
?-1867	William Henry Beare.
1867-68	T. Beare.
1868-69	—. Taylor.
1869-79	Thomas Alfred Burton.
1880-1905	Duncan Hume.
1905-46	James D. Chandler.
1946-53	Charles R. Palmer.
1953-66	Michael D. Peterson.
1966-67	Harry Victor Sayles.
1967-68	Frederick Stanley Hewitt.
1969-	Cyril Knight.

Assistant Curates

1851-52 *George Irving Davies,* M.A., Oxon. Later Rector of Kelsale, Suffolk.

1852-55 *H. L. Dodds.*

1853-54 *Edward Kelson Yeatman,* M.A., Oxon. Ordained in 1852, Yeatman came to St. Peter's from Potterspury, Northants. In 1854 he emigrated to Australia and was Rector of Auburn in the Diocese of Adelaide from 1882.

1855-56 *John M. Maguire.*

1856 *James Henry Moore,* M.A., Durham. Left St. Peter's to become incumbent of Vobster, Somerset. Later Rector of St. Mary's, Truro, and Honorary Canon of Truro Cathedral.

1857-59 *Alfred Brook,* M.A., Oxon. Assistant curate at East Retford, Notts., before coming to St. Peters.

1860-75 *Samuel Robinson Waddelow,* M.A., Cantab. Came to St. Peter's in 1860 and remained until his death on 5th January 1875. He was Morden Bennett's senior curate for upwards of 13 years. His work for Bournemouth's sick people, especially at the National Sanatorium and the Firs Home, made him much loved and respected in the locality. He was appointed as a colonial bishop in 1866 but was prevented from accepting because of bad health.

1860-72 *Edward Wanklyn.* Left the staff of St. Peter's to become the first vicar of St. Michael's, Bournemouth. He died in 1881.

1863-68 *Robert Scott McDowall,* M.A., Oxon. Came to Bournemouth in 1863 having been assistant master at Newark Grammar School. He left in 1868 for Powerstock, where he was assistant curate until 1872 and again from 1876 to 1884. Between his spells at Powerstock he was assistant curate at St. Giles, Camberwell. During his second curacy at Powerstock he held the rectory of North Poorton, Dorset. He became vicar of Yetminster in 1884.

1863-80 *Alexander Sykes Bennett,* M.A., Oxon. Son of the first vicar of St. Peter's, Alex. Bennett was ordained deacon in 1861 and spent two years as assistant curate at Wilton. Upon his ordination as priest in 1863 he returned to Bournemouth. He was responsible for several of the St. Peter's missions and was the first priest-in-charge of St. Swithun's. He gave up his appointment during the difficulties which followed his father's death, the congregation having petitioned the patron that he should be nominated as the new vicar. In 1882 he became the first vicar of the new Church of St. Stephen, Bournemouth, which had been built as a memorial to his late father. He resigned the incumbency of St. Stephen's in 1911 and died in 1912.

1864-67 *Henry Raymond Smythies,* M.A., Cantab. From 1878 he was Rector of Southacre, Norfolk.

1865-67 *Thomas Anderson,* M.A., Cantab. Came to St. Peter's from Sudbury, Suffolk. He was vicar of St. James, Pokesdown from 1868 to 1886.

1866-68 *William Knowlton Hampshire,* M.A., Cantab. Held assistant curacies in Sussex before coming to St. Peter's and in Devon after leaving Bournemouth. He was later vicar of Bampton.

1868-69 *Percy Serjeant Newell.*

1869 *James N. Nicholson.*

1869-71 *William Walton Herringham,* M.A., Cantab. In 1873 he was appointed Rector of Old Cleeve, Taunton.

1870-71 *Franklin Tonkin,* M.A., Cantab. Later Vicar of Madron and Morvah, Cornwall.

1870-71 *Arthur Kevill Davies Edwards,* B.A., Oxon. Ordained deacon in 1869, Edwards was assistant curate of Islington, Devon. He came to St. Peter's in the following year after his ordination as priest and spent eighteen months in charge of Moordown district. In 1871 he became Vicar of Vernham Dean, near Andover. During his incumbency at Vernham Dean he held the chaplaincy of St. Bartholomew's, Dinard (1877-89), and chaplaincies at St. Paul's, Durban, and Maritzburg, Natal (1894-97).

1871-72 *Ambrose C. B. Cave.*

1871- *Norman Coles.* Succeeded Edwards in charge of Moordown district.

1872-73 *Walter Francis Wrottesley.* Died in February 1873, aged 27.

1875-80 *Charles Rowland Haydock Hill,* M.A., Oxon. Hill came to St. Peter's as a deacon in 1875. After Morden Bennett died he went as assistant curate to St. Michael's, Bournemouth, later joining Alex. Bennett at St. Stephen's. From 1885 Hill held several incumbencies in Dorset, ultimately becoming vicar of Holy Trinity, Dorchester, in 1898.

1878-79 and 1918-20 *John William Barrow*. A missionary from South Africa, he was attached to St. Ambrose Church, leaving in 1879 to become Vicar of Alderholt. Subsequently he held five other country incumbencies in Dorset and Somerset, returning to St. Ambrose in 1918.

1878-80 *Henry Pole Fraser,* M.A., Oxon. Fraser came to St. Peter's after gaining experience at Southampton and Andover. He left the parish when Ryan became vicar and then held assistant curacies at Sunningdale (1880-84) and Ascot (1884-86), before being presented Vicar at Westbury, Bucks., in 1886. In 1901 he became Rector of Ryton, Salop., where he remained for a great many years.

1880 *Charles Arthur LeGeyt,* B.A., Oxon. A young priest who only stayed at St. Peter's for a few months. He left to take an assistant curacy at another Street Church (Ryde, Isle of Wight). Later he was Vicar at Truro Cathedral and priest-in-charge of South Huish, Devon.

1880 *Robert Halcott Paul Ash*. Former Vicar of Emery Down, Hants. On leaving St. Peter's Ash went to Cheshire as Chaplain at Arley (1880-86). He was later Vicar of Appleton-Thorn, Cheshire.

1880-81 *Willis Fleming Aston Lambert,* M.A., Oxon. Came to Bournemouth from Bradford. From 1881 to 1884 he was assistant curate at Windsor and subsequently Curate and Clerk-in-Orders at St. James, Westminster, and Vicar of Peterchurch (1887-96).

1880 *G. H. Bateson Wright*.

1880-81 *J. K. Stow*.

1880-84 *William Hubert Groom,* M.A., Cantab. Came to St. Peter's as a deacon and was ordained priest in 1881. Later he became Rector of Monk-Soham, Suffolk.

1880 *William Hamlyn,* B.A., London. Assistant curate at Bishop's Teignton, Devon, before coming to St. Peter's, and at Brixton and St. Leonards-on-Sea afterwards. From 1890 to 1896 he held an incumbency on Prince Edward Island.

1881-83 *William Paxton Thorp*. Came to St. Swithun's from Hatcham, Surrey. He was later assistant curate at Reigate and at Wateringbury. In 1895 he was appointed Rector of Little Yelsham.

1881-99 *George Herbert West,* M.A., D.D., Oxon. Came to Bournemouth as a deacon in 1881 and was attached to St. Swithun's. Ordained priest in 1882, he took his doctorate in 1889 and retired to Eastbourne in 1899.

1881-84 *James Frank Warden Gompertz,* B.A., Cantab. After a first curacy at St. Peter's Gompertz became a Chaplain in the Indian Army.

1881-86 *Henry Spencer Kenrick Bellairs,* M.A., Oxon. Was an assistant curate in Oxford before joining the staff of St. Ambrose. He was later Professor of English at Bombay University and a lecturer at Oxford.

1882-83 *Percy Brent,* M.A., Cantab. Senior assistant curate at St. Peter's under Ram, Brent left in 1883 as incumbent of Enfield, Middlesex. He later held other livings in Hereford and Kent.

1882 & 1888 *Frederick Glyn Montagu Powell.* Vicar of Milborne St. Andrew, Dorset. Temporary priest-in-charge at St. Swithun's. He was later Chaplain to the Duke of Buccleuch and Vicar of St. Luke's, Southampton.

1882-95 *John Radclyffe Husband,* M.A., Cantab. After thirteen years as a young assistant curate at St. Peter's and St. Swithun's Husband held the Rectory of Laverstoke from 1895 to 1903, when he returned to Bournemouth to assist at St. Stephen's under Alex. Bennett. In 1913 he was inducted to Keble's old living at Hursley where he remained for many years. Died 1948.

1883-85 *Frank Cossor.* Came from St. James, Keyham, Devonport, and had to give up his work in 1885 because of ill health. While at St. Peter's Cossor had special charge of the Terrace Road Mission District. He took the long sea voyage to Australia in the hope of regaining his health, but died in 1888.

1883-86 *Arthur Fraser Forbes,* M.A., Oxon. Former Rector of Badger, Salop. Later he became Vicar of St. James, Southampton.

1883 *Edmond Bennet Brackenbury,* B.A., Oxon. Formerly a Minor Canon at Bristol Cathedral, he later served as Assistant Chaplain of the Memorial Church of St. George at Cannes.

1884-85 *Gavin F. Saxby,* M.A. A former Fellow of St. Augustine's College at Canterbury and Principal of St. Boniface's Missionary House at Warminster, Saxby was senior priest under Ram until he was appointed to the living of Monk's Kirby in 1885.

1884 *Robert Copeman,* B.A., Cantab. Temporary assistant curate between appointments at Sopley and Leicester. Later he was Rector of Stoke-Albany.

1885 *James Acton Butt,* M.A., Oxon. Later Vicar of Weston, Herts.

1885-90 *John Frank Buxton,* M.A., Cantab. Before succeeding Saxby as senior priest at St. Peter's Buxton had been assistant curate at Eton (1875-81) and assistant chaplain at St. Petersburg (1881-85). After Ram died he went to St. Leonards-on-Sea. He later became Vicar of St. Giles with St. Peter's at Cambridge and Vicar of St. Peter's, Eltham.

1885 *William Nicholson.* Left Bournemouth to take an assistant curacy at St. Martin's, Scarborough. In 1886 he became Vicar of Warter, Yorks.

1885-88 *Duncan Travers,* M.A., Cantab. Came to Bournemouth to take charge of St. Ambrose after being Chaplain to Bishop Smythies with the Universities Mission to Central Africa. In 1888 he returned to Africa, serving in Zanzibar, Nyasaland and Northern Rhodesia. From 1889 to 1924 he was Secretary of the U.M.C.A. and from 1915 a Canon of Zanzibar. He retired to Kent in 1925.

1886-92 *John Trelawny Ross,* M.A., B.D., D.D., Dublin. Before coming to St. Peter's Ross was assistant curate in Ireland and a Minor Canon at Llandaff. From 1892 he was Vicar of Paignton.

1887-94 *Edward Healey,* M.A., Oxon. Master of Ascham School and part-time assistant curate at St. Swithun's. He resigned in 1894 to become a schoolmaster on a full-time basis.

1887-88 *Henry Longueville Graham,* B.A., Cantab. Left St. Peter's on being presented to the living of Riseley, near Bedford. He was later Vicar of St. Anne's, Eastbourne.

c.1887 *Edward Robert Phelps,* M.A., Oxon.

1888-95 *Charles Henry Wood,* M.A., Cantab. St. Peter's was Wood's fourth assistant curacy; later he held similar positions at Feltham and Radlett. He died in 1937.

1888 *Herbert Geldart.* U.M.C.A. priest who went with Travers to Zanzibar and died there in 1889.

1888-1922 *John Irwin Patterson,* M.A., Oxon. Came to take charge of St. Ambrose after spending four years as assistant curate at St. John's, Chatham. He retired to Surrey when St. Ambrose was constituted a separate parish. By far the longest-serving assistant priest of St. Peter's; only the first Vicar, Alexander Morden Bennett, spent longer in the parish. Patterson may claim to be the founder of St. Ambrose Church as we know it today.

1890-93 *John Marshall Collard,* M.A., Cantab. Later assistant curate at St. Stephen's, Bournemouth, and vicar of West Fordington, near Dorchester, Dorset.

1890-91 *Herbert Reginald Scott,* M.A., Oxon. Having been an assistant curate at Whittington, Salop., since ordination in 1884, Scott spent a year at St. Peter's until his appointment as Vicar of Kilmeston with Beauworth, Hants., a living he held from 1891 to 1901. Later he was a curate at Parkstone.

1892-94 *Frederick Arthur Potts.* M.A., Oxon. Came to Bournemouth after serving as assistant curate at Salford, Lancs., and St. Leonard's, Sussex. He left St. Peter's to be Vicar of Burton, Cheshire.

1893 *J. Simpson Jones.* At St. Peter's for one month only, January, 1893.

1893-97 } *William Ward Goddard,* M.A., Oxon. A former Vicar of St. Saviour's, Hoxton (1882-91), Goddard was a
1904-16 } voluntary helper at St. Ambrose before being taken

on to the permanent staff of the parish. He lived in Bournemouth during his retirement and returned to St. Peter's under Daldy. He died in 1916.

1893-94 *John Genn Hooton.* Assistant curate at Sydenham and at Harlesden before coming to Bournemouth, and at Chislehurst and Camden Town after leaving St. Peter's, but his health was not strong enough to bear the continual strain of work at St. Peter's.

1894-96 *Robert William Harrison Acworth,* M.A., Oxon. Came to St. Peter's immediately after ordination and served as assistant curate at Sunningdale from 1896 to 1903. He was then Vicar of Twyford until 1919 when he returned to Sunningdale as Vicar.

1894-99 *Philip Marmaduke Cramer Johnstone,* M.A., Oxon. Former assistant curate at Kenwyn, Cornwall, and at Kimberley in the Diocese of Bloemfontein (1892-94). He left St. Peter's in 1899 to become Vicar of St. Michael's, Woolwich, but he returned to Bournemouth in 1903 as Vicar of St. Katherine's, Southbourne. He was later Vicar of All Saints, Cheltenham and Honorary Canon of Gloucester Cathedral.

1895-1900 *Hubert Burges Hunt,* M.A., Oxon. Came to St. Peter's from Tenbury, Gloucestershire, where he had been Vicar for three years. In 1900 he became assistant curate at Clewer, Berks.

1895-1905 *Duncan Woodroffe,* M.A., Oxon. Assistant curate of Grantham, Lincs., under Fisher (1875-85) and then Rector of Stroxton, Lincs., for ten years prior to coming to Bournemouth as priest-in-charge of St. Swithun's. Later Rector of Banstead, Surrey. He died in 1917.

1896 *Arthur Henry Finn.* Missionary priest from Burma who gave temporary assistance at St. Peter's while in England on furlough in 1896.

1896-99 *George Owen Apthorp,* M.A., Cantab. Came to St. Peter's as a deacon in 1896. In 1909 he was inducted as Rector of Rewe, near Exeter.

1898 *Thomas Samuel Kendall.* Temporary assistant for three months during the summer of 1898.

1897 *William Macdonald Bottome,* M.A., Dickinson College, Carlisle, U.S.A. An American who was a retired English country parson, father of Phyllis Bottome, the writer. Temporary senior priest at St. Peter's.

1897 *James Morgan.* Came to St. Peter's after serving at Southwark and Wincanton.

1899-1903 *Frederick Gosnal Jameson Page,* M.A., Cantab. A former assistant master at King's School, Warwick (1885-99), Page was attached to St. Swithun's while headmaster of Ascham School, Bournemouth. He was later headmaster of St. Christopher's School at Eastbourne, Vicar of Mountfield, and Master of Lord Leycester's Hospital, Warwick.

1900 *Edward Grigson,* B.A., Cantab. Formerly Rector of Whinburgh with Westfield, East Dereham, Norfolk.

1900-02 *Frank Urch,* M.A., Oxon. Came to St. Peter's after a first assistant curacy at Shepton Beauchamp, Somerset. When he left Bournemouth he went to Rhodesia and was priest-in-charge at Umtali. Later he held a number of chaplaincies and assistant curacies in London and the Home Counties.

1901-04 *Charles Paulet Cunningham Seagrim,* B.A., Cantab. Senior priest under Fisher, and succeeded by Jourdain after Daldy's induction. Ordained at Bloemfontein in 1889, Seagrim worked in Basutoland and Cape Colony until 1895 when he returned to England as assistant curate at Hamble In 1904 he was appointed Vicar of Ashmansworth.

1901-04 *Arthur Robert Fernsby,* M.A., Oxon. Came to Bournemouth after serving assistant curacies at Leeds, Durban and Battersea. From 1904 until 1918 he was assistant curate of St. Peter's, Parkstone. Later he became Vicar of Shaldon, near Teignmouth.

1903-04 *Harry Hamilton Taylor,* M.A., Durham. For four years prior to coming to St. Peter's he was assistant curate at All Saints, Battersea Park. In 1904 he took a similar position at Tunbridge Wells. Later he was Vicar of St. Mark's, New Brompton, Kent.

1903-05 *Charles Wright.* Assistant priest at St. Swithun's.

1904 *Carew Hervey St. John Mildmay,* M.A., Cantab. Former Rector of St. Mary's, Stamford, and Chaplain in South Africa during the Boer War.

1904-07 *Reginald Towle Jourdain,* M.A., Oxon. Came to Bournemouth in 1904 after spending five years in Calcutta with the Oxford University Mission. In 1907 he was sent to the Assam as an S.P.G. missionary. Later he became Vicar of Woodham, Surrey, and Commissioner for Assam.

1904-09 *Ernest Marling Roberts,* M.A., Oxon. Priest-in-charge of St. Swithun's. In 1909 he was appointed Vicar of St. Philip's, Kensington. Later he became Vicar of St. Mary Abbots and Rural Dean of Kensington.

1904-06 *Harry de Trevelec.* Left in 1906 to join the staff of St. Michael's, Bournemouth.

1905-08 *George Porter,* M.A., Cantab. Former Rector of Wickford, Essex, who retired to Bournemouth.

1905-06 *Ernest Morgan Trevor Williams,* M.A., Cantab. Came to St. Peter's for a few months between assistant curacies at Paddington and at St. John's, Surrey Road, Bournemouth. He was later Vicar of East Preston, Sussex.

1906-14 *Edgecombe Walter Leachman,* A.K.C. After several assistant curacies (including one at St. Clement's, Boscombe from 1899 to 1901) he came back to Bournemouth in 1906 as senior priest under Daldy.

He was author of the history of St. Peter's, published in 1915, and Vicar of Christchurch from 1914 to 1915. Later he was assistant secretary of the Church of England Men's Society and assistant curate at Holy Trinity, Hastings. He died in 1945.

1906-13 *William George Iremonger,* M.A., Oxon. Came to St. Peter's from St. Mary's, Southampton and left in 1913 to become priest-in-charge of Langford, near Bristol, a position he held for a great many years.

1906-08 *Harold Gordon Peile,* M.A., Oxon. Came to Bournemouth in 1906 from All Saints, Acton, where he had been assistant curate. In 1908 he was appointed Clerical Organising Secretary of the S.P.G. for Schools and King's Messengers. He served at Singapore Cathedral and later returned to All Saints, Acton, as Vicar.

1906-08 *Eric Arthur Shattock,* M.A., B.Litt., Oxon. Worked at St. Peter's as a newly ordained deacon. He was later Vicar of St. Mark's, Purley.

1907-13 *Kenneth Hovil McMaster,* M.A., Oxon. Formerly assistant curate at Kilburn and Maidenhead. Later Vicar of All Saints, Alton (1917-21) and Warden of St. Thomas' Home at Basingstoke (1921-27).

1908-19 *Ernest Augustus Causton,* M.A., Cantab. Priest-in-charge of Christ Church, Westbourne. He started his clerical career at St. John's, Boscombe (1891-94), and then went to India with the Church Missionary Society.

1908 *Alfred William Flux,* M.A., Oxon. Former Vicar of Roxwell (1896-98) who stayed for only a short time at St. Peter's before moving to All Saints, Branksome, as assistant curate. In 1910 he was appointed Rector of Carlton, near Worksop.

1909-11 *Adolph Conrad Muller,* B.A., London. After two assistant curacies in London, Muller spent eight years in South Africa before coming to St. Peter's. In 1911 he moved to All Saints, Branksome, and from 1915 to 1923 was Vicar of Redlynch, near Salisbury. Then he went to Canada and held several Church appointments there.

1909-14 *Herbert Schacht Holt,* M.A., Cantab. Former Vicar of Molash, near Canterbury. On leaving St. Peter's in 1914 Holt went as assistant curate to St. Peter's, Parkstone.

1910-20 *Arthur Stephen Withers Moore,* M.A., Oxon. Assisted at St. Swithun's for many years without remuneration. In 1920 he left Bournemouth to become incumbent of Markbeech, Kent. He died in 1924 and lies buried in the Wimborne Road Cemetery at Bournemouth.

1911-19 *Edward Hamilton Blyth,* M.A., Oxon. Came to Bournemouth from missionary work in Egypt. From 1916 he was senior priest at St. Peter's. In 1919 he became

Vicar of Holy Trinity, Weymouth, and later Vicar of Milton Lilbourne.

1912-16 *Frederic Godfrey Guy,* M.A., Oxon. Vicar of Manea, Cambs., from 1894-1912, Guy came to Bournemouth in 1912 and succeeded McMaster in 1914 as priest-in-charge of St. Swithun's. After the war he held chaplaincies at Algiers, Nice and Venice.

1913-17 *Thomas John Hardy,* M.A., Cantab. Came from London and returned there after four years at St. Peter's.

1913-16 *Leslie Marcus Quehen,* B.Litt., Toulouse. Served assistant curacies at Alderney, Christchurch and Romsey before coming to St. Peter's. From 1916 he was Rector of St. Sampson, Guernsey, and subsequently Vicar of St. Stephen's, Guernsey, and Vicar of Fulwell, Middlesex.

1915-17 *James Lyne Beaumont James,* M.A., Cantab. Came to St. Peter's after five years as assistant curate of St. Luke's, Southampton. In 1917 he was inducted as Rector of Millbrook, Southampton, and remained there until 1951. He died in 1952. James was the uncle and Godfather of the present Vicar of St. Peter's.

1916-23 *Arthur Gerald Sayer,* M.A., Oxon. Ordained in 1911, Sayer came to St. Peter's in 1916 after serving in Swindon and Folkestone. He was Daldy's personal assistant and private secretary, and also assistant organist of St. Peter's. He took charge of the parish when Daldy resigned and stayed on as senior priest of St. Peter's under Green-Wilkinson. From 1923 he was Vicar of Westend, Southampton. Later he became a Prebendary of Bodmin.

1916-21 *Maurice Roach Bailey,* M.A., Oxon. Came from Otterbourne, Hants., as priest-in-charge of St. Swithun's. Later he was Vicar of East Coker and Rector of Corston, Somerset.

1917-21 *Eustace Edward Arthur Heriz-Smith,* M.A., Cantab. Came to St. Peter's after two years as assistant chaplain at Sherborne School. While on the staff of St. Peter's he was temporary chaplain to the Forces (1918-20). He left Bournemouth to become Rector of Holy Trinity, Winchester (1921-25) and then went back to teaching. He was Honorary Canon of St. John's Pro-Cathedral at Buenos Aires in 1937 and Vicar of Radley from 1939 to 1941.

1917-18 *William Kyle Patrick Hogan,* M.A., Dublin. Came from Chingford and left for a Church Army chaplaincy during the war.

1919-21 *Arthur David Phillips,* M.A., Oxon., B.D., London. Came from St. Luke's, Reading, as senior priest of St. Peter's. From 1921 to 1924 he was assistant curate of St. Luke's, Winton, Bournemouth. After a short incumbency at Colden Common Phillips became assistant priest at another Street Church, St. Saviour's, Eastbourne.

1919-21 *Trevor Hope Lingley,* B.A., Durham. Formerly Vicar of Bothenhampton, he succeeded Causton as priest-in-charge of Christ Church, Westbourne, and became first Vicar there when Christ Church was separated from St. Peter's and made a Conventional District.

1921-25 *Ernest Harrington Holden,* M.A., Oxon. An experienced priest engaged by Green-Wilkinson to take charge of St. Swithun's, Holden came from St. John's, Clifton. From 1925 to 1928 he served under Daldy at St. Mary's, Southampton.

1921-30 *Charles Overton Rockett.* Gave up the Rectory of Shaftesbury to join Green-Wilkinson at St. Peter's. From 1933 to 1947 he was Vicar of St. John's, Surrey Road, Bournemouth.

1922-28 *William Parker Jones,* M.A., Durham. Formerly Rector of Toft.

1923-24 *George Cuthbert Scarlin.* A missionary from Costa Rica. He left St. Peter's for an assistant curacy at Basingstoke. He died in 1938.

1924-28 *Claud William Trench,* M.A., LL.B., Cantab. Joined staff from Leamington and had charge of the Mission Room and its district. He later officiated at St. Mary Magdalen's, Wandsworth Common, and at Tetbury, Gloucestershire (1929-43), finally retiring to Boscombe.

1925-31 *Rupert Russ Pitter,* M.A., Oxon. A former Vicar of East Cowes on the Isle of Wight, Pitter became priest-in-charge of St. Swithun's in succession to Holden.

1928-29 *Willis Mansfield Feast,* M.A., Cantab. A young assistant curate from Swaffham, Norfolk.

1928 *Joshua Withers,* L.Th., Durham. Assistant curate in a large number of parishes since 1886, including ten years (1918-28) at St. James, Pokesdown. He left St. Peter's after just a few months.

1928-36 *Henry Ellerker Lewin.* An Australian, Lewin took charge of the parish during the vacancy between Marsh and Burrows. He was appointed Vicar of Burton, near Christchurch, in 1936, and died on 12th February, 1946.

1929-32 *Charles Palmer.* Formerly a Vicar in New Zealand, Palmer was at St. Aldhelm's, Branksome from 1923 to 1929, before coming to St. Peter's.

1930-32 *Frederick William Thompson Greenwood,* D.D., Oxon. Associate priest at St. Peter's following his retirement as Vicar and Rural Dean of Blandford Forum, Dorset.

1932-36 *Walter Leonard Freeman,* A.K.C. Came to St. Peter's after serving two assistant curacies in Yorkshire. From 1935 to 1936 he was in charge of St. Swithun's. Later Vicar of Hardingstone, Northants.

1932-33 *William John Hawtrey Bankes.* Came to St. Peter's when ordained deacon and left to become assistant curate at Andover. More recently he has been a chaplain in the Royal Navy and an incumbent in Tobago.

1933-35 *William Richard Spalding Wray,* M.A., Cantab. Formerly an assistant curate at Ely and Wisbech, Wray came to Bournemouth as priest-in-charge of St. Swithun's. He left in 1935 to save the parish having to pay his salary. Later he was incumbent of several parishes in the North of England.

1936-38 and 1955-56 *Percy Steed,* B.A., Durham. After gaining wide experience both in England and overseas (in Canada, Honduras and Jamaica) Steed was priest-in-charge of St. Swithun's in two spells, one under Burrows, the other under Williams. Between these periods in Bournemouth he was Vicar of Upperby, Cumberland, Rector of Preston Bagot, Warwickshire, and Rector of St. Mary's, Barnes, Surrey. In 1957 he returned to Jamaica. He died in 1968.

1936-41 *Frederick Alexander Sanders,* B.Sc., London. Priest-in-charge of St. Swithun's from 1938. Came to St. Peter's from Southampton, leaving Bournemouth in 1941 as Vicar of East Meon, Hants. Later he became Rector of Overton, Rural Dean of Whitchurch, and an Honorary Canon of Winchester.

1938-40 *Henry William Moorcroft Hearsey,* M.A., Oxon. Came to St. Peter's in 1938 after a first assistant curacy at All Saints, Southbourne. In 1940 he became a Chaplain to the Forces. Since 1949 he has been Chaplain of Holy Trinity, Nice, and St. George's, Cannes. He is also an Honorary Canon of Malta Cathedral. In 1964 Canon Hearsey was awarded the O.B.E.

1941-44 *Nevil Francis Tucker.* Took the place of Sanders as senior priest at St. Peter's under Burrows. He is now an incumbent in Canada.

1942-45 and 1968- *Robert Peel Price,* M.A., Oxon. Priest-in-charge of St. Swithun's, he accepted the Vicarage of Christchurch two days before Boyd died and remained at the Priory until 1961 when he succeeded Burrows as Dean of Hereford. While at Christchurch he was a Chaplain to the Queen and an Honorary Canon of Winchester. Price resigned from Hereford in 1968 and is now Dean Emeritus. He returned to St. Swithun's as priest-in-charge in October, 1968.

1944-46 *Cuthbert Edwin Thomas Wills,* A.K.C. Part-time assistant at St. Peter's and St. Swithun's. A much travelled priest, having held Church appointments in England, Las Palmas, Cairo, Colombo and Vienna.

1945-51 *Claude Beckwith,* M.A., Oxon. Honorary assistant at St. Peter's; formerly Vicar of East Meon, Hants.

1946-52 *John Coutts,* M.A., B.Litt., Oxon. After an assistant curacy at Haigh, near Liverpool, from 1941 to 1943, Coutts went to Banbury, under Williams, and came to

St. Peter's with Williams in 1946. In 1952 he was appointed Vicar of Holybourne.

1946-51 *Keith Edgar Hollyer Parkinson,* B.D., M.Th., London. Assistant curate under Williams at Banbury (1941-43), Parkinson came from Weeke to rejoin Williams in 1946 as priest-in-charge of St. Swithun's. Since 1952 he has been vicar of St. Augustine's, Bournemouth.

1951-53 *Alfred Barrow Milner,* M.A., L.Th., Durham. Former Hampshire incumbent and Honorary Canon of Winchester. He was honorary assistant at St. Peter's during his retirement.

1951-53 *Ebenezer Parker Pelloe,* M.A., Dublin. Retired priest who became honorary assistant at St. Peter's. Among his previous appointments he had been assistant curate at St. John's, Boscombe, 1903-06, and Rector of Chiddingfold, Surrey from 1923.

1951-55 *George Francis Helm,* M.C., M.A., Oxon., T.D. Came to St. Peter's upon his retirement as Rector and Rural Dean of Dursley, Gloucestershire. Helm was a Canon Emeritus of Gloucester and a former Chaplain to the King. He moved to Tewkesbury in 1955 and died in 1958.

1952-55 *Peter John Chandler,* B.A., London. Came to St. Swithun's from Leicestershire. In 1955 he was appointed Vicar of North Baddesley, Hants. From 1964 to 1967 he was Archdeacon in Cyprus and Chaplain of Nicosia and Kyrenia. He is now Vicar of Andover, Hants.

1953-57 *Henry Grindley Johnson,* M.A., Cantab. Formerly incumbent of parishes in the Midlands, he became an honorary assistant priest at St. Peter's during his retirement.

1953-57 *Thomas Barton McKee,* M.A., Cantab. Came to St. Peter's from St. James, Pokesdown, where he had been assistant curate under Fox Robinson. Later McKee was a missionary in Bulawayo (1957-60) and then incumbent of St. James, Darlington. He is now the Secretary of the Actors Church Union.

1956-57 *Joseph Palanque Byng,* A.K.C. Formerly Rector of Weston-in-Gordano, Somerset (1923-31), and Vicar of Aldborough Hatch, Essex (1931-51), who retired to Southbourne and became honorary assistant at St. Peter's.

1956-58 *Leslie Stanley Brasnett,* M.A., Oxon. Canon Emeritus of Chester, former incumbent of parishes in Oxfordshire and Cheshire, and Rural Dean of Great Budworth and Frodsham. On leaving St. Peter's he joined Parkinson at St. Augustine's, Bournemouth.

1957-63 *Arthur Harold Gordon Clinch.* Formerly in the Indian Police and latterly Rural Dean of Worcester and Honorary Canon of Worcester Cathedral, Clinch retired to Bournemouth in 1956 and became priest-in-charge of St. Swithun's. the following year. He succeeded Evans as Director of the Bournemouth Samaritans.

1958-61 *William Gordon Roe,* M.A. (later D.Phil.), Oxon. Came to St. Peter's as a deacon and was ordained priest in 1959. Since 1961 he has been priest-in-charge of St. Michael's, Abingdon.

1958-62 *Thomas Eric Evans,* M.A., Oxon. Came from Margate Parish Church as senior assistant curate of St. Peter's under Fox Robinson. He was the founder of the Bournemouth Samaritans. Evans became Honorary Canon and Diocesan Youth Chaplain of Gloucester where he is now Diocesan Missioner.

1960- *Eric Hugh Pepler Norton,* M.A., Cantab. Honorary assistant priest at St. Peter's. Formerly Vicar of Carlton (1938-45), Vicar of Birkenshaw (1943-53) and Vicar of Almeley (1953-59).

1961 *John Lawrence Rowley Presswell,* A.K.C. Temporary assistant priest who left St. Peter's to take up an appointment as Chaplain to St. John's College at York. Later Vicar of St. Faith's, Wandsworth.

1961-64 *Colin George Sykes,* M.A., Cantab, B.D., M.Th., London. Came to St. Peter's as a deacon in 1961 and ordained priest in 1962. On the staff of Llandaff Cathedral from 1964 to 1966. Sykes is now Librarian and Lecturer at St. Michael's Theological College, Llandaff, and Lecturer in the Philosophy of Religion at the University College of South Wales and Monmouthshire. He has been Examining Chaplain to the Bishop of Llandaff since 1965.

1962-65 *David Haslam,* B.A., Durham. Former assistant curate at Manston, near Leeds. Vicar of East and West Worldham and Hartley Mauditt, with Kingsley and Oakhanger, near Alton, Hants, until 1971, when appointed Vicar of St. Andrew's, Boscombe.

1962 *David Osamu Tsukada,* B.A., B.D. Temporary assistant curate from the Anglican Church in Japan.

1963 *Webster Wulfstan Hwiridzai Nechironga,* L.Th. Temporary assistant from Southern Rhodesia. After leaving he was assistant curate at St. Mary's, Portsea, and he is now incumbent of a new parish at Rusape, Rhodesia.

1964 *Francis Lester Msokosela.* Temporary assistant from Northern Rhodesia, recommended to St. Peter's by Archbishop Green-Wilkinson, son of the former vicar.

1964-67 *Brian Dudley Simmons.* A former master mariner who came to St. Peter's upon his ordination as deacon. In 1967 he became Missions to Seamen Chaplain at the Sea Training School, Gravesend.

1964-66 *Peter Graham Cecil Brett,* M.A., Cantab. Former assistant curate at Tewkesbury. Now Chaplain at Durham University.

1966-67 *John Noel Yarrow,* B.A., Leeds. Former Vicar of South

Elmsall, near Pontefract (1941-61) and Honorary Canon of Wakefield. After his retirement to Bournemouth he assisted at St. Stephen's before coming to St. Peter's. He is now assistant priest of St. Luke's, Winton, Bournemouth.

1967- *Paul Robert Iles,* M.A., Cantab., F.R.C.O. Ordained in 1961 Iles was assistant curate at St. Michael's and Chaplain of Bishop Wordsworth School at Salisbury until he came to Bournemouth as James' senior assistant curate in 1967.

1967-71 *Christopher John Stark Jones,* B.A., London. Formerly assistant master at Ringwood Grammar School Bournemouth, and assistant curate of St. Luke Stanmore, Winchester, before joining the staff of St. Peter's in 1967. Now resident priest at St. Birinus, Booker, in the parish of West Wycombe.

1970- *Anthony Douglass Caesar,* M.A., Cantab., Mus.B., F.R.C.O. Resident priest at St. Stephen's. Before joining the clerical staff of the parish he was Chaplain to the Royal School of Church Music and a Priest in Ordinary at the Chapel Royal.

Photographic Acknowledgements

THE AUTHOR received assistance from a number of sources whilst collecting together the photographic section of this book. The origin of four of the pictures is mentioned in captions. Of the others, the bulk are printed by courtesy of Bournemouth Public Libraries. They provided the originals for all the uncredited plates up to that with the date 1919. The 1938 picture of *St. Peter's Clergy* is from the "Parish Magazine" for December of that year. *'The Vicar goes aloft,'* is reproduced by courtesy of the Evening Echo, Bournemouth. Lastly, the photograph of the Rev. Colin James was kindly provided by the B.B.C.

Index Of People